Current Issues in Auditing

Third Edition

Edited by

MICHAEL SHERER
and
STUART TURLEY

P·C·P
Paul Chapman
Publishing Ltd

Paul Chapman Publishing Ltd
A SAGE Publications Company
6 Bonhill Street
London EC2A 4PU

British Library Cataloguing in Publication Data

Current issues in auditing. – 3rd ed.
  1. Auditing
I. Sherer, Michael II. Turley, Stuart
657.4'5

ISBN 1 85396 365 8

Typeset by Anneset, Weston-super-Mare, Somerset
Printed and bound in Great Britain by Athenæum Press Ltd,
Gateshead, Tyne & Wear

D E F G H   9 8

Contents

Preface

With each edition of *Current Issues in Auditing*, and this is now the third one, we present a snapshot of the state of auditing at a particular point in time. But each time we also hope to do a little more than that. Some of the chapters discuss critically the development of an issue over the previous few years, for example independence and regulation. Some chapters are concerned to describe and document current best practice, for example in audit methodologies and audit risk. And the remaining chapters attempt to look forward to possible future developments in audit practice and their consequences, for example the increasing use of information technology in the audit process and the extent to which there are viable solutions for the expectations gap.

In accepting the wisdom of the old adage, 'if it ain't broke, there is no need to fix it', we have only made significant changes from the second edition where feedback from students and lecturers indicated that such changes were essential. Thus, we have expanded the discussion of auditing and the law beyond the issue of third-party liability, we have given more space to the recent developments in audit methodologies and techniques, and we have omitted one or two chapters where the content is no longer a 'current issue' or has been incorporated into other chapters. There are also several new chapters which reflect the emergence of issues since the previous edition. We now include a survey of developments in audit automation, a discussion of the nature and development of the audit market, both in the UK and the European Union, and an assessment of the impact on auditing of the Cadbury Report on corporate governance, with particular attention to the role of audit committees.

Because it is such a distinctive feature of the book, we have continued the practice from previous editions of including contributions from both academic and practitioner authors. We have once again asked our contributors to include some discussion questions at the end of their chapters to help provide a focus for class and seminar discussions.

We are grateful to Paul Chapman Publishing for enabling us to work together again on another edition of *Current Issues in Auditing*. We would especially like to thank all the contributors for their excellent chapters and for (nearly) meeting the deadlines we imposed on them. And, of course, we would like to say a very special thank you to Marianne Lagrange whose patience must have worn thin on many occasions but who nevertheless cajoled and nudged us along to deliver the finished book.

MJS
WST
March 1997

Part I

The Framework and Context of Auditing

1
Debating Audit Expectations
Christopher Humphrey

In the first edition of *Current Issues in Auditing*, Sherer (1985, p. 1) wrote that auditors had 'come out of the closet. Gone were perceptions of auditing as dull, boring and even insignificant. With a new public image, auditing was heralded as facing an exciting, if sometimes controversial, future (p. 12). Twelve years on, the growth of auditing has led some to suggest that we are now living in the 'Audit Society' (see Power, 1994) yet the audit function still stands surrounded by mystique and paradox. Indeed, the expanding reliance placed on the audit function in processes of organizational and social control has been accompanied over the last two decades by a research literature which has cast doubt over the role of auditing and questioned what is both expected of, and provided by, auditors. As Power (1994, p. 7) notes, 'the great puzzle of financial audit is that it has never been a more powerful and influential model of administrative control than now, when many commentators talk of an auditing crisis'. The professional accountancy press provides witness to such concern, most notably through the notion of the 'audit expectations gap', a debate fuelled by major financial scandals (including 'infamous' corporations such as Barlow Clowes, Ferranti, Atlantic Computers, BCCI, Maxwell, Polly Peck, etc.) which regularly place the audit function under the public microscope. The purpose of this chapter is to reflect on the role and changing status of the audit function. By offering an overview of the literature on audit expectations and analysing the issues which have been the major focus of debate, the chapter seeks to facilitate understanding of a function which is varyingly claimed to be misunderstood, misrepresented, contradictory or simply unhelpful and of limited use.

STATEMENTS OF COMPANY AUDIT OBJECTIVES

Concern that the fundamentals of the rationale for auditing were misunderstood has led numerous writers over the years to call for the publication of better defined and clearly communicated statements of audit objectives. If such statements were available and had the acknowledged approval of interested parties, they would certainly provide a solid basis for answering any expectations gap problem. What can be gleaned from an analysis of contemporary professional statements on the limited company external audit function (i.e. auditing standards published by the Auditing Practices Board) is that the audit is being portrayed primarily as a process designed to assess the credibility of information contained in a company's financial statements. Auditing is not regarded as an exact science, designed to specify to 100 per cent accuracy the information contained in the financial statements. It is more a process of judgement, concerned to ensure that the information is reasonably accurate, true and fair, not true and correct, sufficient rather than absolute.

However, the heavy reliance in such professional statements, and also in any statutory declarations on auditing, on subjective terms such as reasonable, materiality, adequacy, reliability, relevance and judgement tends to cloud the audit process with a large degree of uncertainty. In particular, there remains one question (fundamental to any analysis of audit expectations) which is largely left unanswered: 'Why audit?' Why is an audit needed? What are the reasons justifying its existence and particular form and content? The obvious, but rather unhelpful, response is to say that audits are performed because statutes require them. But why was such a requirement invoked in the first place? The question remains the same. Interestingly, in this respect it is worth noting the findings of Turley and Cooper's (1991) investigation of the audit methodologies of twenty-one large UK accountancy firms. A quarter of the firms' audit manuals (the closest one can get to an ABC approach of how to audit) did not contain any definition of auditing activity and, generally, very few of the manuals gave any significant discussion to explaining conceptual factors such as the need for independence, the benefits of an assessment of the credibility of the financial statements, etc. Turley and Cooper concurred with the view of Mautz and Sharaf (1961, p. 1) that auditors prefer to view the audit in procedural terms: 'to them, auditing is a series of practices and procedures, methods and techniques, a way of doing with little need for the explanations, descriptions, reconciliations and arguments so frequently lumped together as theory'. Given this, it does seem rather ironic that the cover illustration for the published version of one firm's audit manual at one stage comprised solely the dictionary definition of the verb 'to think' (Thornton Baker, 1983)!

The concepts of auditing

One way of attempting to understand the audit function and the status of associated audit expectations is to move from a procedural perspective to one which explores any underlying concepts – the bases on which the audit function is constructed. Again, such consideration offers possibilities with respect to closing any audit expectations gap. As Lee (1970, p. 296) noted, 'if auditors do not fully comprehend their auditing role in society, then how can non-accountants be expected to understand it?'

Shifting from procedures to concepts unfortunately makes redundant a whole number of auditing texts. In the auditing literature the conceptual approach has tended to be dwarfed by the number of writers seeking to provide practical, technical guides as to how to perform an audit. Nevertheless, some auditing texts (see, for example, Mautz and Sharaf, 1961; Lee, 1986; Flint, 1988; Sherer and Kent, 1988; Dunn, 1996) have sought to address the philosophical basis of auditing. As Flint argues, there has to be an explanation of why auditors do what they do, what they believe they achieve, and what the public believes they achieve. There has to be an explanation of the nature, purpose, possibilities and limitations of auditing so that members of society who seek to draw benefit from the function can understand what they can expect to obtain (Flint, 1988, p. 4).

Starting from such a premise, the general approach of these writers has been to identify a number of basic concepts and postulates about the audit function. Lee (1986), for instance, identified justifying, behavioural and functional postulates, stressing (among other things) the importance of credibility assessment to investment decisions and stewardship functions, auditor independence and accountability, and the ability to obtain audit evidence in a cost-effective manner. While providing a representation of the assumptions underlying the present statutory audit requirement for limited companies, however, such approaches tend to fall short on philosophical analysis. The emphasis is more on the way that auditors should behave than on exploring the reasons why auditors may behave differently and why their performance may not live up to expectations. In particular, they fail to give appropriate consideration to alternative perspectives on the nature of professionalism. As such the views of Flint (1988, pp. 14–15) that auditing is wholly utilitarian, and Mautz and Sharaf (1961) that 'a profession exists . . . to serve society' sit uneasily with Collin's opinion (quoted in Haskell, 1984, p. 181) that 'professionals are wolves in sheep's clothing, monopolists who live by the rule of caveat emptor, but lack the integrity to admit it', or with Turley and Cooper's (1991) finding that the benefits stressed by the methodologies of major audit terms are not expressed in terms of any societal role of auditing, but as a commercial service to the management of the company they are auditing.

Market-based approaches

In response to the conflicting views over the nature of, or existence of, professionalism, market-based approaches to auditing have argued that the persistence of audits through time in unregulated environments (where auditing is not a mandatory statutory requirement) provides evidence that auditing services are valued by their consumers. If auditing was not providing the necessary benefits, in a free market, the resources currently expended on auditing would be switched to more preferred products (Wallace, 1980). In examining why audits have been demanded and the valued characteristics of the audit service, such approaches have developed a number of hypotheses and propositions about auditing which are seen as expanding the basic concepts ingrained in the above-mentioned 'philosophical' texts. Wallace (1980), for example, identified three hypotheses in explaining the demand for auditing: the stewardship (monitoring) hypothesis; the information hypothesis; and the insurance hypothesis. The added insight provided by such hypotheses is nicely illustrated by the use of agency theory in explaining the stewardship hypothesis. According to agency theory, the demand for auditing can be generated by the agent rather than the principal (by the directors rather than the shareholders or other users contractually related to the company). The rationale for this argument is that principals are basically indifferent to the use of monitoring activities because they always have the ability to protect themselves from the risk of loss (incurred by agents spending the company's resources on personally related items, e.g. a holiday or other unsanctioned perquisites) by paying lower wages/salaries for the services of the agent. Thus, agency theory purports to establish that agents have an incentive to subject their stewardship of the principal's resources to external monitoring if the benefits of monitoring (in terms of avoiding or minimizing wage reductions through the guarantee/protection provided by the monitoring to the principal) are greater than the costs (in terms of monitoring/audit fees). Again, with the insurance hypothesis, Wallace (1980) provides additional insights on the rationales for auditing. She notes the 'deep pockets' of auditors relative to ailing or bankrupt corporations (the victims of undetected fraud) and concludes that auditors can provide some protection from an otherwise uninsurable business risk.

This consideration of the economics of information can also be used to examine the type of monitoring applied to the activities of the agent. Wallace (1980) concluded that principals (and agents) will prefer attestation of financial statements by independent, external auditors if the cost of such work is less than the accumulated cost of each principal individually undertaking the monitoring activities him- or herself. The application of cost-benefit analysis to the role and functioning of external auditing has also been utilized by Moizer (1992) in considering the likelihood of audit cheating. He has sought to analyse whether a rational economic person could be expected to 'tell the truth' – whether it would be in such an auditor's economic interests to report detected errors and omissions of management. Moizer's thesis is that such an auditor would have to weigh up the expected value of the economic interest that will be lost (if he or she is dispensed with by management for disclosing a breach) against the reduction of future net auditing revenues that will occur as a result of the loss of reputation suffered by the auditor if the misconduct (of not reporting a detected breach) is made public. The benefit of this approach is that it helps to address the aforementioned conflict between the alternative perspectives of auditors acting as altruistic, ethical professionals and profit-seeking monopolists. In one of his earlier articles, Moizer (1985) concluded that, even in the extreme case of an auditor acting purely on grounds of economic self-interest, there are many occasions when such an individual would choose to act in an independent manner. Interestingly, though, in a later (1992) article, he presents a rather gloomier picture with regard to the auditor's choice of audit quality, when arguing that auditors really have an economic incentive to ensure only that the quality of audit work does not fall below the minimum specified by the law (and endorsed by the auditing profession). The relative unobservability of higher quality audit work was seen as such that it would have little impact on the reputation, and hence earning power, of the audit firm. Thus, instead of expecting auditors independently to improve the quality of their audit work, Moizer saw the stronger economic incentive being to improve their image with company management and with users of financial statements through public relations activities, etc. In a similar fashion, Kaplan (1987) has questioned market-based presumptions of auditor independence by highlighting the apparent immunity of audit firm reputations to any 'fall-out' following a publicized audit failure.

Alternative conceptions of audit practice

In recent years, a third identifiable contribution to audit theory has developed, initially through attempts to move away from traditional, laboratory-style, audit judgement research. Taking as its cue the latter's failure to explain adequately the nature of auditors' decision processes and the functioning of audit techniques (e.g., see Abdolmohammadi and Wright, 1987; Johnson, Jamal and Glen Berryman, 1989), such research has begun to explore the socially constructed nature of auditing and the processes by which the conflicts and pressures in the auditor's working environment are accommodated (e.g., see Humphrey and Moizer, 1990; Pentland, 1993; Power, 1992, 1995).

The findings emanating from such research have started to expose some of the mystiques associated with audit practice, revealing its ideological character and the questionable nature of certain taken-for-granted assumptions about audit work and processes of audit regulation. Conceptually, auditing practices appear not as 'natural' or 'unchallengeable' but as contextually dependent, with considerable commercial demands on the part of client company management affecting the general design of audit methodologies, audit planning systems and statistical sampling/'risk-based' audit techniques. In Humphrey and Moizer's (1990) study, for example, audit plans were seen by auditors not to be concerned purely with credibility assessment but also with enhancing a decreasingly valued audit product by identifying the scope to provide other services to client management – 'our planning is not just audit planning. It is planning to give the client the service he wants' (p. 231). Their discussions with audit managers illustrated the loosely constructed status of audit techniques in terms of the task of credibility assessment, but audit 'philosophy' was clearly not absent. Rather, it was ever present but in the form of keeping the customer (i.e. client company management) satisfied – a philosophy deriving from business and not from any direct concern with social obligation or notions of public interest. Similarly, Power's (1992) historical analysis of the development of statistical sampling techniques argued that such a sampling discourse had arisen to legitimate, rationalize and improve practices that were already in place – that partial investigation procedures had already been introduced, largely to keep costs down, by audit firms. In concluding, Power lamented the way that much of what has passed for audit judgement research has seemed more intent on sustaining, than on exploring, the auditor's claims and bases of expertise.

Such questioning of the nature of audit practices has also been used to explore processes of audit regulation and the growing extension of the audit function to organizations and society where it has hitherto had little significance (e.g., see Power, 1994; Sikka and Willmott, 1995). Such research has attempted to broaden analysis from one dominated by 'rational' economic motives and perspectives to one which recognizes the sociological and political nature of audit practice and its regulation; from one which does not presume auditor expertise but which seeks to examine the construction and application of audit practices in their local contexts. An interesting illustration of the growing impact of such research is illustrated by Lee's most recent (1993) auditing text, *Corporate Audit Theory*. While retaining the normative and prescriptive tone of three editions of his preceding company auditing book, Lee states that he had consciously chosen to incorporate relevant alternative analyses of audit practice. Key motivations were his concern with 'the fundamental lack of understanding' among practising auditors as to the nature of the corporate audit function and the diet of 'conventional and uncritical theory' being fed to a measurable proportion of accountancy students and the need for more challenging and critical audit education (p. xiv).

By necessity, the above review of theoretical studies of the nature of auditing has been able to provide only a broad overview of key concepts and issues. However, what is striking is the contrasting theoretical stances with regard to expectations of the purpose and operation of the audit function. Most notable is the distinction between views of auditing as a socially orientated function (in which auditors are portrayed as ethical, socially responsible individuals) and the views of auditing as a monopolistic business (with auditors hiding behind the profitable mystique of professional judgement). Some reconciliation of this conflict can be provided through reference to theories of information economics and market-based approaches to auditing but even here there are divergent views and some critical commentaries on the benefits of a self-regulating audit function. Such diversity and conflicts in theoretical perceptions provide a strong indication of why discussions about audit expectations are often concerned with the existence of an 'expectations gap'.

The remainder of this chapter attempts to summarize the major strands of the debate on the expectations gap, including some examination of the strategies that have been put forward or implemented in order to close the gap, and the relative degree of success or impact such strategies have had. The chapter concludes with a discussion of where the debate will move in the future, considering among other things whether it is in the interests of the audit profession for the gap to be closed.

THE AUDIT EXPECTATIONS GAP

Defining the expectations gap

As might be expected from the diversity of views about the audit function, described above, a variety of definitions has been provided for the audit expectations gap. Some have seen it purely as a role-perception gap, leading to comparisons of the views of shareholders (and/or other users of audited financial statements and/or the general public) regarding the role of the audit with a predetermined, sometimes legalistic notion of what can reasonably be expected of auditors (or with what auditors believe should be expected of them). This has led to talk of an 'ignorance gap' – a gap that can be closed by the professional auditing bodies educating the recipients of audit services (and in some cases the auditors) as to what can reasonably be expected from an audit. Others have sought to broaden the definition of an expectations gap by incorporating a service delivery element – specifically considering whether auditors are performing, or are perceived to be performing, the duties that can reasonably be expected of them. A few have even sought to break down this latter category into the adequacy of current professional auditing standards and the quality of auditors' service delivery (CICA, 1988).

The difficulty in operationalizing these various categorizations of the audit expectations gap is that they rely heavily on the use of the word 'reasonable', and the implicit assumption that there exists one real, absolute way of looking at the audit function. For the purposes of this chapter, the expectations gap will be regarded in more general terms, as a representation of the feeling that *auditors are performing in a manner at variance with the beliefs and desires of those for whose benefit the audit is being carried out.*

The history of the expectations gap

The first use of the phrase 'expectations gap' can be traced to the United States, where the phrase has until recently been given much more public prominence. In early 1974 the Commission on Auditors' Responsibilities (frequently referred to as the Cohen Commission, after its chairman) was set up by the American Institute of Certified Public Accountants (AICPA) with the specific task of making recommendations on the appropriate responsibilities of auditors. In doing so, the Commission's terms of reference stated that it was to consider 'whether a gap exists between what the public expects or needs and what auditors can and should reasonably expect to accomplish'. The AICPA had been prompted to establish the Cohen Commission by the growing public concern about the criticisms of the quality of auditors' performance. The failure of auditors to detect or disclose failures or wrongdo-

ings by publicly owned corporations (such as Equity Funding) was also officially stated as the reason for the US government establishing a Senate subcommittee (known commonly as the Metcalf Committee) in the autumn of
1975 to investigate and suggest ways of improving the accountability of publicly owned corporations and their auditors. This was followed in 1976 by
the setting up of the House (of Representatives) Subcommittee on Oversight
and Investigations of the House Commerce Committee (usually referred to
as the Moss Committee, again after its chairman), which was also concerned
with standards of corporate accountability. In Canada similar concerns led
the Canadian Institute of Chartered Accountants (CICA), in 1977, to establish a group called the Special Committee to Examine the Role of the Auditor,
which became known as the Adams Committee and reported in 1978, soon
after the Cohen Commission.

Whilst the phrase 'expectations gap' may well have had its roots in North
America, similar concerns about the role and accountability of auditors were
concurrently being expressed in the UK (again following a number of major
corporate scandals and a growing demand for greater corporate accountability – the latter reflected in the issue of the Accounting Standard Committee's
Corporate Report in 1975). Several Department of Trade investigations in
the 1970s were critical of auditing practices and such concern led to the
accountancy profession setting up a joint disciplinary scheme to investigate
cases of public interest concerning auditors, and the Auditing Practices
Committee (APC), which published its first set of auditing standards in 1980.

A gap that would not go away

A feature common to many of these studies and investigations was the finding that a gap between performance and expectation did exist, and that this
was not due just to ignorance on the part of users of accounting information. According to the Cohen Commission, users generally had reasonable
expectations of auditors' abilities and of the assurances they can give. It
attributed the expectations gap more to the public accounting profession's
failure to react and evolve rapidly enough to keep pace with the changing
business and social environment. Similar conclusions were reached by the
Metcalf Commission, which in calling for more visible regulatory procedures
noted that 'the public is not willing to accept things on faith today.
Government and business leaders must demonstrate that they are worthy of
the trust they ask of the public' (Metcalf Committee, 1978, p. 90).

The congressional findings that an expectations gap existed and that auditors were underperforming were challenged. Benston (1985) undertook a
detailed analysis of the congressional recommendations and came to the conclusion (p. 74) that:

> there is little evidence of collusion and other anticompetitive actions by
> CPA firms. Audit failures appear to be fewer than the optimal amount as
> a consequence of enforced minimum standards. Therefore, there would

seem to be few valid arguments for additional regulation in the public interest.

In fact, the arguments made in the Moss Report (1976) and in the Metcalf Committee's Staff Report (1976) are almost completely devoid of empirical or logical support. If enacted, they would increase auditing and regulatory costs and reduce competition. In any event, a principal aspect of the demand for regulation by legislators, journalists, academicians, and public interest activists appears to have been fulfilled. The legislators have had publicity, journalists have gotten copy, academicians received data and the opportunity of writing papers like this, and some public interest activists have had a shot at authority.

However, historical evidence and experience would suggest that the notion of an expectations gap would seem to be more than an imaginary problem. With time such problems could be expected to disappear, but the issue of audit expectations has continued to remain at the forefront of debate throughout the 1980s and 1990s.

In the USA, in 1985, the accountancy profession was again put under the spotlight of government investigation with the establishment of two congressional committees. The Brooks Committee (officially the Legislation and National Security Subcommittee of the House Committee on Government Operations) was concerned with the quality of CPA audits of federal expenditure, which had been reported as being substandard (with frequent non-compliance with professional auditing standards). The second committee, the Dingell Committee (officially the Subcommittee on Oversight and Investigations of the House Committee on Energy and Commerce) was established to investigate the 'effectiveness of independent accountants who audit publicly owned corporations and the effectiveness of the SEC who audits those accountants'. Again the setting up of this committee came after a number of notable corporate failures where the role of the auditor had once more been called into doubt (e.g. the cases of ESM Government Securities Inc. and Beverly Hills Savings and Loan Association).

While the Dingell Committee's hearings were in progress the National Commission on Financial Reporting (a private sector accounting-funded development, chaired by James Treadway, which became known as the Treadway Commission) was established. The Treadway Commission reported in October 1987 with a number of recommendations including restatements of the auditor's responsibility for fraud detection and quarterly reporting. At the same time as the Treadway Commission was conducting its investigations, the profession's Auditing Standards Board (ASB) launched a number of projects with the aim of reducing the expectations gap. These produced a series of new statements on auditing standards (becoming known as the 'expectations gap' standards), covering such issues as the detection of fraud and illegal acts, the assessment of internal controls and audit reporting.

The audit expectations gap has also continued to figure prominently on the international auditing stage over the last decade. In 1986 the Canadian

Institute of Chartered Accountants (CICA) established the Macdonald Commission (where the majority of members were not chartered accountants) with the specific task of investigating the 'public's expectations of audits'. This found considerable evidence of a gap between the public's expectations of auditors and auditor performance. As with the earlier 1970s studies it concluded that for the most part public expectations of auditors are reasonable and achievable. In the Commission's view expectation gaps would only be narrowed by the profession's acceptance of the need for change and improvement, and its detailed report contained fifty recommendations as to ways in which the expectations gap could be narrowed.

In Britain, the ICAEW's working party on the future of the audit (ICAEW, 1986) concluded that 'there appears to be a considerable gap between the public's perception of the role of the audit and auditor's perception of that role'. According to Tweedie (1987), the need for the profession to address this issue was the prime reason for the establishment of the Emerging Issues Task Force in early 1987. Similarly, in Australia in 1987, the president of the Institute of Chartered Accountants called on the profession to respond to public concern about the role of the auditor and to seek ways of narrowing the expectations gap.

In the 1990s there has been no let up in the debate on audit expectations. In Britain, for example, the Auditing Practices Board published a paper in November 1992 designed to promote discussion on the future of the audit (known as the Macfarlane Report – APB, 1992). This explored various issues concerning the role, scope and structure of the auditing function. However, in the light of (often) critical responses from the auditing profession and perceived conflicts with a subsequently published report in December 1992 by the Cadbury Committee, *The Financial Aspects of Corporate Governance*, the APB published a revised future framework for auditing in its 1994 publication, *The Audit Agenda* (APB, 1994). Not to be outdone, the Institute of Chartered Accountants in Scotland published a monograph entitled *Auditing into the Twenty-First Century* (ICAS, 1993) which specified a range of proposals for ensuring that external corporate audits satisfy reasonable public expectations (p. iii).

The growing significance of the issue of an audit expectations gap has also been reflected in a range of research studies (often sponsored by the accounting profession) seeking to measure or position the gap in a wide range of countries including Britain, the USA, Canada, Denmark, Spain, New Zealand, Australia, South Africa, Belgium and Japan (e.g., see Sikka *et al.*, 1992; Humphrey, Moizer and Turley, 1992, 1993; García Benau *et al.*, 1993; Gloeck and De Jager, 1993; Porter, 1993).

A striking finding to have emerged from such research has been that the audit expectations gap, while existing officially in name for just over twenty years, has a much longer history in terms of content. Ambiguities in the role, responsibilities and performance of auditors have existed for over a hundred years. Humphrey, Moizer and Turley (1992), for example, show how the content of public speeches and articles in reaction to corporate scandals in the

1880s and the 1930s bears considerable similarity to the issues being raised via contemporary audit expectation gap discussions. The respective comments by the president of the ICAEW to the London Students' Society in 1885 and the AICPA secretary in 1939 in the aftermath of the McKesson Robbins scandal provide excellent illustrations of such arguments:

> Audits performed by us are described as useless, wasteful and dangerous; as deceitful and fraudulent pretences, and as traps laid to catch fees and deceive confiding clients and the public. . . . In my experience I have found men of ordinary business ability holding the most ridiculous opinions as to the power of a professional accountant to detect fraud and error. . . . Let us be open and frank with the public and our clients, endeavour to create a true public opinion of the value of our services, and the scope and limits of our capacity.   (Griffiths, 1885, p. 27)

> We find that the public has believed that the certified public accountant was an infallible superman; that the signature of a CPA invariably meant that everything was perfect; that it was unnecessary to read the accountant's certificate or the financial statements to which it was appended as long as the three major letters were in evidence. . . . Whether through its own fault or not, the accounting profession seems to have been oversold. Its limitations have been overlooked, while its abilities have been emphasized. Now the public has been somewhat shocked to find that even auditors can be fooled by clever criminals.   (quoted in Miller, 1986, p. 35)

Historical analysis of this form serves to sensitize interpretations of the audit expectations gap debate. Its clear implication is that the longevity and resilience of the 'gap' need to be explored not just in terms of failures in professional accounting education and communication programmes. Attention also needs to be directed to structures governing the provision of audit services and the inherent conflicts in any self-regulated audit function.

THE CONTENT OF THE EXPECTATIONS GAP

Within the confines of this chapter, it is clearly not possible to analyse all the findings and recommendations of the various investigations that have studied the issue of audit expectations even in just the last twenty years, let alone the last century. From a review of this literature, however, it would appear that the debates about audit expectations have tended to focus on four main aspects of the audit function:

(1) audit assurance;
(2) audit reporting;
(3) audit independence;
(4) audit regulation and liability.

Many of the relevant issues are covered in much more depth in other chapters of this book. As such, the aim here is not to provide an exhaustive coverage of these issues but, rather, to highlight the key elements of concern and in so doing help to illuminate some of the deep-rooted factors underlying the audit expectations gap.

The provision of audit assurance

In reviewing studies of audit expectations and attitude surveys of users of financial statements, what is most striking is the exacting nature of perceptions of the functions performed by the present statutory external corporate audit. Rather than being seen as a probabilistic statement, the audit report has been viewed frequently as a certification, a guarantee of accuracy, even among auditors (Lee, 1970). The audit is also seen as something more than an information credibility assessment. Beck (1973), for example, found considerable support for the view that the audit is designed to give assurance on the efficiency of management and the financial soundness of the company. Such studies have been criticized for methodological weaknesses (see Davidson, 1975) but a similar pattern of findings has continued over the last two decades, with users of audited accounts continually perceiving a broader audit function than that performed, or perceived as legitimate, by auditors (for summaries, see CICA, 1988; Humphrey, Moizer and Turley, 1993).

The usual response to such findings among the auditing profession, and unfortunately, at times, among auditing academics, is to stress the general lack of understanding of the audit function, and to highlight the unreasonable nature of such expectations. Such comments tend, however, to gloss over what is a more fundamentally controversial area. For instance, the view that the audit function is designed to assess management performance does not look that unreasonable when set in the context of public sector auditing. For example, various National Audit Offices around the world undertake 'value-for-money', or operational, audits in seeking to ensure the accountability of local and central government organizations. Indeed, it could only be a matter of time before such investigations become a normal part of the external audit of limited companies. For instance, legislation in the 1980s establishing new regulatory frameworks in the financial services sector and for banks and building societies would seem to add support to this view. One aspect of this legislation laid great stress on auditors assuming a responsibility to assess the adequacy of the internal control systems of financial organizations. Such an issue received a heightened profile when the Cadbury Committee (1992) recommended that company directors should make a statement in the company's annual accounts as to the effectiveness of its system of internal control and that 'the company's auditors should report thereon'. The Auditing Practices Board subsequently recognized in its *Audit Agenda* (1994) that in the longer term auditors may extend their published reports to all aspects of a company's system of internal control. Its specific discussion paper on the matter (APB, 1995), however, has produced a generally negative response from the large accounting firms, with only Touche Ross standing out publicly as being in favour of such a development in auditors' responsibilities.

The controversial nature of audit expectations with respect to the nature of auditor assurance is perhaps best illustrated by considering the auditor's responsibility for fraud detection. According to the original Explanatory Foreword to the Auditing Standards and Guidelines, issued in 1980, the primary responsibility for the prevention and detection of irregularities and fraud rests with an enterprise's management. The auditor's principal responsibility is seen as reporting on the truth and fairness of the enterprise's financial statements, and any duty in respect of fraud detection is restricted to planning the audit so as to have a reasonable expectation of detecting any resultant material misstatements in the financial statements (which implies that auditors who executed their audits in a reasonable manner would not be held responsible for any failure to detect material fraud). This all reads very conclusively until it is recognized that until the 1940s the detection of fraud was still seen by auditors as the primary objective of the audit (Brown, 1962). Since that time pronouncements of the professional auditing bodies throughout the world have tended to displace it with the broader objective of reporting on the truth and fairness of a company's financial statements. Lee (1986, p. 23) asserted that such a switch reflected the growing concern of users with the quality of financial information and the tendency of company management to assume more responsibility for fraud prevention and detection (through the development of internal control systems). In his view, the increased scale of business transactions was such that the cost of searching out fraud and error by external audit was largely acknowledged as having become uneconomic.

Other writers, however, attribute a much more proactive and self-interested role for the audit profession in bringing about such a change. Brown (1962) suggested that the profession's down-playing of this responsibility was largely a response to the massive undetected fraud revealed in the McKesson and Robbins case of the late 1930s. As Willingham (1975, p. 19) notes:

> perhaps the discussion of the auditor's responsibility for the detection of fraud has not yet diminished because it was a stated audit objective for over 400 years and was removed as an objective by the profession rather than by a change in the demand of clients of accounting firms. A solicitous consuming public could reinstate it.

Gwilliam (1987) expressed concern at the scarcity of explanation for the changed emphasis with regard to fraud detection, particularly when it was clear that courts or regulatory bodies have continually stressed the importance of the auditor's responsibility in this respect.

The pressure for auditors to assume a broader responsibility for fraud detection has continued in the 1980s. For instance, in the mid-1980s in the UK the government, in response to a serious questioning of the role of the auditor in such scandals as DeLorean and Johnson Matthey Bank (the latter resulting in its auditors paying a reported £49.5 million in out-of-court settlements) and to a growing concern as to levels of corporate fraud, 'invited' the auditing profession to rethink its role regarding fraud detection (*Accountancy*

Age, 25 October 1985, p. 4). The deep-rooted and complex nature of the debate over audit expectations is well illustrated by the fact that some five years elapsed before auditing guidance on the auditor's responsibilities in relation to fraud and other illegal acts was finally approved. The difficulty the profession has had in defining such responsibilities was such that the ASB's predecessor, the Auditing Practices Committee, found itself in the position of issuing a revised Explanatory Foreword to Auditing Standards and Guidelines, which, unlike its predecessor, remained silent on the fundamental matter of fraud.

In the 1990s there have been further twists in the tale of the auditor and fraud. The 1990 guideline lasted for only another two years before a new draft guideline appeared, eventually resulting in two final guidelines in 1995 (see SAS 110 and SAS 121, reprinted in *Accountancy*, March 1995). In commenting on the development of standard guidance with respect to fraud responsibilities, Humphrey, Turley and Moizer (1993) highlighted the largely defensive attitude of the profession, concluding that while it had given some ground in relation to fraud reporting responsibilities it had avoided any extension in detection responsibilities. Such views were backed by opinions emanating from the DTI, which was reported as being of the view that 'management and shareholders see an important role for auditors generally, and the prevention and detection of fraud in particular and there is a wide gap between these expectations and the view of the auditors' responsibilities offered in the proposed guidelines' (as reported in *Accountancy Age*, 9 March 1989, p. 3). Humphrey, Turley and Moizer argued that in recent years the profession had made some of its strongest public acknowledgments of the limited capacity of the statutory audit to detect fraud, particularly in relation to senior management fraud. Such statements were seen to be especially ironic given that several of the major accounting firms had, at the same time, started to offer specialist fraud investigations (called 'forensic' audits) as an additional chargeable service to client company management. Humphrey, Turley and Moizer stressed the need for more analysis and debate on the practical capabilities of the statutory audit with regard to fraud detection and the extent to which audit failure was disguised by continuing corporate success (also see Power, 1993).

Much of the concern with audit practice appears to rest in the degree of trust placed by auditors in client company management. For example, the 1990 fraud guideline stated that the auditor 'should neither assume that management is dishonest nor assume unquestioning honesty when planning, performing and evaluating audit work'. Such a stance was criticized by the Trade and Industry Select Committee. Drawing on the case law judgement in *Re Kingston Cotton Mill* (1896) that the auditor is a 'watchdog not a bloodhound', the Committee argued that what society needed were auditors who acted more like 'rottweilers'. An editorial in *Accountancy* magazine, the official journal of the ICAEW, argued that 'a profession of rottweilers would be a dangerous and anti-social innovation' (July 1990, p. 1), which produced letters from readers questioning whether auditors approached their work in such a naive fashion that they were capable of detecting only innocent management errors or employee-led fraud. The 1995 fraud guideline subsequently stated that auditors should plan and perform their work with an attitude of 'professional scepticism' and there have been more recent initiatives which have stressed the need for auditors to be more assertive in terms of fraud detection duties. However, the inherent contradiction between having audits to check on 'untrustworthy' directors and auditors having to 'trust' management assurances in the conduct of their work questions whether the future will be little different from the scenario portrayed in another *Accountancy* editorial in January 1991 (p. 1):

> There will be a gigantic fraud. The auditors will fail to detect it, and will be surprised when they read about it, at the same time as everybody else, in the pages of *The Sunday Times*. The profession will be heavily criticized. The auditing guideline on fraud will be reviewed. . . . There will be nothing new under the sun.

Audit reporting

Given the differing views and misunderstandings of the nature of audit assurance identified in studies of the role of auditing, it is not surprising to find that research on perceptions of the form and content of audit reports has produced similar results. The CICA's (1988) study, for example, found that a significant proportion of the reader/investor public believes that an unqualified audit opinion is only ever issued in circumstances where the company is not presently experiencing financial problems. As Tweedie (1987) noted, in discussing the functioning of the audit report as an early warning/burglar alarm system, it is difficult for lay people to understand how a company can suffer serious financial difficulties, or even collapse, shortly after having received an unqualified opinion. Divergences between the intended message of an audit report and the impression/meanings attributed to it by users have also been revealed in studies of qualified audit reports (for summaries, see Craswell, 1985; Holt and Moizer, 1990). In certain cases audit qualifications designed to alert readers to material errors in the financial statements have been found not to have influenced subsequent investment decisions by users relying on those financial statements (see Estes and Reimer, 1977; Estes, 1982).

Such findings have served repeatedly to direct discussions on audit expectations to the form and content of the audit report. As such, the expectations gap has been framed very much in terms of a codification problem – that if users better understood the code being used by auditors in reporting their opinions, they would more accurately perceive the messages being given by the various forms of audit reports. Consequently, one of the most frequent solutions that has been put forward as a way of closing the expectations gap has been to change the format of the audit report. In the late 1970s short-form, standardized reporting was typically in favour, in the hope that it would reduce the inconsistency and complexity of audit reports and generate 'at-a-glance' understanding. The continuance of the expectations gap in the 1980s somewhat discredited this exception-based approach to audit reporting and longer-form reporting has come back into favour (albeit in many cases in a standardized form). Typical of this movement was the ICAEW's (1986) *Future of the Audit* report, which called for more consideration of positive reporting and the inclusion in the audit report of explicit statements of assurance regarding each aspect of the auditor's responsibilities. The stylized, short-form reports were seen as employing a rather complex codification system and emphasis was now placed on the 'adoption of a language more understandable to non-expert readers of reports'. Versions of this latter form of reporting have been subsequently adopted in the USA, Canada and the UK.

Historical analysis, however, does not hold out much hope that such changes to the audit reporting format will provide a resolution to the audit expectations gap. If, underneath all the apparent 'confusion' regarding the work of auditors, there was one all-embracing definition of the audit function, the outcome of such an educative initiative would be far less problematic. As has been shown above, however, theoretical analyses continue to offer sharply distinctive perspectives on the role, responsibilities and conceptual underpinnings of the audit. Given such divergent theoretical, and, indeed, legal (see below) views, the audit expectations gap debate begins to resemble a struggle in which the various parties to the audit process seek to ensure that their particular view of the audit remains in, or rises to, the ascendancy. In such a context, educational initiatives become possible mechanisms for buttressing or legitimating certain preferred positions. This is very much the impression with longer-form audit reporting. Critics, for instance, have highlighted the considerable degree of standardization in the claimed 'long-form' reports and the way they provide generalized descriptions of the audit process but little detailed information on the precise level of audit testing and operational levels of audit materiality and risk. The intention appears to be to give readers of an audit report more information about auditing rather than more information about the results of specific audits. Not surprisingly, in the USA, for example, some commentators have argued that changes in the audit report will not be seen as unselfish, socially orientated concessions on the part of the auditor, but as a self-serving retreat from responsibility by the audit profession (for example, see Neebes and Roost, 1987).

Similar criticisms have been directed at published professional Auditing Standards, as a way of explaining the heavy utilization of subjective terms such as reasonable, material, sufficiency and judgement. As Hopwood (1990, p. 84) noted, the profession's regulatory organizations have 'rarely adopted either a consistent or a proactive stance. They have also tended to avoid too close an involvement with the detailed functioning of the auditing craft.' Interestingly, work in this area has started to highlight the double-edged status of professional communications in that the more specific they become, the more they undermine the mystical qualities of professional expertise and judgement (a frequently noted critical factor underlying the power base of a profession). This raises the paradox that, if the general public really knew the full extent of the work performed by auditors, it may conclude that the audit service is overrated, which is presumably the last impression auditors would want to give. As stated in the CICA's (1988) investigation of the audit expectations gap (p. 149):

> it may be of little comfort to the profession to know that a vast majority of the general and reader/investor publics are satisfied with the performance of auditors, if the profession concludes that the views of a substantial portion of both publics are based on a misperception of the role of the auditor.

The Macdonald Commission concluded that better communication of the respective roles of auditors and management could have only a limited effect in reducing the expectations gap. In coming to the same conclusion as the earlier Cohen, Metcalf and Adams investigations (that a gap did exist and that public expectations of the auditor are generally reasonable and achievable), it saw a need for the audit profession to be more adaptive and receptive to change, stressing that any public trust in the profession was a fragile commodity that 'could easily be shattered by a few highly publicized instances of apparent audit failures' (CICA, 1988, p. 4).

Audit independence

If any topic can be classified as going to the heart of the audit expectations debate, it is the issue of auditor independence. All the above-mentioned investigations of the audit function in the 1970s and 1980s have highlighted the importance of auditors performing and being seen to perform, in an unbiased, impartial manner. The Metcalf Report, for example, regarded independence as the auditor's single most valuable attribute.

In terms of the expectations gap, the concern has been that auditors have not been operating in a sufficiently independent fashion. Both the Cohen and Metcalf Commissions, for example, were worried that competitive pressures were affecting audit quality. The pressure to acquire or maintain audit clients was seen to be such for Metcalf to conclude that 'accounting firms have often cut costs to the point where the integrity of the audit is impaired' (Metcalf Committee, 1978, p. 93). Similar concerns were expressed by the Dingell investigation in the mid-1980s. Its chairperson summarized such doubts at the start of the inquiry:

> The system begins with the corporate managers and directors, whose actions are to be audited, going out and choosing the auditor. They hire the independent audit firm, determine the fees to be paid and have the power to fire the auditor for any reason. The independent audit firm often provides tax and management consulting services to the same corporation it audits. Can we really expect an audit firm to remain independent when

its audit fees, and perhaps substantial consulting fees, are directly related
to pleasing the corporate managers being audited?

                                                    (quoted in Miller, 1986, p. 31)

The particular issue of auditors providing non-audit services has been the
subject of frequent discussion in the last three decades, although it should be
stressed that all the major investigations have focused on the potential threat
to independence, having found little evidence of cases where the provision of
such services had compromised independence. This lack of evidence was
picked up by Hall (1988, p. 26), who commented that 'nothing was broken
that required fixing. Critics, regulators, the profession itself had conjured up
a problem, based on assumption and repetition, not facts and then busily
engaged themselves in finding a cure.' Hall believed that the profession had
been too flaccid in fighting off its critics with concessions, and that some
members had been unwitting allies of the critics because they had deplored
the change from the profession they knew and thought should continue. Hall
was confident that in today's litigious environment no firm could afford to
stay in practice if it was not committed to high quality audit performance
and that those who strayed from these standards would be taken care of by
the market. This argument, however, pays little regard to the difficulty of
knowing whether an auditor has failed to act independently given the relative unobservability of audit work – a point emphasized by John Dingell, at
the Committee's first hearing.

> The accounting firms which audit publicly owned corporations are private
> organizations which do not file public reports. It may sometimes be hard
> to understand the operations of their corporate clients from the public
> reports filed, but it *is* impossible to understand the operations of the audi-
> tors themselves since all we know is the little they choose to tell us.
> Likewise, when auditors make mistakes, we often do not know the causes
> of those mistakes because the investigation results are sealed from public
> view as a condition of an out-of-court settlement.
>
>   (quoted in Miller, 1986, pp. 30–1)

Given such descriptions of the provision of audit and non-audit services, it
is understandable why the lack of empirical evidence of the latter compromising independence has not failed to quell concern. As the Metcalf
Committee stressed, the auditor must be independent in both fact and appearance. Over the last thirty years a whole host of recommendations have been
put forward (including peer review systems, the development and strength-
ening of audit committees, the rotation of auditors, the prohibition of auditors performing non-audit services for a company they also audit, the
declaration in the company's financial statements of non-audit fees paid to
the auditor, etc.) as ways of bolstering audit independence. And yet the doubts
still remain that commercial pressures and the disproportionate power of
company management *vis-à-vis* the auditor are hindering in some way the
quality of audit work. The CICA (1988) saw much merit in stronger audit

committees and less flexible standards of financial reporting (as did the Cadbury Committee and the Accounting Standards Board in the UK in the 1990s), but believed that ultimately the most effective strategy to ensure that audit quality was not compromised by commercial pressures was a determination and dedication to professionalism on the part of auditors.

There are others, however, who see such a strategy as rather naive, wishful thinking. Apart from the fact that research studies have generally shown that user groups have much stricter views than auditors regarding situations which could jeopardize audit independence, there is a feeling that the days of the disinterested professional are long gone. Stevens (1988), in a survey of the impact of commercialism on the 'Big 8' accounting firms, was one of the first to highlight the increasing 'business' (as distinct from 'professional') orientation in audit work:

> The exploding scope of practice is transforming the cultures of the firms themselves. Salesmanship, once a dirty word to accountants, is now critical to the management process and, in many cases, has become the fastest route to promotion and partnership. When Arthur Young or Touche Ross or Price Waterhouse wins a new audit client (more than likely on the basis of a loss leader fee), it uses that opening to bombard the client with sales pitches designed to develop business for the firm's full inventory of services.
>
> (Stevens, 1988, p. 41)

Such work has been developed, most notably in the UK, by a range of authors who increasingly refer to the 'audit profession' as the 'audit industry' as a way of emphasizing its increased commercial emphasis (e.g., see Mitchell and Sikka, 1993). Such research has highlighted concerns with the audit profession's commitment to 'public interest' issues (see Willmott, 1990), emphasized the loosely constructed, ritualistic nature of audit practice and the ability of economic pressures to influence such practice behind the protective veil of claims to professional independence and judgement (see Humphrey and Moizer, 1990; Pentland, 1993; Power, 1995). One of the most striking observations has been the regular contrast drawn between the rising global economic power of the large accounting firms and the apparent persistence of the audit expectations gap – a clear sign that the latter debate is well within the control (and working to the benefit) of the audit profession.

Audit regulation and liability

Concerns with the persistence of the expectations gap, the regular frequency of audit scandals and doubts over public interest commitments of the profession have increasingly been translated into debates over the regulation of auditing firms. The traditional theoretical justification for a regulatory system has been that it offers a valuable way of ensuring that auditors provide quality work and discourages the provision of substandard work through a system of active monitoring and the punishment of poor quality work. The institutionalization of reducing to acceptable levels the risk of unsatisfactory audits is seen as particularly crucial in auditing given the difficulty that audit service recipients have in observing audit quality, either *ex-post* or *ex-ante*.

In recent times, however, another dimension of an audit regulatory system has been highlighted. Moving from the economics of auditing to the politics of auditing, a number of writers have highlighted the self-serving nature of what is in a large part a self-regulated audit system. A stream of papers has emphasized the self-serving nature of a regulatory system where auditors regulate themselves (e.g., see Willmott, 1990; Hooks, 1992; Humphrey, Moizer and Turley, 1992; Preston *et al.*, 1995; Sikka and Willmott, 1995). Self-regulation is seen as a way of the profession protecting itself from external threat and of preserving the status quo. Thus, in times of a major audit scandal, it becomes essential for the audit profession to be seen to be doing something, to be reacting to crisis, to reassure the public that nothing is wrong with the existing audit system despite appearances to the contrary. It is claimed to matter less that little happens to prevent similar scandals occurring in the future – the appearance of action is what really counts. Such lines of thinking have been used to criticize the closed nature of professional investigations into audit failure and the resulting lack of disciplinary action by professional regulators particularly in cases involving large audit firms, the limited operational use of professional auditing standards and guidelines and the self-interested nature of changes to statements of professional ethics. Classic criticism of the UK audit regulatory system has been the relative infrequency of regulatory visits (for some chartered accounting firms it was estimated that investigators would visit only once every fifty years), its lack of impact in terms of improving large firms' audit practices (most criticisms have been directed at small audit firms) and the fact that the regulators are concerned with the existence (or lack) of appropriate procedures to ensure high quality audits. This latter observation has led to comments that the regulators are regulating only compliance with audit regulations not audit quality *per se*, a degree of distancing from primary activities that has been seen to be evident in the growing expansion of audits across a range of organizational contexts (see Power, 1994, p. 6).

The general tone of such sentiments concerning the politics of audit regulation were nicely captured in an article by Fogarty, Heian and Knutson (1991). In a conflict-ridden environment, the task of the profession is to buttress itself against change, to give an appearance of a willingness to change but to give little ground in reality, to keep audit scandals out of court rather than run the risk of audit responsibilities being extended as a consequence of a detailed investigation of the practical limits of current audit work. Interestingly, the task of 'doing nothing' was seen to be an exhausting one, requiring the profession to battle for its case on a seemingly endless stream of investigating committees, reviews and public debates – a case of fighting to stand still. Similar conclusions have been drawn by a number of other writers in highlighting the control that the profession is able to exercise over any self-regulatory system (e.g., see Humphrey, Moizer and Turley, 1992; Sikka *et al.*, 1992).

Conceptually, such discussion has focused significantly on the conflicts inherent in a self-regulated audit system – and whether it can be reasonably expected that a professional body can act as both a regulator of audit practice and a 'trade' association designed to promote the best interests of its members. Increasingly, this has led to calls for more evidently independent regulation. In the UK, for instance, there have been suggestions that the regulatory system should be managed by either an Audit Commission or State Auditing Board (appointing and regulating auditors) or a Public Oversight Board (overseeing a self-regulated audit process, as is operated in the USA).

The demands for regulatory reform have also been heightened in the last five years by the changing legal liability environment facing auditors. On the one hand auditing firms have launched major publicity campaigns to highlight what they perceive as an unfair and overly punitive legal framework. Citing the huge sums that they have had to pay out in out-of-court settlements in cases of suspected audit failure, they have sought to secure the removal of joint and several liability terms that have been traditionally applied to (unlimited liability) partnerships and to ensure that a cap (monetary limit) is placed on auditors' liability in any cases where negligence is proved (as exists in Germany but which is prevented in the UK by the 1977 Unfair Contract Terms Act). Additionally, they have advocated the implementation of a principle of proportionate liability, as a way of avoiding the situation where auditors are only 1 per cent to blame for a corporate collapse but, because of their attractive 'deep pocket' insurance cover, attempts are made by litigants to ensure that they are held 99 per cent liable. Recently, audit firms have attracted considerable press coverage through decisions to register as limited partnerships in Jersey (as a way of reducing potential liability) or incorporating as a limited company for auditing services (where the price of limited liability is the requirement to publish annual accounts).

For critics of the auditing profession, such moves have for a long time been viewed with a fair degree of suspicion. As *The Economist* (1992, p. 28), a fairly conservative journal, noted pointedly a few years back, it would be foolish to let accountants off the liability hook without getting something from them in return. Liability is one of the few threats that keep auditors up to the mark.' Coming on top of the 1990 *Caparo* legal decision, which narrowed considerably the auditor's responsibility to third parties, the profession's liability campaign has been held out as further evidence of it putting its own business interest before considerations of public interest.

CONCLUSION

The purpose of this chapter has been to cast some light on the role of auditing and the nature of audit expectations. Both from examinations of theoretical perspectives on auditing, and from more practically based studies of the auditing services environment, it is quite clear that the auditing function is not a unitary phenomenon and can be taken as meaning different things to different people. There are a number of competing conceptual perspectives on the role and purpose of auditing and the nature of professionalism which portray some quite radically different scenarios of what can be expected of auditors. When this is coupled with the low visibility of audit work and the resultant uncertainty about what it comprises, it is not surprising to find that auditing has a problem of an expectations gap. Moreover, while the term 'expectations gap' has gained prominence over the last few years, the issues it has been seen to incorporate have been in existence for a good deal longer. Fraud detection, public interest reporting, the provision of non-audit services and reliance on management representations have at varying times been the subject of much debate. Indeed, on occasions the similarity of issues giving rise to a questioning of the audit function is of a level where it could almost be said for 1980 read 1970 or 1940 or even 1890.

What is also noticeable is that the major crises to have hit the audit profession, and the major investigations into the nature of the audit services market and its regulation (in both the UK and North America), have been closely related to the failure of auditors either to detect a number of major frauds or to provide an advance warning of an impending corporate collapse. These investigations have then tended to produce a whole host of recommendations as to ways by which the performance of auditors, or perceptions of auditor performance, could be enhanced, followed by a gradual quietening down of debate until the next major scandal. Some have seen this as the natural way of life for the audit profession. Others have argued that corporate crisis (defined broadly to include corporate collapse, undetected major frauds or even social disquiet at any abuse of corporate power) leads to new expectations of and requirements for accountability, which in turn lead to new demands on the audit function and in due course produce changes in auditing standards and practice (Tricker, 1982).

This chapter has argued that such a view should not be allowed to disguise the fact that the same issues have frequently recurred in many debates over auditing expectations. For example, there is a remarkable similarity between many of the recommendations of the Cohen (which is generally regarded as being largely ignored by the profession) and Metcalf Commissions in the late 1970s and those of the Treadway and Dingell Commissions in the 1980s. Tricker's (1982) analysis almost has too cosy an appearance about it, in suggesting that corporate crisis leads to demands for regulation and accountability, which in turn lead to changes in audit practice. This implies a relatively passive profession, continually responding to the changing expectations of society. From an analysis of the response to the varying historical crises, what appears more appropriate is evidence of a wealth of concern and investigation, followed by reflection and reconsideration on the part of the auditing profession, leading to some change as well but also a watering down of controversial reforms and a settling of the auditing services market until the next crisis or scandal (when more often than not the same issues are addressed and similar recommendations for change put forward).

The great difference between the above two views is the active consideration that the latter gives to the interested nature of the actions of the audit profession in both framing the content of the expectations gap and recommending and implementing strategies to close the gap. A lack of attention to such matters would seem to be a general failing of much of the audit expectations literature, with solutions being proposed without adequate attention being given to the lessons of history. There is often an apparent inability to recognize the way (failed) solutions of a few decades ago get reinvented, reimplemented and subsequently returned to the shelf to await the next search for a 'new' solution to the expectations gap.

The persistent similarity of the expectations gap debate raises questions as to whether it is a debate firmly in the control of the profession or a concept which serves its interests by allowing it to convey an impression of responding to public concern, repeatedly asserting its independence and directing questioning away from the existing audit system to the limitations of proposed audit reforms. Alternatively, the recurrent defensiveness of the audit profession has been claimed to be a reflection of serious, if not inherent, conflicts within a self-regulated audit system. These are seen to rest in the structural position of auditors where their appointment and work is capable of being, or being seen to be, influenced significantly by those (corporate management) on whom they are reporting. Additionally, auditors face a number of conflicting pressures having to satisfy parties with potentially differing interests in, and demands on, the audit function either as shareholders, creditors, potential investors, government and regulatory bodies and the audit firms themselves. The nature of audit assurance (which implies that auditors can routinely be expected to miss a number of material errors and irregularities) is another factor often quoted as making the audit expectations gap somewhat of an inevitability, especially given the fact that audit communications which seek to clarify such a probabilistic status can serve to undermine audit profitability by reducing the (publicly) perceived level of audit assurance.

The dominant view to emerge from such analysis is that the expectations gap is unlikely to be reduced if responses to it are left solely in the hands of the audit profession. In Britain this has led to a swell of opinion for more openness in audit regulation and support for the establishment of an independent body charged with regulating the audit function, although the precise shape and responsibilities of any such body have yet to be determined. Such issues demand careful thought and design because the possible impact of any such body on the expectations gap, despite its current popularity, remains open to question (not least given the fact that the USA has had both a Public Oversight Board and an expectations gap for the last twenty years).

In recommending regulatory reform, even the most severe critics of the audit profession appear vulnerable to the claim that they retain considerable faith in the capacity of audits to detect major fraud and error and to report in a timely and enlightening manner. To coin a phrase, 'everything would be fine if we could get some proper auditing being undertaken and the exercise of professional audit judgement'. What 'proper auditing' or 'professional audit judgement' can achieve appears to be based on hope rather than any analysis of past history. Likewise, there appear to be considerable inconsistencies between 'radical' demands for less pressure on audit fees and the outlawing of low-balling – the implication being higher audit fees for already economically profitable firms – or for more competition (and by implication lower audit fees and reduced independence) by the abolition of the statutory audit requirement for limited companies.

Frequently, there is a worry that reformers appear rather conservative in that the typical response to regulatory failure is frequently yet more regulation. To get away from a never ending, increasing spiral of regulation, some have called for more localized, less hierarchical and more facilitative forms of monitoring and control (see Power, 1994; Hatherly, 1995). Underlying such views is a belief in the need to develop greater understanding of what can be reasonably expected and achieved of auditing and other forms of monitoring, to see the process of regulation as a shared activity between corporate stakeholders. In this regard, there continues to be a need to develop understanding of the practical activities of auditors, not from the basis of hypothetical laboratory experiments but from detailed studies of the lived experiences of auditors in real contexts – or what Power (1995) refers to as the development of a sociology of audit technique. Such a research agenda can seem threatening to auditing practitioners. However, with the audit now such a significant mechanism in processes of organizational and social control and capable through its practice of shaping and changing the lives of so many people, the concept of auditing practitioners needs to be viewed in broad terms to include both those promoting, practising and being audited. The debate also needs to move from one concerned with the proportional liability of auditors to the proportional benefits provided by the purchase of audit services. Ultimately, it may mean that society generally comes to get the audit function it both wants and supports. It will at least get auditors off the uncomfortable hook of having to defend a service which is not providing what people want and mean that the type of statements about auditing that have been made in response to recent major corporate collapses are once and for all consigned to the history books:

> An auditor is not like a ferret who is pointed at a rabbit warren just to see how many rabbits he catches. Someone is meant to tell him how many rabbits are down there to get and then he can decide whether they are big, or bad or what.
> (Coopers & Lybrand partner in response to court questions on the role of Maxwell's auditors, the *Financial Times*, 20/21 January 1996, p. 4)

REFERENCES

Abdolmohammadi, M. and Wright, A. (1987) An examination of the effects of experience and task complexity on audit judgements, *The Accounting Review*, Vol. 53, pp. 1–13.

AICPA (1987) *Report of the National Commission on Fraudulent Financial Reporting* (Treadway Commission), AICPA, New York.

American Institute of Certified Public Accountants (AICPA) (1978) *Report Conclusions and Recommendations of the Commission on Auditors' Responsibilities* (Cohen Commission), AICPA, New York.

Auditing Practices Board (APB) (1992) *The Future Development of Auditing: A Paper to Promote Public Debate*, APB, London.

Auditing Practices Board (APB) (1994) *The Audit Agenda*, APB, London.

Auditing Practices Board (APB) (1995) *Internal Financial Control Effectiveness: A Discussion Paper*, APB, London.

Auditing Practices Committee (APC) (1989) Explanatory foreword to Auditing Standards and Guidelines (revised), in *Auditing and Reporting*, Institute of Chartered Accountants in England and Wales, London.

Beck, G. W. (1973) The role of the auditor in modern society: an empirical appraisal, *Accounting and Business Research*, Spring, pp. 117–22.

Benston, G. J. (1985) The market for public accounting services – demand, supply and regulation' *Journal of Accounting and Public Policy*, Vol. 4, pp. 33–80.

Brown, R. G. (1962) Changing audit objectives and techniques, *Accounting Review*, Vol. 37, no. 4, pp. 696–703.

Cadbury Committee (1992) *The Financial Aspects of Corporate Governance*, Gee, London.

Canadian Institute of Chartered Accountants (CICA) (1988) *Report of the Commission to Study the Public's Expectation of Audits* (Macdonald Commission), CICA, Toronto.

Craswell, A. (1985) Studies of the information content of qualified audit reports, *Journal of Business Finance and Accounting*, Spring, pp. 93–116.

Davidson, L. (1975) *The Role and Responsibilities of the Auditor: Perspectives, Expectations and Analysis*, unpublished background paper for the AICPA Commission on Auditors' Responsibilities.

Dunn, J. (1996) *Auditing: Theory and Practice*, 2nd ed. Prentice-Hall International, Hemel Hempstead.

Estes, R. (1982) *The Auditor's Report and Investor Behavior*, Lexington Books, Lexington, Mass.

Estes, R. and Reimer, M. (1977) A study of the effects of qualified auditors' opinions on bankers' lending decisions, *Accounting and Business Research*, Autumn, pp. 250–9.

Flint, D. (1988) *Philosophy and Principles of Auditing – An Introduction*, Macmillan, Basingstoke.

Fogarty, T. J., Heian, J. B. and Knutson, D. L. (1991) The rationality of doing nothing: auditors' responses to legal liability in an institutionalized environment, *Critical Perspectives on Accounting*, Vol. 2, pp. 201–26.

García Benau, M. A., Humphrey, C., Moizer, P. and Turley, S. (1993) Auditing expectations and performance in Spain and Britain: a comparative analysis, *The International Journal of Accounting*, Vol. 28, pp. 281–307.

Gloeck, J. D. and De Jager, H. (1993), *The Audit Expectation Gap in the Republic of South Africa*, School of Accountancy Research Series, Research Report No. 93(1), University of Pretoria.

Griffiths, J. G. (1885), Accountants and the public, *The Accountant*, 26 December, re-printed in M. Chatfield (ed.) *The English View of Accountants' Duties and Responsibilities 1881–1902*, Arno Press, New York, 1978, pp. 25–9.

Gwilliam, D. (1987) *A Survey of Auditing Research*, Prentice-Hall/ICAEW, London.

Hall, W. D. (1988) An acceptable scope of practice, *The CPA Journal*, February, pp. 24–33.

Haskell, T. L. (1984) Professionalism versus capitalism: R. H. Tawney, Emile Durkheim and C. S. Pierre on the disinterestedness of professional communities, in T. L. Haskell (ed.) *The Authority of Experts: Studies in History and Theory*, Indiana University Press, Bloomington.

Hatherley, D. J. (1995) The case for the shareholder panel in the UK, *The European Accounting Review*, Vol. 4, no. 3.

Holt, G. and Moizer, P. (1990) The meaning of audit reports, *Accounting and Business Research*, Vol. 20, no. 78, pp. 111–22.

Hooks, K. (1992) Professionalism and self interest: a critical view of the expectations gap, *Critical Perspectives on Accounting*, Vol. 3, pp. 109–36.

Hopwood, A. G. (1990) Ambiguity, knowledge and territorial claims: some observations on the doctrine of substance over form: a review essay, *British Accounting Review*, Vol. 22, pp. 79–88.

Humphrey, C. and Moizer, P. (1990) From techniques to ideologies: an alternative perspective on the audit function, *Critical Perspectives on Accounting*, Vol. 1, no. 3, pp. 217–38.

Humphrey, C. G., Moizer, P. and Turley, S. (1992) The audit expectations gap – plus ça change, plus c'est la même chose, *Critical Perspectives on Accounting*, Vol. 3, pp. 137–61.

Humphrey, C. G., Moizer, P. and Turley, S. (1993) The audit expectations gap in Britain: an empirical investigation, *Accounting and Business Research*, Vol. 23, no. 91A, pp. 395–411.

Humphrey, C. G., Turley, S. and Moizer, P. (1993) Protecting against detection: the case of auditors and fraud?, *Accounting, Auditing and Accountability Journal*, Vol. 6, no. 1, pp. 39–62.

ICAEW (1986) *Report of the Working Party on the Future of the Audit*, ICAEW, London.

ICAS (1993) *Auditing into the Twenty-First Century*, Institute of Chartered Accountants of Scotland, Edinburgh.

Johnson, P. E., Jamal, K. and Glen Berryman, R. (1989) Audit judgement research, *Accounting, Organizations and Society*, Vol. 14, pp. 83–99.

Kaplan, R. L. (1987) Accountants' liability and audit failures: when the umpire strikes out, *Journal of Accounting and Public Policy*, Vol. 6, pp. 1–8.

Lee, T. A. (1970) The nature of auditing and its objectives, *Accountancy*, Vol. 81, no. 920, pp. 292–6.

Lee, T. A. (1986) *Company Auditing* (3rd edn), Van Nostrand Reinhold, Wokingham.

Lee, T. A. (1993) *Corporate Audit Theory*, Chapman & Hall, London.

Mautz, R. K. and Sharaf, H. A. (1961) *The Philosophy of Auditing*, American Accounting Association, Sarasota, Fl.

Metcalf Committee (1978) Improving the accountability of publicly owned corporations and their auditors, *Report of the Subcommittee on Reports, Accounting and Management of the Committee on Governmental Affairs*, United States Senate, Washington (reproduced in *The Journal of Accountancy*, January 1978, pp. 88–96).

Miller, R. D. (1986) Governmental oversight of the role of auditors, *The CPA Journal*, September, pp. 20–36.

Mitchell, A. and Sikka, P. (1993) Accounting for change: the institutions of accountancy, *Critical Perspectives on Accounting*, Vol. 4, pp. 29–52.

Moizer, P. (1985) Independence, in D. Kent, M. Sherer, and S. Turley (eds.) *Current Issues in Auditing*, Harper & Row, London.

Moizer, P. (1992) State of the art in audit market research, *The European Accounting Review*, Vol. 1, no. 2, pp. 333–48.

Neebes, D. L. and Roost, W. G. (1987) ASB's ten 'expectation gap' proposals – will they do the job?, *The CPA Journal*, October, pp. 23–5.

Pentland, B. T. (1993) Getting comfortable with the numbers: auditing and the micro-production of macro-order, *Accounting, Organizations and Society*, Vol. 18, no. 7/8, pp. 695–620.

Porter, B. A. (1993) An empirical study of the audit expectation–performance gap, *Accounting and Business Research*, Vol. 24, no. 93, pp. 49–68.

Power, M. (1992) From common sense to expertise: reflections on the prehistory of audit sampling, *Accounting, Organizations and Society*, Vol. 17, no. 1, pp. 37–62.

Power, M. (1993) The politics of financial auditing, *The Political Quarterly*, pp. 272–84.

Power, M. (1994) *The Audit Explosion*, Demos, London.

Power, M. (1995) Auditing, expertise and the sociology of technique, *Critical Perspectives on Accounting*, Vol. 6, pp. 317–39.

Preston, A. M, Cooper, D. J, Scarborough, D. P. and Chilton, R. C. (1995) Changes in the Code of Ethics of the US accounting profession, 1917 and 1988: the continual quest for legitimation, *Accounting, Organizations and Society*, Vol. 20, no. 6, pp. 507–46.

Sherer, M. (1985) Auditing today: opportunities and threats, in D. Kent, M. Sherer, and S. Turley (eds.) *Current Issues in Auditing*, Harper & Row, London.

Sherer, M. and Kent, D. (1988) *Auditing and Accountability*, Paul Chapman, London.

Sikka, P. and Willmott, H. (1995) The power of 'independence': defending and extending the jurisdiction of accounting in the United Kingdom, *Accounting, Organizations and Society*, Vol. 20, no. 6, pp. 547–81.

Sikka, P., Puxty, T., Willmott, H. and Cooper, C. (1992) *Eliminating the Expectations Gap?*, Research Report No. 28, The Chartered Association of Certified Accountants, London.

Stevens, M. (1988) No more white shoes, *Business Month*, April, pp. 39–42.

Thornton Baker (1983) *Audit Manual*, Nova Communications Ltd, London.

Tricker, R. I. (1982) Corporate accountability and the role of the audit function, in A. G. Hopwood, M. Bromwich and J. Shaw (eds.) *Auditing Research: Issues and Opportunities*, Pitman, London.

Turley, W. S. and Cooper, M. (1991) *Auditing in the UK*, Prentice-Hall/ICAEW, Hemel Hemstead.

Tweedie, D. (1987) Challenges facing the auditor: professional fouls and the expectation gap, the Deloitte, Haskins and Sells Lecture, University College, Cardiff, 30 April.

Wallace, W. A. (1980) *The Economic Role of the Audit in Free and Regulated Markets*, University of Rochester, New York.

Willingham, J. J. (1975) Discussant's response to the relationship of auditing standards to the detection of fraud, *The CPA Journal*, April, pp. 18–21.

Willmott, H. (1990) Serving the public interest? a critical analysis of a professional claim, in D. J. Cooper and T. Hopper (eds.) *Critical Accounts*, Macmillan, London.

DISCUSSION QUESTIONS

1. The expectations gap is due to public ignorance about auditing. Discuss.
2. To what extent have developments in audit responsibilities arisen only due to public pressure forcing change on an unwilling profession?
3. The expectations gap is a symptom of the fact that auditing is now a business rather than a profession. Discuss.
4. What strategies would you recommend to reduce or eliminate the expectations gap in auditing?

2

Auditors' Responsibilities with Respect to Corporate Fraud – A Controversial Issue

Brenda Porter

INTRODUCTION

In recent years corporate fraud has cost British businesses many millions of pounds: between 1989 and 1994 reported fraud amounted to £2.2 billion (KPMG, 1995) and it is estimated that reported fraud represents less than 10 per cent of total frauds (*Financial Times*, 1993, p. 8). It is evident that corporate fraud is a serious problem. Such fraud, especially that committed by senior executives and directors, usually comes to light when companies fail unexpectedly. When such failures occur, invariably the question asked is, 'Where were the auditors?'

The role of external auditors in detecting and reporting corporate fraud is a highly controversial issue. Not only do opinions vary widely among auditors, it is also the issue which makes the greatest contribution to the audit expectation–performance gap (discussed in Chapter 1) – the gap between what society expects of auditors and what it perceives it receives from them (Porter, 1993). Whilst numerous surveys have shown that politicians, the courts, financial journalists and the public expect auditors to detect and report fraud, the auditing profession has, in general, downplayed its responsibility in this regard. Instead it has emphasized that detection of fraud is management's responsibility and that audits are not designed, and cannot be relied upon, for this purpose (Porter, 1991). This position is illustrated by the following quotations:

It is obvious that a company's auditor should spot a few million dollars being paid for work that doesn't exist, or coming from phoney customers. Obvious but wrong. Contrary to popular belief and common sense, the job of an auditor is not to identify these kinds of transactions.

(Cowe, 1989, p. 16)

Surely auditors who can measure the value of profits or assets down to the last pound note ought to be able to notice when a few million go missing, or certainly when £215m went walkabout at Ferranti? Not so say the auditors, this is to misunderstand their role. (Riley, 1990, p. 1).

In this chapter we examine the issue of auditors' responsibility to detect and report fraud. After defining what is meant by fraud, we trace the historical development of auditors' legal and professional duties with respect to corporate fraud and discuss reasons for the changes which are evident. We then compare the position in the United Kingdom with that pertaining in other Anglo-American countries, more particularly, the United States, Canada, Australia and New Zealand (NZ). Before concluding the chapter we explore some of the factors which contribute to the controversial nature of auditors' responsibilities to detect and report fraud and ensure that it will remain a difficult issue to resolve.

DEFINITION OF FRAUD[1]

For the purposes of this chapter, 'fraud' is defined to mean each of the following:

(1) the use of deception, such as manipulation, falsification or alteration of accounting records or other documents, in order to obtain an unjust or illegal financial advantage;
(2) intentional misstatements in, or omissions of amounts or disclosures from, accounting records or financial statements;
(3) intentional misapplication of accounting principles relating to amounts, classification, manner of presentation or disclosure;
(4) misappropriation of assets or theft.

HISTORICAL DEVELOPMENT OF AUDITORS' DUTIES TO DETECT AND REPORT CORPORATE FRAUD

The historical development of auditors' duties to detect and report fraud may be discussed conveniently with reference to four phases, namely:

(1) the pre-1920s phase, when detecting fraud was recognized as a primary audit objective;
(2) the 1920s to 1960s phase, during which the importance of fraud detection as an audit objective declined until it became 'a responsibility not assumed';

(3) the 1960s to 1980s phase, when auditors' duty to detect fraud was partly reinstated;

(4) the post-1980s period, during which auditors' duties to detect and, more particularly, report fraud have become more firmly established and expanded.

Pre-1920s phase

Prior to the 1920s, fraud detection was accepted as a primary audit objective. This is clearly evidenced by the auditing texts of the time. For example, Dicksee (1898) stated that the objective of an audit was made up of three parts: the detection of fraud, the detection of technical errors and the detection of errors in principle. Similarly, Montgomery (1912) referred to the prevention and detection of fraud and error as the 'chief objects' of an audit. Nevertheless, notwithstanding the importance accorded to fraud detection as an audit objective, the courts were concerned to ensure that auditors' responsibilities were kept within reasonable bounds. For example, in the case of *In re London and General Bank (No. 2)* [1895] 2 Ch. 673, Lindley LJ stated that it was the auditor's duty to report to shareholders any dishonest acts which had occurred and which affected the propriety of the information contained in the balance sheet. However, he also said that the auditor could not be expected to find every fraud committed within the company. That would be asking too much; the auditor was not an insurer or guarantor. What was expected of the auditor was reasonable skill and care in the circumstances. Similarly, in *In re Kingston Cotton Mill Co. Ltd (No. 2)* [1896] 2 Ch. 279, Lopes LJ, expanding on Lindley LJ's remarks, stated: 'An auditor is not bound to be a detective or . . . to approach his work with suspicion or with a foregone conclusion that there is something wrong. He is a watchdog not a bloodhound. [However], if there is anything to excite suspicion he should probe it to the bottom.'

These two landmark cases established that auditors are required to conduct their audits with reasonable skill and care appropriate to the circumstances. In the absence of suspicious circumstances they are not required to seek out every fraud but, if their suspicions are aroused, they are required to investigate the matter thoroughly. This remains the legal position in the UK as well as in countries such as Australia and NZ.

1920s to 1960s phase

During the period from the 1920s to the 1960s, the auditing profession acknowledged progressively less responsibility for detecting fraud. By the end of the period, it was, in general, denying all but an incidental responsibility in this regard. Instead it maintained that the prevention and detection of fraud were the responsibility of company management and that the primary purpose of an audit was to lend credibility to financial statements.

This change in audit objectives is often explained in terms of auditors responding to changes in the socio-economic environment. During the 1920s to 1960s period, companies grew in size and complexity and various tasks, including the collection and processing of accounting and other information, were delegated to employees. In order to control the activities of employees and, more particularly, to prevent or detect errors and irregularities (i.e. fraud) in the accounting and other records, company managements established systems of internal control. At the same time, as companies grew in size so did the volume of their transactions and it soon became infeasible, within the limits of reasonable time and cost constraints, for auditors to check every entry in the accounting records. As a consequence, auditing procedures changed from meticulous checking of every transaction to evaluating the company's internal controls and testing a sample of transactions.

Additionally, following the First World War and, later, the depression of the 1930s, a new class of small investors emerged. Unlike the shareholders of earlier years, who were few in number but closely bound to the companies they partly owned, the new class of investors were little interested in the fortunes of 'their' company *per se*. They were concerned primarily with the returns their investment generated and, if they perceived better returns could be earned elsewhere, they readily switched their allegiance to another company. This changed attitude of investors stimulated a change in focus with respect to financial statements. Instead of being seen as documents which reflected the stewardship of company managers entrusted with the shareholders' resources, they came to be regarded as a basis for investment decisions. As a result, attention focused on the fairness with which financial statements portrayed the position and performance of the reporting entity (see, for example, Lee, 1986). Reflecting these changes in the socio-economic environment, audit objectives shifted away from detecting fraud and error towards assessing the truth and fairness of the information contained in financial statements.

By the end of the 1920s–1960s period, as noted in Montgomery's (1957) auditing text, fraud detection had become 'a responsibility not assumed' by auditors (reported in the Commission on Auditors' Responsibilities (CAR), 1978, p. 34). This is also reflected in the professional promulgations of the time. For example, in 1951 the American Institute of Certified Public Accountants (AICPA) stated in its *Codification of Statements on Auditing Procedure*:

> The ordinary examination incident to the issuance of an opinion respecting financial statements is not designed and cannot be relied upon to disclose defalcations and other similar irregularities, although their discovery frequently results. In a well-organized concern reliance for the detection of such irregularities is placed principally upon the maintenance of an adequate system of accounting records with appropriate internal control. If an auditor were to discover defalcations and similar irregularities he would have to extend his work to a point where its cost would be prohibitive.
>
> (AICPA, 1951, pp. 12–13)

Although the demise in fraud detection as an audit objective may be explained in terms of the auditing profession responding to changes in the socio-economic environment, some commentators have suggested that the profession was rather more instrumental in effecting the change. Brown (1962), for example, has argued that the profession, at least in the USA, downplayed auditors' responsibility for detecting fraud as a defensive move, following the huge McKesson and Robbins fraud (1938) which auditors failed to uncover. Further, notwithstanding the profession's denial of responsibility for detecting corporate fraud, numerous surveys (for example, Lee, 1970, in the UK; Beck, 1974, in Australia; CAR, 1978, in the USA; the Commission on the Public's Expectations of Audits (Macdonald Commission), 1988 (CICA, 1988a), in Canada; Steen, 1989, in the UK; Porter, 1993, in NZ) have consistently found that the majority of financial statement users, other members of the financial community, the general public, and – possibly surprisingly – auditors, believe otherwise. This seems to lend support for Willingham's (1975, p. 19) contention that 'the detection of fraud . . . was the stated objective for over 400 years and was removed as an objective by the [auditing] profession rather than by a change in the demand of clients of accounting firms'. Humphrey, Turley and Moizer (1993, pp. 42–3) have suggested that the profession's desire to minimize auditors' responsibility for detecting fraud is reflective of the conflict inherent in any self-regulated profession. As cases involving massive frauds, which auditors failed to detect, reached the courts, so the profession sought to minimize auditors' responsibility in this regard: it sought to protect its own members' interests rather than pursuing its public duties and obligations.

1960s to 1980s phase

By the 1960s, the profession's denial of responsibility for detecting fraud was subject to criticism from both inside and outside the profession. Morison (1970), for example, drew attention to the fact that neither the press nor the general public shared the view expressed in accounting literature that an audit is not intended to detect fraud. He noted that they considered that if an audit is not meant to uncover major frauds it must be of very little use. He also observed that it is absurd for auditors to state that financial statements are reliable, 'that they are "all right" ', and then to add, 'they are all right subject of course to the possibility that undetected fraud may have made them all wrong' (p. 414). In similar vein, the investment analyst whose solo efforts were responsible for exposing the notorious *Equity Funding* fraud raised the pertinent question: 'If routine auditing procedures cannot detect 64,000 phoney insurance policies (two-thirds of the total number), $25 million in counterfeit bonds, and $100 million in missing assets, what is the purpose of audits?' (reported by Woolf, 1978, p. 62).

In the light of the widespread criticism, it became clear that the 'responsibility not assumed' stance of the profession could not be sustained. Professional pronouncements were amended to acknowledge that, when conducting an audit, auditors have a responsibility to be aware that fraud may exist and that 'material irregularities . . . will normally be brought to light by sound audit procedures' (Institute of Chartered Accountants in England and Wales (ICAEW), 1961, p. 27). It should be noted that requiring auditors to be aware that fraud may exist seems to recognize a duty for auditors to remain alert to suspicious circumstances. If such circumstances are encountered, auditors have an obligation to 'probe the matter to the bottom' (*Kingston Cotton Mill* case (see above), per Lopes LJ). Thus, this requirement, together with the acknowledgement that sound auditing procedures should uncover major frauds, indicates that auditors were, once again, accepting some responsibility to detect fraud. For most of the 1960s–1980s period, however, the profession continued to downplay auditors' role in the fraud arena and to emphasize that auditors do not have a duty to search for fraud and that an audit is not designed, and cannot be relied upon, to disclose irregularities (for example, ICAEW, 1961, para. 27; AICPA, 1972, section 110.05).

Nevertheless, the profession continued to move in the direction of recognizing increased responsibility for detecting fraud. At the end of the period, the *Explanatory Foreword to Auditing Standards* (Auditing Practices Committee (APC), 1980) still insisted that 'responsibility for the prevention and detection of fraud rests with management' (para. 8), and that 'the auditor's duties do not require him specifically to search for fraud' (para. 9), but it also stated (para. 10):

> the auditor should recognise the possibility of material irregularities or fraud which could, unless adequately disclosed, distort the results or state of affairs shown by the financial statements. The auditor should, therefore, plan his audit so that he has a reasonable expectation of detecting material misstatements in the financial statements resulting from irregularities or fraud.

Post-1980s period

Since the early 1980s there has been a continuing shift in the profession's stance with respect to corporate fraud. This has been stimulated by the increasing size and incidence of corporate fraud[2] and the growing criticism of auditors by politicians, the courts, financial journalists and the public for failing to uncover even major frauds in companies and, in general, denying a responsibility to do so. Although fraud detection as an audit objective has not reached the prominence it held in the pre-1920s phase, auditors throughout the Anglo-American world acknowledge some responsibility to detect fraud. Additionally, led by the auditing profession in the UK, auditors throughout the region have begun to accept a duty to report fraud (or suspected fraud) detected during the course of an audit to regulatory authorities. However, the level of responsibility for detecting and reporting fraud acknowledged by the auditing profession in different countries varies quite markedly. In the next section we examine auditors' duties in the UK with respect to fraud and then compare the UK position with that pertaining in other countries with similar legal and corporate systems, namely the USA, Canada, Australia and NZ.

AUDITORS' DUTIES IN THE UK TO DETECT AND REPORT CORPORATE FRAUD

The 1980s witnessed intense activity by the auditing profession in the UK in relation to auditors' duties with respect to fraud. The reasons for this probably lie in the high level of public and political concern about the escalating extent of corporate fraud, especially in the financial services sector. In the mid-1980s Fletcher and Howard, successive Ministers of Corporate and Consumer Affairs, were very vocal in their criticism of auditors for failing to play a more active role in the fight against fraud (Smith, 1985; Allen, 1985). They also made it clear that, if auditors did not voluntarily accept greater responsibility to detect and report corporate fraud, it would be forced on them through legislation. The stance of the politicians was supported by officers of the Fraud Investigation Group who stated that they considered it both practical and desirable, within the limits of cost and auditing procedures, for auditors to accept a general responsibility to detect and report fraud (Smith, 1985).

In response to the political pressure exerted on auditors, the main professional bodies for auditors established working parties to investigate the issue. These working parties were, in general, supportive of the view that auditors have an important role in curtailing corporate fraud but, as the following extracts show, they were strongly opposed to extending auditors' duties to detect fraud:

> We do not believe . . . that it would be either realistic or cost effective to expand the existing requirements for the auditor to detect fraud.
>
> (ICAEW, 1985a, para. 2.48)

> The auditor's responsibilities are already heavy and we do not think it is necessary or practicable to extend his existing duties in this respect.
>
> (ICAEW, 1985b, para. 3.11)

> In examining the detection function we believe that it is impractical and inefficient to extend generally and indiscriminately the auditor's role.
>
> (ICAS, 1985, para. 4.1)

The strength of the opposition to extending auditors' duty to detect fraud is reflected in a statement by the chairman of the ACCA's working party:

> It would be quite impossible for auditors to accept responsibility for detecting fraud – the cost would be astronomical. The government has no idea how an audit is conducted, what it can achieve and what it is there for. . . I don't believe the profession should roll over and play dead and accept an increase in its responsibilities.   (Nelson, quoted by Barclay, 1985, p. 1)

The working parties' reports gave far less prominence to the issue of auditors detecting fraud than to auditors reporting fraud. This is probably a consequence of the government's apparent general satisfaction with the level of responsibility acknowledged by auditors for detecting fraud. This is reflected, for example, in the statement by Howard, Minister of Corporate and Consumer Affairs, at the 1985 joint ICAEW/Law Society Conference on Financial Fraud: 'I would accept that to impose a general duty of detection on the auditor would be unrealistic; on that issue I believe we are on common ground' (ICAEW, 1985c, p. 12).

Given the situation outlined above, it is not surprising that there has been relatively little change in the wording of professional pronouncements since 1980 with respect to detecting fraud. This may be seen by comparing the following extracts from the current Auditing Standard (SAS 110: *Fraud and Error*; Auditing Practices Board (APB), 1995) with those quoted above from the *Explanatory Foreword to Auditing Standards* (APC, 1980):

> It is the responsibility of the directors to take such steps as are reasonably open to them to prevent and detect fraud (para. 10). . . . It is not the auditors' function to prevent fraud and error . . . (para. 17). Auditors plan, perform and evaluate their audit work in order to have a reasonable expectation of detecting material misstatements in the financial statements arising from error or fraud. However, an audit cannot be expected to detect all errors or instances of fraudulent or dishonest conduct (para. 18).

The major change in auditors' duties in the corporate fraud arena in recent years concerns reporting fraud which has been detected during an audit. The profession's working parties were supportive of an extension of such duties. The Davison Committee (ICAEW, 1985a), for example, stated that the ICAEW should encourage auditors to report to regulatory authorities suspected cases of serious fraud by management. In similar vein, the Benson Committee (ICAEW, 1985b, para. 3.18) stated:

> We are satisfied that the duties put upon the auditor by statute, case law decisions and professional standards would require him to include a qualification in his audit report if fraud by directors arises. . . . We think that such matters cannot fail to affect the truth and fairness of the accounts put before the shareholders or they call into question the integrity of the accounting records and accounts.

Just as the minimal attention given by the profession's working parties to auditors' duty to detect fraud may be linked to the government's apparent satisfaction with the status quo, their support for an extension to auditors' reporting duties may well have been prompted by threats by politicians such as Fletcher and Howard to impose extended reporting duties on auditors if the profession did not accept them voluntarily. The strength of the government's desire for auditors to assume greater responsibility for reporting corporate fraud (overriding, in appropriate cases, their duty of confidentiality to their clients) is reflected in Howard's statement at the 1985 joint ICAEW/Law Society Conference on Financial Fraud:

there is little or no point reporting management fraud ... to the perpetrators themselves. In such circumstances I hope it can be generally
accepted that there is a clear duty on the auditor to report the matter to
the regulatory authorities.... [T]here will be some cases where ... giving the client advanced warning may amount to nothing less than a tip
off. I am quite clear the public interest requires the auditor [in appropriate cases] to report to the regulatory authorities without first informing
his client. ... I do not think that recognition of such a duty is in any way
inconsistent either with the best traditions and practices of the auditor's
profession or with his duty to his clients. Even auditors are not islands.
You have duties to the rest of the community of which you are part, and
you owe that community a more compelling duty which must on occasion take first place. Public expectation must be given full weight in these
matters.   (ICAEW, 1985c, pp. 12–13)

That the government's intention of imposing reporting duties on auditors, if
the profession failed to accept them voluntarily, was no idle threat was made
clear with enactment of the Financial Services Act 1986. This Act requires
all investment businesses in the UK to be duly authorized and to comply with
strict rules laid down by the Securities and Investments Board (SIB) or relevant self-regulating organization (SRO) to which the SIB has delegated regulatory powers. The Act includes a requirement for auditors of authorized
investment businesses to report matters of concern arising from their duties
as auditors (including detected or suspected fraud) to the appropriate regulatory authority. Similar provisions have been included in the Building
Societies Act 1986, Banking Act 1987 and Friendly Societies Act 1992. In
each case, legislative protection has been provided for auditors against action
by their clients for breach of confidentiality or defamation, provided the
information is given to the regulatory authorities in good faith.

In response to the political and public pressure on auditors to assume
greater responsibility with respect to corporate fraud, and the recommendations of the working parties and committees established to investigate the
issue, two auditing guideline exposure drafts (APC, 1985, 1988) were issued,
followed by the auditing guideline (APC, 1990). The latter contained provisions similar to those proposed in the 1988 exposure draft but the assertive-
ness of the draft document was softened somewhat. For example, the
exposure draft stated that, 'since fraud invariably has an impact on either
the accounting records or the financial statements, it is generally accepted
that auditors should plan their audits so that they have a reasonable expectation of detecting material misstatements caused by fraud' (APC, 1988,
Foreword). The subsequent guideline contains what might be regarded as a
weaker assertion in terms of detecting fraud, namely that auditors have a
responsibility 'properly to plan, perform and evaluate [their] audit work so
as to have a reasonable expectation of detecting material misstatements in
the financial statements, whether they are caused by fraud, other irregularities or errors' (APC, 1990, para. 9). Further, the guideline provides no

acknowledgement that fraud invariably impacts on either the accounting records or the financial statements.

Nevertheless, the guideline signals a major shift in the stance of the auditing profession with respect to reporting fraud. Of greatest significance, however, is the guideline's recognition that, when it is in the public interest to do so, auditors may report fraud or suspected fraud to a 'proper authority' (para. 31). The guideline allays auditors' concerns about the effect of breaching their duty of confidentiality by stating: 'Where it is in the public interest to disclose and where information is disclosed to an appropriate body or person, and there is no malice motivating the disclosure, the auditor is protected from the risk of breach of confidence or defamation' (para. 34). However, the guideline warns that auditors' qualified privilege applies only in cases where matters of concern are reported to the proper authority, which depends on the nature of the matter to be reported. Possible authorities cited in the guideline include the Serious Fraud Office, the police, the International Stock Exchange, the SIB and the various SROs under the Financial Services Act 1986 (para. 35).

It is pertinent to observe that, in promulgating the provisions relating to auditors reporting to regulatory authorities, the APC went as far as the law would allow. As Tweedie (1991, p. 30), Chairman of the APC at the time, explains:

> The APC has taken legal advice on the present state of the law . . . The auditor certainly owes a duty of confidentiality to the company. That duty is not broken by disclosure to its management or shareholders . . . The duty would, however, be broken by disclosure to third parties. Counsel has advised that in the present state of the law the furthest that it is possible to go in encouraging disclosure by auditors to third parties is to say that there will be some cases in which an auditor, although not bound in point of law to disclose information to a third party, is entitled to do so. . . . In certain circumstances information which would otherwise be confidential would cease to be so if the information was such that disclosure was justified in the 'public interest' and should consequently be reported to a third party.

Statements such as that quoted above, and analysis of the auditing guideline and its predecessor exposure draft, suggest that, had the APC been able to do so, it would have gone further and imposed a duty on auditors to report detected (or suspected) fraud to regulatory authorities in certain circumstances. This has, in fact, occurred in the APB's SAS 110 (1995). This (current) standard requires auditors who become aware of an actual, or suspected, instance of fraud, which they believe should be reported to a proper authority in the public interest, to notify the directors (in writing) of their view, unless the directors themselves are implicated. If the directors do not report the matter to a proper authority, the auditors are required to do so (paras. 50 and 51). Similarly, if the directors are implicated in the suspected or actual fraud, the auditors are required to 'make a report direct to

a proper authority in the public interest without delay and without informing the directors in advance' (para. 52).

By converting auditors' voluntary right to report to a proper authority in
appropriate circumstances to a duty to do, SAS 110 has strengthened auditors' reporting duties from those in the APC's auditing guideline (1990).

AUDITORS' DUTIES IN THE UK COMPARED WITH THOSE IN THE USA, CANADA, AUSTRALIA AND NZ

Comparison of the relevant auditing standards[3] reveals that auditors' duties
in the UK with respect to detecting fraud are similar to those of auditors in
the USA, Canada, Australia and NZ. In each case, auditors are required to
plan and perform their audits so as to have a reasonable expectation of
detecting material misstatements in financial statements resulting from fraud,
and with an attitude of professional scepticism. However, whilst in the USA
and Australia auditors are told they should not assume that management is
dishonest or assume unquestioned honesty, auditors in the UK and NZ are
permitted, in the absence of evidence to the contrary, to accept representations as truthful and records and documents as genuine. In Canada, an attitude of professional scepticism is defined to mean that the auditor is alert
to, among other things, evidence which contradicts the assumption of management's good faith (CICA, 1991, sec 5135, para. 05). This seems to be akin
to the UK and NZ provision noted above.

Although auditors' duty to detect fraud in the various countries is similar,
detailed analysis of the professional promulgations reveals that the tone of
the US standard indicates more exacting duties for auditors in the USA than
elsewhere. For example, in the USA, SAS no. 53 (AICPA, 1988, para. 8)
requires auditors to 'exercise (a) due care in planning, performing and evaluating the results of audit procedures, and (b) the proper degree of professional skepticism to achieve reasonable assurance that material errors or
irregularities will be detected'. In none of the other countries are auditors
explicitly required to gain reasonable assurance of detecting material fraud
through both planning, performing and evaluating their audit work and exercising the proper degree of professional scepticism: in the other countries one
or other requirement is emphasized.

Like auditors' duty to detect fraud, their duty to report fraud to management and to shareholders is very similar in each of the countries considered
here. In each case, when auditors encounter an actual or suspected fraud,
they are required to:

(1) inform the appropriate level of management (or the audit committee or
    board of directors); and
(2) consider the effect of the fraud on the financial statements. In cases where
    auditors consider that the truth and fairness of the financial statements
    have been impaired as a result of fraud, they are required to qualify their
    audit reports.

Beyond this, auditors' reporting duties differ significantly between the USA, Canada and NZ on the one hand, and Australia and the UK on the other. In the USA, Canada and NZ, the auditor's duty of confidentiality to the client is, in general, regarded as paramount and overrides 'public interest' considerations. In special circumstances, such as in response to a subpoena or where an audit client is subject to a particular regulatory regime, auditors may also have an obligation to report to a regulatory authority. Nevertheless, in these countries, auditors' ability or duty to report to third parties is limited and narrowly prescribed. The situation in Australia and the UK is somewhat different.

In Australia, AUS 210: *Irregularities, Including Fraud, Other Illegal Acts and Errors* (Australian Accounting Research Foundation (AARF), 1995, para. 31) points out that, if the auditor is unable to obtain all the information and explanations he or she considers necessary (for example, when seeking to confirm or dispel a suspicion that fraud has occurred) the matter should be reported in the audit report.[4] It also notes that, when there are compelling reasons to do so, the auditor may disregard his or her normal duty of confidentiality to the entity and report matters concerning the entity's affairs to a third party, without first obtaining permission from the entity's management to do so (para. 32). Further, the Companies Act and Codes, section 285 (10) requires auditors to report to the national Companies and Securities Commision if they find the Code has been breached and the matter will not be dealt with adequately by comment in the audit report, or by referring it to the directors. The NCSC (1990, para 8) has cited fraud as a matter likely to require such reporting.

At first sight, auditors' reporting duties in Australia may appear to resemble those pertaining in the UK. However, analysis of the relevant provisions in AUS 210 (AARF, 1995) and SAS 110 (APB, 1995) reveals that the tenor of the two documents is very different. In contrast to the assertive tone adopted in the UK standard, and the apparent willingness of the APC (and, presumably, its successor body, the APB) to extend auditors' duty to report fraud as far as the law allows (see quotation from Tweedie, 1991, above), the Australian standard conveys reluctant acceptance of duties imposed on auditors by statute, and its tone does not encourage auditors to go beyond the legal minimum. The difference in the tenor of the two standards may be illustrated by comparing their respective paragraphs relating to auditors' duty to report to third parties:

> Confidentiality is an implied term of the auditor's contract. The duty of confidentiality, however, is not absolute. In certain exceptional circumstances auditors are not bound by the duty of confidentiality and have the right or duty to report matters to a proper authority in the public interest.
>
> (SAS 110 (APB, 1995), para. 53)

The auditor's duty of confidentiality to the entity would ordinarily preclude reporting any matters concerning the entity's affairs to a third party, without the express permission of the entity's management. This rule would be followed unless there are compelling reasons to the contrary.

(AUS 210 (AARF, 1995), para. 32)

Reasons for the international differences

It is evident that auditors' duties to detect fraud in the various countries are broadly similar, although detection duties in the USA appear to be rather more exacting than elsewhere. As regards reporting fraud, auditors' duties to report detected or suspected fraud to management and shareholders are similar in all the countries but there are marked differences with respect to auditors reporting detected fraud to third parties, reflecting different positions on the relative importance of reporting in the public interest and maintaining a duty of confidentiality.

Given the broad similarity of the socio-economic environments of the various countries, it may be asked why these differences in auditors' duties with respect to fraud have arisen. It is suggested that the answer may be found in the relative importance of corporate fraud as a social and economic issue, the level of public and political concern it has generated and, more especially, the strength of the political pressure which has been brought to bear on the auditing profession. As has been noted, in the UK corporate fraud reached particularly serious proportions in the mid-1980s and became the focus of public and political attention. Politicians made it clear that they expected auditors to be in the front line of the public's defences in the fight against fraud and to extend their duties in this regard. They also made it clear that, if the profession failed to respond appropriately, legislative action would be taken (Smith, 1985; Allen, 1985). The nature of the reporting duties auditors could expect to be imposed on them was indicated by provisions incorporated in the Financial Services Act 1986, the Building Societies Act 1986 and the Banking Act 1987.

In the USA criticism of the auditing profession was rife in the 1970s and 1980s. Senator Metcalf and Congressman Moss were particularly scathing in their attacks on auditors in the mid- to late 1970s, and Congressman Dingell has been similarly critical since the mid-1980s. However, unlike the UK, where public and political criticism of auditors focused almost entirely on their failure to play a more active role in combating fraud, in the USA criticism of auditors has embraced all the 'expectation gap' issues and, in particular, auditors' role in detecting and reporting illegal acts (other than fraud). Interest in the latter issue came to the fore in the USA as a consequence of the revelations which led to the passing of the Foreign Corrupt Practices Act 1977. The multiple focus of criticism in the USA is reflected in the fact that SAS no. 53 (AICPA, 1988) was promulgated as one of nine 'expectation gap standards' which covered a wide range of issues (Guy and Sullivan, 1988). Additionally, in the USA, auditors have not been exposed to the specific political threat of having reporting duties imposed on them through legislation nor has legislation been passed, like that in the UK, which embodies reporting duties for auditors. In the prevailing socio-political environment in the USA, auditors have acknowledged a duty to detect fraud which is similar to, if not more exacting than, that of their UK counterparts, but they deny any responsibility to report detected or suspected fraud to third parties, except in very restricted and clearly specified circumstances.

In Australia, Canada and NZ auditors have not come under the intense critical scrutiny which the profession in the UK and USA has experienced. Nevertheless, in Australia, largely as a consequence of some major corporate scandals in the 1980s, a statutory duty to report to the National Companies and Securities Commission (NCSC) has been imposed on auditors. This duty is invoked when auditors encounter breaches of the Companies Act and Codes and the matter cannot be dealt with adequately other than by the auditor reporting it directly to the Commission. As noted earlier, fraud is one of the matters specified by the NCSC as likely to require direct reporting by auditors. In this political climate, auditors' duties in Australia to detect and report corporate fraud are similar to, but, in the case of reporting fraud, less exacting than, those of auditors in the UK. In Canada and NZ, where auditors do not have a general statutory duty to report to a regulatory authority like that in Australia, auditors acknowledge a similar level of responsibility for detecting fraud as elsewhere in the Anglo-American world but, in general, they deny a responsibility to report fraud to third parties.

AUDITORS' DUTY TO DETECT AND REPORT FRAUD REMAINS A CONTROVERSIAL ISSUE: WHY?

The issue of auditors' duty with respect to corporate fraud is a significant factor in the audit expectation–performance gap: it displays the greatest disparity between what society expects of auditors and what it perceives it receives from them. It is also an issue which is frequently and hotly debated in auditing circles – some members of the profession argue for increased responsibility, others for less. The question arises: why is auditors' responsibility for detecting and reporting fraud prone to differing opinions and expectations? In this section we explore some of the factors which help to explain why this issue is both controversial and difficult to resolve. The factors fall into two main groups:

(1) those associated with the nature of the external audit: these tend to support limiting auditors' responsibilities to detect and report corporate fraud;
(2) those associated with society's expectations: these tend to support extended responsibilities for auditors.

Nature of the external audit

The UK Companies Act 1985 (section 235) requires auditors to report to the company's shareholders stating whether, in their opinion, the company's financial statements give a true and fair view of the company's state of affairs and its profit or loss for the financial year, and have been properly prepared in accordance with the 1985 Act. Auditors are also required (by section 237) to carry out such investigations as will enable them to form an opinion as to whether:

(1) proper accounting records have been kept by the company, and proper returns adequate for their audit have been received from branches not visited by them;
(2) the financial statements are in agreement with the underlying accounting records;
(3) the information given in the directors' report is consistent with the financial statements.

In any case where auditors consider that one or more of these requirements has not been met, and/or if they consider they have not received all the information and explanations they have required for the purposes of their audit, they are required to state that fact in their audit report.

The Companies Act 1985 does not mention auditors having a duty to detect fraud. Therefore, it may be presumed that any responsibility the auditor may have for detecting corporate fraud relates to his or her duty to form an opinion on the truth and fairness of the financial statements and/or on the adequacy of the accounting records and information and explanations received. This seems to define auditors' fraud detection duties fairly narrowly and deviates significantly from the general duty to detect corporate fraud which surveys have shown is expected of auditors by society. However, it could be argued legitimately that every major fraud committed in a company will, to a greater or lesser extent, affect the truth and fairness of the financial statements and/or involve improperly kept accounting records and/or generate inadequate information and explanations. Further, as noted earlier, it was established in the *London and General Bank* case over a century ago that, when performing their duties, auditors must exercise reasonable skill and care appropriate to the circumstances of the audit. Thus, if an auditor fails to detect a fraud which affects the truth and fairness of the financial statements, or which is facilitated by the company failing to keep proper accounting records, the auditor could potentially be held liable for negligence.

Nevertheless, in the *London and General Bank* case, Lindley LJ held that auditors are not bound to exercise more than reasonable skill and care, even in situations where their suspicions about a possible fraud have been aroused. Lopes LJ, in the *Kingston Cotton Mill* case, was even more specific. He stated:

> Auditors must not be made liable for not tracking out ingenious and carefully laid schemes of fraud when there is nothing to arouse their suspicion, and when those frauds are perpetrated by tried servants of the company and are undetected for years by the directors. So to hold would make the position of an auditor intolerable.

Thus, although case law has established that, in some circumstances, auditors have a duty to detect fraud, the courts have attempted to keep that duty within reasonable bounds. Nevertheless, difficulties arise because opinions differ in society as to the circumstances in which auditors have a duty to detect fraud.

Apart from the absence of a general legal requirement to detect corporate fraud, the auditing profession has pointed to the nature of fraud as a reason for not accepting extended detection duties. One of the characteristic features of a fraud, as distinct from an error, is that its perpetration is usually accompanied by attempts to conceal it. As the APB (1995, para. 22) notes in SAS 110, this applies particularly in the case of fraud committed by management, who may have the power to, for example, introduce complexity into the corporate structure, transactions or systems, override internal controls, influence accounting policies, and manipulate evidence.

The auditing profession has pointed out that, given the nature of fraud and the ability of its perpetrators to conceal it, audit procedures which are designed to enable the auditor to form an opinion about the truth and fairness of the financial statements and the other matters specified in the Companies Act 1985 may not be appropriate for discovering fraud. The APB (1994, para. 4.25) also notes:

> the type of forensic work necessary to follow up suspicions of fraud is time consuming, demands a high level of skill and experience and is consequently expensive and in the final analysis may not be conclusive. The annual audit of a company's financial statements is not the place to undertake such work.

However, this reference is not to the (initial) detection of fraud, but to following up suspicions of fraud, something it has been established auditors should 'probe to the bottom' since the *Kingston Cotton Mill* case in 1896. In relation to forensic work, Humphrey, Turley and Moizer (1993, p. 56) observe that, in recent years, the auditing profession has made some of its strongest public statements about the limited capacity of the statutory audit to detect fraud at the same time as some of the large international accountancy firms have been promoting their ability to provide specialist fraud audits as additional, chargeable extras to the normal statutory audit. It appears that the techniques and expertise to detect corporate fraud are available within audit firms but, rather than using these to satisfy the public's expectations of auditors establishing the absence (or otherwise) of fraud as part of their 'normal' duties, they are offered to management as an additional service. As Humphrey, Turley and Moizer (ibid.) have noted, 'the auditor's fraud detection obligations [are] increasingly appearing to be framed by accountancy firms as a service to management rather than a check on management'.

This raises questions regarding the parties for whom the audit is conducted. In practice, the shareholders normally delegate their (legal) responsibility for appointing auditors to the company's directors and the latter are also made responsible for fixing the auditors' remuneration. Given that the appointment and payment of auditors is controlled by company directors, it does not seem unreasonable for auditors to be more concerned with the directors', rather than the shareholders', perceptions of them providing value for money.

Additionally, the nature of an audit is such that it relies on the co-oper ation and integrity of the audit client's directors and management. Apart from management affecting such things as the ease with which the auditor can access accounting records and other documents, and make inquiries of vari- ous employees, much audit evidence rests on the willingness of management to provide information and respond fully and honestly to the auditor's inquiries. Without management's co-operation and integrity, an effective audit is extremely difficult, if not impossible. The importance of management's rep- resentations to the successful conduct of an audit is reflected in the fact that the Companies Act 1985 (section 389A) makes it a criminal offence for any officer of a company knowingly or recklessly to make a statement (written or oral) to the company's auditors which 'is misleading, false or deceptive in a material particular'.

The need to maintain a high level of mutual trust and co-operation between the audit client's personnel and the auditor raises problems for the auditor in respect of reporting fraud. In the case of suspected or detected employee fraud, reporting this to management, the board of directors or the audit committee may result in auditee personnel regarding the auditor as a 'spy' and 'informer', and withdrawing their trust and co-operation. Similarly, if the auditor reports detected or suspected fraud to a 'proper authority' without first informing the client, he or she faces the danger of being regarded as 'a possible mole or sneak' by the client's directors and management – and possibly by others in the finan- cial and business community who hear of it – and the integrity of the profes- sion may be destroyed (ICAEW, 1985b, para. 2.3).

Society's expectations

Despite the absence of a general legal requirement for auditors to detect and report fraud and the difficulties they face in performing these duties, they are nevertheless expected, by the majority of the financial and business commu- nity and the general public, to detect all – or at least all material – corpo- rate fraud. One key reason for this is the fact that auditors are the only independent professionals who routinely visit companies and have the oppor- tunity, if not a duty, to 'find out what is going on': they alone have a legal right of access to all the company's accounts, books and records and the right to seek the information and explanations they require from the company's officers and employees.

This 'detective' role of auditors has been accentuated in recent years as auditors, seemingly, have been cast in the role of quasi-agents of regulatory bodies. The Financial Services Act 1986, Building Societies Act 1986, Banking Act 1987 and Friendly Societies Act 1992 have given the auditors of entities in the financial services sector the duty or the right (depending on the cir- cumstances) to report to the relevant regulator when they consider it appropriate to do so in order to protect the interests of depositors and/or share-holders. It is suggested that, by enacting legislation requiring auditors to report matters of concern encountered during an audit to regulatory author-ities, the government has given a clear message that it expects auditors to play a greater social role in combating corporate fraud and, thus, to extend their duties in this regard.

This accords with the view expressed by Knox (1994), deputy director of the Serious Fraud Office, who regards the detection of fraud by auditors as an element of their 'social responsibility'. He notes, 'law enforcement is a matter for the whole community, and [given that] the only independent exam-ination of company accounts is by the auditors – it is not surprising that auditors would wish to detect any malpractice' (p. 128). Knox also suggests that auditors are likely to want to detect fraud for two further reasons:

(1) uncovering fraud within a company is likely to be regarded as good ser-vice by the company's directors (assuming they themselves are not involved); and
(2) discovering fraud by an audit client's directors and/or management will provide a warning for the auditor of the risk of continuing to act for the client.

An area where the auditing profession is acknowledging increased responsi-bility in relation to detecting fraud is that of companies' internal controls. The profession has long emphasized that prevention and detection of fraud are best achieved through an effective system of internal controls but in recent years it has begun to acknowledge that auditors also have a role to play in this regard. More specifically, professional bodies such as the Research Committee of ICAS (1993, p. 33) and the APB (1994, para. 4.42) have expressed the view that auditors should be required to examine the effec-tiveness of an auditee's internal controls with respect to to fraud, to report to the entity's board of directors and, if it has one, its audit committee, any weaknesses detected, and to express an opinion in the entity's annual report on the adequacy of the internal controls for preventing and detecting fraud.

These views of the professional bodies accord with those of the Committee on the Financial Aspects of Corporate Governance (the Cadbury Committee, 1992), which recommended that the directors of listed companies should make a statement (in the company's annual report) on the effectiveness of their sys-tem of internal control and that auditors should report on the directors' state-ment. However, faced with strong opposition from both company directors and auditors (based principally on apparently unresolvable questions as to how the effectiveness of internal controls can be judged), the proposal for directors to report on the effectiveness of their system of internal control has been dropped; additionally, 'system of internal control' has been limited to 'system of internal *financial* control'. The directors of listed companies are now required to report that they have reviewed the effectiveness of the company's system of internal financial control without expressing an opinion thereon. On this point, McInnes and Stevenson (1996, p. 13) have observed: 'the public are not going to get the reassurances they are entitled to as long as boards of directors and auditors are unwilling or (more worryingly) unable to express an opinion on the effectiveness of these systems'. They suggest that auditors reluctance in this area may be affected by fear of litigation.

An inherent conflict

It is well established in the literature on professions that a profession exists to satisfy a societal need. It has a specialist body of knowledge which enables it to provide a service to members of society which they are unable to provide for themselves. The nature of the profession's expertise is such that it is generally beyond the ability of those receiving the service to judge its quality. Thus, the profession's governing body is expected, among other things, to ensure that its members act in the public interest and satisfy the need in society which underpins the profession's existence. The governing body is also expected, by the profession's members, to protect their interests. This dual responsibility of protecting both the public's and members' interests generates an inherent conflict in any self-regulatory profession.

In the case of auditing, society has a general expectation that auditors will help to fulfil the need to detect corporate fraud. *Prima facie*, the professional body has a responsibility to ensure its members meet this expectation. However, a question arises as to the level of fraud which it is reasonable to expect auditors to detect. It is generally accepted that it would not be reasonable to expect detection of all minor pilfering within companies or very ingeniously concealed fraud. However, opinions differ as to the cut-off point between what is reasonable and unreasonable to expect of auditors.

It is suggested that part of the reason the auditing profession has sought to deny its responsibility for detecting fraud – other than that which gives rise to material misstatements in the financial statements – is because, in its view, the public's expectations of auditors in this regard are not always reasonable. Its view of what is reasonable (or otherwise) has probably been influenced by the rising tide of litigation resulting from unexpected corporate failures which have been accompanied by major frauds the auditors failed to detect: the profession perceives that auditors are being held responsible for *business* failures rather than *audit* failures. However, notwithstanding the profession's denial of responsibility, the public has continued to expect external auditors to detect, at least material, fraud. As Singleton-Green (1990, p. 34), Editor of *Accountancy*, has noted:

> We cannot get away from the fact that the layman expects the auditor to discover all serious frauds. . . . [I]f auditors did not have a responsibility to find fraud, people would not waste time and money suing those who fail to find it. Auditors might as well face up to their responsibilities and try to sound positive about them. The negative approach will do nothing to diminish the auditor's duties, but it will help to discredit the profession.

In its *Audit Agenda*, the APB (1994, para. 4.24) reflects the inherent conflict the professional body faces in attempting to protect, simultaneously, the profession's and the public's interest. It first downplays auditors' responsibility even to detect fraud which has a material effect on the financial statements, noting that this is 'an aim rather than a requirement of the audit'. It then observes that there is 'a need for ... greater realism both within and outside the profession about the possibilities of finding fraud, whether material or not'. However, it also calls for 'greater commitment on the part of the profession to meeting this aim' (ibid.) and recommends steps the profession may take as part of this increased commitment. The steps include:

(1) auditors reporting to company boards of directors and/or audit committees on the adequacy of the company's system of controls for preventing and detecting fraud – and, in particular, their adequacy to detect fraud by the directors or senior employees (APB, 1994, paras. 4.27(a) and 4.53);
(2) the professional bodies considering whether sufficient attention is given in pre- and post-qualifying education to fraud detection and the behavioural aspects of individuals under pressure (ibid., para. 4.27(b));
(3) the professional bodies holding seminars on a regular basis to ensure that directors and auditors are continually aware of the common symptoms of fraud and the characteristics of people who perpetrate it (ibid., para. 4.27(c)).

CONCLUSION – AND A WAY FORWARD

Over the last hundred or so years, whilst society consistently has expected auditors to detect corporate fraud, the auditing profession has changed its stance from one extreme of recognizing fraud detection as a primary audit objective, to the other of denying responsibility in this regard. In more recent years, responding to public and political pressure, the profession has once again acknowledged some responsibility to detect fraud: more particularly, it recognizes a duty for auditors to plan and perform their audits so as to have a reasonable expectation of detecting material misstatements in financial statements caused by fraud. The profession has also begun to accept a responsibility to evaluate the adequacy of the internal control systems established by corporate managements to prevent and detect fraud. Further, in recent years, the auditing profession has accepted extended reporting duties: in addition to its duty to report fraud detected during an audit to management and, in appropriate cases, to shareholders, it has accepted a duty to report detected fraud to a proper authority, when it is in the public interest to do so.

Despite the changes to auditors' duties, corporate fraud continues to be a major and apparently escalating social and economic problem, and it is clear that auditors' duties – or the performance of those duties – still fall short of society's expectations.

Auditors face significant difficulties with respect to detecting and reporting corporate fraud. Fraud (especially by management) may be carefully concealed. The audit process requires mutual trust and co-operation between the auditor and auditee which may be undermined if the auditor reports suspected or detected fraud. Further, there is no general agreement in society as to the minimum size or type of fraud which it is reasonable to expect auditors to detect. Nevertheless, if the auditing profession is to avoid continued public and political criticism – and further erosion of its credibility – it needs to move closer to meeting society's expectations with respect to detecting and reporting fraud. The APB, in *The Audit Agenda* (1994), has outlined some steps the profession can take. In its follow-up document, *The Audit Research Agenda* (1996), the APB identified the profession's fraud responsibility as a priority area (para. 31) and identified (in para. 32) questions it considered worthy of research:

(1) How can an auditor's ability to detect fraud be improved?
(2) To what extent can assessment of the control environment assist in detecting the risk of fraud?
(3) What level of demand exists for more detailed forensic work by auditors?

History has shown that auditors' responsibility to detect and report fraud is a controversial issue and one which is not easy to resolve. It requires greater realism about what auditors should be expected to detect, and greater commitment by the profession to meeting society's realistic expectations. The APB has identified steps the auditing profession can take as part of, and to demonstrate, this increased commitment. If these are taken, the gap between what society expects from auditors and what it perceives it receives from them should be narrowed quite significantly.

NOTES

1. This definition is derived from definitions of fraud and/or irregularities provided in Statement of Auditing Standards (SAS) 110: *Fraud and Error* (APB, 1995); Statement on Auditing Standards (SAS) no. 53: *The Auditor's Responsibility to Detect and Report Errors and Irregularities* (AICPA, 1988); the Canadian Institute of Chartered Accountants' (CICA) Handbook Section 5135 (CICA, 1991); and Auditing Standard (Aus) 210: *Irregularities, Including Fraud, Other Illegal Acts and Errors* (AARF, 1995).
2. For example, in 1985 it was reported that, in London alone, corporate fraud had risen from £260 million in 1981 to £776 million in 1984, and that the average size of frauds had increased over the same period from £0.65 million to £1.09 million (ICAEW, 1985c).
3. SAS 110 (APB, 1995; UK); SAS no. 53 (AICPA, 1988; US); CICA Handbook Sections 5300 and 5135 (CICA, 1988b and 1991, respectively; Canada); AUS 210 (AARF, 1995; Australia); Auditing Guideline (AG) 9 (New Zealand Society of Accountants (NZSA), 1986; NZ).
4. A similar provision was included in the APC's auditing guideline (1990, UK) but was omitted from the APB's SAS:110 (1995).

REFERENCES

Allen, R. (1985) Fraud and the auditor: for sleuth read sneak?, *Accountancy Age*, 12 March, p. 17.

American Institute of [Certified Public] Accountants (AICPA) (1951) *Codification of Statements on Auditing Procedure*, AICPA, New York.

American Institute of Certified Public Accountants (AICPA) (1972) *Statement on Auditing Standards no. 1*, AICPA, New York.

American Institute of Certified Public Accountants (AICPA) (1988) *Statement on Auditing Standards no. 53, The Auditor's Responsibility to Detect and Report Errors and Irregularities*, AICPA, New York.

Auditing Practices Board (APB) (1994) *The Audit Agenda*, APB, London.

Auditing Practices Board (APB) (1995) *Statement of Auditing Standards 110: Fraud and Error*, APB, London.

Auditing Practices Board (APB) (1996) *The Audit Research Agenda*, APB, London.

Auditing Practices Committee (APC) (1980) *Explanatory Foreword to Auditing Standards and Guidelines*, ICAEW, London.

Auditing Practices Committee (APC) (1985) *Exposure Draft of an Auditing Guideline: Fraud and Other Irregularities*, ICAEW, London.

Auditing Practices Committee (APC) (1988) *Exposure Draft of an Auditing Guideline: The Auditor's Responsibility for Detecting and Reporting Fraud and Other Illegal Acts*, ICAEW, London.

Auditing Practices Committee (APC) (1990) *Auditing Guideline: The Auditor's Responsibility in Relation to Fraud, Other Irregularities and Errors*, ICAEW, London.

Australian Accounting Research Foundation (AARF) (1995) *Auditing Standard 210: Irregularities, Including Fraud, Other Illegal Acts and Errors*, AARF, Melbourne.

Barclay, S. (1985) Certifieds to hold out against fraud changes, *Accountancy Age*, 22 August, p. 1.

Beck G. W. (1974) *Public Accountants in Australia – Their Social Role*, AARF, Melbourne.

Brown, R. G. (1962) Changing audit objectives and techniques, *The Accounting Review*, Vol. 37, no. 4, pp. 696–703.

Canadian Institute of Chartered Accountants (CICA) (1988a) *Report of the Commission to Study the Public's Expectations of Audits* (Macdonald Commission), CICA, Toronto.

Canadian Institute of Chartered Accountants (CICA) (1988b) *Members Handbook. Auditing Recommendations Section 5300*, CICA, Toronto.

Canadian Institute of Chartered Accountants (CICA) (1991) *Members Handbook. Auditing Recommendations Section 5315*, CICA, Toronto.

Commission on Auditors' Responsibilities (CAR) (1978) *Report, Conclusions and Recommendations* (Cohen Commission), AICPA, New York.

Committee on the Financial Aspects of Corporate Governance (1992) *Report of the Committee on the Financial Aspects of Corporate Governance* (Cadbury Committee), Gee, London.

Cowe, R. (1989) No mystery of watchdogs that don't bark, *Guardian*, 19 September, p. 16.

Dicksee, L. R. (1898) *Auditing: A Practical Manual for Auditors* (3rd edn), Gee & Co., London.

Financial Times (1993) *Fraud against companies trebles*, 24 February, p. 8.

Guy, D. M. and Sullivan, J. D. (1988) The expectation gap auditing standards, *Journal of Accountancy*, Vol. 165, no. 4, pp. 36–46.

Humphrey, C., Turley, S. and Moizer, P. (1993) Protecting against detection: the case of auditors and fraud, *Accounting, Auditing and Accountability Journal*, Vol. 6, no. 1, pp. 39–62.

Institute of Chartered Accountants in England and Wales (ICAEW) (1961) *General Principles of Auditing, Statement on Auditing U1*, ICAEW, London.

Institute of Chartered Accountants in England and Wales (ICAEW) (1985a) *Report of the Working Party on Fraud* (Davison Report), ICAEW, London.

Institute of Chartered Accountants in England and Wales (ICAEW) (1985b) *The Auditor and Fraud: Report of Lord Benson's Committee*, ICAEW, London.

Institute of Chartered Accountants in England and Wales (ICAEW) (1985c) *Financial Fraud – What Next?*, The Proceedings of Joint ICAEW and Law Society Conference on Financial Fraud, ICAEW, London.

Institute of Chartered Accountants of Scotland (ICAS) (1985) *The Auditor's Role with Respect to Fraud and Irregularities in the Financial Services Sector*, memorandum submitted to the Department of Trade and Industry, ICAS, Edinburgh.

Institute of Chartered Accountants of Scotland (ICAS) (1993) *Auditing into the Twenty-First Century*, ICAS, Edinburgh.

Knox, J. (1994) Why auditors don't find fraud, *Accountancy*, Vol. 113, no. 1206, p. 128.

KPMG (1995) *Fraud Barometer*, KPMG, London.

Lee, T. A. (1970) The nature of auditing and its objectives, *Accountancy*, Vol. 81, no. 920, pp. 292–6.

Lee, T. A. (1986) *Company Auditing* (3rd edn), Van Nostrand Reinhold, Wokingham.

McInnes, W. M. and Stevenson, J. E. (1996) *The Expectations Gap: An Exploration of Auditors' Responsibilities in Regard to Fraud*, Discussion Paper no. 96/01, Department of Accountancy and Finance, University of Stirling.

Montgomery, R. H. (1912) *Auditing, Theory and Practice*, The Ronald Press, New York.

Montgomery, R. H. (1957) *Auditing, Theory and Practice* (8th edn), The Ronald Press, New York.

Morison, A. M. C. (1970) The role of the reporting accountant today, *The Accountants' Magazine*, Vol. 74, no. 771, pp. 409–15.

National Companies and Securities Commission (NCSC) (1990) *Practice Note no. 356: Auditors' Duty to Report to Commission*, CCH pp. 95–140, Australia.

New Zealand Society of Accountants (NZSA) (1986) *Auditing Guideline 9, Fraud and Error*, NZSA, Wellington.

Porter, B. A. (1991) Narrowing the audit expectation–performance gap: a contemporary approach, *Pacific Accounting Review*, Vol. 3, no. 1, pp. 1–36.

Porter, B. A. (1993) An empirical study of the audit expectation–performance gap, *Accounting and Business Research*, Vol. 24, no. 93, pp. 49–68.

Riley, B. (1990) Getting the measure of accountants, *Financial Times*, 9 December, p. 1.

Singleton-Green, B. (1990) The new auditing guideline on fraud, *Accountancy*, Vol. 105, no. 1160, pp. 33–4.

Smith, T. (1985) Expectation gap trips up fraud fight's 'front line', *Accountancy Age*, 22 August, p. 10.

Steen, M. (1989) *Audits and Auditors: What the Public Thinks*, KPMG Peat Marwick McLintock, London.

Tweedie, D. P. (1991), Fraud – managements' and auditors' responsibility for its prevention and detection, in M. Sherer, and S. Turley (eds.) *Current Issues in Auditing* (2nd edn), Paul Chapman, London, chapter 2.

Willingham, J. J. (1975) Discussant's response to the relationship of auditing standards to the detection of fraud, *The CPA Journal*, April, pp. 18–21.

Woolf, E. (1978) Profession in peril – time running out for auditors, *Accountancy*, Vol. 89, no. 1014, pp. 58–65.

DISCUSSION QUESTIONS

1. The pendulum representing auditors' acknowledged responsibility to detect corporate fraud has swung from the one extreme of 'a primary audit objective' to the other of 'a responsibility not assumed'. It is currently resting at some intermediate point between the two extremes. At the same time as the auditing profession has changed its stance, the majority of the financial and business community and the general public have maintained a fairly static position of expecting auditors to detect fraud.

   Discuss reasons which may explain:

   (a) the auditing profession's changing position in respect of detecting corporate fraud;

   (b) the disparity between the position of the auditing profession on the one hand and that of the financial and business community and the general public on the other.

2. Describe auditors' duty under statutory and common (case) law to detect corporate fraud and show how the courts have demonstrated a concern to keep auditors' duty to detect fraud within reasonable bounds.

3. Discuss the conflicts which arise between the auditor's duty of confidentiality to the client and the desirability of reporting suspicions of fraud encountered during an audit to regulatory authorities.

4. The socio-economic environments of the UK, USA, Canada, Australia and New Zealand are broadly similar and it may, therefore, be expected that auditors' duties to detect and report corporate fraud in these countries would be similar.

   (a) Outline the similarities and differences in auditors' duties to detect and report fraud in the countries named above.

   (b) Give reasons which may explain the differences which are evident.

5. If the auditing profession is to avoid continuing public and political criticism, it must better meet society's expectations as regards detecting and reporting fraud. Discuss ways in which the match between society's expectations of auditors and auditors' performance in the corporate fraud arena may be improved.

3

Independence

Peter Moizer

All men are liable to error; and most men are, in many points, by passion or interest, under temptation to it.

> (from *An Essay Concerning Human Understanding*,
> Chapter 20, section 17, by John Locke)

INTRODUCTION

At the heart of the audit process is a belief about human nature. Human beings will speak the truth, unless there is sufficient to be gained by being dishonest. As the managers of an organization are assumed to be able to benefit personally from reporting dishonestly in their organization's published financial statements, there is a presumption that managers will tend to manipulate the financial statements so as to make their performance look better than it actually is. In contrast, auditors are assumed to have no incentive to be dishonest. They are presumed to be independent of both the organization being audited and its managers and so they can be employed to report on the truthfulness of the managers' financial statements.

If auditors were truly independent of their client this chapter would end here, but they are not. Restricting our attention to company auditing, it can be seen that the directors of a company effectively appoint the company's auditors and also effectively determine the size of the audit fee. The word 'effectively' is used because, strictly, a company's shareholders appoint the auditors and approve their remuneration, but in practice the shareholders merely rubber-stamp the recommendations of the directors. Hence, if the auditors conclude that the financial statements do not show a true and fair view and qualify their audit opinion, they know that there is a possibility

Peter Moizer is Professor of Accounting at the University of Leeds.

either of losing the audit or of having their fee reduced. There is also a sense of loyalty that is built up between an auditor and the managers being audited. An auditor may be reluctant to jeopardize the career of a manager who is a personal friend.

Having allowed that auditors are not truly independent and that they may have some incentive not to report truthfully, there is then a rather interesting paradox. Managers cannot be relied upon to subordinate their own self-interest to the demands of honesty but auditors can. Why auditors can be assumed to act honestly, even though they are not truly independent, is the subject of this chapter.

TECHNICAL COMPETENCE

Before addressing the issue of independence, it is helpful to analyse the concept of technical competence, as technical competence can be used to mask dishonest reporting. For the report of the auditor to have any value to the readers of the financial statements, the auditor must be both technically competent and honest. A technically competent auditor will have the necessary expertise to discover all the significant errors and omissions present in a set of financial statements. An honest auditor will ensure either that all significant errors and omissions are corrected or that they are fully disclosed in the auditor's report.

In reality, the concepts of competence and honesty can become interrelated. A dishonest auditor may choose to act in such a way that errors or omissions are not discovered, i.e. to behave in a technically *incompetent* fashion. An illustrious example of the practice was given in 1801 at the Battle of Copenhagen, when Nelson put his telescope to his blind eye to avoid seeing the signal commanding him to withdraw his ships from battle. He was reported as saying, 'I have only one eye – I have a right to be blind sometimes . . . I really do not see the signal!' (Southey's *Life of Nelson*, Chapter 7). Auditors can choose to act in a similar fashion by studiously avoiding those areas where errors or omissions might be found. Since the audit tests have failed to produce any embarrassing revelations, the auditor can produce an unqualified opinion without apparently compromising his or her integrity. In cases of audit failure, where subsequent events have shown that the auditor's report was incorrect, it is often difficult to decide whether the auditor made an honest mistake or whether he or she deliberately chose not to examine a particular area or to make some technical error. In this chapter we will assume that the auditor is technically competent and concentrate on the issue of whether the auditor can be expected to act honestly in particular circumstances.

ANALYSING THE MOTIVATIONS OF AUDITORS

The main issue to be addressed in this chapter is why auditors should behave honestly, even when they are not economically independent of their clients and hence have some economic interest to lose by being honest (either the whole or part of the present value of the net revenues expected to be received from the client in the future). A necessary condition for honesty is that an auditor must have an independent attitude of mind, since an auditor who does not have an independent outlook cannot be relied upon to be honest. This view is echoed in Lee's (1993, p. 98) conclusion that 'there is a general agreement that independence is an attitude of mind which does not allow the viewpoints or conclusions of the corporate auditor to become reliant on or subordinate to the influence and pressures of conflicting interests'. There are several approaches to analysing an individual's attitude of mind, but the approach that will be followed here is to use the principles of ethical reasoning and an economic analysis of the motivations of self-interested individuals.

Ethical reasoning

Two types of ethical reasoning can be distinguished: *consequentialism* and *deontology*. In consequentialism actions are judged in terms of the consequences that result, whereas in deontology the view is taken that some acts are morally obligatory regardless of their consequences. The distinction between deontology and consequentialism can be seen by asking:

> Are all the guides to conduct that we want people to follow, and all the constraints on conduct that we want them to accept, of the form – act so as to bring about X as far as is possible (consequentialism); or of the form – do (or do not do) things of kind Y (deontology)?
>
> (Mackie, 1977, pp. 154–5).

The debate between consequentialists and deontologists has often centred on the doctrine of 'the end justifies the means' (a doctrine which teaches that evil means may be employed to produce a good result). Such a doctrine is an extreme version of consequentialism, however, because it implies that the moral difference between ends and means is such that only the end is important; the means to achieve it having no moral significance at all. The more usual consequentialist view is that there is no morally relevant distinction between means and ends and hence that any badness in the proposed means has to be balanced fairly against the expected goodness of the end. It is therefore possible to justify the use of evil means to achieve a good end, provided that the end is sufficiently good to outweigh the bad created by the means. The deontological view differs, because it assumes that particular aspects of an action determine its moral quality absolutely. Thus a proposed action could be analysed in terms of its moral character and a decision could be made whether it is morally obligatory or morally wrong on the basis of this analysis alone, without considering what else is involved.

In terms of auditor independence and reporting honestly, the ethical position adopted by an auditor will influence his or her decision. Thus an auditor could adopt the deontological stance that it is wrong to be dishonest.

Such a person would therefore not write an audit opinion which he or she knows to be wrong, even if the consequences of issuing an honest opinion are expected to be disastrous for a large number of people. Such a person would conform to Aristotle's concept of a sincere or truthful man (*aletheutikos*):

> A man is truthful both in speech and in the way he lives because he is like that in disposition. Such a person would seem to be a good type; for a lover of the truth, who speaks it when nothing depends on it, will speak it all the more when something does depend upon it.
>
> (Ethics, translated Thomson, 1976, p. 165)

In contrast, a consequentialist auditor will be concerned about the consequences of issuing a truthful opinion and hence will have to wrestle with his or her conscience when making damaging revelations in the audit report. Perhaps one of the most damaging reports that an auditor can issue is the so-called 'going concern' qualification, in which the auditor casts doubt on the organization's ability to continue as a viable entity, because of its potential inability to meet its obligations to its creditors. One inevitable consequence of such a report is that the organization has a greater chance of being put into the hands of a receiver or liquidator. The auditor is therefore aware that his or her report can mean the break-up of an organization which could spell considerable hardship for a large number of people. In such circumstances a consequentialist auditor may well conclude that it would be better to say nothing and produce a dishonest report.

The conclusions of the ethical analysis are therefore ambiguous. Auditors who are concerned only with performing the action that is morally obligatory (deontologists) will always report in an honest fashion, but auditors who are concerned about the consequences of their actions may on occasion report in a dishonest way. The profession's ethical guidelines on the subject are somewhat ambiguous. For example, the first two fundamental principles in the Guide to Professional Ethics of the Institute of Chartered Accountants in England and Wales (ICAEW, 1997, p. 174) are as follows:

1. A member should behave with integrity in all professional and business relationships. Integrity implies not merely honesty but fair dealing and truthfulness.

2. A member should strive for objectivity in all professional and business judgements. Objectivity is the state of mind which has regard to all considerations relevant to the task in hand but no other.

In the context of the present discussion, such fundamental principles leave open to the individual the choice of which 'considerations are relevant to the task in hand but no other'. The question of whether the consequences of the auditor's actions are considerations relevant to the decision are not made clear. Sometimes, a professional body will suggest that its members should occasionally think about the consequences of their actions, as in the following extract: 'The council therefore recommends that members . . . should not disclose past or intended civil wrongs, crimes . . . or statutory offences *unless they feel that the damage to the public likely to arise from non-disclosure is of a very serious nature*' (emphasis added) (Institute of Chartered Accountants of Scotland, 1971, para. 10).

The question of the extent to which auditors do ignore the consequences of their actions is impossible to answer, because the data to answer the question are unobtainable. However, it has to be allowed that there are ethical reasons why on certain, admittedly rare, occasions an auditor may prefer to report dishonestly from entirely *altruistic* motives (i.e. taking account of the interests of others rather than the auditor's own self-interest).

However, whilst the preceding discussion draws attention to the fact that consequentialist auditors may act dishonestly because they think that such a course of action will bring the greatest happiness to the greatest number, the more usual threat to independence is that a consequentialist thinker will be more concerned about the consequences to himself or herself. A more plausible assumption (or, at least, the assumption that the more cynical readers of audited financial statements are likely to make) is that auditors are consequential *egoists*, interested only in the effects on their own welfare. The question, therefore, that remains to be addressed is whether consequential egoists, concerned solely with their own self-interests, can be expected to behave in an independent fashion. Surprisingly, the answer is 'Yes' in certain circumstances and these will now be discussed.

The self-interested auditor (a rational economic person)

Perhaps the best model of a consequentialist egoist was developed by economists and termed by them 'rational economic man'. Rational economic individuals act in such a way as to maximize their own utility (self-interest). This goal is usually considered to have two aspects: the maximization of an individual's economic wealth, i.e. the present value of the stream of future cash flows accruing to the individual; and the minimization of the risk attached to these future cash flows. Antle (1984) has produced a one-period game-theoretical analysis of the situation in which there are three parties: the owner, the manager and the auditor. The language of the paper is difficult to understand, but the result of the analysis is essentially simple. If each party acts purely to maximize his or her self-interest, the implication of the model is that the manager and the auditor should conspire together to the detriment of the owner. This result applies for one period only, the model being too complex to extend to a multi-period situation.

In order to examine the more realistic setting of many periods (so that the auditor is reporting not just once but on a regular basis), it is necessary to use a less exact form of economic analysis. To understand this analysis, the nature of the auditing service needs to be understood. If a set of financial statements is produced without an audit, a rational economic reader will expect that the management of the organization will have biased the financial statements, in some way, to make the performance of the organization seem better than it actually is. Errors resulting from genuine mistakes may be present as well as deliberate ones. Accordingly, the value of an audit can, in principle, be measured by how much confidence the reader of the audited financial statements has that they are free from the impact of both types of error. By its nature, the audit cannot be expected to uncover all possible errors, since cost considerations prevent the auditor from examining all the transactions that the organization has undertaken in the period and so the auditor has to make a decision on how much audit work needs to be undertaken. This process forms the substance of Part II of this book, but for the present we need note only that the auditor makes a judgement on how much audit work he or she considers necessary in order to give an opinion on the financial statements. Different auditors will make different decisions based on their training and their attitudes to risk. As a result it is possible to speak of different qualities of audits. Quality can be measured either by input measures (how much work has been performed) or output measures (the probability that the audited financial statements do not contain a significant error or omission). However, the difficulty faced by consumers of the audit service (the readers of the financial statements) is that there is no way in which they can determine the quality of the audit work performed. Unqualified audit reports are documents noted for their consistency across different audit firms. Reading an unqualified audit report conveys the impression that the audit work carried out complies with auditing standards and guidelines, but this is only at a general level and gives no idea of the actual level of audit quality employed. The only assurance that the reader has is that he or she knows that if the auditor is found to have behaved in a negligent fashion the auditor will be liable to a claim for damages. A rational economic auditor can therefore be expected to perform an audit which will reduce the chances of a successful negligence suit to a level which is acceptable to the auditor. In the language of economics, the auditor should perform audit work until the cost of undertaking more work is equal to the benefit that the auditor derives because there is only a negligible chance of being successfully sued for damages. This then represents the minimum amount of work that the reader can expect the auditor to perform. However, all auditors are individuals with different attitudes to risk and return and so one auditor's minimum standard of audit work will not necessarily be that of a colleague.

One further point needs to be considered which relates to the reputation of the auditor or audit firm. There have been a number of studies which show that different firms have different reputations (see, for example, Moizer, 1989). An economic analysis of markets where reputations exist shows that those firms with an above average reputation for performing work of above average quality can earn higher fees than the average. Such firms can earn a 'rent' for their reputation. In the audit context, if an audit firm has a reputation for performing above average quality work (in the sense that the financial statements of companies that it audits have a lower chance of containing significant errors), readers will have more confidence in the financial statements. In a world of rational economic individuals who are wealth maximizers and risk minimizers, this increase in confidence means that there is less risk of error and this decrease in risk should be worth paying for (the insurance industry is built on this concept). Hence, auditors with higher reputations can be expected to earn higher fees because their reports are more highly valued. There is thus the possibility that, if an auditor performs work of an above average standard, eventually the reputation of the auditor will rise and he or she will be able to charge more for his or her services. There is, therefore, an incentive mechanism in the market for the auditor to improve or at least maintain the existing quality of work, although the auditor will have to decide whether the costs of improving quality are justified by the increase in future audit fees which might arise once the improvement in quality has been recognized by the consumers of the audit service.

How then does this economic analysis relate to independence or the need to report honestly? Every time that an auditor makes a statement which he or she knows to be false, that individual is risking two things: firstly, the costs of a successful legal action for negligence (this could be a mixture of money that has to be paid directly to the aggrieved party as a result of a legal settlement and the higher insurance premiums that will inevitably arise if part of the legal settlement is covered by insurance) and, secondly, the costs of a loss in reputation resulting from the reduction in fee income that the auditor can command. Thus, the self-interested auditor has to balance the costs of reporting honestly (the present value of the reduction in net fee income expected to be received from the client) against the long-term benefits of honest reporting (the avoidance of legal costs and the loss of income derived from a good reputation).

The above analysis concentrates on the position of a single economic rational auditor, but there is also a collective perspective, since it can be argued that auditors as a group benefit from being perceived as independent, technically competent individuals. Hence, the analysis has to be extended to cover the audit profession and the benefits which all members could lose if one of its members were seen to be acting dishonestly.

The economic value of a self-governing audit profession

Section 25 of the Companies Act 1989 requires that for a person to be eligible for appointment as a company auditor he or she must be a member of a recognized supervisory body and be eligible for the audit appointment under the rules of that body. There are at present five recognized supervisory bodies in the UK: the Institute of Chartered Accountants in England and Wales, the Institute of Chartered Accountants of Scotland, the Institute of Chartered Accountants in Ireland, the Association of Chartered Certified Accountants, and the Association of Authorized Public Accountants. The professional bodies are self-governing and receive little governmental interference, which should confer substantial benefits on the audit profession. For example, entry into the profession can be limited by examinations and practising certificate requirements; secrecy can be encouraged (e.g. until the mid-1980s professional audit firms were prevented from advertizing by the rules of the profession); the regulation of accounting and auditing practice is carried out by the profession rather than government; and misconduct can be judged by fellow professionals rather than by some central licensing body such as the Securities and Exchange Commission (SEC) in the USA. All these benefits provide a potentially higher income stream than would be possible under a state scheme and also give the profession's members more flexibility in their work. It might be expected, therefore, that there should be a strong desire on the part of the auditing profession to maintain its self-regulating monopoly and avoid governmental intervention. Government tends to respond to public anxiety, which is usually fuelled by some *cause célèbre*, when the work of the auditing profession is deemed to be of unacceptable quality. Consequently, there is the additional need to report honestly in an independent fashion, because every occasion when dishonesty is discovered increases the possibility of governmental intervention and hence the loss of the self-regulatory monopoly that the profession currently enjoys.

One way that the profession attempts to ensure that its members behave with integrity is by promulgating and enforcing a code of ethics. Such codes lay down the minimum standards of behaviour expected of members of the profession and hence can be said to constitute the moral rules of the profession. An egoistical explanation of the profession's morality would be that all the benefits arising from being regarded as a competent, trustworthy auditor stem from the existence of a stable, well-thought-of profession; the observance of certain moral rules is a necessary condition of such a profession; hence auditors have an interest in maintaining the moral order of the profession. However, there is also an altruistic explanation for the profession's morality which would argue that the preceding discussion based on egoism proves only that an auditor has an interest in *other* auditors abiding by the moral rules of the profession. It does not prove that it is in the interest of an individual auditor to abide by the rules, since the central argument of altruism is that the explanation of morality cannot be reduced to self-interest. An altruist would argue that it is the interest in people for their own sake that is a necessary condition for morality. This notion of the altruistic professional is not confined to auditing, e.g. Johnson (1972, p. 13) has noted that professions may be distinguished from other occupations by their altruism which may be expressed in the service orientation of professional men. However, to conclude on the subject of the altruistic nature of professionals, one can perhaps do no better than quote Haskell (1984, p. 181):

> The image of the disinterested professional lingers on, but reactions to it range from mild scepticism to curt dismissal. Some modern writers regard it as a harmless myth, possessing like all myths a grain of truth and serviceable as an ideal, perhaps, but certainly not an adequate representation of the actual motives of most professionals, most of the time. Others share Collin's hostile conviction that professionals are wolves in sheep's cloth-

ing, monopolists who live by the rule of caveat emptor, but lack the integrity to admit it.

EXISTING WAYS OF IMPROVING INDEPENDENCE

The foregoing sections analysed the motivational forces acting upon auditors. They reflect what auditors might do given no regulatory restrictions. However, in order to strengthen public confidence in the independence of the auditing profession, a number of rules and guidelines of behaviour have been laid down by Parliament and by the profession itself. These rules assume that auditors are self-interested and that the way to ensure independence is to reduce the auditor's economic dependence on company management.

To understand the basis behind these rules and regulations, it is necessary to reconsider some of the economic forces which could potentially affect the behaviour of auditors. In terms of professional and legal rules and regulations, four economic factors are relevant:

(1) the value of the auditor's economic interest that will be lost if the auditor discloses some error or omission by company management;
(2) the probability that the client will dispense with the auditor's services if he or she reports that the financial statements are misstated;
(3) the financial loss that will occur as a result of a legal settlement if the auditor fails to report a significant error or omission; and
(4) the loss of future net revenues that will occur as a result of the loss of reputation suffered by the auditor when any misconduct is made public.

The last two factors have not been considered by regulators as ways of improving auditor independence. In the case of the last factor, the reason is presumably because it is too nebulous a concept to legislate for (although the heated discussions which took place on the subject of 'brand accounting' show that the concept of the value of a brand's reputation is accepted by some accountants). The third factor relating to the costs of legal settlements has been discussed in the political arena, but not from the point of view of increasing the size of legal settlements (and hence one would suppose increasing independence), but from the viewpoint that legal settlements are too high and that some way should be found of reducing them.

Most of the rules and regulations designed to protect auditor independence can be seen as relating to the first two factors identified above: reducing the size of the auditor's economic interest and reducing the probability that the auditor will lose the audit by reporting unfavourably on the financial statements. These two factors will now be considered in more detail.

Limiting the size of the auditor's economic interest

In the modern commercial world, auditors usually provide numerous other services to complement their audit work. Such services include accountancy and bookkeeping assistance, legal assistance, management consultancy services, personnel recruitment assistance, investigation work, corporate finance advice and tax advice. In some cases the fees from the non-audit services can dwarf the audit fee. Consequently, the cost of losing a client can be considerably more than simply the audit fee. For some audits (e.g. local government audits) auditors are not allowed to be consultants, but for company audits there is no existing legal restriction on the amount of non-audit fee income that an audit firm can receive from a client. However, the mood of the EU countries is against auditors also being advisers and so the position in the UK may change.

In the consultative document issued by the Department of Trade and Industry (DTI) on the implementation of the EU Eighth Directive, comments were invited on the possibility of introducing a prohibition on auditors providing non-audit services to audit clients. No legislation on this point was subsequently introduced in the Companies Act 1989, other than Statutory Instrument 1991/2128 'The Companies Act 1985 (Disclosure of Remuneration for Non-Audit Work) Regulations 1991' which required the disclosure in companies' annual accounts (for financial years beginning after 1 October 1991) of any fees paid to auditors for non-audit services.

If the EU does set out to prevent audit firms from providing non-audit services, the audit profession could do worse than use the interesting defence proposed by Goldman and Barlev (1974). They argue that the more non-audit services are provided to the client, the greater will be the dependence of company management on the audit firm and hence the greater will be the management's desire not to lose the services of that audit firm. Paradoxically therefore, the greater the audit firm's economic interest, the greater will be its independence.

At present, the only restriction on the provision of 'other services' is contained within the ethical guides of the various professional bodies. For example, section 4.2 of the Guide to Professional Ethics issued by the Institute of Chartered Accountants in England and Wales instructs members that an auditor 'should not accept an audit appointment or similar financial reporting assignment from any entity which regularly provides him or an office within the firm with an unduly large proportion of his or its gross practice income' (ICAEW, 1997, p. 183). An unduly large proportion would normally be 15 per cent, or in the case of listed or other public interest companies the appropriate figure would be 10 per cent. The logic behind this instruction is that an auditor will be seen to be more independent of a client if revenues from the client form only a small part of the individual partner's or the office's total fee income. The recent series of mergers between the medium-sized accounting firms should help in this regard.

Likelihood of losing an audit client

This area has attracted the most interest from legislators and the professional bodies as a way of bolstering the independence of auditors. Sections 384 to

394 of the Companies Act 1985 regulate the appointment, removal, resignation and remuneration of the auditor. Auditors have the right to speak against any resolution at a company's general meeting which proposes their replacement and they can also have written representations distributed to shareholders at the company's expense. Hence, company law attempts to place the dismissal of auditors in the hands of the shareholders and not the directors. Unfortunately for auditors, the decisions of the shareholders are likely to be heavily influenced by the view of the directors. In the UK the large majority of shareholders are institutions which are interested principally in achieving above average portfolio returns and which are therefore unlikely to 'rock the boat' as far as the auditors are concerned.

Further support for auditors is provided by the ethical rules of the Institutes. For example, section 1.206 of the Guide to Professional Ethics of the Institute of Chartered Accountants in England and Wales instructs its members as follows:

'It is necessary . . . for a member who is asked to act by a prospective client . . . to communicate with the existing auditor or advisor and for the latter to reply promptly as to any considerations which might affect the prospective auditor or advisor's decision whether or not to accept the appointment' (ICAEW, 1997, p. 222).

This recommendation appears to be effective for public companies listed on the UK Stock Exchange, principally because of the publicity that surrounds the replacement of auditors. Lack of communication with the old auditor would diminish the reputation enjoyed by the new auditor.

Section 390A of the Companies Act 1985 ensures that the remuneration of auditors is determined at the annual general meeting, but apart from this there is little to protect them from a reduction in either audit fees or fees from non-audit work should they upset client company management. There has been an increasing tendency to put audits 'out to tender' with the ostensible aim of reducing audit fees, but this may be a way of making the removal of an audit firm more acceptable to the public at large, as well as lowering fees. In such cases, company management must decide whether the set-up costs of a new audit firm are worth paying (e.g. the new audit firm will have to waste company employees' time learning about the company).

Another feature of the modern audit environment which might be expected to give some support to the independence of auditors is the existence of accounting and auditing standards and guidelines. If these were comprehensive and enforced in a vigorous and visible manner the power of the auditor would be increased. Both auditors and company management would know that all audit firms would reach a similar conclusion as to what ought to appear in the company's financial statements and hence that the advantages of changing audit firms would be non-existent. That this is not the case can be seen from the prevailing practice of 'opinion shopping', where client management will telephone various audit firms asking their opinion on a particular aspect of its company's financial statements. The effect of such practices is to weaken the position of existing auditors, once company management can say that another audit firm would act differently.

One further form of support for auditors that is employed is the use of audit committees. These committees are manned by members of the board of directors, including several non-executive directors. These committees can provide a buffer between the audit firm and company management, although their degree of effectiveness will depend on the independence of the non-executive directors. As most non-executive directors are people with a reputation to lose, the presumption is that they will act in an honourable fashion and hence support the auditors when their cause is a fair one.

ADDITIONAL WAYS OF IMPROVING INDEPENDENCE

The preceding section outlined what presently exists to support the independence of auditors. In this section we shall examine further ways that have been suggested.

Legal prohibition of financial interests in client companies

At the present time, there are no legal requirements to prevent an auditor from having a financial interest (such as holding shares) in a client company. There are not even any legal requirements that an auditor should disclose such financial interests. The ethical guidelines of the professional bodies make clear that financial interests in clients should be avoided and the large accounting firms regularly produce lists of the companies in which members of the firm cannot invest. The effect of a legal requirement not to hold shares will probably therefore have little effect in most cases, although it should improve the outside world's perception of the independence of auditors. The reasoning behind this last statement is subtle and runs like this: beneficial shareholdings in audit clients create an incentive for the auditor to act in such a way as to maintain the market value of the client; maintaining a false market value of a company is against the interests of future shareholders at whose expense an existing shareholder (such as the auditor) could profit by selling shares at an inflated value; hence an auditor shareholder has an incentive to mislead potential shareholders and therefore not to act in an independent manner. Furthermore, an auditor has access to insider information (information not yet in the public domain) and could potentially profit by this information, although such insider dealing would be a criminal offence under section 52 of the Criminal Justice Act 1993.

Rotation of audit appointments

One suggestion to reduce the dependence of the auditor is that audit appointments should be rotated on a regular basis such as every five years. This system should mean that the loss of economic interest will be minimized, since the audit fee income would last for only a short period. If auditors know that they are due to be replaced soon, they are less likely to be concerned about the attitudes of a company's management. The obvious drawback with the suggestion is that there will inevitably be set-up costs every time the audit changes.

Peer review

Another suggestion designed to improve performance is that one audit firm's audit working papers should be reviewed by another firm. This 'peer' review would check that the original audit firm had performed all the audit work that was necessary and that all discovered significant errors and omissions had been either corrected or disclosed in the audit report. The principal drawback of this system is deciding who should bear the costs of the review: the client or the profession. Neither appears particularly willing. Most audit professionals would argue that the monitoring units of the professional bodies perform a similar function and that peer review as such would add little.

Independent audit-appointing and fee-setting body

The intention behind this proposal is to reduce the power of directors over the appointment of auditors. A governmental body would be set up under the auspices of the Department of Trade and Industry or some specially con-stituted State Auditing Board. This body would be responsible for the appointment of auditors and determining the size of their remuneration. The audit fee could also be paid by the governmental body out of a system of levies on companies. The main disadvantage of such a system is that it would be difficult and costly to implement.

SUMMARY

Individuals who use company financial statements when making decisions need to be reassured that the information contained in the financial state-ments is reliable. The audit is the main mechanism for providing this re-assurance. An analysis of the ethical position for *altruistic* auditors (who have an unselfish concern for the welfare of others) shows that in the vast major-ity of cases the ethical decision is to tell the truth. However, it is possible to envisage situations in which an altruistic auditor, concerned about the con-sequences of reporting honestly, might ethically justify dishonest reporting on the ground that the bad caused by the act of dishonesty is outweighed by the expected overall increase in good arising from the dishonesty.

In contrast, for *egoistical* auditors (preoccupied with their own interests and welfare), there are personal incentives which could make them act in a non-independent fashion, since modern auditors are effectively hired, and their remuneration determined, by the directors of their client companies. Accordingly, there is an economic incentive for an auditor not to offend the directors and hence for the auditor not to be independent. Fortunately, there are also economic reasons why egoistical auditors *should* act in an independent manner. If an auditor fails to report some error or omission in the financial statements, there are two directly associated economic costs: the costs of a legal settlement for negligence and the costs associated with a drop in the levels of fee income that the auditor can command as the auditor's reputation among users falls. There is also an indirect cost to the firm in that every case of auditor negligence reduces the esteem in which the audit profession is held by the general public and therefore increases the likelihood that the self-regulatory monopoly which the profession currently enjoys will be withdrawn by government.

In order to increase the independence of egoistical auditors, it is necessary to reduce the expected gains from not telling the truth. Therefore, it is necessary either to reduce the size of the auditor's interest in the client or to reduce the powers of the directors of the client company to sack the audit firm or reduce its income from the company. A number of methods for supporting and improving auditor independence are in use and have been suggested. A common thread linking all of them is that someone (be it directors, auditors or shareholders) must make some sacrifice. Consequently, proposals to improve independence can succeed only if backed by an effective means of producing this sacrifice. The most obvious way is via specific legislation, although there is a role for self-regulation by the profession, provided the enforcement procedures are tough enough.

REFERENCES

Antle, R. (1984) Auditor independence, *Journal of Accounting Research*, Spring, pp. 1–20.

Aristotle, *Ethics*, translated by J. A. K. Thomson, (1976), Penguin, Harmondsworth.

Goldman, A. and Barlev, B. (1974) The auditor–firm conflict of interests: its implications for independence, *The Accounting Review*, Vol. 49, no. 4, pp. 707–18.

Haskell, T. L. (1984) Professionalism versus capitalism: R. H. Tawney, Emile Durkheim and C. S. Pierre on the disinterestedness of professional communities, in T. L. Haskell (ed.) *The Authority of Experts: Studies in History and Theory*, Indiana University Press, Bloomington.

Institute of Chartered Accountants in England and Wales (1997) *Members Handbook*, Volume 1, ICAEW, London

Institute of Chartered Accountants of Scotland (1971) *Statement of Professional Conduct No. 4: Unlawful Acts or Defaults by Clients of Members*, ICAS, Edinburgh.

Johnson, T. J. (1972) *Professions and Power*, Macmillan, London.

Lee, T. A. (1993) *Corporate Audit Theory*, Chapman & Hall, London.

Mackie, J. L. (1977) *Ethics – Inventing Right and Wrong*, Penguin, Harmondsworth.

Moizer P. (1989) The image of auditors, chapter 8 of *Auditing and the Future*, Institutes of Chartered Accountants of Scotland and in England and Wales, Edinburgh and London.

FURTHER READING

Further discussion of the issues raised in this chapter can be found in the following:

Carey, J. L. and Doherty, W. O. (1970) The concept of independence – review and restatement, in W. S. Boutell (ed.) *Contemporary Auditing*, Dickenson Publishing, Belmont, California.

Flint, D. (1988) *Philosophy and Principles of Auditing – An Introduction*, Macmillan, Basingstoke, pp. 54–86.

Lee, T. A. (1993) *Corporate Audit Theory*, Chapman & Hall, London, pp. 93–114.

Mautz, R. K. and Sharaf, H. A. (1961) *The Philosophy of Auditing*, American Accounting Association, New York, pp. 204–31.

Sherer, M. and Kent, D. (1983), *Auditing and Accountability*, Pitman, London, pp. 24–35 (reprinted 1988, Paul Chapman, London).

DISCUSSION QUESTIONS

1. Explain what is meant by the concept of auditor independence.
2. Given that the directors of a company effectively hire the company's auditors and determine the size of their audit fee, explain to a non-accountant why he or she should rely on the audit report contained in a company's financial statements.
3. Suggest ways in which an audit firm can acquire a reputation for performing audit work of a particular quality.
4. Discuss the ethical arguments that an auditor should always tell the truth.
5. Compare the threats to independence facing an external company auditor with those facing a chartered surveyor advising a client on a house purchase.
6. Discuss why company shareholders allow their directors so much power in the appointment, removal and remuneration of their company's auditors.

4

Corporate Governance and Audit Committees

Paul Collier

WHAT IS CORPORATE GOVERNANCE?

Corporate governance has received close scrutiny over the past few years due to the debate surrounding the recommendations of the Cadbury Committee (1992) on the Financial Aspects of Corporate Governance. The term 'corporate governance' is much used but rarely defined. Tricker (1984, p. 7) distinguished corporate governance from management by observing that, if management is about running the company, corporate governance is about ensuring that the company is run properly, and the *Financial Times* (6 April 1992) suggested that 'Corporate governance is all about finding ways to make companies run better.' Keasey and Wright (1993) distinguished corporate governance, which concerns the structures and processes associated with production, decision-making, control and other activities within an organization, from accountability, which was specified as a sub-set of corporate governance which involves the monitoring, evaluation and control of organizational agents to ensure that they behave in the interests of shareholders and other stakeholders.

This chapter focuses on the auditing implications of corporate governance, which are concerned largely with accountability, and concentrates upon the board of directors and its relationships with auditors. The chapter discusses the Cadbury Committee recommendations on auditing before focusing on audit committees and examining their structure, development, benefits and effectiveness. The discussion uses the corporate governance framework in Figure 4.1.

The framework emphasizes two key concerns of corporate governance

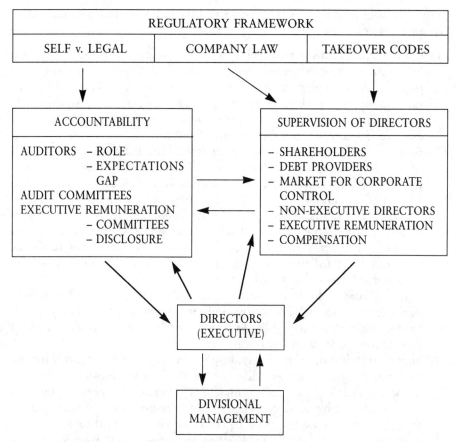

Source: Reproduced from Keasey and Wright (1993)

Figure 4.1   The corporate governance framework

which derive from the separation of ownership and control in large companies. First, the need for the supervision and monitoring of the executive and, secondly, mechanisms for ensuring that management is accountable to shareholders and other stakeholders. The framework includes the involvement of auditors as independent third parties and links the accountability problems of the auditors' role and the expectations that derive from audit activities with the supervisory role of non-executive directors through audit committees. The link between corporate governance and the audit is consistent with the societal approach to the corporate audit function (Flint, 1988, p. 15), which holds that its principal task is perceived as one which assists in corporate governance and managerial accountability

THE CADBURY COMMITTEE

The setting up of the Cadbury Committee reflected a gradual increase in dissatisfaction throughout the 1980s with the system of corporate governance in the UK. Whittington (1993) has identified the following four themes under-pining these concerns:

(1) Creative accounting – throughout the 1980s there was a steady increase in the use of creative accounting methods which sought to present company results in unduly favourable terms (e.g. Griffiths, 1986). The failure of monitoring systems to protect shareholders by controlling this activity led commentators to suggest that the system of corporate governance failed to control the actions of directors.

(2) Business failures and scandals – in the late 1980s and early 1990s a series of spectacular failures and scandals (for example, Johnson Matthey, British and Commonwealth, Ferranti, Polly Peck, Coloroll, BCCI and the Maxwell companies) were attributed in part to deficiencies in corporate governance systems. This led to debate about the advisability of one-man-dominated companies and the role of non-executive directors. In addition, the perceived failure of the accounts to warn that problems were imminent led to a 'crisis of confidence' in the accounting profession and a focus on auditor/board relations.

(3) Directors' pay – the expansion of directors' stock options and well-publicized pay increases for directors and senior managers, especially in privatized utilities, led to public disquiet at the lack of shareholder control over the rewards of these groups.

(4) Short-termism – the perceived failure of British industry to invest for the long term, for instance as evidenced by the lack of research and development investment (see, for example, DTI, 1992). This phenomenon has been attributed by some commentators to the pressures on management from the stock market to deliver performance in the short term as otherwise the company might be subject to an opportunistic takeover bid.

In addition, the classical UK model of corporate governance which linked the power to govern the company with ownership has also been undermined by a rise in institutional shareholdings, as reported by Gaved and Goodman (1992, pp. 38–40), who found that between 1981 and 1990 institutional ownership of voting capital rose from around 75 to 85 per cent and commented that 'the general trend is towards increasing control and ownership of major British companies by institutional fund managers'. The objectives of institutional fund managers are determined by their responsibilities as trustees and therefore such investors do not influence corporate governance mechanisms other than in extreme situations. The passivity of institutional shareholders in these matters compared with the USA, Germany and Japan has been criticized (for example, Bank of England, 1989). Further evidence that this situation persists is provided by recommendations from both the Institutional Shareholders' Committee (1991) and the Cadbury Committee (1992) to the effect that institutional shareholders should take a positive interest in the composition of boards of directors, the presence of appropriate checks and balances in the corporate governance system, and the appointment of sufficient non-executive directors of the necessary calibre, experience and independence.

In essence, the Cadbury Committee recommendations attempt to spread 'best practice' so as to improve information to shareholders, reinforce self-regulation and strengthen auditor independence. The section on 'Auditing' (Cadbury Committee, 1992, pp. 36–47) commences by stating that the crucial question is 'not whether there should be an audit, but how to ensure its objectivity and effectiveness' in the face of a number of problems, which include:

(1) the scope which accounting standards and practice allow boards to present the financial outcomes of various situations and the difficulties for the auditor in insisting on one permitted treatment against another;

(2) the formal appointment of the auditors and the fixing of their remuneration by the shareholders hides the lack of any real involvement of the shareholders in this decision. In practice it is the company's directors who appoint the auditors, determine the scope of the audit and set the fee; this opens up the possibility of auditor independence being compromised;

(3) despite ethical guidelines, the threat of litigation and the need to maintain a professional reputation, it is possible that competition between audit firms may drive down audit fees to below the level at which a proper audit can be done;

(4) the audit 'expectations gap' especially in the light of the position set out in the *Caparo* case, which limited the auditors' duty of care in normal circumstances to the company and the shareholders as a body.

The Code of Best Practice (Cadbury Committee, 1992, p. 59) put forward the following proposals on reporting and controls to meet these concerns:

4.1 It is the board's duty to present a balanced and understandable assessment of the company's position.

4.2 The board should ensure that an objective and professional relationship is maintained with the auditors.

4.3 The board should establish an audit committee of at least three non-executive directors with written terms of reference which clearly deal with its authority and duties.

4.4 The directors should explain their responsibility for preparing the accounts next to a statement by the auditors about their reporting responsibilities.

4.5 The directors should report on the effectiveness of the company's system of internal control.

4.6 The directors should report that the business is a going concern with supporting assumptions or qualifications as necessary.

The Cadbury Committee Code of Best Practice covered all listed companies registered in the UK and required that companies should make a statement about their compliance with the Code and reasons for non-compliance with any sections in the report and accounts. Compliance is not mandatory; however, the London Stock Exchange backed the Code by requiring all listed companies to state their degree of compliance so that shareholders are aware of the situation (para. 12.43(j) of the new Stock Exchange rules on admission of securities to listing). The involvement of the Stock Exchange is limited to ensuring that the degree of compliance is stated and that reasons are given for any non-compliance. The Stock Exchange does not specify the standard of the corporate governance systems employed, nor does it determine the adequacy of any reasons given for non-compliance.

Overall, the Cadbury Committee recommendations reflected a considerable input from the auditing profession and adopted many of the solutions being advanced by the profession (for example, reporting on internal control, going concern and compliance with the Code). The Committee also sought to protect auditors from corporate governance problems. The major recommendation with this aim was the promotion of the formation of audit committees (1992, para. 4.3) and this will be the subject of the remainder of the chapter.

AUDIT COMMITTEES

In recommending that all listed companies should establish an audit committee, the Cadbury Committee (1992) followed the US National Commission on Fraudulent Financial Reporting (Treadway Commission, 1987) and the Canadian Macdonald Commission (1988). The Cadbury Committee (1992, pp. 27–8) justified this recommendation partly on the grounds that US experience shows audit committees have 'proved their worth' and become essential committees of the board and partly because recent research (Collier, 1992, p. 165) had shown that the majority of UK companies with an audit committee are enthusiastic about them.

There is no accepted definition of an audit committee but most have the following features:

(1) it is a formally constituted subcommittee of the main board;
(2) it is composed exclusively, or predominantly, of non-executive directors but with the finance director, and representatives of the external and internal auditor, in attendance as appropriate;
(3) it has responsibility for reviewing the financial statements and the accounting principles and practices underlying them, liaising with the external and internal auditors, and reviewing the effectiveness of internal controls.

Structure of an audit committee

An audit committee should be formally constituted with written terms of reference as a subcommittee of the main board, to which it reports and is answerable. The terms of reference should be straightforward and should be discussed with the internal and external auditors prior to approval by the main board. A specimen terms of reference taken from the Annex to the Cadbury Report (1992) is shown in the Appendix to this chapter. The principal points to note are:

(1) the limiting of the membership to non-executive directors;
(2) the requirement that at least once a year the committee meet with the external auditors without executive board members present;
(3) the suggested regularity of meetings, which should be held at least twice a year – in practice to consider the interim and final accounts;
(4) the delegation of authority to carry out investigation on any activity within its terms of reference and to obtain outside legal or other independent professional advice; and
(5) the wide range of duties, covering financial reporting and internal and external auditing.

The development of audit committees in the UK

Audit committee developments in the UK reflect the impact of North American experiences. The first article on audit committees to appear in a UK professional journal was in the *Accountant* (Beedle, 1974). The author was a professor from the University of British Columbia who argued that audit committees were 'a peculiarly North American phenomenon'. The idea of adopting audit committees grew quickly and in 1976 the editorial in the 1000th issue of *Accountancy* (Woolf, 1976) was headed 'Introduce audit committees *now*'. However, the adoption of the practice in companies was slow. Surveys by Tricker (1978) and Chambers and Snook (1979) found that few companies had formed audit committees by 1977. This observation was confirmed by the Accountants International Study Group (AISG, 1977, p. 1), which stated that in the UK audit committees were unusual but not unknown and that the concept of audit committes had not been generally accepted. Subsequent work by Marrian (1988) and Collier (1992, pp. 59–60) showed that up to the Cadbury Committee audit committees gradually became more widespread among the larger companies and that by 1991 around 55 per cent of the top 250 industrial organizations from the Times 1000 had formed an audit committee. Since the Cadbury Committee, the pressure to conform has increased and Collier (1995) found that by 1994 the proportion of UK listed companies which had formed an audit committee had risen to over 80 per cent.

The benefits to companies of having an audit committee

One major motivation for companies to form audit committees voluntarily would derive from the benefits they bring. Supporters contend that the benefits from audit committees are extensive. The Cadbury Committee Report

(1992, App. 4, para. 4, pp. 68–9) suggested that audit committees can provide a range of benefits provided they are effective in carrying out their functions. Current literature on audit committees from professional firms (see, for example, Peat Marwick McLintock, 1987 or Coopers & Lybrand Deloitte, 1990) and professional bodies (see, for example, AISG, 1977; Canadian Institute of Chartered Accountants, 1981; Marrian, 1988) also supports this view.

The benefits of audit committees can be summarized from the viewpoints of the parties involved.

The board of directors

The audit committee could assist directors to meet their statutory and fiduciary responsibilities, especially as regards accounting records, annual accounts and the audit. Further, the audit committee should improve communication between the board and the external auditors. A typical audit committee would meet the external auditors on several occasions during the year and be able to evaluate the annual accounts, the audit and the quality of internal controls more thoroughly than would be possible if the review of these matters was left to the full board, which might see the auditors only once a year. The audit committee can also act as a filter that ensures that the board considers only the most important items relating to audit, accounting and internal control.

Non-executive directors

The audit committee can strengthen the role of independent non-executive directors by formalizing their work in a key business area. Involvement by non-executive directors through the audit committee should assist them to improve their knowledge and understanding of the business's financial reporting practices and accounting and control systems, and the nature and scope of statutory audit and internal audit. Thus, the audit committee acts as a catalyst which enables non-executive directors to bring their wider business knowledge to bear on accounting, auditing and internal control issues.

External auditors

It is contended that reporting to an audit committee will enhance the external auditor's independent position since the external auditor can communicate directly with those directors who are not actively engaged in the management of the company. This view was supported by a Canadian study (CICA, 1981, p. 52), which reported that 72 per cent of external auditors indicated that the existence of an audit committee 'enhanced their perceived independence, making it easier for them to be objective and not to be subject to undue influence by management'. It should be noted that, as Wolnizer (1987) comments, the capacity of audit committees to enhance external auditor independence and provide an independent review is limited by the education, experience and independence of the members of the audit committee. Important factors in achieving the latter and avoiding the problems identified by Vicknair, Hickman and Carnes (1993) are the initial selection process for recruiting non-executive directors, the mechanism for appointing the audit committee, and limiting audit committee membership to non-executive directors. At a minimum, however, the audit committee should pressure management into acting on the recommendations made by the external auditor. As mentioned above, the audit committee will improve communications between the external auditor and the directors. The audit committee causes the external auditor and a subset of directors to meet on a normal and regular basis and overcomes the difficulties identified by Mautz and Neumann (1970, p. 87), who reported that in firms without an audit committee there was little communication between boards and external auditors because external auditors were reluctant to go over the heads of operating management to the board.

Internal auditors

An audit committee provides the opportunity for internal auditors to report to board members and thus improve communication between the board and the internal audit function. Prior to the introduction of audit committees, it was rare for internal auditors to report to more than one board member, and certainly not to a director without management responsibilities. The audit committee provides a forum in which a subset of directors can consider the scope and results of internal audit work and filter matters for consideration by the main board. This facility should give four benefits: first, it will raise the status of the internal audit function; secondly, it may encourage internal auditors to enhance the quality of their work; thirdly it will pressure management into acting on the recommendations made; and, finally, it will raise their esteem among the company's managers who will be aware that the internal auditors have this line of communication.

As with external auditors, reporting to an audit committee should enhance the independence of internal auditors. Because of concern for internal auditor independence, the Treadway Commission (1987) discouraged the situation where the internal audit function reports to the senior officer directly responsible for preparing the accounts. Instead it advised that internal auditors report to the chief executive officer, and in many companies there is a dual reporting responsibility to the chief executive and the audit committee (see, for example, Williams, 1988, describing the position at Warner-Lambert Company). Miller (1988) suggests that the 'best liability insurance coverage a corporate board can have is an effective internal audit department' and argues that the audit committee is crucial in determining the effectiveness of the internal audit department as it ensures the independence of the function and reviews the scope, results and quality of its work. The Institute of Chartered Accountants of Scotland report (ICAS, 1993, pp. 36–9) also recognizes this need to enhance the independence of internal auditors and the crucial role they can play in improving internal controls.

Internal controls

Responsibility for the effectiveness of the internal control systems of an organization rests with management. As can be seen from the appendix to this chapter, the list of duties for an audit committee includes reviewing the company's statement on internal control systems prior to endorsement by the board, ensuring the effectiveness of the system of internal financial control, and determining the adequacy and appropriateness of the directors' statement on internal controls. In carrying out this overview, the audit committee will need to consider:

(1) confirming the existence of an integrated control environment including written policies, procedures, organization structure and codes of conduct;
(2) monitoring the integrated control environment to ensure that the controls are functioning properly;
(3) assessing the management strategy for evaluating the risks and control objectives;
(4) analysing the main business risks and changes thereto, for example increased foreign currency exposure or the impact of new computer systems;
(5) evaluating the results of the internal and external auditors' work on internal controls; and
(6) checking the adequacy of procedures for reporting control weaknesses and instigating corrective action.

The link between the internal auditors and the audit committee in fulfilling this task is well illustrated by the following quotation from the 1994 financial statements of Guinness plc:

> The Group Internal Audit function formally reports to the Audit Committee which approves its plans in advance and reviews the conclusions of its work. Lessons learned are disseminated within the Group as appropriate. Audit plans are drawn up based on an assessment of the control risks in each operating unit and their materiality in a Group context. The Audit Committee has reviewed the system of internal controls and has reported to the Directors on the result of this review. Accordingly, the Directors are satisfied that the Group continues to have an effective system of internal controls.

Shareholders and other users of financial statements

It is argued that the existence of an audit committee increases the credibility and objectivity of financial reports by demonstrating the board's intention to give due weight to reviewing external reporting, auditing, internal controls and other related matters. This argument presupposes that share-holders understand the relevance of an audit committee and that the company discloses the existence of the audit committee. Both Marrian (1988, p. 13) and Collier (1992, p. 153) found that a significant minority of companies with an audit committee did not disclose in the accounts that they had one and few drew attention to its role. This position has changed, however, as is demonstrated by the fairly full note in Coats Viyella's 1994 financial statements, which specifically reinforces the role of the committee in ensuring the independence of the auditors by specifying that the external auditors have direct access to the chairman of the audit committee:

> The Audit Committee is formally constituted with written terms of reference. Its membership comprises the non-executive Directors. The Chairman, Chief Executive, Finance Director and Company Secretary are not members but are invited to attend. The Group Internal Auditor acts as Secretary and the Committee meets at least three times a year. The external auditors also attend for part or the whole of each meeting and they have direct access to the Chairman of the Committee without the presence of the executive Directors for independent discussions. The minutes of the Audit Committee are reported by the Chairman of the Committee to the next full Board Meeting and formally recorded. The Audit Committee may examine any matters relating to the affairs of the Group and to the Group's internal and external audits; this includes reviews of the annual accounts and announcements, internal control procedures, accounting policies, compliance with accounting standards, the appointment and fees of external auditors and such other related functions as the Board may require.

Reservations about audit committees

A review of the literature suggests that the claimed advantages of audit committees are not always realized in practice and that the support for audit committees is based upon anecdotal information on their effectiveness rather than objective evidence. Kalbers and Fogarty (1993, p. 24), after a review of research into the effectiveness of audit committees, found that 'little empirical research has been conducted to investigate the effectiveness of audit committees' and concluded that the evidence collected to date is weak. Certainly Collier (1992, p. 70) reported 'good corporate practice' rather than specific advantages as the main reason for companies forming an audit committee. Sommer (1991, p. 91) suggested that 'there is considerable anecdotal evidence that many, if not most, audit committees fall short of doing what are generally perceived as being their duties'. Menon and Williams (1994) support this contention with findings which showed that companies which had nominally formed an audit committee were often reluctant to rely upon it. The researchers concluded that audit committees 'are often created for the purposes of appearances rather than to enhance stockholders' control of management' (1994, p. 137). Confirmation of this is provided by Verschoor (1989, 1990), who explored the ineffectiveness of the audit committee in two major corporate failures, and Campbell (1990), who reported a number of major corporate failures in the 1980s among Canadian companies that had maintained an audit committee for a number of years. One possible reason for these shortcomings was identified by Vicknair, Hickman and Carnes (1993), who raised severe doubts about the impartiality of directors on audit committees and suggested that the existence of 'grey' area directors, who are not wholly independent of management, may undermine the position of audit committees as truly independent corporate governance entities and imperil auditor independence. Any failure of audit committees to act effectively compromises their important roles in assessing the level of the audit fee to ensure that it is not too low for audit quality to be maintained, arbitrating fairly in any auditor–management disputes, and approving the appointment and change of auditors.

Overall, it may be concluded that the support for audit committees is based largely on opinions about their effectiveness and reflects an 'act of faith' rather than a decision founded on hard evidence.

Allied to doubts about the effectiveness of audit committees, questions have been raised by industrialists and academics about the possible dangers which arise from their operation. Collier (1992, pp. 11–12) identified the following four main dangers:

(1) encroachment on the functions of the executive and dilution of executive authority;
(2) diversion of non-executive directors from their strategic and other roles;
(3) creation of divisiveness between the executive and non-executive directors; and
(4) reduction in the contact between the auditors and the main board.

Further, Bradbury (1990) pointed out that a recommendation for companies to operate an audit committee as a monitoring mechanism had the following disadvantages:

(1) it imposes costs unevenly across companies if differences exist between companies in the costs and benefits of monitoring packages;
(2) it could lead to companies transferring resources from existing, and perhaps more effective, monitoring activities on the assumption that monitoring expenditure is limited; and
(3) it may prevent companies from signalling information by the choice of an audit committee as a monitoring mechanism.

CONCLUSION

This chapter has briefly discussed the concept of corporate governance and has linked it to auditing through a review of audit committees as these bodies are central to the interface between internal and external auditors and the board. The promotion of audit committees by the Cadbury Committee (1992) is premised on the assumption that audit committees are effective at remedying some of the deficiencies in corporate governance systems. However, as Kalbers and Fogarty (1993) indicate there is only weak empirical evidence to demonstrate that audit committees are effective. The reasons for this situation could include the following:

(1) audit committees are formed merely to provide the appearance of monitoring in order to satisfy external constituencies such as shareholders, the providers of finance and regulators rather than to enhance stockholders' control of management;

(2) the position of audit committees as truly independent corporate governance entities is undermined by non-executive directors who are not impartial;

(3) deficiencies in the effective operation of individual audit committees which lead to them failing to operate properly; and

(4) the concept of audit committees is flawed.

It will be interesting to see whether corporate governance and auditing are improved by their widespread introduction.

APPENDIX

Cadbury Report – Specimen Terms of Reference for an Audit Committee

FOR GUIDANCE ONLY

Constitution

1   The Board hereby resolves to establish a Committee of the Board to be known as the Audit Committee.

Membership

2   The Committee shall be appointed by the Board from among the Non-Executive Directors of the Company and shall consist of not less than three members. A quorum shall be two members.

3   The Chairman of the Committee shall be appointed by the Board.

Attendance at meetings

4   The Finance Director, the Head of Internal Audit, and a representative of the external auditors shall normally attend meetings. Other Board members shall also have the right of attendance. However, at least once a year the Committee shall meet with the external auditors without executive Board members present.

5   The Company Secretary shall be the Secretary of the Committee.

Frequency of meetings

6   Meetings shall be held not less than twice a year. The external auditors may request a meeting if they consider that one is necessary.

Authority

7   The Committee is authorized by the Board to investigate any activity within its terms of reference. It is authorized to seek any information it requires from any employee and all employees are directed to co-operate with any request made by the Committee.

8   The Committee is authorized by the Board to obtain outside legal or other independent professional advice and to secure the attendance of outsiders with relevant experience and expertise if it considers this necessary.

Duties

9   The duties of the Committee shall be:

(a) to consider the appointment of the external auditor, the audit fee, and any questions of resignation or dismissal;

(b) to discuss with the external auditor before the audit commences the nature and scope of the audit, and ensure co-ordination where more than one audit firm is involved;

(c) to review the half-year and annual financial statements before submission to the Board, focusing particularly on:
   (i)   any changes in accounting policies and practices;
   (ii) major judgemental areas;
   (iii) significant adjustments resulting from the audit;
   (iv) the going concern assumption;
   (v)   compliance with accounting standards;
   (vi) compliance with stock exchange and legal requirements;

(d) to discuss problems and reservations arising from the interim and final audits, and any matters the auditor may wish to discuss (in the absence of management where necessary);

(e) to review the external auditor's management letter and management's response;

(f) to review the Company's statement on internal control systems prior to endorsement by the Board;

(g) (where an internal audit function exists) to review the internal audit programme, ensure co-ordination between the internal and external auditors, and ensure that the internal audit function is adequately resourced and has appropriate standing within the Company;

(h) to consider the major findings of internal investigations and management's response;

(i) to consider other topics, as defined by the Board.

Reporting procedure

10   The Secretary shall circulate the minutes of meetings of the Committee
to all members of the Board.

REFERENCES

Accountants International Study Group (AISG) (1977) *Audit Committees – Current Practices in Canada, the United Kingdom and the United States*, AISG, London.

Bank of England (1989) *Corporate Governance and the Market for Control of Companies*, Panel Paper, Bank of England, London.

Beedle, A. (1974) *The audit committee: a North American phenomenon, The Accountant*, 21 March, pp. 349–51.

Bradbury, M. E. (1990) The incentives for voluntary audit committee formation, *Journal of Accounting and Public Policy*, Vol. 9, no. 1, pp. 19–36.

Cadbury Committee, Committee on the Financial Aspects of Corporate Governance (1992) *Report of the Committee on the Financial Aspects of Corporate Governance*, Gee, London.

Campbell, N. (1990) Holding audit committees accountable, *Canadian Business Law Journal*, Vol. 16, no. 2, pp. 134–59.

Canadian Institute of Chartered Accountants (CICA) (1981) *Audit Committees*, CICA, Toronto.

Chambers, A. D. and Snook, A. J. (1979) *1978 Survey of Audit Committees in the United Kingdom: A Summary of Findings*, Working Paper No. 10, The City University Business School.

Collier, P. A. (1992) *Audit Committees in Large UK Companies*, Institute of Chartered Accountants in England and Wales, London.

Collier, P. A. (1995) *Audit Committees in Smaller Listed Companies*, unpublished report, Institute of Chartered Accountants in England and Wales, London.

Coopers & Lybrand Deloitte (1990) *Audit Committees: The Next Steps* (2nd edn), Coopers & Lybrand Deloitte, London.

Department of Trade and Industry (DTI) (1992) *The UK R&D Scoreboard*, Company Reporting Ltd, Edinburgh.

Flint, D. (1988) *Philosophy and Principles of Auditing – An Introduction*, Macmillan, London.

Gaved, M. and Goodman, A. (1992) *Deeper Share Ownership*, The Social Market Foundation, London.

Griffiths, I. (1986) *Creative Accounting*, Sidgwick and Jackson, London.

Institute of Chartered Accountants of Scotland (ICAS) (1993) *Corporate Governance – Directors' Responsibilities for Financial Statements*, ICAS, Edinburgh.

Institutional Shareholders' Committee (1991) *The Role and Duties of Directors – A Statement of Best Practice*, ISC, London.

Kalbers, L. P. and Fogarty, T. J. (1993) Audit committee effectiveness: an empirical investigation of the contribution of power, *Auditing: A Journal of Practice & Theory*, Vol. 12, no. 1, pp. 24–49.

Keasey, K. and Wright, M. (1993) Issues in corporate accountability and governance: an editorial, *Accounting and Business Research*, Corporate Governance Special Issue, Vol. 23, no. 91A, pp. 291–303.

Macdonald Commission, Canadian Institute of Chartered Accountants (1988) *Report of the Commission to Study the Public's Expectation of Audits*, Toronto, CICA.

Marrian, I. F. Y. (1988) *Audit Committees*, ICAS, Edinburgh.

Mautz, R. K, and Neumann F. L. (1970) *Corporate Audit Committees*, University of Illinois, Urbana.

Menon, K. and Williams, J. D. (1994) The use of audit committees for monitoring, *Journal of Accounting and Public Policy*, Vol. 13, pp. 121–39.

Miller, H. D. (1988) Internal audit's safety, *Directors & Boards*, Vol. 12, no. 4, pp. 30–3.

Peat Marwick McLintock (1987) *The Audit Committee*, London.

Sommer, A. A. Jr (1991) Auditing the audit committee: an educational opportunity for auditors, *Accounting Horizons*, Vol. 5, no. 2, pp. 91–3.

Treadway Commission (1987) *Report of the National Commission on Fraudulent Financial Reporting*, New York.

Tricker, R. I. (1978) *The Independent Director: A Study of the Non-Executive Director and the Audit Committee*, Tolley, Croydon.

Tricker, R. I. (1984) *Corporate Governance*, Gower, Vermont.

Verschoor, C. C. (1989) A case study of audit committee ineffectiveness at Sundstrand, *Internal Auditing*, Vol. 4, no. 4, pp. 11–19.

Verschoor, C. C. (1990) Miniscribe: a new example of audit committee ineffectiveness, *Internal Auditing*, Vol. 5, no. 4, pp. 13–19.

Vicknair, D., Hickman, K. and Carnes, K. C. (1993) A note on audit committee independence: evidence from the NYSE on 'grey' area directors, *Accounting Horizons*, Vol. 7, no. 1, pp. 55–7.

Whittington, G. (1993) Corporate governance and the regulation of financial reporting, *Accounting and Business Research*, Corporate Governance Special Issue, Vol. 23, no. 91A, pp. 311–19.

Williams, J. D. (1988) The board of directors' reliance on the internal auditor, *Internal Auditor (US)*, Vol. 45, no. 8, pp. 31–5.

Wolnizer, P. W. (1987) *Auditing as Independent Authentication*, Sydney University Press, Sydney.

Woolf, E. (1976) Introduce audit committees now, *Accountancy*, December, p. 1.

DISCUSSION QUESTIONS

1. Explain what is meant by corporate governance.
2. What factors led to the formation of the Cadbury Committee?
3. What are the main implications of the Cadbury Committee Code of Best Practice for auditors?
4. Summarize the benefits of audit committees from the viewpoint of the board of directors, non-executive directors, external auditors, internal auditors and users of financial statements. Are there any dangers in establishing an audit committee?
5. 'A review of the literature suggests that the claimed advantages of audit committees are not always realized in practice and that the support for audit committees is based on anecdotal information on their effectiveness rather than objective evidence.' Discuss.

5

Audit Firms and the Audit Market

Chris Pong and Stuart Turley

INTRODUCTION

Several of the chapters in this volume discuss different aspects of the demand for audit sevices, that is, the nature and quality of the service auditors are expected to provide. For example, questions about the assurance auditors should give on the financial statements and whether or not they should attempt to detect fraud concern the nature of the functional roles through which the demand for auditing can be satisfied, while issues such as the need for auditors to be independent from their client companies and for technical standards to be set at an appropriate level reflect demand for particular qualities in the way audit services are delivered. In considering how the current debates on auditing might be resolved, it is also important to have an understanding of the supply side of the audit market, and in this chapter we review some of the characteristics of the supply of audit services.

Auditing is a regulated activity, and a full consideration of the supply side of auditing should include the ways in which it is regulated. Statutory requirements governing many different kinds of enterprise establish rules concerning which individuals or entities can act as suppliers of audit services, and a framework of technical standards and guidelines regulate how audits are carried out. As audit regulation is discussed in full in other chapters, the emphasis in this chapter is confined to some of the economic characteristics of the suppliers of audit services, that is, the audit firms, and the markets in which they operate. There are several interesting questions about auditing which depend on analysis of the auditing market and the firms, for example:

(1) *Is there effective competition between audit firms?* If the structure of the market is highly competitive the possibility arises that commercial pressures will influence the quality of service provided. Equally, if the market is dominated by just a few suppliers they may be able to exercise considerable market power.

(2) *What sort of factors influence the level of audit fees charged by suppliers, and is there any relationship between fees and the quality of service provided?* The output of an audit is a very standardized report comprising just a few paragraphs, yet the fees paid for this report vary considerably. It is of interest to know what determines prices charged for audit services, and what constitutes value for money in audit fees.

(3) *How do different audit firms differentiate their services in order to compete with one another?* Given standardized reporting, audit quality is difficult to measure and observe. The audit firms may therefore have to compete on the basis of other factors.

Drawing on the results of research studies on the economics of the audit market, this chapter examines these and related questions in three main sections. In the first, available evidence about the structure of the audit services market is presented, and in particular the principal suppliers and the degree of market concentration that exists in auditing. Secondly, the pricing of audit services is reviewed and how audit fees are affected by both firm and client characteristics. The third section examines the attributes that can be used for product differentiaton in auditing.

THE STRUCTURE OF THE AUDIT SERVICES MARKET

Understanding the structure of the audit market is important because, according to the structure–conduct–performance paradigm, there can be a direct causal link from structure, through conduct, to performance (Reid, 1987). In other words, aspects of market structure, such as the level of concentration, diversification, the existence of barriers to entry to the market and scale economies, can influence the nature of the service actually performed by auditors. Below we review evidence on concentration, the effects of internationalization and the existence of barriers to entry in the audit services market.

Market concentration

On 2 February 1995 *Accountancy Age* carried the statement that 'the big six accountancy firms control more than nine out of ten of the top 500 company audits'. This statement refers to the market share of the biggest audit suppliers, or, in the language of the economics of industrial organization, the level of supplier concentration in the market for auditing services. Market concentration is one important aspect of the study of industrial organization.

The degree of supplier concentration in the audit services market is the extent to which a relatively small number of audit firms account for a significant proportion of the total volume of audit work carried out. Supplier concentration is of interest because it is likely to be a major determinant of audit firms' market behaviour. A high degree of concentration is usually associated with an oligopolistic market where supply is dominated by a small number of large firms. Dominance of the market by large firms could lead to a sub-optimum allocation of resources and the creation of internal inefficiencies in the firms, because the decisions taken by one supplier are heavily influenced by the possible reactions of that supplier's few competitors. In order to reduce uncertainty and improve profits, it is generally argued that oligopolists will adopt some form of collusion (Moizer and Turley, 1989).

A number of research studies have investigated concentration in the UK audit market. The results are summarized in Table 5.1 and Figure 5.1. The vertical axis in the figure represents the level of concentration and the horizontal axis the number of firms the measure relates to. Thus a figure of 0.6 for CR4 would indicate that the four largest audit firms enjoy 60 per cent of the audit market on the basis of a particular measure.

It should be noted that the studies included in the table do not give directly comparable concentration figures as they are based on different samples of the audit market and make use of slightly different concentration measures, which can have an effect on the level of concentration reported (Moizer and Turley, 1987). Briston and Kedslie's (1985) study was based on all UK domestic listed companies, while Moizer and Turley (1989) looked only at the companies included in the FT500 share index and Beattie and Fearnley (1994) covered all UK quoted companies including those on the USM. The main measures used to calculate the level of concentration are the number of audits

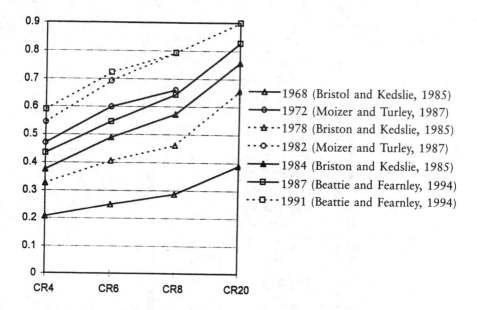

Figure 5.1   Supplier concentration in audit services, 1968–1991

Table 5.1 UK evidence on supplier concentration in audit services

Time	Measure	Sample	CR4	CR6	CR8	CR20
1968 (Briston and Kedslie, 1985)*	Number of audits	All domestic listed	0.207	0.250	0.287	0.389
1972 (Moizer and Turley, 1987)†	Audit fees	FT500 Share Index	0.470	0.599	0.660	N/A
1978 (Briston and Kedslie, 1985)*	Number of audits	All domestic listed	0.326	0.406	0.462	0.657
1982 (Moizer and Turley, 1987)†	Audit fees	FT500 Share Index	0.544	0.692	0.794	N/A
1984 (Briston and Kedslie, 1985)*	Number of audits	All domestic listed	0.375	0.489	0.572	0.758
1987 (Beattie and Fearnley, 1994)*	Number of audits	All domestic listed (including USM)	0.434	0.546	0.643	0.828
1991 (Beattie and Fearnley 1994)*	Number of audits	All domestic listed (including USM)	0.589	0.723	0.793	0.900

* Based on Beattie and Fearnley (1994), Table 8.
† Based on Moizer and Turley (1987), Tables 1 and 2.

(Briston and Kedslie, 1985, and Beattie and Fearnley, 1994) and the level of audit fees (Moizer and Turley, 1987). Audit fees represent the most appropriate measure of the size of the market and, as larger companies will tend to have larger fees, a measure based on number of audits alone may understate the real size of the firms' market shares. A measure based on the number of audits does, however, facilitate analysis of shifts in concentration due to auditor changes and is also consistent with the regulatory regime developed by the three Chartered Institutes, which focuses on the absolute number of listed clients which each audit firm has.

Although based on slightly different measures and samples, the studies show a consistent pattern of increasing concentration over the period of the last twenty-five years or so. Beattie and Fearnley (1994) report that in 1991 72.3 per cent of all domestic listed and USM companies were audited by the Big Six and 90 per cent by the top twenty audit firms. Measures using audit fees to show value-based market shares would have shown even higher concentration ratios. Indeed, by July 1996 the position for the top 100 UK companies was that only one company had a firm of auditors from outside those firms recognized as the Big Six, and one further company was jointly audited by a Big Six and a non-Big Six firm (*Accountancy*, July 1996, p. 9). Figure 5.1 also shows that the pattern of increasing concentration is observable at the level of the top twenty audit firms as well as the largest four or six. As market share is increasing even at the level of twenty firms, it must be the case that it is smaller firms outside this grouping that have lost market position. The studies have also reported that market leadership is stable, in other words that the membership of the groupings of the largest firms is not changing. These findings provide evidence that there is likely to be increasing disparity between the large and small suppliers, which should influence the way in which we view the audit market.

The underlying reasons for changes in levels of concentration could include factors connected with audit pricing, the quality of service provided, good marketing and other attributes of the audit. Some of these points are discussed in subsequent sections, although little systematic evidence is available indicating the exact link between, say, pricing and changes in market share. What is apparent, however, is that there are three main ways in which the increases in concentration have come about: mergers between audit firms result in higher combined market share, voluntary changes of auditor tend to favour larger firms and newly listed companies tend to appoint a large firm of auditors, meaning that the distribution of auditors in firms coming to the market is highly concentrated (Moizer and Turley, 1989).

It is interesting to note that the biggest explanation for increasing concentration is that of audit firm mergers. This means that there is more structural change in the audit services market as a result of combinations between firms than is due to the effects of the competitive strategies of firms persuading companies to chose different auditors. Examples of significant mergers among major UK audit firms include Ernst and Whinney with Arthur Young in 1989, Coopers and Lybrand with Deloitte Haskins and Sells in

1990[1] and Spicer and Oppenheim with Touche Ross also in 1990 (Boys, 1989, 1990). Although auditor switching does have some effect in increasing concentration, it is not very common. Beattie and Fearnley (1994) reported that, for the years 1988 to 1991, the annual rate of change of audit firm was between 3.8 per cent and 6.1 per cent. Where changes do take place, they tend to favour larger firms; among listed companies most switches involve a change from a non-Big Six firm to a Big Six firm.[2] This situation has led to claims by some middle-tier firms that the Big Six are actively taking away their clients through lowballing (the practice of charging very low initial fees to induce an audit change) (see, for example, *Accountancy*, June 1995, p. 13). Finally, auditor concentration among newly listed companies tends to favour the Big Six: 'The Big Six act as accountants to 85% of the new issues on the London Stock market ... the four leading firms – KPMG, Coopers and Lybrand, Ernst and Young, and Price Waterhouse – alone accounted for over two-thirds of the 180 companies that gained a listing in 1994' (*Accountancy Age*, 2 March 1995).

Overall, the change in concentration has led to a situation where 'audit services has reached the limit of a tight oligopoly, which is characterised by few rivals, stable market share and medium-to-high entry barriers' (Beattie and Fearnley, 1994, p. 308). What is less clear is whether this is having any effects on the nature of competition in the audit services market. While as long ago as 1977 a US Senate report suggested that the level of concentration even then was reaching levels which 'constitute evidence of a serious lack of competition'(Metcalf Committee, 1978), two reports commissioned by the European Commission have both concluded that audit service markets in Europe are not anti-competitive, despite the high market shares of individual suppliers, and that audit firms are not behaving in a way which is contrary to the public interest (NERA, 1992, Buijink *et al.*, 1996).

Internationalization

The analysis above has focused primarily on some of the structural characteristics of the audit services market in the United Kingdom. A further factor which has influenced developments in both the competitive position of the audit firms and the markets in which they operate is the rapid international growth in the firms in recent years. International accounting service provision is not entirely a development of the late twentieth century. A number of firms have offered services internationally since the early 1900s, but the development in the more recent past has had greater effects on the structure of firms. The creation of transnational partnerships and affiliations has resulted in what might be considered as international brand names for professional services. It is no longer meaningful to describe particular audit firms as, say, British or American, as, although they may have grown from a particular national base, they now have significant operations in many markets internationally.

The pattern and methods of internationalization adopted by firms vary.

Only a few are truly international firms, the majority preferring models involving affiliation between national firms or international co-operative organizations. While methods vary, however, the objectives of internationalization are consistent – to preserve or enhance a firm's competitive position in markets for professional services, including auditing.

The competitive position of individual firms can be enhanced by the effects of internationalization on both revenues and costs. Revenue effects will result both because of the possibility of work which has to be undertaken on behalf of an international affiliate and, perhaps more importantly, because the availability of an international network provides an additional attribute through which a firm in any country can compete for domestic business. The benefits from internationalization also include the possibilities of cost sharing. For example, technical research and development of audit methods may be organized internationally, reducing costs for an individual national firm, and the major audit firms now use the same audit methodology worldwide. Similarly, there may be cost advantages in areas such as staff training.

The existence of international firms can also be expected to have effects on the audit services markets in individual countries. This impact is clear from the international evidence on market concentration. Studies in many different countries have drawn similar conclusions to those that were reported in the preceding section concerning the United Kingdom (for example, see Walker and Johnson (1996) for a general international summary), although there are some exceptions. For example, in Germany the Big Six firms held only 54 of the top 100 company audits in 1989, compared to 80 of the French top 100, 88 in the United Kingdom and 97 in Belgium (NERA, 1992). Not only is there a common pattern of increasing concentration, but it is also the same grouping of firms that constitute the market leaders in different countries. In other words, it appears to be very difficult for an audit supplier to maintain a significant position in a national market without being part of an international firm. As noted by Daniels, Thrift and Leyshon (1989, p. 79), 'one of the key processes sustaining the concentration, and to some extent the diversification, of accounting firms has been their growing involvement in overseas markets'. Internationalization will also have an impact on national audit service markets through possible effects on pricing (discussed below) and on 'product innovation' and the availability of particular services which might be transferred between international partners.

Barriers to entry

Before leaving the structure of the audit services market, a final point which should be noted is the existence of 'barriers to entry' which might affect competition and the supply of services.

In auditing services, an initial barrier to entry may be identified in the statutory regulations which control audit appointments. For example, the Companies Act 1989 implemented the European Union Eighth Directive on company law, which included rules concerning the licensing arrangements on who can be permitted to undertake audits. Thus, only those satisfying the qualification and other requirements can be appointed as auditors to a company. This type of regulation effectively provides accounting firms with a legal monopoly over auditing and protects them from competition from, say, law firms.

Perhaps of more significance for the development of market structure are barriers which result from:

(1) The need for compliance with regulations governing audit practice: compliance imposes costs on suppliers which can affect ability to compete. One view of the regime of auditing standards, which in the past have tended to codify what is existing best practice among the larger firms, is that it has imposed the cost structures of the large firms on their smaller competitors, and so may affect the terms of competition, with consequences for market structure.

(2) The existence of economies of scale and economies of scope: these factors will again make it more difficult for smaller suppliers to compete with larger firms. For example, investing in technical development in audit methods or computerized audit packages may be relatively more costly for a small firm. Similarly, offering a wide range of services to clients, with the associated economies of scope, will be more difficult for a small firm than a large.

These barriers to entry do not involve legal restriction on competition but do result in effective economic restriction on some competition, at least for the audits of listed and large private companies. They are likely to result in both market segmentation, where only certain firms can compete for particular types of client, and also market stability. Indeed, as has already been pointed out, the evidence is that the realignments and changes in market structure in auditing tend to be associated more with mergers between firms than with the generic growth of individual suppliers. These effects are likely to be reinforced by the pressures of internationalization.

PRICING OF AUDIT SERVICES

It has been claimed that the audit fees charged to British companies are among the highest in the world and that UK firms take substantially longer than the international average to produce the auditor's report (*Financial Times*, 28 December 1991). Certainly, large amounts of money are earned by the major firms providing professional accounting services. For example, in 1994/5 British Petroleum and Nat West Bank paid, respectively, Ernst and Young and KPMG audit fees of £5.6 and £3.8 million and the largest 100 companies spent nearly £350 million on their auditors (*Accountancy Age*, 1 June 1995). Table 5.2 shows the audit and accounting (excluding tax, consultancy and insolvency) fee income of the top fifteen UK firms.

In return for the audit fee, the company receives a very standardized report and the audit opinion is captured in just a few lines. Obvious questions there-

Table 5.2 Audit and accountancy fee income of top fifteen accounting firms

	1994/5 (£m)	1993/4 (£m)	Growth (%)
Coopers & Lybrand	253.0	253.0	0
Arthur Andersen	128.0	151.07*	-15
KPMG	223.7	200.1	12
Ernst & Young	158.0	167.6	–6
Price Waterhouse	163.3	158.8	3
Touche Ross	121.8	134.9	–10
Grant Thornton	41.7	37.3	12
BDO Stoy Hayward	49.7	37.3	33
Pannell Kerr Forster	31.0	37.0	–16
Clark Whitehill	36.3	35.2	3
Kidsons Impey	28.4	29.4	–3
Moore Stephens	17.7	15.8	12
Robson Rhodes	12.0	12.0	0
Neville Russell	20.7	20.1	3
Moores Rowland	16.0	15.9	1

*£63.9m for Binder Hamlyn and £87.1m for Arthur Anderson.
Source: *Accountancy Age*, 8 June 1995 and 9 June 1994.

fore arise about whether companies get value for money from their spending on audit, what constitutes a fair price for audit services and what determines the prices actually charged. For example, the Glasgow-based firm JDH Consultants surveyed 688 non-financial listed companies and noted some large discrepancies in the audit fees paid by similar sized companies in the same sector:

> Why does Savoy Hotels (audited by Coopers & Lybrand) pay £211,000 when City Centre Restaurants (audited by Ernst & Young) pays only £52,000, when their level of sales is very similar? Is the Savoy four times more complicated? What takes a week at City Centre takes a month at The Savoy? Perhaps the audit staff like to spend longer at The Savoy.
>
> (Accountancy Age, 17 November 1994)

The response from auditors to such questions is that it is impossible to make comparisons of audit fees based simply on turnover because so many other factors determine the fee for an individual client. Trying to identify what are the determinants of audit fees has been a significant research theme for some time.[3] Below we outline the main factors that have been investigated for a possible relationship to fees charged. These can conveniently be divided into two groups: characteristics of the company being audited (the auditee) and characteristics of the audit firm.

Auditee characteristics

While individual studies have looked at a wide range of company charac-teristics, the three most notable are size, complexity and risk (Chan, Ezzamel and Gwilliam, 1993; Pong and Whittington, 1994).

Size

Research to date has shown consistently that the size of the auditee is by far the most important determinant of audit fees. Total assets and turnover are the most commonly utilized measures of the size of an auditee. The former is a proxy for efforts in balance sheet audits while the latter is a proxy for efforts in systems audits. Generally, increases in size are associated with increases in audit fees. However, the relationship between size of auditee and audit fee is not constant because there may be many economies of scale in auditing, i.e. large audits cost less, per unit of assets or transactions audited, than do small audits.

Complexity

The level of business complexity of the auditee also influences audit fees. Complexity reflects the nature and diversity of the business of the auditee, locations, the quality of internal controls, the existence of unusual transac-tions, etc. For example, the nature and volume of audit work will be affected if an auditee has very diversified operations, as there is likely to be a sep-arate accounting system for each type of business. Similarly, more subsidiaries operating at different locations may imply a greater amount of work in con-solidating the financial statements and eliminating intra-group transactions. Audits of subsidiaries in foreign countries, in particular, require higher audit monitoring and control costs.

Risk

Some types of asset could be considered as particularly prone to errors. For example, particular audit efforts may be needed to verify assets such as stocks and debtors. Consequently, auditees with substantial amounts of stocks and debtors could be expected to incur higher audit fees. If an auditee has a high risk of fraud or bankruptcy, the auditor might take additional steps to ensure that the audit opinion is appropriate. However, studies which have attempted to test whether audit firms make adjustments to fees based on the riskiness of the client have tended to conclude that there is little evidence of real risk pemiums being charged by auditors.

While size, complexity and risk are the most commonly tested auditee characteristics, some studies have looked at other factors which could have an impact on fees. Chan, Ezzamel and Gwilliam (1993) also considered audi-tee profitability and ownership control. When an auditee faces financial pressure, management are likely to seek to control all overhead costs which might lead to lower audit costs. However, such circumstances also suggest higher auditee risk and thus the auditor might perform additional work, which means higher fees. Diverse ownership structure could require a more extensive and higher quality audit in order to satisfy the needs of individual shareholders. Thus, diverse ownership structures could increase audit fees. However, it might be argued that the thoroughness of audit work should simply be a reflection of the legal obligation on auditors, which is invariant across different levels of ownership control.

Auditor characteristics

Characteristics of the audit firm which have been tested for a relationship with prices are the size of the firm, willingness to offer reduced initial fees (lowballing) and the provision of additional services to auditees.

Size of audit firm

Tests of the effect of audit firm size on fees charged typically divide suppliers into Big Six and non-Big Six firms. If Big Six firms charge higher audit fees compared to smaller firms, the premium may represent either a monopoly rent or a payment for a higher quality product. Since audit quality is difficult to observe, it is not possible to be categoric about the reason for any Big Six premium. Lower Big Six audit fees, in contrast, might indicate the existence of economies of scale.

Studies of whether a price differential exists between large and small firms have obtained mixed results. In the USA, Simunic (1980) reported no price difference between, as it was then, the Big Eight and non-Big Eight for both small and large auditees. However, Palmrose (1986a) and Francis and Simon (1987) did find evidence of a Big Eight premium in the small auditee market and suggested the existence of Big Eight product differentiation. Francis (1984) and Francis and Stokes (1986) recorded similar results for the Australian market. In the United Kingdom Chan, Ezzamel and Gwilliam (1993) and Pong and Whittington (1994) reported the existence of a Big Eight premium, but no differentiation was made between large and small auditees in these studies.

Lowballing

Lowballing occurs when an auditor reduces the quote for an initial fee in the hope of attracting a new audit client. This practice is believed to prejudice auditor independence since the auditor needs to retain the audit for several years to recover the initial costs incurred in setting up the audit at less than normal fees. It is not immediately obvious that, having incurred initial set-up costs, the auditor will be in a worse competitive situation than in the absence of such costs, since any competitor for the audit would incur similar costs.

Recently, some medium-sized firms have criticized the large firms for low-balling:

> our clients regularly receive phone calls from other firms willing to do the work for a lot less than we do. (Tim Richmond, Pannell Kerr Forster, quoted in the *Financial Times*, 16 May 1991)

> Without a doubt lowballing does exist, although it is marginally better than it was. (Jim Gemmell, Clark Whitehouse Association, quoted in *Accountancy Age*, 9 November 1995)

When BDO Stoy Hayward lost the audit of the Royal Automobile Club to Price Waterhouse for a tendered audit fee for 1995 of £160,000, compared to an actual audit fee in 1994 of £304,000, they appealed directly to the membership of the Club, accusing their rivals of 'pricing the audit as a loss leader for other services'. The action was unsuccessful and Price Waterhouse were confirmed as auditors, but the row prompted an inquiry by the ICAEW. A working party was set up, headed by an independent outsider, Elizabeth Llewellyn-Smith, principal of St Hilda's College Oxford. The group concluded that there was no evidence that large audit clients were damaged by competitive pricing (see *Financial Times*, 9 November 1995). The results were not accepted by the medium-sized firms, however: 'It was unsurprising, given the timescale, that the working party could not explore the question of the independence of the audit and the provision of other services' (John Wosner, managing partner of Pannell Kerr Forster, quoted in *Accountancy Age*, 9 November 1995).

The position of the working party is consistent with the idea that lowballing does not impair independence but is, rather, a competitive response to the expectation of future quasi-rents to incumbent auditors (DeAngelo, 1981). Such quasi-rents could arise because of the technological advantage an audit firm has over competitors once the initial set-up has been undertaken and because of the costs to the auditee of switching auditor. Magee and Tseng (1990) also showed that the value of the auditor's incumbency presents a threat to independence only under limited circumstances.

However, theoretical arguments based on psychology can be advanced to show that the auditor might feel unduly dependent on the support of the management of the auditee firm. Simon and Francis (1988, p. 266) stated that:

> in the context of price cutting, a considerable investment is made to obtain a new client. So the prior decision to discount the audit fee could motivate the auditor's desire to not lose the client, even in the presence of serious auditor–client disagreements. This desire to not lose the client, because of the prior investment commitment (although it is a sunk cost and should not be relevant) could lead to an additional auditor independence problem during the period of investment recovery, over and above the normal independence problems.

Outside the United Kingdom, studies by Francis (1984), Palmrose (1986a) and Francis and Simon (1987) have failed to detect price cutting or cannot be generalized due to very small samples. Simon and Francis (1988) reported a significant fee reduction in the initial engagement year that averaged 24 per cent of normal fee levels for ongoing engagements, an average fee reduction of 15 per cent for the next two years, and by the fourth year the fee had increased to normal levels for continuing engagements. One UK study (Pong and Whittington, 1994) also identified a tendency for new auditors to charge less, on average, than continuing incumbent auditors.

Provision of additional services

Income from consultancy services represents a large proportion of the total income of accountancy firms. In many cases, as can be seen in Table 5.3, the consultancy services income is higher than that from audit services. Again this is of interest because it raises the possibility that auditors may concede to management in disagreements in order to ensure that they continue to provide the consultancy services. Thus it has sometimes been suggested that firms should not provide both audit and consultancy services to the same client. The counter-argument is that provision of both services increases efficiency and does not threaten independence.

Simunic (1984) found that the purchase of management advisory services (MAS) from the auditor was associated with a significant increase in audit

Table 5.3 Comparison of top fifteen accounting firms audit/accountancy and consultancy income, 1994/5

	Audit/ accountancy (£m)	Consultancy/ tax (£m)
Coopers & Lybrand	253.0	269.0
Arthur Andersen	128.0	293.4
KPMG	223.7	195.7
Ernst & Young	158.0	209.4
Price Waterhouse	163.3	192.6
Touche Ross	121.8	166.2
Grant Thornton	41.7	38.7
BDO Stoy Hayward	49.7	31.0
Pannell Kerr Forster	31.0	28.4
Clark Whitehill	36.3	17.1
Kidsons Impey	28.4	19.3
Moore Stephens	17.7	19.0
Robson Rhodes	12.0	14.5
Neville Russell	20.7	9.3
Moores Rowland	16.0	12.8

Source: *Accountancy Age*, 8 June 1995.

fees. This result would arise if the production of auditing generates knowledge that is useful for MAS or if the production of MAS reducees the marginal cost of auditing and the demand is relatively elastic. Palmrose (1986b) also provided evidence of a positive relationship between fees for audit services and non-audit services. However, the relationship was observed whether both kinds of service were provided by the same or different accounting firms. She suggested that non-audit services might require greater audit effort, an idea supported in some other research (Davis, Ricchiute and Trompeter, 1993).

To summarize, research so far has provided consistent evidence that audit fees increase as the size and complexity of an auditee increase. Big Six firms charge higher audit fees compared to smaller firms, but the premium may represent either a monopoly rent or a payment for a higher quality product. There is also evidence that the purchase of consultancy services from an auditor is associated with an increase in fees, but the causal relationship is not clear. Further evidence is needed to establish lowballing practice and to determine the relationship between audit fees and the risk of the auditee.

PRODUCT DIFFERENTIATION

Having looked at the evidence on audit fees, including that relating to price competition between firms, it remains to consider the other 'product attributes' of auditing through which firms can differentiate their services and compete with one another.

As has been commented above, the visible output from an audit is very limited. Audit reports are very brief and follow prescribed formats. It is impossible to judge the quality of an audit from this type of output. The content of the audit is also required to meet certain professional regulations. Given such a standardized product, it is sometimes argued that the identity of the firm which performs the audit should be irrelevant. In this situation, we would expect purchasers always to select the cheapest available supplier.

Clearly, this is not the case in practice. Purchasers do distinguish between audit suppliers and, as we have noted, price differentials have often been identified. This suggests that some form of product differentiation affects purchasers' decisions. If audit suppliers can differentiate their services, this provides a possible source of market competition and a means whereby some suppliers can maintain higher prices than others. Below we consider three possible types of product differentiation which could affect auditing: the auditor's contribution to organizational control, the credibility of different suppliers (Dopuch and Simunic, 1980) and the provision of additional services.

Contribution to organizational control

As well as producing the audit opinion which accompanies the financial statements, auditors normally report to management, giving details of control weaknesses that they may have discovered during the audit, making observations on operations and recommending actions which could improve control or even reduce future audit costs. This form of reporting will enable management to form impressions about the quality of the auditors and their value to the organization based on their contribution to the maintenance and improvement of effective organizational control. An audit firm can therefore differentiate its service from others by devoting attention to this aspect of the audit, and may be able to improve its security of tenure or protect the level of fees it is able to charge on the basis of this quality differential.

Credibility

Secondly, purchasers may have a preference for certain auditors because they have higher credibility with financial statement users. If some firms have a higher reputation than others then users may judge the financial statements that those firms are associated with as being of higher quality or more reliable. How audit firms obtain a reputation for high quality is likely to be a complicated process given the unobservability of quality on individual audits. The existence of firm reputations is close to the idea of branding – that certain audit firms' names are equivalent to premium brands in other markets. Credibility will include the firm's reputation for audit quality and the perceived independence of the firm. It will also include the issue of auditor liability, in that beliefs about an audit firm's potential to meet liability claims will affect its credibility with financial statement users. Evidence that differentiation does exist on the basis of reputations is provided both by the audit fee studies which have shown a large firm price differential (referred to above) and studies which have shown that companies often change auditor to a firm with more established reputation when seeking a stock market listing for the first time (Simunic and Stein, 1987).

Additional services

While the contribution to organizational control discussed above arises as a by-product as audit services are executed, audit firms may also compete through the interrelationship between auditing and other services. Purchasers may choose a particular audit firm because of perceived synergies with other services or because they prefer to use a single supplier for a range of professional services and their selection is driven primarily by non-audit considerations. Audit firms, therefore, can attempt product differentiation through their portfolio of and approach to additional services.

A possible problem concerning the above aspects of product differentiation is that in the case of both the contribution to organizational control and additional services, the quality differential between firms is visible primarily to management rather than to the generally recognized intended beneficiaries of audit services, such as investors. As a result the manner in which firms compete through product differentiation could be more influenced by the concerns of management, whose perceptions of quality and the service attributes of firms will guide their recommendations on audit appointments, than by service to audit beneficiaries. In contrast, the credibility differential relies on reputation with a much wider set of interest groups than management alone.

SUMMARY

There has not been space within this chapter to discuss all aspects of the audit services market in detail. We have concentrated on a limited number of factors which have been significant in the development of the audit services market in recent years and which are most related to fundamental questions about the supply of audit services – the nature of competition, pricing and quality, and the characteristics of the services supplied. The audit market has changed considerably over the last two decades and is likely to continue to do so. It is clear that the overall pattern of development in the audit market has involved increasing supplier concentration and the creation of international supply networks. There is also some evidence of differential pricing between classes of firms and of price competition to attract new audit business as well as the possibility of non-price factors creating product differentiation between firms. While this chapter has looked mainly at the behaviour of suppliers, the audit firms, it should be remembered that the development of the market does not depend on them alone, but involves interaction and transactions between suppliers and purchasers. Evidence such as that presented in this chapter about the structure of the market and supplier behaviour will continue to be relevant to debates about important auditing issues such as the need for regulation and auditor independence.

NOTES

1. Outside the UK most of the international firm of Deloitte Haskins and Sells merged with Touche Ross, hence the existence of the merged trading name of Deloitte & Touche.
2. For a discussion of the factors influencing decisions on auditor change, see Beattie and Fearnley (1995).
3. A useful summary of research studies on audit fees can be found in Chan, Ezzamel and Gwilliam (1993).

REFERENCES

Beattie, V. and Fearnley, S. (1994) The changing structure of the market for audit services in the UK – a descriptive study, *British Accounting Review*, Vol. 26, pp. 301–22.

Beattie, V. and Fearnley, S. (1995) The importance of audit firm characteristics and the drivers of auditor change in UK listed companies, *Accounting and Business Research*, Vol. 25, no. 100, pp. 227–39.

Boys, P. (1989) What's in a name, *Accountancy*, January, pp. 100–2, February, pp.

138–9, March, pp. 96–7, April, pp. 118–19, May, pp. 88–91, June, pp. 98–99, July, pp. 102–4, August, pp. 82–3, September, pp. 80–2, October, pp. 158–60, November, pp. 22–3, December, pp. 134–5.

Boys, P. (1990) What's in a name, *Accountancy*, January, pp. 132–4.

Briston, R. and Kedslie, M. (1985) Must smaller firms continue to lose out? *Accountancy*, March, pp. 163–4.

Buijink, W., Maijoor, S., Meuwissen, R. and van Witteloostuijn, A. (1996) *The Role, Position and Liability of the Statutory Auditor within the European Union*, Maastrict Accounting and Auditing Research Centre.

Chan, P., Ezzamel, M. and Gwilliam, D. (1993) Determinants of audit fees for quoted UK companies, *Journal of Business Finance and Accounting*, November, pp. 765–86.

Daniels, P. W., Thrift, N. J. and Leyshon, A. (1989) Internationalisation of professional producer services: accountancy conglomerates, in P. Enderwick (ed.), *Multinational Service Firms*, Routledge, London.

De Angelo, L. (1981) Auditor independence, 'low balling', and disclosure regulation, *Journal of Accounting and Economics*, Vol. 3, pp. 113–27.

Davis, L. R., Ricchiute, D. N. and Trompeter, G. (1993) Audit effort, audit fees and the provision of nonaudit services to audit clients, *The Accounting Review*, January, pp. 135–50.

Dopuch, N. and Simunic, D. (1980) The nature of competition in the auditing profession: a descriptive and normative view, in J. Buckley and F. Weston (eds.) *Regulation and the Accounting Profession*, Lifetime Learning Publications, Belmont, California.

Francis J. R. (1984), The effect of audit firm size on audit prices – a study of the Australian market, *Journal of Accounting and Economics*, Vol. 6, pp. 133–51.

Francis J. R. and Simon, D. T. (1987) A test of audit pricing in the small client segment of the US market, *The Accounting Review*, January, pp. 145–57.

Francis J. R. and Stokes, D. J. (1986) Audit prices, product differentiation and scale economies: further evidence from the Australian market, *Journal of Accounting Research*, Autumn, pp. 383–93.

Magee, R. P. and Tseng, M. C. (1990), Audit pricing and independence, *The Accounting Review*, April, pp. 315–35.

Metcalf Committee (1978) *Improving the Accountability of Publicly Owned Corporations and their Auditors*, Report of the Subcommittee on Reports, Accounting and Management of the Committee on Governmental Affairs, United States Senate, Washington (reproduced in *Journal of Accountancy*, January 1978, pp. 88–96).

Moizer, P. and Turley, S. (1987) Surrogates for audit fees in concentration studies, *Auditing: A Journal of Practice and Theory*, Fall, pp. 118–23.

Moizer, P. and Turley, S. (1989) Changes in the UK market for audit services: 1972–1982, *Journal of Business Finance and Accounting*, Spring, pp. 41–53.

NERA (National Economic Research Associates) (1992) *Competition in European Accounting*, Dublin, Lafferty Publications.

Palmrose, Z. (1986a) Auditor fees and auditor size: further evidence, *Journal of Accounting Research*, Spring, pp. 97–110.

Palmrose, Z. (1986b) The effect of nonaudit services on the pricing of audit services: further evidence, *Journal of Accounting Research*, Autumn, pp. 405–11.

Pong, C. and Whittington, G. (1994) The determinants of audit fees: some empirical models, *Journal of Business Finance and Accounting*, December, pp. 1071–95.

Reid, G. C. (1987) *Theories of Industrial Organisation* (1st edn), Oxford, Basil Blackwell, chapter 2.

Simon, D. T. and Francis, J. R. (1988) The effects of auditor change on audit fees: tests of price cutting and price recovery, *The Accounting Review*, April, pp. 255–69.

Simunic, D. (1980) The pricing of audit services: theory and evidence, *Journal of Accounting Research*, Spring, pp. 161–90.

Simunic, D. (1984) Auditing, consulting and auditor independence, *Journal of Accounting Research*, Autumn, pp. 679–702.

Simunic, D. and Stein, M. (1987) *Product Differentiation in Auditing: Auditor Choice in the Market for Unseasoned New Issues*, Monograph 13, Canadian Certified General Accountants' Research Foundation.

Walker, K. B. and Johnson, E. N. (1996) A review and synthesis of research on supplier concentration, quality and fee structure in non-US markets for audit services, *International Journal of Accounting*, Vol. 31, no. 1, pp. 1–18.

DISCUSSION QUESTIONS

1. Discuss the implications of the evidence that is available on market concentration and the pricing of audit services for the debate on the regulation of auditing.

2. If audit fees from a client are high, concerns about auditor independence are raised, but if low prices are quoted in a tender bid, the same concern is expressed. Are these arguments inconsistent?

3. As a purchaser of audit services, describe how you would attempt to measure the quality of services received for the price quoted by an audit firm.

4. Discuss the view that over the last twenty years, the large accounting firms have come to dominate the audit services market and that they dictate the terms on which smaller firms must compete with them.

5. Produce a list of factors that you believe ought to influence the level of fees charged for an audit assignment, and indicate how these factors might result in differential prices between companies.

6
Changes in the Legal Environment
David Gwilliam

INTRODUCTION

The legal environment within which auditors work is one which evolves and develops over time. In recent years in the UK changes have been introduced by statute but there has also developed a significant body of case law focusing on the common law duties of the auditor in contract and in tort. This chapter provides a brief overview of relevant statutory change but focuses primarily on this body of case law and on the manner in which it adds to our knowledge of what are appropriate auditing standards and to whom, and in what circumstances, a duty of care is owed. Particular attention is paid to two important recent cases – *ADT* v. *BDO* and *Hughes* v. *Merrett*[1] – in which these issues are examined in some detail.

The larger accounting and auditing firms operate on a global basis but clearly the legal environment within which auditors work is not uniform around the world. Statutory requirements and obligations vary as do legal concepts and interpretation (for example, the law of negligence in most Scandinavian countries is very different from that in the UK). Even in Commonwealth countries where the development of the law has essentially followed a UK pattern there are now significant statutory differences (for example, there is no direct UK equivalent to the Australian Trade Practice Act) between the countries and common law interpretations may diverge more widely now than in previous years. Although the USA has inherited much of the UK legal tradition the interplay between state and federal law and the variety of jurisdictions makes it impossible to identify any one single US legal environment (Brecht, 1989). In these circumstances this chapter focuses primarily on developments in UK law although reference is made to cases decided outside the UK where these are of particular significance and are likely to influence UK courts.

STATUTORY CHANGE

The changes in statute which have impacted the legal environment within which auditors in the UK operate have been largely peripheral rather than central to the major issues of what constitutes an adequate audit performance and to whom an auditor owes a duty of care. There have been various extensions of the statutory requirement for audit, for example under the Financial Services Act and in the public sector. In the company sector audit is no longer compulsory for very small companies. Following the publication of the Bingham Report (Bingham, 1992–3) there was statutory amendment of the rules relating to disclosure of information to regulators. The regulatory environment has changed in part as a result of the need to conform to the Eighth Directive.

One area where there has been a significant change is that audit firms are now able to incorporate and thus take advantage of limited liability. In fact few firms have taken advantage of this opportunity and as yet only KPMG of the larger UK firms has actually incorporated part of its audit practice although the other large UK firms are keeping the situation actively under review and considering the possibility of basing their partnerships offshore. It would appear that the benefits in terms of removing the spectre of partners being personally liable for action or inaction over which they had little, if any, personal control (as was strikingly illustrated in the Australian case *Cambridge Credit*,[2] where litigation effectively directed against the activities of one partner wiped out a medium-sized Australian firm and confronted individual partners with the prospect of liability far in excess of their personal means) have until now been outweighed by more prosaic considerations relating to taxation, issues of organization and control and disclosure of partnership income. However, the recent decision of the lower court in *ADT* v. *BDO*, in which damages of £65 million plus interest were awarded against one of the (then) larger second-tier auditing firms, has refocused attention on this issue.

One other statutory change with implications for auditor liability has been the relaxation of the prohibition in section 310 of the Companies Act 1985 on a company purchasing indemnity insurance for its officers (including the auditors). Although few companies, if any, have seen fit to purchase insurance on behalf of their auditors any increase in the extent of insurance cover carried by other company officers may have implications in respect of the choice of action of potential plaintiffs and any settlement negotiations.

THE REQUISITE STANDARD OF CARE AND SKILL

In accepting an appointment as the auditor of a company the auditor enters into a contract with that company. This contract will require the auditor to carry out the statutory duties of an auditor as specified in company legislation (principally contained in sections 235–237 of the Companies Act 1985), in particular in terms of providing an opinion as to whether the annual accounts have been properly prepared in accordance with the Act and whether or not they give a true and fair view, and certain other duties which the courts consider to be implicit within the contract to audit. In the performance of these duties the auditor will be expected to exercise 'reasonable care and skill'. A classic statement of this requirement was given in *Kingston Cotton Mill*, where Lopes LJ observed:[3]

> It is the duty of an auditor to bring to bear on the work he has to perform that skill, care, and caution which a reasonably competent, careful, and cautious auditor would use. What is reasonable skill, care, and caution must depend on the particular circumstances of each case.

Although the requirement to use reasonable skill and care has not changed in the last 100 years it is clear that what actually constitutes the fulfilment of this requirement has changed. In the UK in *Thomas Gerrard*, Pennycuick J emphasized the relative rather than the absolute nature of the concept of reasonable skill and care:[4]

> I am not clear that the quality of the auditor's duty has changed in any relevant respect since 1896. Basically that duty has always been to audit the company's accounts with reasonable care and skill. The real ground on which *In re Kingston Cotton Mill Co. (No. 2)* is, I think, capable of being distinguished is that standards of reasonable care and skill are, upon the expert evidence, more exacting today than those which prevailed in 1896.

In Australia, similar sentiments were expressed by Moffitt J in *Pacific Acceptance*:[5]

> It is not a question of the court requiring higher standards because the profession has adopted higher standards. It is a question of the court applying the law which by its context expects such reasonable standards as will meet the circumstances of today, including modern conditions of business and knowledge concerning them.

The two decades before the outbreak of the First World War saw the establishment of a body of case law in which the essentially subjective criterion of the exercise of reasonable skill and care was interpreted and applied to a number of specific audit situations. These cases, which included *London and General Bank*,[6] *Kingston Cotton Mill*, *Irish Woollen Co v. Tyson*,[7] *London Oil Storage*,[8] *Henry Squire Cash Chemist*,[9] and *Republic of Bolivia Exploration Syndicate*,[10] dealt with, *inter alia*, the auditor's responsibilities in respect of cash, stock and the detection of fraud, and the need for the auditor to familiarize himself or herself with the constitution of the company as set out in the memorandum and articles of association. Up until the Second World War decided cases involving allegations of audit negligence continued to be heard before the courts and to add to the *corpus* of case law. These cases included *Calne Gas Company*,[11] *Arthur Green* v. *Central Advance*,[12] *City Equitable Fire Insurance*,[13] *Armitage* v. *Brewer*,[14] *Westminster Road Construction*,[15] and *SP Catterson*,[16] and threw further light on responsibilities with regard to cash, debtors and stock, the suitability of certificate evidence, the respective responsibilities of directors and auditors, and duties with regard to the detection of fraud.

The decades following the Second World War saw a marked reduction in the number of reported cases involving auditors. Whether this was the result of changes in the nature and quality of auditing, increased complexity and cost of litigation, a less litigious society or a greater propensity to settle cases out of court is unclear. Some of the cases that did come before the courts were important (as noted below, in *Candler*[17] the Court of Appeal affirmed the doctrine of privity of contract and *Thomas Gerrard*, although not specifically distinguishing *Kingston Cotton Mill*, clearly highlighted changes in the auditor's responsibilities with regard to stock), others were optimistic, for example *Luscombe* v. *Roberts and Pascho*.[18] In this case a solicitor who had misused his client's funds sought to claim against his accountant on the grounds that the exercise of reasonable care and skill by the accountant would have detected the irregularities at an earlier stage and thereby saved the solicitor from loss (including the overpayment of tax). Although the accountant was found to have been negligent in failing to supervise adequately young and inexperienced staff, the claim failed because of the illegality of the solicitor's actions.

From the 1970s onward the incidence of claims against auditors appears to have increased, particularly in terms of those directed against the larger auditing firms. Again it is impossible to identify clearly any single cause for this upturn in claims. Factors contributing wholly or in part to this upsurge in legal activity may include a greater importance attached by society to audited financial information as parties which previously sought protection by other means have come to rely more heavily upon the auditor's work; the possibility of pursuing claims for economic loss outside contract following the *Hedley Byrne*[19] decision; changes in the nature and quality of the work of the auditor resultant upon greater competition within the audit services market; an increasingly litigious society or perhaps a greater willingness to see auditors and their insurers as a mechanism for spreading risk within society.

The propensity to settle claims out of court has continued to limit the number of reported cases involving auditors, and those cases which have proceeded to trial have often turned on issues (discussed below) as to the scope of the duty of care and of causation rather than on the question of the proper fulfilment of the auditor's duties. In *JEB Fasteners*[20] negligence (principally in respect of the valuation of stock at what transpired to be an overly optimistic market value rather than cost) was not strongly contested. In *Twomax*[21] failure to make physical checks at the stock count and failure to circularize debtors were seen as indicative of negligent auditing (negligence with respect to proper commission accruals was conceded) but, as in *JEB Fasteners*, the judgement was essentially directed at the duty of care and reliance issues. In *Lloyd Cheyham* v. *Littlejohn*[22] the case against the auditors turned on the suitability of the accounting policies employed by the company. In the outcome, the judge found that the relevant policies were appropriate and the action failed (see Gwilliam, 1986). In an Irish case, *Kelly* v. *Boland*,[23] an auditor who failed to attend a single stocktake over a period in excess of twenty years was found to have been negligent. In *McNaughton*[24] a lower court found an audit firm to have been negligent in the preparation and audit of a set of accounts, but this was not reported and the Court of Appeal decision turns only on the duty of care issue. In *Berg*[25] the auditor was found to have been at fault in not qualifying the audit report on uncertainty grounds in respect of the collectability of certain bills of exchange. This constituted a breach of contract with the company. In particular, the auditor relied upon unsupported representations (confirmed in writing) from both the management of the company and from the party from whom payment was due as to both the extent of the liability and the prospect of payment. In the circumstances in which the auditor had no other information about the debtor (which was based in Abu Dhabi) or its resources the auditor should have qualified the accounts on a 'subject to' basis.

Other cases, for example *Al-Saudi Banque*,[26] *Caparo*[27] and *Morgan Crucible*,[28] were decided purely upon the issue of a duty of care, and in *Galoo*[29] the case came before the court in respect only of the issues relating to causation and duty of care with no discussion of the underlying allegation of negligence.

However, in two recent cases – *ADT* v. *BDO* and *Hughes* v. *Merrett* – the court has given more detailed consideration to what constitutes an adequate performance of an auditor's duties in circumstances where very large claims were made against audit firms. We take each case in turn.[30]

In early 1990 ADT acquired Britannia Securities Group (BSG) by means of an agreed take-over. BSG's main business was the sale, leasing and maintenance of domestic and commercial security alarms and this business was conducted primarily through a wholly owned subsidiary, Britannia Security Systems (BSS). BSS was audited by a small firm of auditors, McCabe & Ford, but BSG was jointly audited by BDO Binder Hamlyn (Binders) and McCabe & Ford. ADT subsequently brought an action against Binders alone relating to their audit of BSG's accounts for the year ended 30 June 1989. ADT alleged that these accounts did not show a true and fair view in respect of a range of interrelated issues including matters pertaining to debtors, sales, terminations, capitalization of costs and depreciation of installations, together with some more specific issues relating to accounting for associated companies and fair valuation on acquisition.

BSS made relatively few outright sales of equipment – the majority of the transactions involved the leasing of installations. Leased equipment was capitalized in the books of BSS and depreciated over a ten-year life. The capitalization was based on both direct costs and significant amounts of overhead costs (including all selling and marketing costs). The accounting systems of BSS were not adequate to cope with the large number of customers and this gave rise to particular problems when contracts were terminated, for example when the ownership of a property changed or when a customer discontinued a lease in other circumstances. Although BSS could recover the installed equipment, in practice they rarely did. Furthermore, the customer was likely to continue to be billed even though the contract had been effectively terminated, and even if it was legally enforceable the prospects of recovery were very low. This could and did result in BSS's accounts showing an asset at a figure well above its market value and sales and debtors which were either invalid or unenforceable.

On the general issue of what constituted reasonable skill and care the judge emphasized the relevance of complying with generally acceptable standards in the profession: 'It is uncontroversial that the standard of professional competence required of Binders in relation to the 1989 audit to enable them to express an audit opinion is that of ordinarily skilled auditors – see *Bolam* v. *Friern Hospital Management Committee* [1957] 1 WLR 582 at 586.' On the basis of the evidence before him, including expert witness evidence, the judge held that Binders had failed to satisfy this test, concluding that Binders 'did submit to pressure from their client to certify accounts whose profits did not show a true and fair view'. The planning of the audit was insufficient with no evidence that the time pressure evident in 1988 was avoided in 1989 with the result that decisions were taken at the very last moment upon inadequate evidence. This resulted in the auditors acquiescing in significant under-provision for bad debts, acceptance of an estimate of outright sales significantly less than a true figure (which resulted in capitalization of costs for assets not owned by BSS) and capitalization of costs which should more appropriately have been expensed as service costs.

Apart from the underlying questions as to the valuation of the installations and the recoverability of debtors, two other separate issues were also considered by the court. BSG was the effective 49 per cent owner of a loss-making French security alarm business, Actron France. Three days before the BSG results were due to be announced BSG informed Binders of its intention not to equity account Actron France on the ground that BSG was not in a position to exercise control and influence over the company. Binders accepted, solely on the basis of management representation, that BSG had no representation on the board of Actron France or any right of access to its books and records. Examination of documentary evidence would have shown this to be untrue and during the course of the action Binders conceded that they had been negligent in this respect. However, no negligence was found with respect to the profit on the disposal of a property, Titan House, part of the assets of a company acquired by BSG in October 1988. Contracts for the sale of this property for a consideration of £1.8 million were exchanged in June 1989 with completion in September 1989. A fair value on acquisition of £1 million was attributed to the property and a net profit on sale of £764,000 shown in the financial statements. Although the fair valuation was based on a (rounded-down) valuation by a qualified valuer of slightly more than £1.1 million, this valuation was the result of a brief inspection in October 1988 by a valuer apparently not familiar with the area in question. Furthermore, there were grounds for supposing that the valuation was not at arm's length (the chief executive of BSG was chairman of the company providing the valuation) and written confirmation of the valuation was not provided until June 1989. Although ADT contended that the circumstances were such that this valuation should not be accepted, the judge found that Binders had addressed the issues in question, they were appropriately sceptical and their judgement that a professional valuation (whose honesty was not challenged) could be accepted should not be regarded as having been negligently made.

Hughes v. *Merrett* was part of the raft of litigation (some of it directed at auditors) arising out of the losses sustained in the Lloyd's insurance market in the 1980s. In this case actions were brought by Lloyd's names on a particular syndicate in respect of the failure to keep open the accounts of the syndicate in the presence of uncertainty as to the amount and outcome of future claims related primarily to asbestosis and environmental pollution. In addition to direct insurance the syndicate had also entered into a number of 'run-off' contracts whereby the syndicate had, in exchange for a premium, taken on the liabilities of other syndicates and insurers. These run-off contracts greatly enhanced the exposure of the syndicate to the risks associated with this type of 'long-tail' business. The plaintiffs alleged that the uncertainty as to the eventual outcome was such that the syndicate's year of account should have first been left open in 1979 and, this not having happened, in subsequent years up to and including the 1984 year of account before the 1985 account was finally left open.[31] The action lay against the managing agents of the syndicate for the decision to close the year of account by reinsurance into the subsequent year of the syndicate for each of these years and also against Ernst & Whinney, the auditors of the syndicate, for their failure to disclaim an opinion on the closed year accounts on the grounds of fundamental uncertainty. The amounts involved were large; the judge noted that by 1993 the loss on the 1985 open year was already £164 million, with a projected final deficit of £724 million to be shared among the syndicate members. The case was complicated both by the changing nature of the audit reporting requirements at Lloyd's over the relevant period and by the fact that for some time the managing agents concealed from the auditors the existence of the highly risky run-off contracts.

On the basis of a review of previous authority the judge derived a number of propositions as to the requisite standard of care. These highlighted the need to consider standards prevailing at the relevant time without the benefit of hindsight; that the exercise of judgement which turns out badly is not in itself proof of negligence – a judgement should not be impugned merely because it is wrong; a professional person should command the *corpus* of knowledge which forms part of the professional equipment of the ordinary member of his profession; that where a variety of practice is accepted as proper the preference by the court for any one practice is no basis for a finding of negligence; that the determination of what is a reasonable average standard of ordinary skilled persons professing a particular skill is the responsibility of the courts.

In the outcome the decision by the managing agents to close the 1979, 1980 and 1981 accounts was not found to have been made negligently in that the relevant uncertainties were not so great as to prevent closure of these years nor were they so great as to require the auditors to disclaim an opinion. Therefore the case against the auditors in respect of these years also failed notwithstanding the acceptance by the judge that in at least one year there had been a breakdown in communication and organization in the course of the audit and that in all the years the audit approach was open to criticism with regard to the need for appropriate audit evidence (the actions were concerned only with the failure to keep open the years in question and not with the quantum of an appropriate reinsurance to close to which these audit failings may have been relevant). In respect of the 1982 year of account, however, the judge concluded that the year should have been left open and that a reasonably competent Lloyd's auditor would have disclaimed an opinion on the grounds of fundamental uncertainty. In circumstances where, *inter alia*, knowledge of the potential uncertainties relating to the future outcome of these claims was widespread, the syndicate was highly exposed to such claims, previous estimates of outcomes had proved to be inaccurate, and the auditors had failed adequately to test management representations as to the future development of such claims and also to ensure that they were provided with sufficient information as to the run-off contracts with the result that they had inadequate audit evidence in relation to these contracts, the decision not to disclaim an opinion was negligently taken. In that the 1982 accounts had not been so qualified similar considerations applied to the failure to qualify the 1983 and 1984 closed year accounts.

Outside the UK, in countries with a similar legal and commercial environment, there have been rather more decided cases in which the actual performance of the audit work has been at issue. Since the comprehensive exposition of an auditor's duties by Moffitt in *Pacific Acceptance,*[32] other significant Australian cases have included *Simonius Vischer,*[33], *Cambridge Credit,*[34] *WA Chip*[35] and *AWA v. Deloitte.*[36] Although the circumstances of each individual case are different,[37] these cases have emphasized the importance of the auditor assessing the internal control environment and reporting in a timely fashion to management where the control environment is such that there is the potential for loss to the company. Furthermore, if the auditor is aware that management is not acting on warnings given, he or she needs to consider further action including if necessary reporting to shareholders. In Canada *HE Kane*[38] and *Revelstoke*[39] emphasized the need for auditors to guard against placing excessive reliance upon either management representations or the operation of systems and thereby reducing the extent of year-end vouching and verification.

Auditing firms frequently provide services other than audit to their clients and a significant proportion of the litigation directed against audit firms has related to the provision of these other services. Two recent UK cases – *Lowes v. Clark Whitehill*[40] and *Nederlandse*[41] – have shed further light on how the courts will interpret what constitutes an adequate performance of professional duties in the particular contexts of taxation advice and advice as to the valuation of a potential acquisition.

In *Lowes v. Clark Whitehill* the plaintiff alleged loss caused by inadequate advice as to the possibility of obtaining roll-over relief on the disposal of a business. In determining whether there had been a breach of professional duty Walker J considered both whether the advice proffered should be given in writing[42] and the extent to which advice should be comprehensive. He did not hold that it was an absolute requirement that advice, even on technical and important matters, should be in writing, but he did state that 'if the adviser puts nothing in writing, he is taking on a considerable burden of seeing that his advice is clear and understandable, and is in fact understood'. Nor was it necessary that tax-planning advice should be comprehensive in the sense of covering every possibility whether or not it is likely to be appropriate to the particular circumstances. Indeed such a course of action was likely to run up unnecessary fees and risk confusing the client. However, it was important for a professional adviser to recognize which areas called for close examination and full advice and it was the failure of the defendants to pursue with their client the possibility of structuring the disposal in a manner which would attract roll-over relief which constituted a breach of their duty as professional advisers.

In *Nederlandse* the plaintiffs failed to establish their case that their professional advisers had been negligent in the provision of advice as to valuation. Colman J noted that the advisers, Bacon & Woodrow (an actuarial firm) and Ernst & Young, were obliged to exercise all reasonable care, the appropriate standard being measured by the quality of work reasonably to be expected from a professional firm possessed of the skills required to undertake the work in question. Where that skill was a specialist skill the appropriate reference point should be the work of a specialist professional. More specifically he held that the magnitude of the possible loss that the client might suffer if the advice turned out to be wrong was also a material factor in setting the standard of professional care to be expected. In the case of advice as to valuation given for the purpose of enabling a client to decide whether to purchase a company there is a clear risk of irrevocable loss to the client if the advice is ill-founded, and this was sufficient to persuade Colman J that the necessary standard of care was higher than that in providing identical valuation advice to a company client. He stated: 'I therefore accept that the standard of care required both from Bacon & Woodrow and Ernst & Young was somewhat higher than that to be expected from accountants or actuaries whose function was to advise a company in respect of its annual accounts or its annual setting of loss reserves.'

TO WHOM IS A DUTY OF CARE OWED?

In the UK before the path-breaking decision in *Hedley Byrne*[43] extra-contractual responsibility for economic loss arising out of negligent mis-statement was, in the absence of deliberate deceit, minimal. In the accounting context this had been clearly illustrated in *Candler*,[44] where an auditor who had negligently prepared a set of accounts for a client company knowing that they were intended to be shown to a prospective investor, and were in fact delivered to that investor by the auditor, was found not to owe a duty of care to that investor.

From *Hedley Byrne,* which was not an accounting case, emerged the concept of a duty being owed only if there was a special relationship between the non-contractual parties. No clear consensus as to what did or did not constitute such a relationship emerged from the various judgements given in the House of Lords, although there was reference to the possibility of such a relationship being established by means of a voluntary assumption of responsibility. Subsequent interpretation by the courts significantly widened the scope of the duty of care until, in *Anns*,[45] the need for a special relationship was reduced to little more than a requirement of reasonable foresight of harm constrained only by relevant policy considerations. In order to establish a *prima facie* duty of care all that was required of the relationship between the alleged wrongdoer and the person who has suffered damage was 'sufficient relationship of proximity or neighbourhood such that, in the reasonable contemplation of the former, carelessness on his part may be likely to cause damage to the latter'.[46]

This approach was followed by the lower courts in a number of accounting cases. In both *JEB Fasteners*[47] and *Twomax*[48] the auditor of a company was found on the basis of the *Anns* test to owe a duty of care to third parties who invested in that company. In both instances the court emphasized the auditor's knowledge of the likely or actual need of the company to attract outside investment as sufficient to bring the third-party investor within the scope of the duty of care. Subsequently, in *Lloyd Cheyham*,[49] which on the facts was very similar to *Candler* in that the auditor knew of the existence of the specific prospective investor when the accounts were prepared and audited, the existence of a duty of care was effectively not contested. In Ireland the *Anns* test, as interpreted in *JEB Fasteners*, was followed in *Kelly v. Boland*,[50] in which the auditors were held to owe a duty of care to a prospective investor both in respect of accounts which were audited at a time at which the auditor was aware of the existence of the investor and in respect of the audit of the accounts of the previous year (audited when the auditor was unaware of any specific investment interest). However, in none of these cases was the finding as to the duty of care tested in the higher courts and indeed there was soon evidence in the higher courts of a reaction against any widespread extension of responsibility for economic loss outside contract. One means by which the courts limited the scope of the duty of care was by the reinstatement of proximity as a requirement in its own right rather than as an adjunct of reasonable foresight. In *Caparo*,[51] a case in which the plaintiff claimed to have relied upon the audited financial accounts of a company in coming to a decision to acquire that company, both the court of first instance and the Court of Appeal[52] adopted a tripartite test for a duty of care consisting of foreseeability, proximity, and whether it is fair, reasonable and just that a duty of care should exist. Although in the lower court it was held that there was an insufficiently proximate relationship between the auditors and the plaintiffs as shareholders for a duty of care to exist, this was overturned in the Court of Appeal.

The case went to the House of Lords and their Lordships, although not specifically dissociating themselves from the tripartite test, were anxious to emphasize the need for the development of this area of the law incrementally and by analogy to previous case decisions. They cautioned against the search for overarching general principles, three of the Law Lords referring with approval to the view expressed by Brennan J in the Australian High Court:[53]

> It is preferable, in my view, that the law should develop novel categories of negligence incrementally and by analogies with established categories, rather than by a massive extension of a prima facie duty of care restrained only by indefinable 'considerations which ought to negative, or to reduce or limit the scope of the duty or the class of person to whom it is owed'.

A problem which confronted the Law Lords in the application of this approach was that the only directly applicable UK decision untainted by the *Anns* test was that of the Court of Appeal in *Candler*. Not only was this nearly forty years old but, more importantly, had been effectively overruled by *Hedley Byrne*. However, in *Hedley Byrne* their Lordships had specifically approved the dissenting judgement of Lord Denning in *Candler* and from this judgement was drawn out the focus on the need for a statement to be used for the purpose for which it is intended if a duty of care is to be owed in relation to that statement. In *Caparo* Lord Jauncey noted: 'The crucial issue is the purpose for which the report was made. To quote the words of Denning LJ in the *Candler* case ... what was the "very transaction" for which it was provided?' In this context he took the view that the function of audited accounts was primarily to enable existing shareholders to exercise their class rights in a general meeting. In particular: 'Advice to individual shareholders in relation to present or future investment in the company is no part of the statutory purpose of the preparation and distribution of the accounts'.[54]

In that the plaintiffs were using the accounts in a capacity other than that for which they were intended, their case was bound to fail. This key aspect of the *Caparo* decision was set out clearly in the later Court of Appeal judgement in *Morgan Crucible*:[55]

> Their Lordships in *Caparo's* case regarded the purpose of the statutory requirement for an audit of public companies under the Companies Act 1985 as the making of a report to enable shareholders to exercise their

class rights in general meeting – not as extending to the provision of infor-mation to assist shareholders or others as to the making of decisions as to the future investment in the company. These, as we read the decision in *Caparo's* case, were the essential elements of its ratio by which the plain-tiffs' claim on the facts of that case was held to be untenable.

Clearly, this is a very restricted focus on the purpose of statutory accounts. Even in the judgement of Lord Denning on which the House of Lords placed so much emphasis, financial statements were perceived to have a rather wider role. Lord Denning noted: 'the accountant, who certifies the accounts of his client . . . is required to do this, not so much for the satisfaction of his own client, but more for the guidance of shareholders, investors, revenue author-ities, and others who may have to rely on the accounts in serious matters of business'.[56] In other circumstances the courts have taken a much more wide-reaching view of the nature and function of the statutory requirement for the production and filing of audited accounts. For example, in *Devlin* v. *Slough Estates* Dillon J noted:[57]

> The annual accounts of a company are obviously very important docu-ments. They give the only information about the company's affairs which the shareholders are entitled to receive. Beyond that, inasmuch as they have to be filed in the Companies Registry or, with quoted companies, supplied to the Stock Exchange, they give information to the world at large as to the financial position of the company on the basis of which those minded to deal with the company or to buy and to sell its shares can make their plans.

In *Al-Saudi*[58] (decided after the Court of Appeal judgement but before the House of Lords judgement in *Caparo* and a decision approved by the House of Lords in that case) the auditors of a company were found not to owe a duty of care to parties which lent money to that company. Although in *McNaughton*[59] a lower court judge, again hearing the case before the House of Lords judgement in *Caparo*, found that auditors did owe a duty of care to a third party who relied upon draft accounts prepared by a company's auditors when taking over that company, this was overturned by the Court of Appeal following the *Caparo* judgement even though there was evidence that the auditor knew the purpose for which the accounts were being pre-pared and was present at a meeting with the potential purchaser. However, in *Morgan Crucible* the Court of Appeal refused to strike out a pleading that an auditor who allowed representations relating to the audited accounts to be made following an actual bid owed a duty of care to the bidding party, although it did not conclusively determine whether such a duty was owed. In *Berg*[60] the third-party action (which was similar on the facts to that in *Al-Saudi*) failed, but in *Galoo*[61] the Court of Appeal refused to strike out an action based on the existence of a duty of care to a prospective purchaser when the accounts were prepared both for the purpose of the audit and for the fixing of the consideration under the purchase agreement.

Anthony v. *Wright* [62] was an action against the auditors of a company which accepted money from clients for placing in trustee accounts. The company went into liquidation and the money was lost because of the dishonesty of the directors. The plaintiffs argued that there was a special relationship between the auditor and the investors because of their trustee status. The action was struck out on the basis that, in the absence of any assumption of responsibility toward the investors, the close relationship necessary to found a claim was not present.

In *Deloitte Haskins & Sells* v. *National Mutual Ltd*[63] the Judicial Committee of the Privy Council (the Privy Council) had the opportunity to consider a rather different case involving trustee relationships. Deloittes were the auditors of a company receiving deposits from the public. The deposit holders were protected by a trustee and New Zealand statute required the auditor to communicate to the trustee matters which in the auditor's opinion were relevant to the work of the trustee, within seven working days of the auditor becoming aware of the relevant matters. Following the collapse of the company the trustee paid NZ$6.75 million to the depositors which it sought to recover from the auditors. In early 1986, when carrying out the 1985 year-end audit, Deloittes had become concerned as to the collectability of loans to associated companies. However, a report to the trustee was not made until May 1986 and that report did not draw attention to certain relevant matters. In the New Zealand lower court[64] the judge held that although there had been no breach of a statutory duty (because the auditors had not in fact formed an opinion that there were matters that should be reported until May 1986) there was a breach of a common law duty in failing to report by mid-March 1986. However, the trustee had been contributorily negligent and that contribution was assessed at 65 per cent. This decision was upheld by the New Zealand Court of Appeal.[65]

The Privy Council overturned this decision on the ground that there was no common law duty of care owed by Deloittes to the trustee. Although the statute created a relationship of proximity between the auditor and the trustee it did not impose a duty to form an opinion. In these circumstances there was no justification for superimposing a common law duty where statute did not provide for such a duty. Tortious liability could arise only when there had been a failure to exercise reasonable care in preparing a report when statutorily required to do so.

In *ADT* v. *BDO*, as in *Caparo*, the action resulted from the take-over of a public company. There were, however, significant differences between the cases. In *ADT* there was evidence that Binders became aware four days ahead of the final audit clearance meeting on 9 October 1989 that ADT was interested in acquiring BSG and that in consequence they were placed on guard as to possible reliance on their audit report (although it was not argued that this in itself was sufficient to give rise to a duty of care). The key factor which led to the decision of the court that a duty of care was owed was a meeting between the finance director of ADT, the chairman and another representative of BSG and the audit engagement partner, Mr Bishop. This meeting, which took place on 5 January 1990, had been specifically requested by ADT and in it Bishop was asked to confirm that the audited accounts issued on 20 October 1989 showed a true and fair view of the company's financial position as at 30 June 1989. ADT's case was that the provision of an affirmative answer was an assumption of responsibility that gave rise to a duty of care owed by Binders to ADT.

On the basis of a review of previous case law the judge determined that the ingredients of a duty of care were present. Binders professed auditing skills and Bishop attended the meeting on 5 January in his capacity as the audit engagement partner. He was fully aware of the nature of the very transaction ADT had in contemplation. He took it upon himself to give information or advice knowing the purpose for which ADT required that information or advice and knowing that it would be relied upon without further inquiry. Given that the ingredients of a duty of care were present it was necessary for the judge to determine whether in fairness Binders should be determined to have assumed responsibility to ADT for the reliability of the advice or information given. This involved consideration of whether it was fair to hold the defendants responsible in a situation where Bishop was required to answer questions in respect of which he had inadequate notice or time for preparation and where the potential additional liability was enormous; and whether it was fair for the defendants to be taken to have assumed responsibility for the competence of a professional opinion when the work which led to that opinion was in the past and where at the time the extent of their responsibility was limited to that defined in *Caparo*.

In deciding that it was fair to hold the defendants responsible in these circumstances the judge was clearly influenced by the ease with which (in the opinion of the judge) Bishop could have avoided assuming responsibility:

> For all that the crucial questions were short and Mr Bishop had a short time only to consider immediate answers . . . [he] did not have to say yes. He could have declined to answer. He could have given a disclaimer. He could have said that, if ADT were to rely on his answers, he would need to take advice. He could have said words to the effect 'Yes, I do stand by the accounts but this was a difficult audit because . . .'. Rather than doing any of these, he undertook to answer the question posed . . . and gave an unqualified favourable answer.

In a number of Commonwealth cases heard in the 1970s, most notably *Haig* v. *Bamford*[66] in Canada and *Scott* v. *McFarlane*[67] in New Zealand, higher courts were, in certain circumstances, prepared to extend the scope of the auditor's duty of care to include third parties of whose existence the auditor was unaware at the time of the audit. Whereas in *Haig* v. *Bamford* the duty of care was owed to an investor within a known limited class of investors, in *Scott* v. *McFarlane* the duty of care was determined largely by reference to foreseeability alone. The *Caparo* decision is not binding on these jurisdictions but is likely to be influential. For example, in two Canadian cases, *MacPherson*[68] and *Dixon*[69] both heard after the Court of Appeal decision in

Caparo (but before the appeal to the House of Lords), lower courts applied the tripartite test and on the basis of lack of proximity declined to hold that an auditor owed a duty of care to a third-party investor. In *MacPherson* there was some evidence that the auditor knew of the interest of the prospective investor whereas in *Dixon* the reliance was placed upon a press release containing extracts from the financial statements and the auditor had no knowledge of the third party's existence. In an Australian case, *R. Lowe Lippman*,[70] the Victorian Court of Appeal found there to be no duty of care to a third party even in a situation in which the auditor signed the audit report knowing that the client would probably supply a copy of the audited accounts to the client's largest creditor for that creditor to review the loan facility available to the client. In contrast, in *Columbia Coffee*[71] a lower court in New South Wales was prepared to distinguish *Caparo* and find that a third-party investor was owed a duty of care on the basis of an assumption of responsibility flowing from statements in the defendant auditor's audit manual which brought a potential purchaser of shares within the ambit of persons to whom a duty of care was owed.

Local authority auditors are appointed not by the local authority which they audit but by the Audit Commission and they have no direct contractual relationship with the local authority auditee. In *West Wiltshire District Council* v. *Garland*[72] the Court of Appeal was called on to consider, on a striking-out application, whether a duty was owed by the auditors to the audited body. Notwithstanding the auditors' argument that the unique nature of their role and the quasi-judicial aspect of certain of their duties, for example the scrutiny of the legality of transactions, made it invidious to impose such a duty, the Court of Appeal was firmly of the opinion that a statutory duty was owed under the Local Government Act 1982. It was also 'clearly arguable' that a tortious duty was owed although, given the existence of a statutory duty, this issue was largely academic.[73]

In the UK since 1948, experts who consent to the use of their reports in a prospectus have owed a statutory duty of care to persons subscribing for shares on the strength of that prospectus. In *Possfund* v. *Diamond*[74] the question arose whether that duty of care extended to parties (other than or including initial subscribers) who purchased shares in the Unlisted Securities Market subsequent to the initial placing. The case is of particular interest in that whereas the Financial Services Act 1986 appeared to widen the scope of the statutory duty with respect to listed companies to include those parties who subsequently purchased shares in the market, the equivalent legislation relating to the Unlisted Securities Market had never been brought into force. In consequence, the relevant question in *Possfund* v. *Diamond* was whether a common law duty of care was owed. Nineteenth-century case law[75] held there to be no such common law duty but the plaintiffs argued that in the light of changed market philosophy and practice the prospectus has developed the additional purpose of informing and encouraging subsequent purchases in the market. Lightman J considered that on this basis it was at least arguable that a duty of care is assumed and owed to those investors who (as intended) rely on the contents of the prospectus in making subsequent purchases and accordingly refused to strike out the action.

ISSUES OF CAUSATION AND QUANTUM OF DAMAGE

Even if negligence can be established, an aggrieved party has to demonstrate that negligence was a causal factor of the losses incurred if recovery is to be made. In contractual actions, if an auditor negligently fails to detect fraudulent action by an employee or fails to alert management to the potential of loss, the auditor may be found responsible for losses incurred after the date at which the breach of duty ocurred. For example, in *WA Chip*[76] the auditor was responsible for unauthorized and ultimately irrecoverable loans made to an employee after the date at which the auditor should have alerted senior management to the existence of these unauthorized loans. In *AWA* v. *Deloitte*[77] the auditors were held responsible for losses (subject to reduction because of the contributory negligence of the plaintiff) subsequent to their failure to raise at a board meeting their concerns as to the lack of documentation and internal control. However, if the court considers that management would have taken the same course of action even if they had been alerted to particular problems by the auditor then the auditor may not be held to have caused the losses resulting from that action. In the Canadian case, *West Coast Finance*,[78] the British Columbia Court of Appeal took the view that the failure of the auditors to draw the attention of management to inadequate bad debt provisions in the balance sheet was not a cause of the failure of the company management to terminate trading relationships which eventually caused heavy loss to the company

Where an auditor has failed to detect or to report on an overstatement of profit and/or of assets a number of traditional areas of recoverable loss exist in contractual or quasi-contractual (for example, misfeasance proceedings brought by a liquidator on behalf of the company) actions. These include the payment of dividends out of capital (*London & General Bank*,[79] *Thomas Gerrard*,[80] *Segenhoe*[81]), the overpayment of taxation (*Thomas Gerrard*, *Toromont*[82]) and the payment of unwarranted management bonuses (*Westminster Road Construction*,[83] *Toromont*).

In a number of recent cases it has been argued that the auditor should be responsible for losses occasioned by the continued existence of a company in situations where the company might have ceased to trade had it not been for the negligence of the auditor.[84] This was argued in the Australian case, *Cambridge Credit*,[85] where the plaintiffs argued that if the auditor had reported appropriately the debenture holders would have taken action to close the company down and the very large losses subsequently incurred would not have taken place. This argument found favour in the lower court[86] and damages of A$145 million were awarded against the 29-partner defendant firm. This finding with regard to causation was subsequently overturned by a majority in the state appeal court. In the UK a similar line of argument was advanced in the contractual action in *Galoo*.[87] In this case it was alleged that the defendant auditors had been negligent in failing to detect and report on an ongoing, increasing overstatement of stock. This failure had allowed the company to continue trading and to accept loans to support its continued trade with the result that the company racked up losses in excess of £25 million which would not have occurred if the overstatement had been detected at an earlier stage.

This argument was unanimously rejected by the Court of Appeal, which held that the pleaded breach of duty by the defendant auditors gave the company the opportunity to incur and to continue to incur trading losses but it did not cause those trading losses in the sense in which the word 'cause' was used in law. Here the Court of Appeal was anxious to endorse a 'common sense' view of causation rather than to look at it in terms of a combination of causation in fact – a 'but for' test which would necessarily widen the scope of causation, and an overall assessment of whether the defendant should be made responsible for the damage his or her negligence has played some part in causing – which would necessarily entail the making of value judgements and taking into account considerations of policy. Glidewell LJ asked: 'How does the court decide whether the breach of duty was the cause of the loss or merely the occasion for the loss?' and answered himself: 'By the application of the court's common sense.'[88]

The need for the court to exercise common sense in determining whether any breach of duty is an effective or dominant cause of loss or whether it merely provides the opportunity for loss to be sustained was again emphasized in an action against an auditing firm in respect of losses sustained by members of Lloyd's syndicates.[89] Here a key aspect of the plaintiffs' case was that failure by the auditors to uncover allegedly fraudulent transactions between related syndicates in 1983 and 1984 was an effective cause of essentially unrelated losses occasioned by negligent underwriting incurred by the syndicates in 1989 and 1990[90] (in that failure to discover the alleged fraud allowed the underwriter to remain with the syndicates and the misleading results in 1983 and 1984 induced names to remain with or join the ill-fated syndicates). Hearing a striking-out application Gatehouse J described these arguments as 'hopeless', stating: 'Applying common sense, there is no way in which those earlier defaults can be said to be an effective cause of the underwriting losses.'

Outside contract it has also on occasion been difficult for aggrieved parties to demonstrate a causal link between any actual or alleged auditor negligence and losses they have incurred. In *JEB Fasteners*[91] it was held both in the lower court and in the Court of Appeal that the plaintiffs' intention to purchase the company to secure the services of two key personnel would not have been affected even if the accounts had shown the true picture and therefore the negligence of the auditors could not have been held to have caused the plaintiffs' loss. In *Berg*[92] even if the auditors had been found to have owed a duty of care to the third party the action would not have succeeded as the court found no causal connection between the negligence of the auditor in failing to qualify on grounds of uncertainty and the subsequent actions of the third party in advancing money to the company. In *Deloitte* v. *National Mutual*[93] the Privy Council considered that the New Zealand courts had been erroneous in their view that the auditors should compensate the trustee for the depositors for the full amount of the trustee's liability to the depositors. The Privy Council considered that this liability would have been no different even if the auditor had reported to the trustee on the date on which the New Zealand courts considered a report should have been made (or at least that the trustee had failed to prove that it would have been different). Consequently any breach of duty by the auditor did not cause loss to the trustee (of course, as noted above, the Privy Council had already found that there was no breach of duty by the auditor, so strictly speaking this finding had no effect).

In the Canadian case *Toromont*,[94] it was held that the plaintiff would have made their ill-starred investment even if the accounts had not been misstated. Third parties have also had great difficulty in establishing loss in situations where the courts have sought to link errors in financial statements with a measure of loss as determined by a fall in a share price. Commonwealth cases which have failed wholly or partly on this point include the New Zealand cases, *Dimond*[95] and *Scott* v. *McFarlane*,[96] and in Canada the third-party action in *West Coast Finance*.[97]

In *ADT* v. *BDO* causation itself was not in dispute in that the court accepted that ADT would not have gone ahead with the acquisition of BSG at the agreed price if they had not been assured that Binders stood by their audit report. In terms of determining the quantum of damage it was held that the basis for assessment should be the difference between the amount paid for the company and the amount that a willing purchaser would have been prepared to pay if aware of the matters that a full accountant's investigation would have disclosed. Although this was relatively uncontroversial there was still scope for major differences as to what this latter figure would have been, dependent upon assumptions as to the stream of future earnings and differing methods of translating these into present-day values. As compared with the actual purchase price of £105 million the expert witness for ADT produced a valuation of £8.4 million whereas that for Binders gave a valuation range of £50–55 million. In the outcome the judge assessed the 'true' value of BSG at the time of acquisition as £40 million.

CONTRIBUTORY NEGLIGENCE

In both the UK and North America the audit profession has been assiduous in its campaign against the supposed wrongs of a system whereby auditors are said to be held responsible for the entire amount of losses for which they are only partly responsible. The burden of the auditors' complaint is essentially that in both contract and tort they are held responsible for failings which should more appropriately be laid at the feet of company management. In contract the question of the relative responsibilities of company management and auditor has been the subject of debate since the development of the modern audit function in the nineteenth century with, for the most part, the courts seeing these responsibilities as essentially separate.[98] However, in certain circumstances the auditor may be able to put forward a defence of contributory negligence which, if successful, would reduce any award made against the auditor. It would now appear to be accepted that, in the UK at least, contributory negligence is available as a defence in contractual actions where the contractual obligation is expressed in terms of a duty to take reasonable skill and care, and this obligation coexists with a liability in the tort of negligence which exists irrespective of the existence of the contract (Law Commission, 1993). The question of whether there is such a concurrent liability in the auditor/client relationship has not been directly tested in the higher courts in the UK, but it would appear that such a concurrent liability does exist.[99]

Although the defence may be available as a matter of law there are still obstacles to be overcome in mounting such a defence, in particular the argument that such a defence based upon the negligent conduct of an employee or director of a company is not available to an auditor whose duty it is to check the conduct of such persons. This was articulated by Moffitt P in the Australian case *Simonius Vischer*. He stated:[100]

> Where the action for professional negligence is against an auditor, it is difficult to see how a finding of contributory negligence, according to usual concepts, could be made. If, as where the audit is of a public company, the audit contract or the undertaking of an audit is found to impose a duty to be exercised so as to safeguard the interests of shareholders, it is difficult to see how the conduct of any servant or director could constitute the relevant negligence, so as to defeat the claim against the auditor, whose duty is to check the conduct of such persons and, where appropriate, report it to the shareholders.

However, in a more recent Australian case the courts were prepared to reduce an award against an auditor on account of contributory negligence by the plaintiffs in a contractual action. In *AWA* v. *Daniels* the plaintiff company lost large sums of money because of the activities of its foreign exchange manager. The company brought an action against its auditors on the basis of their failure to discover and report on major deficiencies of internal control and accounting record-keeping. The auditors claimed contributory negligence on the part of the plaintiff in terms of its failure to put in place a satisfactory system of internal control and failure to act on warnings given by the auditors.

In the lower court Rogers CJ reviewed at length the case law, both UK and Commonwealth, and North American, relating to contributory negligence in contractual actions against auditors before concluding that it was appropriate to identify the plaintiff corporation with the negligent acts of its senior management and therefore that the plaintiff was guilty of contributory negligence. He reached this decision on a number of grounds, but arguably the overriding consideration was a belief that in the circumstances it would not be equitable not to take into account the behaviour of management. He stated: 'I cannot accept that a corporation is entitled to abdicate all responsibility for proper management of the financial aspects of its operation and then, when loss is suffered, to seek to attribute the entirety of the blame to its auditors.'

In the UK contributory negligence as a defence has not had a major part to play in reported contractual actions against auditors although it was raised in *Hughes* v. *Merrett*. Here the defendants claimed that the damage suffered by the names was partly a result of their own fault on the grounds that they had delegated their responsibilities to the managing agents or to members' agents and had thereby not acted to prevent the closure of the relevant years. Having regard to the unusual and complex structure of the Lloyd's market the judge rejected the notion that the negligence of the agent could be attributed to the plaintiff. Even if it could be so attributed it would not be just or equitable to reduce the award of damages because of any responsibility of the plaintiff.

Outside contract, although contributory negligence is clearly available as a defence in law, again it has had little application in actions against auditors. Here the law has tended to take the view that it is difficult for the reasonable foresight necessary for a duty of care and negligence on the part of the third party to co-exist. In *JEB Fasteners* Woolf referred to this issue in the following terms: 'I do, however, recognize that it may well be that in the case of negligent misrepresentation the scope for contributory negligence is limited since an auditor will only be liable if he should foresee that someone might rely on his accounts and, as I have sought to indicate, this involves it being reasonable for the person concerned to rely on the accounts. If it is reasonable to rely on the accounts, it is difficult to envisage circumstances where as a matter of fact it would be negligent to do so without taking further steps to protect yourself from the consequences of relying on the auditor's certificate.'[101] The situation may be different where the duty of care arises from a voluntary assumption of responsibility. In *ADT* v. *BDO* the judge considered under the heading of contributory negligence Binders' submission that, as a chartered accountant familiar with the industry, ADT's finance director should have studied and understood the considerable volume of information that he was provided with. However, as no submissions as to the relevance of any particular failure to study or understand the information were made the judge did not consider the matter further.

CONCLUSIONS

What can we learn from those cases that have come before the courts in recent years? In terms of the exercise of reasonable care and skill there has perhaps been an even clearer emphasis on the role of standards acceptable within the profession as the yardstick by which what constitutes a proper performance of an auditor's duties is assessed. However, there is still room for dispute as to what acceptable standards are and how far one can fall below best practice without being found to be negligent. Furthermore, the diversity of circumstances within which auditors are required to work (contrast the particular accounting and audit problems posed by overhead allocations in *ADT* v. *BDO* with the need to assess potential liabilities over a twenty-year-plus time scale in *Hughes* v. *Merrett*) means that case-specific factors are likely to be relevant in deciding these issues. What does emerge is the manner in which the actual practice of audit can differ from the textbook model of audit manuals and auditing standards. The reality is, or can be, that auditors are working with uncertain and incomplete information, frequently under significant time pressure and in circumstances where client management can bring considerable pressure to bear on the exercise of auditor judgement. This was clearly illustrated in *ADT* v. *BDO*. Here the auditors did not receive the final consolidation until 7 p.m. on Thursday 5 October and at the first audit clearance meeting on Sunday 8 October there were still at least twenty-two items of suggested adjustment under discussion, Binders proposing adjustments which would have reduced reported profit to £8.73 million. Strangely, the final audit clearance meeting on the following day, 9 October, was not attended by the audit engagement partner (or apparently by any representative of McCabe & Ford, the joint auditors). This meeting was attended by the client service partner (who had been an engagement partner in previous years but who had not reviewed the audit material) and Mr Record the chairman and founder of the client company. In evidence Record agreed that it was an objective to achieve results which were as near as possible to the previous year's results (twelve days previously BSG had announced that profits were unlikely to show any growth on the previous year's figures). It was important that the results were, with the agreement of the auditors, as close as possible to £10 million. In the outcome Binders agreed to a profit figure of £9.32 million (the client insisted on reporting £9.61 million and Binders qualified in respect of £0.29 million).

In *Hughes* v. *Merrett* there were again pressures of time – the judge referred to the audit partner being placed under an unduly heavy burden of work because of the deadlines applying to all Lloyd's syndicates and his particular involvement on a number of problem syndicates. The managing agents were no doubt anxious to close off years of account at a time when syndicate membership was expanding rapidly. There were other pressures, too, which may have contributed to the auditor's decision not to qualify the closed-year accounts. A qualification on a closed year of account was almost certainly not acceptable to the Council of Lloyd's and an intention to qualify would force the managing agents to keep the year of account open (Macve, 1986, p. 212). On another large syndicate audited by Ernst & Whinney a qualification on a 1982 closed year did in fact uniquely result in that year of account being reopened. However, while the Council of Lloyd's would not accept an audit qualification it was nevertheless very anxious to discourage managing agents from running years off (Macve and Gwilliam, 1993, p. 105) and as one of the largest auditors within the Lloyd's market Ernst & Whinney would have been keenly aware of this pressure.

In respect of the extent of a duty of care to third parties the decided cases have added sufficient clarification such that in *Anthony* v. *Wright* Lightman J was able to encapsulate the UK position thus:[102]

> The law is well established that auditors do not in respect of their audits owe a duty of care to anyone other than the company itself save in exceptional circumstances where a special duty has been treated as assumed to a third party. Thus in principle no duty is owed to shareholders or prospective shareholders in respect of investment decisions made regarding the purchase or sale of shares in the company; nor to existing or future creditors who may rely on the audited accounts in leaving debts outstanding or making loans to the company. . . . A special relationship is required and in particular intention (actual or inferred) on the part of the auditors that the third party shall rely, and reliance by the third party, on the audit, before a claim in negligence against the auditor can be maintained: see *Galoo Ltd* v. *Bright Grahame Murray* [1994] BCC 319.

However, as the differing decisions reached in the various cases – *McNaughton, Morgan Crucible, Galoo* and *ADT* v. *BDO* – show, it is not always possible to predict with certainty how this test will be applied. For example, in *Caparo* the House of Lords approved Lord Denning's dissenting judgement in *Candler*, yet in *McNaughton*, which on the facts bore some similarities to *Candler* (draft accounts were prepared in circumstances in which the accountant knew they were to be shown to a prospective purchaser), the Court of Appeal found no duty of care to be owed to the third party.

The accepted view within the auditing profession is that the operation of the law has become onerous in its application to auditors and that change is necessary to protect the interests of both the profession and the public. Currently both the ICAEW and the 'Big Six' firms acting collectively are campaigning for further liability limitation in particular in respect of the law relating to joint and several liability. The APB (1994, 1996) has expressed concerns that issues of auditors' liability may constrain the development of new services and the acceptance of additional responsibilities necessary to meet changing user needs. However, the above review of recent cases does not provide overwhelming evidence that the courts have played any part in placing an undue burden of responsibility upon auditors either in terms of the degree of care and skill they need to exercise in their audit or in the range of parties to whom a duty of care is owed. What the case law does suggest is that in some circumstances auditors have been unable to withstand the very real commercial and psychological pressures which direct them toward compliance with the wishes of their client. Legal sanctions are sometimes haphazard in their operation and involve considerable costs over and above those of any actual award or settlement. Unless auditors are prepared to take a more robust line in their dealings with their clients, however, such sanctions may be a necessary part of any mechanism which seeks to ensure that the audit profession does carry out its ascribed societal role.

NOTES

1. Both these cases are at the time of writing unreported.
2. *Alexander v. Cambridge Credit Corporation Ltd* (1987) 9 NSWLR 310.
3. *Re Kingston Cotton Mill Co. Ltd (No. 2)* [1896] 2 Ch. 279, at p. 288.
4. *Re Gerrard (Thomas) & Son Ltd* [1968] Ch. 455, at p. 475.
5. *Pacific Acceptance* (1970) 92 WN (NSW) 29.
6. *Re London and General Bank* [1895] 2 Ch. 166.
7. *The Irish Woollen Co. Ltd v. Tyson* (1900) 27 Acct LR 13.
8. *London Oil Storage Co v. Seear, Hasluck and Co.* (1904) 31 Acct LR 93.
9. *Henry Squire, Cash Chemist Ltd v. Ball, Baker & Co.* (1912) 106 LT 197.
10. *Re Republic of Bolivia Exploration Syndicate* [1914] 1 Ch. 139.
11. *Calne Gas Co. v. Curtis* (1918) 59 Acct LR 17.
12. *Arthur E. Green & Co. v. Central Advance and Discount Corporation Ltd* (1920) 63 Acct LT 1.
13. *In re City Equitable Fire Insurance Co. Ltd* [1925] 1 Ch. 407.
14. *Armitage v. Brewer and Knott* (1932) 77 Acct LR 25.
15. *Re Westminister Road Construction & Engineering Co. Ltd* (1932) 77 Acct LR 39.
16. *Re Catterson (SP) & Sons Ltd* (1937) 81 Acct LR 62.
17. *Candler v. Crane, Christmas & Co.* [1951] 2 KB 164.
18. *Luscombe v. Roberts and Pascho* (1962) 106 SJ 373.
19. *Hedley Byrne & Co. Ltd v. Heller & Partners Ltd* [1964] AC 465.
20. *JEB Fasteners Ltd v. Marks, Bloom & Co.* [1983] 1 All ER 583, CA, affirming [1981] 3 All ER 289.
21. *Twomax Ltd v. Dickson, McFarlane and Robinson* 1983 SLT 98; 1984 SLT 424.
22. *Lloyd Cheyham & Co. Ltd v. Littlejohn & Co.* [1987] BCLC 303.
23. *Kelly v. Boland* [1989] ILRM 373.
24. *McNaughton (James) Paper Group Ltd v. Hicks Anderson & Co.* [1991] 1 All ER 134, [1990] BCC 891.
25. *Berg Sons & Co. Ltd & Ors vs. Adams & Ors* [1992] BCC 661.
26. *Al-Saudi Banque v. Clark Pixley* [1990] 1 Ch. 313.
27. *Caparo Industries plc v. Dickman* [1990] 2 AC 605.
28. *Morgan Crucible Co. plc v. Hill Samuel & Co. Ltd* [1991] Ch. 295.
29. *Galoo Ltd & Ors v. Bright Grahame Murray* [1994] BCC 319, CA.
30. It should be noted that both these decisions are those of a single judge and may therefore be subject to appeal. However, many of the negligence issues in *ADT* were conceded in the course of the action and the likelihood of any appeal in *Merrett* will almost certainly depend on the success or otherwise of the Lloyd's overall settlement proposals.
31. Space precludes more detailed exposition and analysis of the peculiarities of the accounting and auditing pertaining to Lloyd's syndicates. The interested reader is referred to Macve and Gwilliam (1993).
32. *Pacific Acceptance Corporation Ltd v. Forsyth* (1970) 92 WN (NSW) 29.
33. *Vischer (Simonius) Co. v. Holt and Thompson* [1979] NSWLR 322.
34. *Alexander v. Cambridge Credit Corporation Ltd* (1987) 9 NSWLR 310.
35. *Young (Arthur) & Co. v. WA Chip and Pulp Co. Pty Ltd* (1988) 13 ACLR 283.

36. *AWA Ltd* v. *Daniels t/a Deloitte Haskins & Sells* (1992) 7 ACSR 759, (1992) 9 ACSR 383.

37. In *AWA* v. *Deloitte* Rogers CJ noted: 'Auditors must exercise reasonable care and skill. What that requires of an auditor has been examined in a number of decisions over the last 95 years since the judgment of the Court of Appeal in *In Re [Kingston] Cotton Mill Co (No 2)* (1896) 2 Ch. 279. Although useful by way of illustration none of the decisions apply directly to the problem confronting me.'

38. *Kane (HE) Agencies Ltd* v. *Coopers & Lybrand* (1983) 23 CCLT 233.

39. *Revelstoke Credit Union* v. *Miller* (1984) 28 CCLT 17.

40. Draft judgement handed down 21 December 1995 (as yet unreported).

41. *Nederlandse Reassurantie Groep Holdings NV* v. *Bacon & Woodrow and Ernst & Young*, judgement delivered 2 August 1996 (as yet unreported).

42. The judge noted as a feature of the case the lack of coherent notes or memoranda in the defendants' files and the paucity of letters of advice to the plaintiff.

43. *Hedley Byrne & Co. Ltd* v. *Heller & Partners Ltd* [1964] AC 465.

44. *Candler* v. *Crane, Christmas & Co.* [1951] 2 KB 164.

45. *Anns* v. *Merton London Borough Council* [1978] AC 728.

46. Ibid., at p. 751.

47. *JEB Fasteners Ltd* v. *Marks, Bloom & Co.* [1983] 1 All ER 583, CA, affirming [1981] 3 All ER 289.

48. *Twomax Ltd* v. *Dickson, McFarlane and Robinson* 1983 SLT 98; 1984 SLT 424.

49. *Lloyd Cheyham & Co. Ltd* v. *Littlejohn & Co.* [1987] BCLC 303.

50. *Kelly* v. *Boland* [1989] ILRM 373.

51. *Caparo Industries plc* v. *Dickman* [1990] 2 AC 605.

52. (1988) 4 BCC 144 and (1989) 5 BCC 105, respectively.

53. *Sutherland Shire Council* v. *Heyman* (1985) 60 ALR 1, at pp. 43–4.

54. *Caparo*, at pp. 658 and 662, respectively.

55. *Morgan Crucible Co. plc* v. *Hill Samuel & Co. Ltd* [1991] Ch. 295, at p. 319.

56. *Candler* v. *Crane, Christmas & Co.* [1951] 2 KB 164, at p. 184.

57. *Devlin* v. *Slough Estates Ltd* [1983] BCLC 497, at p. 502.

58. *Al-Saudi Banque* v. *Clark Pixley* [1990] 1 Ch. 313.

59. *McNaughton (James) Paper Group Ltd* v. *Hicks Anderson & Co.* [1991] 1 All ER 134, [1990] BCC 891.

60. *Berg Sons & Co. Ltd & Ors* v. *Adams & Ors* [1992] BCC 661.

61. *Galoo Ltd & Ors* v. *Bright Grahame Murray* [1994] BCC 319, CA.

62. *Anthony* v. *Wright* [1995] BCC 768.

63. *Deloitte Haskins & Sells* v. *National Mutual Ltd* [1993] AC 774, PC.

64. [1990] 3 NZLR 641.

65. (1991) 3 NZBLC 102, 259.

66. *Haig* v. *Bamford* (1976) 72 DLR (3d) 68.

67. *Scott Group Ltd* v. *McFarlane* [1978] 1 NZLR 553.

68. *MacPherson* v. *Schachter* (1989) 1 CCLT (2d) 665.

69. *Dixon* v. *Deacon Morgan McEwan Easson* (1989) 64 DLR (4th) 441.

70. *R. Lowe Lippman Figdor & French* v. *AGC (Advances) Ltd* [1992] 2 VR 671.

71. *Columbia Coffee & Tea Pty Ltd* v. *Churchill & Ors* (1992) 29 NSWLR 141.

72. *West Wiltshire District Council* v. *Garland* [1995] Ch. 297.

73. Perhaps surprisingly, the question whether a local authority auditor owed a

duty of care to the audited body had not previously come before the UK courts. However, similar issues had been considered in a number of previous Commonwealth cases, most notably by the High Court of Australia in *Shire of Frankston and Hastings v. Cohen* 102 (1959–60) CLR 607. The conclusion in this case too was that a statutory duty of care was owed under the relevant local legislation.

74. *Possfund Custodian Trustee v. Diamond* [1996] 2 BCLC 665.
75. *Peek v. Gurney* (1873) LR 6 HL (373).
76. *Young (Arthur) & Co. v. WA Chip and Pulp Co. Pty Ltd* (1988) 13 ACLR 283.
77. *AWA Ltd v. Daniels t/a Deloitte Haskins & Sells* (1992) 7 ACSR 759, (1992) 9 ACSR 383.
78. *West Coast Finance v. Gunderson, Stokes, Walton* (1974) 44 DLR (3rd) 232; (1975) 56 DLR (3rd) 460.
79. *Re London and General Bank* [1895] 2 Ch. 166.
80. *Re Gerrard (Thomas) & Son Ltd* [1968] Ch. 455.
81. *Segenhoe v. Akins* (1990) 29 NSWLR 569. In this case the court held that there was no obligation on the company to seek recovery from the shareholders to whom the illegal dividend had been paid as the requirement to mitigate loss did not include a requirement to undertaken litigation the outcome of which was uncertain.
82. *Toromont* (1976) 62 DLR (3rd) 225; (1977) 73 DLR (3rd) 123.
83. *Re Westminster Road Construction & Engineering Co Ltd* (1932) 77 Acct LR 39.
84. An early example of the rejection by the courts of this line of argument can be found in the lower court judgement of J Vaughan Williams in *Kingston Cotton Mill* [1896] 1 Ch. 331, at p. 349.
85. *Alexander v. Cambridge Credit Corporation Ltd* (1987) 9 NSWLR 310.
86. *Cambridge Credit Corporation Ltd v. Hutcheson & Ors* (1985) 9 ACLR 545.
87. *Galoo Ltd & Ors v. Bright Grahame Murray* [1994] BCC 319, CA.
88. Ibid., at p. 329.
89. *Deeny & Ors v. Walker & Ors* and *Deeny & Ors v. Littlejohn & Co. & Ors* (1996), as yet unreported.
90. As in other actions relating to Lloyd's the amounts involved were not small. The plaintiffs were seeking to recover approximately £220m, itself representing the shortfall in recovery against the negligent managing and members' agents.
91. *JEB Fasteners Ltd v. Marks, Bloom & Co.* [1983] 1 All ER 583, CA, affirming [1981] 3 All ER 289.
92. *Berg Sons & Co. Ltd & Ors v. Adams & Ors* [1992] BCC 661.
93. *Deloitte Haskins & Sells v. National Mutual Ltd* [1993] AC 774, PC.
94. *Toromont* (1976) 62 DLR (3rd) 225; (1977) 73 DLR (3rd) 123.
95. *Dimond Manufacturing Co. Ltd v. Hamilton* [1969] NZLR 609.
96. *Scott Group Ltd v. McFarlane* [1978] 1 NZLR 553.
97. *West Coast Finance v. Gunderson, Stokes, Walton* (1974) 44 DLR (3rd) 460.
98. This was clearly expressed by Lord Alverstone in *London Oil Storage Co. v. Seear, Hasluck and Co.* (1904) 31 Acct LR 93, who stated: 'I entirely agree with the view of the law that the auditor cannot shelter himself for any breach of duty under the neglect of the directors.'
99. In *Caparo* in the Court of Appeal ([1989] 1 QB 653 at p. 682) Bingham LJ

referred to the position thus: 'It is common ground between the parties that an auditor owes a duty to the company which appoints him to exercise reasonable care and skill in conducting the audit and making his audit report. A coincident duty in tort will also arise.' This statement attracted no comment in the House of Lords judgement.

100.   *Simonius Vischer* v. *Holt & Thompson* [1979] 2 NSWLR 322, at pp. 329–30.
101.   *JEB Fasteners Ltd* v. *Marks, Bloom & Co.* [1983] 1 All ER 583, CA, affirming [1981] 3 All ER 289, at p. 297.
102.   *Anthony* v. *Wright* [1995] BCC 768, at p.770.

REFERENCES

APB (Auditing Practices Board) (1994) *The Audit Agenda*, APB, London.
APB (Auditing Practices Board) (1996) *The Audit Agenda – Next Steps*, APB, London.
Brecht, H. (1989) Auditors' duty of care to third parties: a comment on judicial reasoning underlying US cases, *Accounting and Business Research*, Vol. 19, no. 74, pp. 175–8.
Gwilliam, D. (1986) Accounting standards: a guide to negligence, *Professional Negligence*, Vol. 2, no. 6, pp. 175–9.
Law Commission (1993) *Contributory Negligence as a Defence in Contract*, Law Commission (Law Com. No. 219), HMSO, London.
Macve, R. (1986) *A Survey of Lloyd's Syndicate Accounts*, Prentice-Hall, London.
Macve, R. and Gwilliam, D. (1993) *A Survey of Lloyd's Syndicate Accounts* (2nd edn), Prentice-Hall, London.

DISCUSSION QUESTIONS

1. It has been contended that in recent years the operation of the law has been unfair as it has applied to auditors. Do you agree?
2. If a company continues in existence because of the negligence of the auditors then it is right that those auditors should be responsible for its future losses as they would not have been incurred but for the negligence of the auditors. Discuss this statement with particular reference to the *Cambridge Credit* and *Galoo* cases.
3. If anything, the post-*Caparo* cases on the auditor's duty of care to third parties have added confusion rather than certainty to this area of the law. Discuss.
4. What considerations are relevant in determining whether a defence of contributory negligence is likely to be successful in an action against an auditor?
5. Auditors would argue that in many instances the exercise of hindsight is used to identify negligence in circumstances where the issue was in fact one of judgement. Discuss with particular reference to the *ADT* v. *BDO* and *Hughes* v. *Merrett* cases.

7

Regulating the Auditing Profession

Prem Sikka

INTRODUCTION

In little over a hundred years, external audits have become a common way
of regulating a variety of organizations. After the 1878 crash of the City of
Glasgow Bank, the Companies Act 1879 made external audits mandatory for
all banking companies registered thereafter with limited liability. At that time
it was hard to imagine that by the end of the twentieth century, not only
most limited liability companies[1] but also schools, hospitals, universities,
charities, trade unions, housing associations and many other organizations
would be subject to compulsory annual audits. This expansion of the role of
external audit has also been accompanied by an increasingly formal regulation of auditors and the external audit process.

Initially, auditors were regulated by peer pressure, i.e. what the accepted
and reputable accountants of the era did or described in books (for
example, Dicksee, 1892) or magazines.[2] As auditing made a transition from a
voluntary to a public role, courts were often called to settle disputes about
auditor duties, rights and obligations. Common law developments as signified
by court cases began to shape the conduct of an audit (see Gwilliam, 1987 for
further details). For example, cases such as *Irish Woollen Co. Ltd* v. *Tyson
and Others* (1900) 26 Acct LR 13 urged auditors to pay attention to cut-off
procedures and post-balance sheet events; *Fox & Son* v. *Morrish Grant & Co.*
(1918) 35 TLR 126 urged auditors to verify correctness of cash balances held
by companies by referring to documentary evidence (e.g. bank statements);
Arthur E. Green and Co. v. *The Central Advance and Discount Corporation
Limited* (1920) 63 Acct LR 62 urged auditors to consider the likely recovery
of book debts; *Armitage* v. *Brewer and Knott* (1932) 77 Acct LR 28 urged

auditors to pay attention to any unusual alterations in the books of client companies; *Re Gerrard (Thomas) and Son Ltd* (1968) Ch. 455; (1967) 2 All ER 525 urged auditors to make use of third-party circularizations.

By 1948, professionally qualified accountants completed their statutory monopoly of the external audit (Willmott, 1986), but there were no formal auditing standards. Professional bodies were not formally responsible for licensing auditors or monitoring their work. The Institute of Chartered Accountants in England and Wales (ICAEW) began to issue 'Statements on Auditing'[3] in 1961 as its previous strategy of blaming lax accounting practices for audit deficiencies became harder to sustain (Sikka and Willmott, 1995a). Then from the 1970s onwards the regulation of auditors began to become more formalized through the issue of auditing standards, ethical codes, disciplinary, licensing and monitoring arrangements. In the process, professional bodies have also been transformed from mere trade associations to public regulators.

This chapter will focus on the period from the 1970s to the mid-1990s and examine this process of increased regulation of the auditing profession. Like any other regulatory arrangement, it is shaped by broader social, economic and political developments. The mid-1970s banking and property crash, the government's economic policies, the implementation of the European Union's Eighth Directive and some well-publicized corporate collapses in the 1990s have provided the context for increasingly formal regulation of auditors. The influence of each of these on the development of the regulatory processes will be examined in this chapter.

BANKING AND PROPERTY CRASH

The crisis

During the late 1960s and the early 1970s the British economy was going through a period of rapid decline. For example, the average rate of return declined from 13 per cent per annum (in the 1960s) to 4 per cent in 1975, coupled with a balance of payments crisis, double-digit inflation and rising unemployment (Wilson Committee, 1978). The government encouraged the expansion of the financial services sector, with minimal regulation (Clarke, 1986). Qualifications in audit reports were considered to be the prime means of alerting financial regulators to any malpractices even though auditors were not formally appointed by regulators and did not consider fraud detection and reporting to be their main responsibility.

In this rather relaxed regulatory financial environment, speculative activity grew. In the property sector, borrowings trebled between 1971 and 1993 (Coakley and Harris, 1983). Much of it came from the secondary banking sector. Property prices trebled between 1970 and 1973 and led to demand for even more speculative finance. Returns on property and financial dealings were much healthier compared to those from the manufacturing sector. In 1973 the Arab–Israeli war resulted in quadrupling of the oil price and Britain's industrial costs began to rise sharply. Borrowers struggled to meet their loan repayment schedules and secondary banks had difficulty in honouring their obligations to depositors. Lenders who sequestrated assets on which loans were secured had enormous difficulty in selling them as buyers could not find adequate cash to buy them. A banking and property crash followed and spread to insurance, shipping and other sectors.

Questions about auditors

Major secondary banks, such as London and Counties, Cedar Holdings, Moorgate Mercantile, Slater Walker, Keyser Ullman and London and Capital, collapsed. The state eventually bailed out the ailing banking and property sector by spending some £3,000 million of taxpayers' money (Reid, 1982) and in the process had to apply to the International Monetary Fund (IMF) for help. The Department of Trade and Industry (DTI) appointed inspectors to investigate the causes of major collapses (see Sikka and Willmott, 1995b) and the associated audit failures, especially as many companies collapsed within a short period of declaring healthy profits and publishing unqualified audit reports. The resulting DTI reports were highly critical of the quality of audit work. Auditors were charged with failing to spot simple frauds, manipulations and even arithmetical errors. The revelations were sufficient for one influential commentator to conclude that the crisis was fuelled by the

> ease with which eminent firms of auditors turned a blind eye on the wholesale abuse by client company directors of [legal] provisions. [The directors] operated these public companies for the principal benefit of themselves and their families; and most regrettable of all, on the virtual complicity of their auditors, whose efforts are seen to have amounted to a whitewash at best, and a fatuous charade at worst.
>
> (Woolf, 1983, p. 102)

In response to various revelations of poor auditing practices, the quality press expressed disquiet about auditing practices (see Sikka and Willmott, 1995a, for details). This threatened the legitimacy of external audits, and with it the confidence which the public is routinely asked to attach to audited financial statements, especially as further scandals continued to emerge (for example, see Registry of Friendly Societies, 1979). The President of the ICAEW was forced to acknowledge that 'public confidence in the standards of our performance has been badly shaken' (*Accountancy*, November 1976, p. 4). One member of Parliament even introduced a private bill for the creation of a public board for regulating auditors (*Hansard*, March 1977, cols. 1081–8). The attempt was defeated by 35 votes as the government of the time was trying to manage a full-blown economic crisis given visibility by high inflation, rising unemployment, collapses and scandals. It did not have the immediate capacity to tackle auditing problems, but the Secretary of State for Trade found sufficient time to summon the presidents of major accountancy bodies (ICAEW, ICAS, ICAI and ACCA) to his office and told them that 'either they regulated themselves effectively or I would ask Parliament to do it for them' (letter to the author, dated 6 December 1989).

The profession's response

The environment described above gave rise to concerns about regulation of auditors. It should be appreciated that, historically, the UK accountancy profession has sought to blame lax accounting practices for criticisms of auditors (Robson, 1991). But since 1969 a full accounting standards-setting programme fronted by the Accounting Standards Committee (ASC), but entirely under the control of the profession, had been in operation. Thus accountancy bodies and major firms could not easily blame poor accounting practices for audit deficiencies or misleading financial statements. A different card relating to auditing had to be played.

The profession responded in a number of, often contradictory, ways on three broad fronts – auditing standards, ethics and discipline. In 1976 the profession responded by forming the Auditing Practices Committee (APC), a body which remained responsible for formulating auditing standards until 1991 and in that period issued 46 pronouncements. The APC was not a statutory body. It developed auditing standards but the authority to issue them formally remained with the major accountancy bodies. The standards were not mandatory though in the event of dispute the courts could have used them as benchmarks.[5] The explicit purpose of forming the APC was to 'satisfy our critics in political circles and outside' (APC, 1978, p. 50). The APC was staffed largely by part-time unpaid volunteers with auditing experience. As major firms could afford to second staff to the APC, whilst continuing to keep them on its payroll, inevitably the APC came to be populated by major accountancy firms. Most of the voting power was also controlled by major firms, often the very firms whose practices had been severely criticized in the DTI reports (Sikka, Willmott and Lowe, 1989). Despite financing the activities of the APC, neither qualified accountants nor members of the public had any access to APC meetings, minutes or agenda papers though these were made freely available to major auditing firms, thus enabling them to shape the parameters of auditing standards. Some of the auditing standards encouraged auditors to undertake 'passive' auditing (Sikka, 1992) because it minimized audit effort, especially as auditors experienced difficulties in charging additional fees to client companies for additional audit work. Such standards and the influence of major firms on the APC eventually became a source of challenge to the legitimacy of the auditing profession (see below).

The profession also responded to the mid-1970s criticisms by selectively revising its ethical guidelines. The critical DTI reports revealed that in some cases, small auditing firms (DTI, 1981a) had been auditing major companies and deriving a considerable proportion of their income from a single client. Some observers argued that this reliance on one client for a large proportion of the income exerted pressure on auditors and compromised their independence. So the ethical guidelines suggested that auditors should not derive 15 per cent or more of their income from one audit client.[6] Some observers alleged that auditors had been securing favourable commercial transactions with client companies and this special relationship made it difficult for them to report objectively on company affairs (DTI, 1979a). So the guidelines urged that all transactions between auditors and client companies be on normal commercial terms. The auditors of Aveley Laboratories Limited (DTI, 1981b) were criticized for conflict of interests arising out of the acceptance of the office of receiver for their former client. So the guidelines urged auditors not to accept the position of receiver or liquidator where a 'continuing professional relationship' with a client already existed.

The DTI reports on Roadships Limited (DTI, 1976) and Burnholme and Forder Limited (DTI, 1979b) also commented on the influence of non-audit work on auditor independence. For example, the Roadships report concluded: 'We do not accept that there can be the requisite degree of watchfulness when a man is checking either his own figures or those of a colleague . . . for these reasons we do not believe that [the auditors] ever achieved the standards of independence necessary for a wholly objective audit' (DTI, 1976, paras. 249 and 250). The Burnholme and Forder report concluded that 'the principle of the auditor first compiling and then reporting upon a profit forecast is not considered to be a good practice for it may impair their ability to view the forecast objectively and must endanger the degree of independence essential to this work' (DTI, 1979b, p. 271). Any ban on auditors selling non-auditing services to their audit client has the potential to affect firm income and was inevitably resisted by major firms. So the ethical guidelines did not call for any curtailment. Instead, they just urged auditors to avoid conflicts of interest.

The collapse of the Grays Building Society (Registry of Friendly Societies, 1979) amidst a £7.1-million fraud spanning a period of forty years whilst the organization was audited by the same firm persuaded some to call for a compulsory rotation of an auditor's term in office. But the ethical guidelines did not include such proposals. In any case, there were no arrangements for monitoring, or enforcing firm compliance with any auditing standard or ethical guideline. Despite enjoying a statutory monopoly of the external audit function, auditors were not required to publish any information about their affairs. Nevertheless, by appealing to ethical behaviour and residues of professionalism, the profession sought to reassure its critics that it was putting its house in order. This strategy had little immediate cost to the firms or the profession generally.

In addition to introducing auditing standards and revising ethical guidelines, the profession sought to reform its disciplinary arrangements by the creation of the Joint Disciplinary Scheme (JDS). As one observer commented, 'The Department of Trade applied the thumbscrews in the aftermath of the financial scandals of the mid-seventies and the profession came up with the Joint Disciplinary Scheme' (*Accounting Bulletin*, August 1983, p. 10). Historically, the profession has taken a piecemeal approach to disciplining its members. Generally its machinery has been poorly financed as discipline for poor work has been something of an anathema to many practitioners who refute such charges. But in the aftermath of the secondary banking crisis the profession was anxious to provide an alternative to the state taking explicit powers to investigate and prosecute firms implicated in major scandals. Following the Cross Report (1977) and the Grenside Report (1979), the Joint Disciplinary Scheme, funded by the ICAEW, ICAS and the ACCA, was established. The declared objective of the JDS (as per its 1979 constitution) was to 'promote the highest possible standards of professional and business conduct, efficiency and competence ... by providing a system of investigation and regulation of activities of Members and Member Firms so as to secure their adherence to all professional criteria including but not limited to all relevant recommendations and standards promulgated'. The JDS also had lay observers in the hope that this would reassure critics who felt that the profession would hardly condemn one of its own.

In common with the APC, the JDS also came to be dominated by the partners of the very firms implicated in scandals (see, for example, *Accounting Bulletin*, March 1983, p. 9). The lack of financial support and the size of the firms implicated in various episodes meant that the JDS investigation took considerable time to finalize, fuelling suspicions of cover-ups. These became major issues in subsequent years (see below). By introducing machinery for standards, discipline and revision of ethical guidelines, the profession avoided any major institutional reform. However, many of these issues would reappear in subsequent years.

PRESSURES FROM THE UK AND OUTSIDE

Government policies

By the early 1980s the Conservative government had begun to implement its monetarist policies to squeeze inefficiency and inflation out of the economy. Many businesses collapsed and unemployment increased. There was no significant growth in audit business (*Accounting Bulletin*, October 1982, p. 4) though some of the slack was compensated for by extra revenues from the expanding insolvency business. In this environment accountancy firms engaged in aggressive advertising and fierce competition with one another, often undercutting the rival's audit fees ('lowballing'). Soon accounting and auditing provided less than half of the major firms' income (*Accounting Bulletin*, May 1985, p. 6). These trends were also assisted by the state's initiatives with cutting business (accounting) costs and promoting a 'leaner' UK economy. In this, accountancy firms were identified as 'key' advisers.

The government used auditing and accounting disciplines to promote a variety of policies. The public sector was disciplined by the promotion of 'Value for Money' (VFM) auditing (Humphrey, Miller and Scapens, 1993). The VFM philosophy was applied to health, education, transport and other sectors, with accountancy firms, in the vanguard. Following the Local Government Finance Act 1982, the local authority audit sector, previously closed to commercial auditing firms was opened to them. In return, auditing firms agreed to accept a statutory duty to detect and report material fraud to the regulators. The influence of accountancy firms also expanded in the financial sector where, following the Financial Services Act 1986, everyone had to be licensed and needed the services of an accountant. In its attempts to promote finance capital and present the 'City of London' as a clean international financial centre, the government gave financial sector auditors (under the Banking Act 1986, Building Societies Act 1986 and the Financial Services Act 1986) a 'right' to report fraud to the regulators (see Sikka *et al.*, 1992, for further details). Following the panic about rogue directors being able to conduct business through failed and fraudulent companies, the Insolvency Act 1986 granted a statutory monopoly of the insolvency function to accountants (Halliday and Carruthers, 1996). The government policy of privatizing utilities (e.g. gas, electricity, telecommunications, water) created a bonanza for the firms as they reported on profit forecasts and prospectuses and advised the government on suitable flotation prices.

European Union's Eighth Directive

In view of the government's dependency upon major accountancy firms for advancing its policies, a critical scrutiny of the profession was unlikely. However, new challenges were beginning to emerge from outside the UK. Following its accession to the European Union (EU) in 1973, Britain is obliged to implement (albeit with some flexibility) EU directives. The Eighth Directive dealt with regulation of auditors. It required that all auditors be licensed, monitored, disciplined and regulated by independent bodies. As a preparation for implementing the Eighth Directive, the government published proposals for regulating auditors (DTI, 1986). The consultative document raised the possibility of creating an independent body to regulate auditors. In addition, it suggested that, to enhance auditor independence, the sale of non-auditing services by auditors to their audit clients might need to be curtailed, a view publicly espoused by some prominent politicians (Heseltine, 1987).

The government proposals were not a serious threat to the profession as the government's policy of 'self regulation in a statutory framework'[7] was firmly established elsewhere. Nevertheless, the regulatory proposals drew a hostile response from some who preferred the accountancy bodies formally to exercise regulatory functions (Robson *et al.*, 1994). Others were uneasy about such proposals and felt the preservation of self-regulation in a statutory framework would create too many tensions between the accountancy bodies' traditional trade association role and the new explicit role of social regulators (*Accountancy Age*, December 1986, p. 1; *The Accountant*, 3 September 1986, p. 3). Major firms were opposed to any restriction on the sale of lucrative consultancy work (*Accountancy Age*, 23 October 1986, p. 1; Hanson, 1987). Major firms and professional bodies sought to mobilize their members and clients in opposing government proposals, by organizing conferences, favourable surveys and letters (*Accountancy Age*, 16 October

1988, p. 1). The ICAEW issued a soothing report[8] (ICAEW, 1986) defending the traditional privileges of the profession, but also promised reforms.

The organized campaign by major firms and the professional bodies succeeded in silencing the DTI's suggestions. Compliance with the Eighth Directive was secured through the implementation of the Companies Act 1989. To the dismay of auditing firms (*Financial Times*, 19 June 1991, p. 41; 28 September 1991, p. 4; *Independent on Sunday*, 6 October 1991, p. 11), the legislation required companies to disclose fees paid to auditors for non-auditing work, thus keeping alive the possible links between non-audit fees and auditor independence. The parliamentary proceedings also persuaded some Labour politicians to take considerable interest in accounting/auditing matters. The Party was not a keen supporter of self-regulation of accountants. In subsequent years some of its senior politicians mounted a substantial challenge to the profession (see below).

The role of the profession

Following the Companies Act 1989, five separate bodies – the ICAEW, the Chartered Association of Certified Accountants (ACCA), the Institute of Chartered Accountants of Scotland (ICAS), the Institute of Chartered Accountants in Ireland (ICAI) and the Association of Authorised Public Accountants[9] (AAPA) – became regulators and are known as the recognized supervisory bodies (RSBs). The RSB status can be revoked by the Secretary of State for Trade, who needs to be satisfied that the body has adequate auditing standards, rules on independence, ethical codes, procedures for maintaining and enforcing compliance with rules through regular monitoring and disciplinary arrangements. The RSBs also need to have adequate resources and arrangements for investigation of complaints. All RSBs are required to submit an annual report to the Secretary of State.

Only the individuals, firms or companies[10] licensed by one of the RSBs can describe themselves as auditors. To obtain a licence (or a practising certificate) the auditors need to agree to abide by all rules and regulations issued by the relevant RSB, including compulsory professional indemnity insurance. Only individuals holding a qualification from one of the recognized qualifying bodies (RQBs)[11] can apply for a licence. Recognition as an RQB is dependent upon meeting the statutory specified examination, qualification, entry and training requirements. For public information, each of the RSBs has to maintain a register of all authorized auditors. These rules and regulations supplemented the existing legislation (e.g. the Companies Act 1985) relating to auditor appointment, removal, resignation, duties and powers.

The Companies Act 1989 fundamentally changed the position of the accountancy bodies. They became an explicit arm of the state, performing both their traditional trade association role and a new regulatory role. These conflicting roles eventually became a source of tension and criticism (Smith, 1990). As a consequence of the Companies Act the profession also assumed responsibility for investigation of high-profile audit failures, primarily through the JDS. But suitable financial arrangements had not been made to meet these additional obligations and in due course this also became a source of problems (see below). The financial burdens would be considerable, especially as the RSBs could not agree on many things. Each had its own disciplinary, licensing and educational programmes. For some issues, such as audit monitoring, the ICAEW, ICAS and the ICAI agreed to operate jointly through Joint Monitoring Unit Limited (JMU), but the ACCA did not consider these to be appropriate and devised its own monitoring arrangements. The ACCA argued that its licensees would be subject to a monitoring visit at least once every five years whilst the ICAEW, ICAS and ICAI focused their attention on major company auditors, with small practitioners being monitored at random. The resources devoted to JMU suggested that it would take more than fifty years to ensure a monitoring visit to all practitioners (Sikka, Puxty and Willmott, 1992). This was not considered to be a problem, however, because 'the purpose of the visit was not primarily to improve the practices of the firm visited, but to improve the practices of the general population' (Moizer,[12] 1994, para. 4). The financial aspects and public criticisms would continue to be sources of problems. The profession hoped to continue formulating auditing standards through the APC, but further challenges were beginning to take shape.

THE CHALLENGING 1990s

Visibility of auditing firms

Fed by the rapid growth of consultancy, major firms became more aggressive in selling audits – which were seen as a key to securing access to senior management. Major firms' income from accounting/auditing (as a percentage of the total) continued to shrink (*The Accountant*, July 1990, p. 9; *Accountancy*, July 1992, p. 17; July 1993, p. 13). Concentration of audits also increased with the Big Eight firms auditing some 79 per cent of UK listed companies[13] (Beattie and Fearnley, 1994). They diversified into many other fields, ranging from executive recruitment, acting as expert witnesses, forensic accounting, public relations and even laundering money.[14] Firms also engaged in advice on creative accounting and rule avoidance (Smith, 1992). As a Coopers & Lybrand partner put it, 'there is an industry developing. and we are part of it, in rule avoidance' (*Accountancy Age*, July 1990, p. 1). In a stagnant auditing market the firms were faced with a simple dilemma – they could maintain their income by further commercializing their activities or risk being left behind as other groups continued to expand. In a fiercely competitive market trappings of professionalism seemed increasingly remote and irrelevant (Zeff, 1992).

The increasing reliance by the government on auditing-type technologies to regulate businesses and the public sector also led to an increase in the number of financial journalists devoted to reporting accounting stories. These journalists frequently wrote critical comments on accounting/auditing developments. At the same time a number of politicians, notably from the Labour

Party, were also taking more interest in the affairs of the profession. Against the prospects of greater scrutiny, auditing firms continued to lowball audits, often undercutting their rivals by as much as a third (*Accountancy Age*, 9 May 1991, p. 1; 23 May 1991, p. 1; 9 January 1992, p. 1). Some firms were offering free audits in the hope of picking up more lucrative consultancy work (*Accountancy Age*, 20 June 1991, p. 1; 24 October 1991, p. 1). In one case an audit tender by Price Waterhouse to secure the audit of Prudential became public knowledge. In this, Price Waterhouse offered a discount of £900,000 on a proposed audit fee of £2.3 million and a write-off of the £600,000 initial investment. The audit tender went on to say that the firm had 'an acknowledged track record in constructive accounting solutions. Our experience and expertise in financial reporting will enable us to contribute to your discussions on how best to present your results and balance sheet' (p. 2 of the Prudential audit tender).

Some wondered how firms could justify charging so little. Perhaps they were cutting corners or perhaps they were engaged in premature signing-off of audit reports (Willett and Page, 1996). Such concerns coincided with revelation of major frauds. Major businesses, such as the Bank of Credit and Commerce International (BCCI), Polly Peck, Atlantic Computers, Barlow Clowes, Dunsdale, International Signal and Control, Levitt, Maxwell and others, collapsed amid allegations of fraud and within a short time of receiving unqualified audit reports (County Natwest Woodmac, 1991; Mitchell *et al.*, 1991; Smith, 1992). Frauds raised questions about auditor efficiency and independence. The US Senate's investigation of BCCI (Kerry and Brown, 1992) alleged that auditor independence was compromised because auditors received loans, financial benefits, housing and other benefits from the bank. The reputation of the auditing industry was not enhanced when it was learnt that Coopers & Lybrand became joint receivers of Polly Peck even though the ethical guidelines stated that firms should not accept such a position where 'there is continuing professional relationship'. Coopers had audited some Polly Peck subsidiaries and acted as consultants to the company and its chairman. After a two-year campaign by journalists and Austin Mitchell MP, the ICAEW eventually fined partners £1,000 (the maximum permitted under the rules introduced in the 1970s) though the firm probably made £15–20 million from the receivership (Mitchell *et al.*, 1994).

The sudden death of Robert Maxwell and revelations of fraud also raised questions about auditors. In 1991 the Mirror Group of Newspapers was floated with the balance sheet showing shareholders' funds at £840 million. Some £625 million of this related to the titles of newspapers. The titles were valued by Coopers & Lybrand, who also reported on the prospectus and gave unqualified audit opinions on various accounts. Issues about auditor independence and regulation once again began to emerge. Major newspapers and magazines weighed in by adding comments (Sikka and Willmott, 1995a) such as 'The profession has never been less credible. It's seen to be accountable to no one' (*Time Magazine*, 16 March 1992, p. 62); 'People are extremely concerned about the way in which auditors are operating and the way in which the reports they produce are serving the public' (*Accountancy Age*, 12 December 1991, p. 1). Auditors' claims to independence were doubted (*Financial Times*, 4 October 1990, p. 24; *The Times*, 10 February 1992, p. 13). Self-regulation was considered to be flawed and unacceptable (*Guardian*, 27 September 1990, p. 11; *Observer*, 6 January 1991, p. 27; *The Economist*, 17 October 1992, pp. 25–8). Some argued that 'it's absolutely pointless for companies to employ auditors or, indeed, provide audited accounts' (*Independent on Sunday*, 6 October 1991, p. 11).

The profession's response

Previously, the profession sought to mediate the crisis by 're-presenting itself', appealing to notions of professionalism and through selective revision of ethical guidelines and restructuring disciplinary and standard-setting arrangements (see above) together with some soothing reports (e.g. ASSC, 1975; ICAEW, 1986). The same tactics were to be deployed again, with fairly mixed results. Unlike the 1970s crisis, this time the debate was joined and amplified by Labour politicians and some academics (see Sikka and Willmott, 1995a, for further details).

Following the Dearing Report (Dearing, 1988), accounting standards began to be formulated by the Accounting Standards Board (ASB), a body independent of the professional bodies (Turley, 1992). But there were no such plans for the APC and none were mentioned by the ministers or the profession during the debates on the Companies Act 1989. However, following criticisms of the APC by Opposition MPs during the parliamentary passage of the Companies Act 1989 (House of Commons, Standing Committee D, 13 June 1989, cols. 303–4, 310–13) and subsequent dissemination of the same through articles, meetings, parliamentary questions and letters to ministers (Mitchell, 1990a, 1990b), the profession (with prodding from the DTI) made hurried efforts to reform the APC (Sikka, 1994; Pong and Whittington, 1994). In April 1991, the APC was replaced by the Auditing Practices Board (APB), which could issue auditing standards under its own authority. The APB remained under the control of the professional bodies, but half its voting power now rested with non-practitioners. The APB does not hold 'open' meetings, but the public has access to its agenda papers. The continuing criticisms of the APB and the profession's apparent influence on auditing standards have encouraged calls for independent regulation. The profession and its patrons have sought to deflect such criticism by once again issuing soothing reports (Auditing Practices Board, 1992, 1994; Committee on the Financial Aspects of Corporate Governance, 1992) which promise reforms, but more importantly blame directors for auditing problems. In due course, the APB may also slip away from the profession's control and operate independently in a manner similar to that of the ASB (*Accountancy Age*, 29 August 1996, p. 2).

Following the Maxwell revelations ethical guidelines have been revised, forbidding auditors to report on asset valuations which their firms had created. Following the Polly Peck episode insolvency practitioners are now advised not to accept work if there is a 'material professional relationship' with the client. In future, argued the ICAEW, there would be unlimited fines for violation of ethical guidelines. But auditors have not been urged to owe a 'duty of care' to any individual stakeholder. There is no requirement for them to publish any meaningful information about their affairs.

On the disciplinary front, ever since its creation the JDS has been struggling to fulfil its promises. In 1984 it took 384 days to complete an inquiry and publish a report. With increasing burdens and complexity of cases, it reached 1,110 days in 1987. To secure its RSB status, the profession had to agree to investigate and report on the audits of high-profile company failures and frauds. This further exacerbated the crisis. The JDS sought to investigate the role of Price Waterhouse audits in the closure of BCCI (*Observer*, 6 June 1993, p. 26), but Price Waterhouse applied to the courts for judicial review on the ground that any action by the JDS could prejudice the outcome of negligence lawsuits which it was facing. Price Waterhouse's application was granted (*Accountancy*, June 1994, p. 14) and to date there has been no official inquiry into the adequacy of the BCCI's UK audits. In some cases the JDS has investigated and reported on alleged audit failures. An example of this is the 1996 JDS report on the fraud at International Signal Corporation (part of Ferranti) which exonerated KPMG. The cost of the inquiry came to more than £500,000. With internationalization of businesses and firms, any investigation by the profession will be costly and time consuming and requires additional financial resources. The financial demands have exposed tensions among the JDS's sponsoring bodies. With escalating costs, the ACCA has withdrawn from the JDS (*Accountancy Age*, 11 January 1996, p. 1), though at the time of writing negotiations about restructuring the financial arrangements are taking place (*Accountancy Age*, 16 May 1996, p. 1).

A campaign to end self-regulation for auditors has also been building up (Mitchell *et al.*, 1993). The credibility of self-regulation received a further jolt when, despite the ICAEW position that auditor duties are best clarified by auditing standards and professional pronouncements, Lord Justice Bingham's inquiry into the closure of BCCI concluded: 'Determination of the correct relationship between client, auditors and supervisor [i.e. the regulator] raises an issue of policy more appropriate for decision by parliament than by the Bank [i.e. the Bank of England, which is responsible for regulating banks] and the accounting profession' (Bingham, 1992, p. 189). Despite opposition from the ICAEW, Lord Justice Bingham recommended that auditors should have a 'statutory duty' (unlike the previous position where they had only a 'right') to report fraud to the financial sector (i.e. banks, insurance companies, financial services, pension funds) regulators, even without client knowledge. The proposal was accepted by the government (*Hansard*, 6 November 1992, cols. 523–94) and duly legislated (*Hansard*, 15 February 1994, cols. 852–75).

Critics have pointed out that the monitoring and regulatory regime introduced by the Companies Act 1989 is concerned with compliance with rules rather than improvements in audit quality. As the ACCA's 1992 annual report to the DTI on auditor regulation states, 'the main purpose of practice monitoring is to monitor compliance with auditing standards, rather than to obtain statistical information about the quality of work being done' (p. 25). The three chartered bodies (ICAEW, ICAS and ICAI) state that 'The principal purpose of monitoring is to enable the ARCs [Audit Registration Committees] to satisfy themselves that registered auditors comply with the Audit Regulations' (p. 5 of the 1992 ICAEW, ICAS and ICAI annual report on Audit Regulation). Audit monitoring is unpopular with many small practitioners as they have to give up their fee-earning time to explain their conduct (*Accountancy Age*, 26 September 1996, pp. 20–3). The disruption and costs are considerable. For example, Moizer (1994, paras. 9, 50 and 80) estimated that, in 1993, the average number of chargeable days (i.e. the time spent with inspectors as well as preparing for the visit) lost per monitoring visit is 8.8. for the JMU regime and 1.8 for the ACCA regime. In 1993 the total chargeable days lost by practitioners amounted to 3,731. The audit monitoring regime resulted in direct costs of £3,645,000 in 1993 (Moizer, 1994, p. 2) and are expected to rise. Despite the economic costs borne by the practitioners, the RSB operations remain under critical scrutiny because they are not obliged publicly to identify the firms who fare badly in monitoring visits. In addition, the RSBs do not owe an explicit 'duty of care' to their members or the public.

Concerned with recurring criticisms and disquiet of their members, the accountancy bodies have been putting forward various proposals. Under these proposals, professional bodies would retain their Companies Act 1989 role, but would report to a new umbrella body (possibly known as the Review Board) responsible for overseeing their conduct (Swinson, 1995, 1996). This body would not be statutory, but may be given powers to report on the conduct of the RSBs. Such proposals have failed to draw unanimous support from major firms (*Accountancy Age*, 6 July 1995, p. 15). Calls for ending self-regulation have been supported by some major firms and their partners (Llambias, 1995; Roques, 1996; *Accountancy*, June 1995, p. 15) who see self-regulation simply as a means to an end. They feel that public confidence in auditing is unlikely to be restored until auditors are seen to be regulated by bodies independent of the profession.

CONCLUDING COMMENTS

Since the mid-1970s auditors have been subjected to increased formal regulation. Some of the regulations have been the unforeseen outcome of government policies and attempts to manage recurring economic crises. Often the crises have given visibility to the deficiencies in audits and the profession – with support and encouragement from the state – has been obliged to 're-present' itself through the introduction/revision of auditing standards and ethical and disciplinary arrangements.

Following the EU's Eighth Directive, the role of the accountancy bodies has been changed. They now function as both trade associations and public regulators. Inevitably there are tensions. The profession has retained considerable autonomy, but within a statutory framework. Indeed, under the Companies Act 1989 the Secretary of State retains powers to create an independent body for regulating auditors. The present regulatory arrangements have a number of attractions. They offer a kind of political insurance to ministers and civil servants, who in a crisis situation can always 'pass the buck' to the profession (or the RSBs) and escape direct public criticism. By passing the responsibility for licensing, monitoring and investigating auditors to the RSBs the state is also making some savings for the public purse. To some traditionalists, the profession is distinguished from others by ethical codes, standards and disciplinary arrangements for its members. The RSB status conferred upon the accountancy bodies seems to satisfy them. This then leaves the profession open to criticisms from its members for inadequately performing its traditional trade association role and from external critics for failing to perform adequately its public regulatory role. One possibility is that audit standards setting, discipline, licensing and monitoring will slip away from the profession, leaving it to concentrate on its trade association activities, but traditionalists are unhappy, though major firms seem fairly relaxed about this. With the state resisting direct involvement in auditing issues a search for some half-way arrangement (see Swinson, 1995, 1996) is likely. Such arrangements, however, will continue to encounter considerable public scepticism and are unlikely to be durable.

NOTES

1. Small and dormant companies are exempt from compulsory external audits.
2. *The Accountant* was the first English-language weekly accountancy magazine. It frequently contained articles on contemporary accounting and auditing problems by leading practitioners.
3. These were often known as 'U' statements as they formed part of section U in the ICAEW handbook.
4. 'Recommendations on Accounting Principles' began in 1942 and were often known as 'N' statements.
5. Some support for this position is evident from *Lloyd Cheyham & Co* v. *Littlejohn & Co.* [1987] **BCLC** 303(reported in *Accountancy*, February 1986).
6. Such a requirement was unlikely adversely to affect major firms since they were unlikely to derive a large part of their income from one client.
7. This was advocated by Professor Jim Gower (Gower, 1984).
8. The profession has a history of issuing soothing reports at times of crisis. For example, *The Corporate Report* (Accounting Standards Steering Committee, 1975) was issued to placate concerns about accounting practices. Having appeased and disarmed critics, the report was quietly shelved.
9. The AAPA is a small body of about 870 members of whom 500 are auditors. Its licensing, monitoring and other arrangements are handled by the ACCA (*Certified Accountant*, June 1996, p. 15).
10. Prior to the Companies Act 1989 bodies corporate could not become auditors. This has since been changed and auditors can form and operate through limited liability companies.
11. These are essentially the major accountancy bodies.

12. In October 1993 Professor Peter Moizer was asked by the DTI to review the operation of the RSBs' procedures for audit monitoring. His report was submitted to the DTI in February 1994, but has not been published. A copy is held in the House of Commons library.
13. All of the FT 100 companies are audited by Bix Six firms (*The Times*, 5 September 1996, p. 27).
14. See the High Court case of *AGIP (Africa) Limited* v. *Jackson & Co.* [1990] 1 Ch. 265 and *AGIP (Africa) Limited* v. *Jackson & Co.* [1991] 1 Ch. 547.

REFERENCES

Accounting Standards Steering Committee (1975) *The Corporate Report*, ICAEW, London.

Auditing Practices Board (1992) *The Future Development of Auditing*, APB, London.

Auditing Practices Board (1994) *The Audit Agenda*, APB, London.

Auditing Practices Committee (1978) *True & Fair*, No. 10, Winter, APC, London.

Beattie, V. and Fearnely, S. (1994). The changing structure of the market for audit services in the UK – a descriptive study, *British Accounting Review*, Vol. 26, no. 4, pp. 301–22.

Bingham, The Honourable Lord Justice (1992) *Inquiry into the Supervision of the Bank of Credit and Commerce International*, HMSO, London.

Clarke, M. (1986) *Regulating the City*, Open University, Milton Keynes.

Coakley, J. and Harris, L. (1983) *The City of Capital*, Basil Blackwell, Oxford.

Committee on the Financial Aspects of Corporate Governance (1992) *Report of the Committee on the Financial Aspects of Corporate Governance*, Gee, London.

County Natwest Woodmac (1991) *Company Pathology, Equity Briefing Paper 7*; County Natwest Woodmac, London.

Cross Report (1977) *Report of a Committee under the Chairmanship of the Rt. Hon. Lord Cross of Chelsea, Accountancy*, December, pp. 80–6.

Dearing, Sir Ron (1988) *The Making of Accounting Standards*, ICAEW, London.

Department of Trade and Industry (1976) *Roadships Limited*, HMSO, London.

Department of Trade and Industry (1979a) *Peachey Property Corporation Limited*, HMSO, London.

Department of Trade and Industry (1979b) *Burnholme and Forder Limited; Brayhead Limited*, HMSO, London.

Department of Trade and Industry (1981a) *Kina Holdings*, HMSO, London.

Department of Trade and Industry (1981b) *Aveley Laboratories Limited*, HMSO, London.

Department of Trade and Industry (1986) *Regulation of Auditors: Implementation of the EC Eighth Company Law Directive*, DTI, London.

Dicksee, L. R. (1892) *Auditing: A Practical Manual for Auditors*, Gee, London.

Gower, J. (1984) *Review of Investor Protection*/Cmnd 9125/HMSO, London.

Grenside Report (1979) *Report of the Joint Committee Appointed to Consider the Cross Report and Related Matters, Accountancy*, June, pp. 124–32.

Gwilliam, D. (1987) *A Survey of Auditing Research*, ICAEW/Prentice-Hall, London.

Halliday, T. C. and Carruthers, B. G. (1996) The moral regulation of markets: professions, privatization and the English Insolvency Act 1986, *Accounting, Organizations and Society*, Vol. 21, no. 4, pp. 371–413.

Hanson, D. (1987) Unilateral declaration of independence, *Accountancy*, March, p. 18.

Heseltine, M. (1987), *Where There's a Will*, Hutchinson, London.

Humphrey, C., Miller, P. and Scapens, R. (1993) Accountability and accountable management in the public sector, *Accounting, Auditing & Accountability Journal*, pp. 7–29.

Institute of Chartered Accountants in England and Wales (1986) *A Report of the Working Party on the Future of Audit*, ICAEW, London.

Kerry, J. and Brown, H. (1992) *The BCCI Affair*, US Government Printing Office, Washington.

Llambias, D. (1995) English ICA deluding itself on self-regulation, *Accountancy Age*, 5 October, p. 18.

Mitchell, A. (1990a) Learning how to act in the public interest, *Accountancy Age*, 18 October, pp. 22–3.

Mitchell, A. (1990b) Auditing – last bastion of the closed shop, *Accountancy*, November, pp. 21–2.

Mitchell, A., Puxty, T., Sikka, P. and Willmott, H. (1991) *Accounting for Change: Proposals for Reform of Audit and Accounting*, Fabian Society, London.

Mitchell, A., Puxty, T., Sikka, P. and Willmott, H. (1993) *A Better Future for Auditing*, University of East London.

Mitchell, A., Puxty, T., Sikka, P. and Willmott, H. (1994) Ethical statements as smokescreens for sectional interests: the case of the UK accountancy profession, *Journal of Business Ethics*, Vol. 13, no. 1, pp. 39–51.

Moizer, P. (1994) *Review of Recognised Supervisory Bodies: A Report to the Department of Trade and Industry on the Audit Monitoring Process*, Department of Trade and Industry, London.

Pong, C. and Whittington, G. (1994) The working of the Auditing Practices Committee – three case studies, *Accounting and Business Research*, Vol. 24, no. 94, pp. 157–75.

Registry of Friendly Societies (1979) *Grays Building Society*, HMSO, London.

Reid, M. (1982) *The Secondary Banking Crisis 1973–1975: Its Causes and Courses*, Macmillan, Basingstoke.

Robson, K. (1991) On the arenas of accounting change: the process of translation, *Accounting, Organizations and Society*, pp 547–61.

Robson, K., Willmott, H., Cooper, D. and Puxty, T. (1994) The ideology of professional regulation and markets for accounting labour: three episodes in the recent history of the UK accountancy profession, *Accounting, Organizations and Society*, Vol. 19, no. 6, pp. 527–53.

Roques, J. (1996) Who will audit the auditors? *The Times*, 22 February, p. 28.

Sikka, P. (1992) Audit policy-making in the UK: the case of 'the auditor's considerations in respect of going concern', *European Accounting Review*, December, pp. 349–92.

Sikka, P. (1994) Politics of restructuring the regulatory sites of accountancy: the transition from the Auditing Practices Committee into the Auditing Practices Board, *Proceedings of the Fourth Interdisciplinary Perspectives on Accounting Conference*, University of Manchester, July, Vol. 2, no. 13, pp. 13.1–17.

Sikka, P. and Willmott, H. (1995a) The power of 'independence': defending and extending the jurisdiction of accounting in the United Kingdom, *Accounting, Organizations and Society*, Vol. 20, no. 6, pp. 547–81.

Sikka, P. and Willmott, H. (1995b) Illuminating the state–profession relationship: accountants acting as Department of Trade and Industry investigators, *Critical Perspectives on Accounting*, Vol. 6, no. 4, pp. 341–69.

Sikka, P., Puxty, T. and Willmott, H. (1992) Watchdogs must be forced to bark, *The Times*, 19 March, p. 33.

Sikka, P., Willmott, H. and Lowe, T. (1989) Guardians of knowledge and public interest: evidence and issues of accountability in the UK accountancy profession, *Accounting, Auditing and Accountability Journal*, Vol. 2, no. 2, pp. 47–71.

Sikka, P., Puxty, T., Willmott, H. and Cooper, C., (1992). *Eliminating the Expectations Gap?*, Certified Research Report No. 28, Chartered Association of Certified Accountants, London.

Smith, Terry (1992) *Accounting for Growth; Stripping the Camouflage from Company Accounts*, Century Business, London.

Smith, Tim (1990) One supervisory body to serve the public interest, *Accountancy Age*, 3 May, p. 16.

Swinson, C. (1995). *Interim Report of the Regulation Review Working Party*, ICAEW, London.

Swinson, C. (1996) *Regulation – A Way Forward*, ICAEW, London.

Turley, S. (1992) Developments in the structure of financial reporting regulation in the United Kingdom, *European Accounting Review*, Vol. 1, no. 1, pp. 105–22.

Willett, C. and Page, M. (1996) A survey of time budget pressure and irregular auditing practices among newly qualified UK chartered accountants, *British Accounting Review*, June, pp. 101–20.

Willmott, H. C. (1986) Organizing the profession: a theoretical and historical examination of the development of the major accountancy bodies in the UK, *Accounting, Organizations and Society*, Vol. 11, no. 6, pp. 555–80.

Wilson Committee (1978) *Committee to Review the Functioning of Financial Institutions: Interim Report*, Cmnd 7503, HMSO, London.

Woolf, E. (1983) Banks: the substance and the form, *Accountancy*, September, pp. 99–102.

Zeff, S. (1992) The decline of professionalism, *De Accountant*, pp. 264–7.

DISCUSSION QUESTIONS

1. Describe the ways in which auditors have formally been regulated.
2. Earlier parts of this chapter suggested that the profession has been mediating auditing crises by decoupling accounting from auditing and that accounting has usually been blamed for audit failures. What are your views on such a proposition? Support your views with press clippings and/or other analysis.
3. Discuss the role played by the state in regulating auditors.
4. 'Issuing soothing reports, revising standards setting, disciplinary and ethical arrangements is a tried and trusted way of mediating auditing crises.' Discuss.
5. A public meeting has been organized to consider whether auditors should be regulated by a body independent of the profession and the Department of Trade and Industry. After listening to various speakers you have been asked to summarize the main arguments and the issues. Provide your summary.
6. Self-regulation is imaginary. The auditing profession owes its existence to the policies of the state and has always been regulated by the state. Discuss.

8

Audit Markets in the European Union: Regulation in Belgium, Germany and the Netherlands

Roger Meuwissen and Steven Maijoor

INTRODUCTION

Although most of the chapters in this book look primarily at auditing in the United Kingdom, several refer to the variation that can be found between different countries in the roles that auditing serves and how those roles are enforced. International differences are apparent in, for example, the chapters dealing with expectations, fraud and reporting. In this chapter international variation in auditing is considered more explicitly through a comparative analysis of the regulation of audit markets in three European Union countries: Belgium, Germany and the Netherlands.

Markets characterized by substantial information asymmetry are often subjected to extensive regulation (see e.g. Sappington and Stiglitz, 1987). This applies to most markets for professional services and certainly to markets for auditing services. The regulation of professional services can take various forms. Some regulations are designed to protect the users of professional services, whereas others would seem to protect the suppliers. Regulations intended to protect users aim at maintaining the quality of professional services and the integrity of suppliers. However, such regulations will also place costs on users if they restrict competition. Competition is regarded as an efficient method of allocating resources since it encourages service providers to deliver their services in a cost-effective, efficient and innovative way.

Regulations restricting competition, for example through entry requirements, protect the suppliers of professional services. Hence, there is always a trade-off between the aim to provide protection to users and the aim to eliminate anti-competitive practices (see e.g. Beales, 1980). This trade-off is apparently also considered by policy-makers at a European Union level. On the one hand, European audit markets are regulated, for example by audit requirements (e.g. as a result of the Fourth Directive) and auditor education requirements (as a result of the Eighth Directive). On the other hand, concerns have been expressed by European policy-makers regarding the competitiveness of audit markets (see NERA, 1992; MARC, 1996).

The purpose of this chapter is to provide an overview of the regulation of the auditing professions in Belgium, Germany and the Netherlands. In addition, it attempts to outline the effects of this regulation on competition in the markets for auditing services in the three countries covered. This analysis can contribute to our understanding of the consequences of alternative regulatory regimes for the functioning of audit markets. Since regulation influences the conduct in a market, differences in regulation are expected to have a differential impact on the nature of competition.

The economic effects of regulation on audit markets are frequently discussed in the literature (see e.g. Benston, 1985; Wallace, 1987; Maijoor and Van Witteloostuijn, 1996). According to Benston (1985, p. 53), auditors might benefit from regulation in three respects: (1) the erection of barriers to entry, (2) an increased demand for audit services, and (3) the reduction of negative externalities from free-riders. Barriers to entry include, for example, the licensing requirements of auditors (see e.g. Pound and Francis, 1981). Strict educational requirements impede potential competitors' entry to the audit market and thereby limit competition. Furthermore, auditors benefit from regulations imposing an audit requirement for certain types of entity. Such a requirement increases the demand for audit services, and decreases the price elasticity of audit services (see e.g. Eichenseher and Danos, 1981; Maijoor, 1994). Moreover, by introducing auditing standards the audit profession reduces problems resulting from a lower level of performance by some auditors. By imposing sanctions on auditors who do not meet the required auditing standards, the auditing profession is able to protect its reputation. Maintaining user confidence benefits the consumers of auditing services by providing them with a minimum level of auditing quality. However, such auditing standards can go further than protecting users of auditing services. In particular, rules restricting entry to the profession and rules restricting advertising, unsolicited offerings of services and fee-setting are regarded as anti-competitive. The regulatory overview presented in this chapter will focus on those differences in regulation which are expected to have the most profound impact on competition in audit markets. For a more extensive and detailed overview of the laws and regulations regarding auditing in the three countries see, for example, MARC (1996).

The chapter proceeds as follows. The next three sections describe, respectively, the auditing laws and regulations in Belgium, the German regulatory framework, and the laws and regulations of the Dutch audit market. Each of these three sections on national auditing laws and regulations contains an overview of the auditing profession, and covers admission, appointment procedures, independence and liability. The subsequent section discusses the potential effects of the regulatory regimes on the three audit markets covered in this chapter, which then concludes with a summary and some conclusions.

AUDIT MARKET REGULATION IN BELGIUM

Overview of the Belgian auditing profession

The Belgian accounting and auditing profession is organized in two main bodies: the Institut des Reviseurs d'Entreprises/Instituut der Bedrijfsrevisoren (Institute of Auditors) and the Institut des Experts Comptables/Instituut der Accountants (Institute of Chartered Accountants). According to the Act of 21 February 1985, only members of the Institute of Auditors, called *reviseurs d'entreprises/bedrijfsrevisoren*, are eligible to conduct statutory audits. Members of the Institute of Chartered Accountants are not authorized to carry out statutory audits. However, they were given a joint monopoly, shared with *reviseurs d'entreprises/bedrijfsrevisoren*, with respect to contractual audits and other inspection services regarding financial matters.

The 1985 Act encompassed a legislative reform of the auditing profession. The two main forces behind this 1985 reform were the implementation of the Fourth EEC Directive, requiring public and private limited liability companies of a certain size to have their annual accounts audited, and a political agreement on the auditor's obligation to provide workers' councils with the same information as shareholders. In addition, workers' councils obtained the right to veto the appointment of an auditor. Other aims of the legislative reform were to provide auditors with more flexibility in matters of establishment of partnerships and in matters of incompatible activities, and to give chartered accountants their own separate professional organization.

Reviseurs d'entreprises/bedrijfsrevisoren are required to be members of the Institut des Reviseurs d'Entreprises/Instituut der Bedrijfsrevisoren, the professional body which also acts as the regulatory body of the Belgian auditing profession. The profession is under the supervision of the Ministry of Economic Affairs and is assisted in this respect by the High Council for Audit and Accountancy. The main function of a *reviseur d'entreprises/bedrijfsrevisor* is to carry out assignments that are reserved by law for members of the profession, primarily the conduct of statutory audits. In addition, they may perform compatible assignments, such as other inspection tasks (reviewing annual accounts of companies), and may provide consultancy services in accountancy. Nevertheless, these compatible assignments may not form the core services supplied by the auditors. A peculiarity of the Belgian regulations is that auditors are required to have a special licence from the prudential control authorities to be eligible to perform statutory audits of entities under prudential control, like banks, insurance companies and listed companies.

Current audit market regulation[1]

Admission to the profession

In Belgium entry to the profession is regulated by the Royal Decree of 13 October 1987. This application of this Royal Decree is entrusted to the Board of the Institute of Auditors. This Board delegated the supervision of the education of the Belgian auditing profession to the Training Committee, composed exclusively of members of the Board.

In Belgium training for the profession is organized by means of a three-year practical course. In order to be admitted to this traineeship the candidate should fulfil the following conditions – he or she:

(1) should be of Belgian nationality or reside in Belgium;
(2) must not have been deprived of political and civil rights, not be bankrupt and not have been convicted of specific types of offence defined by law;
(3) must have a university degree, or an equivalent foreign university degree, or have a degree of a higher school of vocational training plus five years' practical training or two years' experience as a chartered accountant;
(4) needs to pass the entrance examination; and
(5) must have drawn up an agreement for a traineeship with a supervisor, who has to be an auditor of at least five years' standing.[2]

The entrance examination is organized by the Training Committee and covers a wide range of subjects.[3] Candidates with a university education can obtain exemptions from some or all subjects of the entrance examination if they have already passed those subjects during their university education. Currently, Belgian universities adapt some of their courses to the entrance examination requirements of the Belgian Institute of Auditors to provide candidates with the opportunity to obtain exemptions from the entrance examination. These university courses must be approved by the Training Committee.

During the traineeship candidates are guided by their supervisor, and the Training Committee will supervise the progress of the trainees. Candidates are required to gain at least three years' practical experience in auditing and need to attend several advanced courses. In the first year of practical training there are advanced courses in company law, consolidation, financial accounting law, financial statement analysis and bookkeeping techniques. In the second year candidates are required to follow advanced courses in internal auditing, external auditing and special audit topics. In the second year of the practical training candidates also need to write a paper on a required subject. In the third year of practical training candidates need to attend an advanced course in auditing, and an advanced course in professional conduct.

At the end of the three-year period the Training Committee reviews the practical training. When the Committee decides that the candidate has fulfilled all the traineeship requirements he or she is eligible for the final examination. This examination consists of both a written and an oral part. Although the Training Committee organizes advanced courses and tests, and supervises the record of practical training, the main part of the preparation for the final examination consists of self-study. When a candidate meets all the obligations mentioned above, he or she will be sworn in to become a *reviseur d'entreprises/bedrijfsrevisor*.

Appointment procedure

Auditors are formally appointed by (a majority vote of) the shareholders at the annual general meeting. However, the appointment may be subject to approval by a party other than that appointing the auditor. If an entity has a workers' council, this body is entitled to approve the appointment of the auditor. Further, the supervisory agency for companies subject to prudential control (e.g. banks, insurance companies and listed companies) is also entitled to approve the appointment of the auditor. The period of appointment is fixed for three fiscal years, and is renewable without limitation for periods of three years. Audit firms face restrictions on advertising and the unsolicited offering of services. In Belgium all forms of advertising to the public in general are forbidden. Advertising on a local scale, if factual and objective, is permitted, however. Furthermore, all forms of unsolicited offerings of services are prohibited.

Auditor independence

The most important part in the code of ethics concerns independence, and can be subdivided into regulations to protect independence in general, and rules on independence regarding a particular client. The general legal guidelines with respect to independence prohibit an auditor from being employed outside the auditing profession. Hence, Belgian auditors will lose their licence if they accept employment outside the profession. Auditors are also forbidden to engage in activities that are incompatible with the dignity or independence of the profession.

Independence with respect to a particular client is based on the principle that auditors should refuse to accept an engagement if they:

(1) have been a director or manager of that client in the past three years;
(2) have a personal relationship with the client;
(3) have a commercial relationship with the client;
(4) have a financial interest in the client;
(5) render non-audit services to the client which could question their independence; and/or
(6) become dependent, with regard to fee income, on particular clients.

With respect to non-audit services, audit firms are not allowed to provide other services to an audit client within the same legal entity. In Belgium, however, audit firm networks provide services other than audit services through separate legal entities.

The professional body has wide powers to monitor its members. First, auditors are required to report the number of hours and the fees for all audits to the professional body, which reviews the adequacy of the audit fee and the audit hours spent. This requirement specifically aims at prohibiting low-balling. Secondly, audit firms are subject to a peer review at least once every five years.

Auditor liability

In general, legal actions against the auditor can be undertaken by the audi-tee, its shareholders and any involved third party. The interaction between the auditee's and auditor's liability positions is determined by the liability allocation regime. Belgium has adopted a system of proportional liability, where the liability is placed upon the defendants according to their contri-bution to the damage.

In Belgium it is not possible to reduce the auditor's liability. There is no legal liability cap, that is, a cap which reduces the auditor's liability in cases where auditors are exposed to civil liability at the suit of the other contract party (the auditee), or in cases where auditors together with the auditee are exposed to civil liability in an action initiated by the shareholders or any involved third party. It is also not possible to arrange a contractual liability cap to reduce the auditor's liability to the other contract party (the auditee). A contractual liability cap is not relevant in cases where auditors and audit-tee together are sued by shareholders or any involved third party, since these parties are not contract parties.

Furthermore, the choice of legal form of an audit firm may influence the auditor's liability. In Belgium audit firms can choose between the private lim-ited liability company, (general) partnership and co-operative society. Audit firms cannot be organized in the form of a public limited liability company.

AUDIT MARKET REGULATION IN GERMANY

Overview of the German auditing profession

In Germany two types of auditors are allowed to perform statutory audits: *Wirtschaftsprüfer* and *vereidigte Buchprüfer*. They do not possess equal rights with respect to the provision of audit services. *Wirtschaftsprüfer* are entitled to conduct all statutory audits, whereas *vereidigte Buchprüfer* are allowed to conduct statutory audits of medium-sized private limited liability companies only. German law requires both *Wirtschaftsprüfer* and *vereidigte Buchprüfer* to be members of the Chamber of Auditors (Wirtschaftsprüferkammer), which is a public-law entity charged with disciplinary control over the pro-fession. The Chamber is under the supervision of the Federal Ministry of Commerce and also in the individual states, of the Ministry's state counter-parts. The Chamber of Auditors regulates many aspects of the German audit-ing profession and is supported in this respect by the Institute of Auditors

(Institut der Wirstchaftsprüfer), a voluntary organization of auditors and audit firms.[4] This Institute is involved principally in technical matters and enacts compulsory guidelines for its members.

According to the Act Regulating the Profession of Auditors (Act of 24 July 1961: *Wirtschaftsprüferordnung vom 24 juli 1961*), all auditors need to work in public practice. They can work either as a sole practitioner, as a partner in or employee of an audit firm, or for certain associations of auditors (*genossenschaftliche Prüfungsverbände, Prüfungsstellen von Sparkassen- und Giroverbänden, überortliche Prüfungseinrichtungen für öffentliche Körperschaften und Anstalten*). In public practice the principal task of an auditor is to audit annual accounts, to provide tax services and to render management consultancy services. Auditors are also allowed to accept assignments with respect to trustee management and expert reporting if these activities are compatible with their work as an auditor. The influence of taxation matters on the German auditing profession is considerable. For example, most auditors are also qualified as tax advisers, and taxation matters form a considerable part of the educational programmes for qualifying as an auditor.

Current audit market regulation[5]

Admission to the profession

Under German law, as embodied in the Act of 24 July 1961, candidates are eligible for inclusion as an auditor on the professional register of the Chamber of Auditors when they have passed the German auditor examination. Although the German federal government prescribes the syllabus for the auditor examination, the individual states grant the *Wirtschaftsprüfer* qualification to successful candidates. The qualification granted by one state is equally legitimate in other German states. The course of study leading to the *Wirtschaftsprüfer* qualification consists mainly of self-study. The Chamber of Auditors does not offer an educational programme, and universities do not organize postgraduate programmes. Only the Insititute of Auditors and some private educational institutes or individual professors offer some courses to prepare for the final auditor examination.

The typical course of preliminary training for candidates wishing to commence training for the *Wirtschaftsprüfer* qualification is a university degree in business administration. Other academic studies acknowledged as preliminary training are (business) economics, engineering, law and other studies with an accent on business matters. After their academic training candidates are required to undertake a five-year practical training period. Within this period candidates need to work at least four years in auditing practice.

In addition to this academic route there are three other avenues for candidates to become eligible to sit for the auditor examination. The first of these is to qualify as a tax adviser (*Steuerberater*) or *vereidigter Buchprüfer*. In addition, a total period of five to about nine years' practical training is required. The candidates need to have worked as a tax adviser or *vereidigter*

Buchprüfer for at least five years, and to have at least four years' experience in auditing. The second alternative is to qualify as a tax adviser or *vereidigter Buchprüfer*, and to have worked as such for at least fifteen years. The third is to have worked for an audit firm for at least ten years, and to have spent at least four years working in auditing. So, the total period of practical training involved in this alternative is anything from ten to fourteen years.

After the period of practical training candidates are eligible to sit for the auditor examination. During the practical training candidates are not required to follow courses. Preparation for the final examination consists for the most part of self-study, although candidates can follow some courses at the Institute of Auditors. These courses include most subjects of the auditor examination.[6] The admission to the auditor examination will be granted by the Admittance Committee of the region where the candidate is professionally established or is practising.[7] According to the 1961 Act, the Federal Ministry of Economic Affairs is responsible for conducting the auditor examination. It delegates this task to the individual states. Each state establishes an examination board, which conducts the actual examination. Although the examinations are organized by the individual states, they are intended to have a uniform level. When a candidate successfully completes the examination he or she will be appointed as an auditor after he or she takes an oath.

Appointment procedure

Auditors are formally appointed by (a majority vote of) the shareholders at the annual general meeting. However, the appointment is subject to approval by the supervisory authority for banks (Bundesaufsichtsambt für das Kreditwesen) in the case of banks and that for insurance companies (Bundesaufsichtsambt für das Versicherungswesen) in the case of insurance companies. In contrast with Belgium, there is no fixed period with respect to the term of the auditor's appointment. German audit firms face restrictions on advertising and unsolicited offering of services. All forms of advertising and unsolicited offerings are forbidden. However, an auditor may use the name of his or her firm in academic articles, speeches and seminars.

Auditor independence

As in Belgium there are independence guidelines prohibiting an auditor from being employed outside the auditing profession. Hence, German auditors will lose their licence when becoming so employed. Furthermore, there are a number of regulations on independence with respect to a particular client. These regulations state that auditors should refuse to accept an engagement if they:

(1) have a personal relationship with the client;
(2) have a commercial relationship with the client;
(3) have a financial interest in the client;

(4) render non-audit services which could question their independence; and/or

(5) become dependent, in terms of fee income, on particular clients.

With respect to non-audit services, audit firms are not allowed to provide bookkeeping services to an audit client. Other services may be provided to an audit client within the same legal entity. With respect to the monitoring of audit fees, in Germany there are no explicit regulations on the calculation of audit fees, although auditors are obliged to charge a fair and reasonable fee. Furthermore, audit firms are not required to undergo peer reviews.

Auditor liability

In Germany legal actions against the auditor can be undertaken by the auditee, but not by the shareholders or any involved third party. Furthermore, liability can be capped by law or by contract. There is a legal liability cap, which applies only in cases where auditors are exposed to civil liability initiated by the other contract party (the auditee). The cap is DM 500,000. A contractual liability cap may also be arranged in such cases but may not exceed the legal liability cap. The two caps are applicable only to contract parties since it is not possible for auditors and auditee together to be exposed to civil liability to shareholders or any involved third party.

Furthermore, as stated earlier, the choice of legal form of an audit firm may influence the auditor's liability. Public limited liability company, private limited liability company, incorporated partnership, general partnership and limited partnership are the legal forms which firms of statutory auditors are allowed to take in Germany.

AUDIT MARKET REGULATION IN THE NETHERLANDS

Overview of the Dutch auditing profession

In the Netherlands both certified accountants (*Accountants-Administratie-consulenten*) and registered auditors (*registeraccountants*) are allowed to give a written opinion regarding annual accounts. Registered auditors were granted this right by the 1962 Act on Registered Auditors (28 June 1962: *Wet op de registeraccountants*), which came into force in 1967. Registered auditors are listed in the register of their professional body, the Royal Dutch Institute of Registered Auditors (*Koninklijk Nederlands Instituut van Registeraccountants*). Certified accountants, associated in the Dutch Association of Certified Accountants (*Nederlandse Orde van Accountants-Administratieconsulenten*) were granted the right to perform audits by the 1993 Act on Certified Accountants (6 August 1993: *Wet op de Accountants-Administratieconsulenten*). The 1993 Act is a substantial revision of the 1974 Act on Certified Accountants due to the implementation of the EEC Eighth Directive into Dutch legislation. Before the revision of the Act, certified accountants were not allowed to render auditing services. They provided mainly bookkeeping, tax and consultancy services. Currently, the right of certified accountants to perform audits applies to those who completed the new education programme for certified accountants or to certified accountants who enrolled in a transitional programme. The two professional bodies are public-law entities, and are charged with regulating the auditing profession. They are responsible for licensing statutory auditors and issuing auditing standards as authoritative guidance for their members.

Both registered auditors and certified accountants are permitted to perform statutory audits as well as contractual audits. No limitations are placed on rendering non-audit services, as long as these activities are compatible with their audit services.[8] Moreover, they are not required to work in public practice. Currently, only about 40 per cent of the total number of auditors are engaged in public practice.

Current audit market regulation[9]

Admission to the profession

There are two educational programmes leading to qualification as a registered auditor. Candidates can follow either the educational programme of the Royal Dutch Institute of Registered Auditors or that organized by universities. The education of registered auditors is, according to the Act on Registered Auditors, entrusted to the Royal Dutch Institute of Registered Auditors. The Institute established an Educational Board, responsible for the educational programme. In addition, an independent Examination Bureau was established to monitor the final auditor examination and the post-doctoral auditor examinations at the universities. The doctoral examinations organized by universities are under the responsibility of their faculties of economics and business administration.[10]

The educational programme of the Royal Dutch Institute of Registered Auditors (the NIVRA programme) extends over eight years of part-time study. Candidates follow the NIVRA programme while being employed by an audit firm or elsewhere. The typical way to enter the NIVRA programme is after completing secondary school.[11] Candidates can also enrol in the NIVRA programme after finishing a four-year course in accountancy or business administration in a higher school of vocational education.

The NIVRA programme consists of three stages. The first extends over two and a half years, and includes introductory subjects in economics and business administration, bookkeeping, information systems/computer science, (tax) law, and mathematics/statistics. The second stage is a two-year general stage, including the subjects of management and organization, law, finance, information systems/computer science, management accounting, tax law, financial accounting and an introduction to auditing. In the final stage, which extends over three and a half years, candidates need to pass tests in advanced financial accounting, administrative organization and auditing. Candidates pass the final stage after taking both written and oral tests in the required subjects, and after successfully defending a written paper.

Candidates can also follow a university education in business administration, and a post-doctoral programme, in order to become a registered auditor. The course of study for the university programme consists of a one-year preliminary course (*propaedeuse*), a three-year doctoral course and a two-year post-doctoral course.[12] The one-year preliminary course and the three-year doctoral course are offered by Dutch universities in a full-time, four-year degree programme in *Bedrijfseconomie*.[13] After completion of the degree programme, candidates start working at an audit firm or elsewhere and follow the post-doctoral programme on a part-time basis. This post-doctoral programme is equal to the final stage of the NIVRA programme.

After passing either the NIVRA programme or the university programme, candidates can apply for inclusion on the professional register of the Royal Dutch Institute of Registered Auditors. Together with their application, candidates need to confirm that they are not bankrupt, not placed under guardianship by court order, and have not been convicted of certain types of offence which prohibit rendering services as a registered auditor. When candidates meet all these requirements they are eligible for recognition as a registered auditor.

In contrast to Belgium and Germany, candidates are not currently required to have practical experience in auditing to achieve qualification as a registered auditor. Due to the implementation of the Eighth Directive, however, practical experience will become compulsory for candidates who qualify as an auditor after September 1999. These candidates are required to have at least three years' practical training in auditing. In practice this implies that these candidates will have to have commenced practical training in September 1996.

Appointment procedure

Statutory auditors are formally appointed by (a majority vote of) the shareholders at the annual general meeting. No approval is required from anyone other than the party appointing the statutory auditor. As in Germany, there is no fixed period with respect to the term of the appointment of the auditor. In the Netherlands audit firms also face restrictions on advertising and unsolicited offerings. Advertising is allowed but should be limited to factual and objective information and needs to comply with professional ethics. All forms of unsolicited offerings are forbidden.

Auditor independence

Auditors will not, in contrast to Belgium and Germany, lose their license when becoming employed outside the auditing profession. Regulation on independence with respect to a particular client requires that auditors should refuse to accept an engagement if they:

(1) have a personal relationship with the client;
(2) have a commercial relationship with the client;
(3) have a financial interest in the client; and/or
(4) become dependent, in terms of fee income, on particular clients.

With respect to non-audit services, audit firms are allowed to provide any services to an audit client within the same legal entity. Regarding the monitoring of audit fees, there are no explicit regulations on the calculation of audit fees. However, there is a general requirement that the fees should reflect the amount of work spent on the audit. Furthermore, audit firms are currently not required to undergo peer reviews.

Auditor liability

In the Netherlands legal action against the auditor can be taken by the auditee, its shareholders and any involved third party. The interaction between the auditee's and auditor's liability positions is in principle determined by a system of proportional liability. There is no legal liability cap, but it is possible to arrange a contractual liability cap. Finally, Dutch audit firms are allowed to take any legal form, although the Dutch professional bodies are in certain circumstances entitled to restrict the legal forms which auditing firms may take. However, in practice the professional bodies seem to be liberal on this issue.

THE EFFECTS OF REGULATION ON AUDIT MARKETS

In this section we will compare the audit market regulations in Belgium, Germany and the Netherlands and outline the potential effects of these regulations on each of the three audit markets. The focus will be on regulations affecting competition. Hence, we will first discuss the differences in entry requirements and then the regulations covering the appointment procedure and auditor independence.

According to the Eighth Directive of the European Union, statutory auditors are required to have at least three years' practical experience in auditing. Although all three countries have implemented the Eighth Directive, there is a difference with respect to the date of operation of this practical experience requirement. Belgium and Germany have had a practical experience requirement for several decades, whereas in the Netherlands a practical experience requirement will come into operation in September 1999. Furthermore, as a consequence of their practical experience requirement, Belgium and Germany require candidates to secure a traineeship before starting the educational programme. Such a requirement impedes entry to the profession. Hence, with respect to practical experience, it can be concluded that the requirements are more strict in Belgium and Germany. In addition to achieving a qualification, in Belgium and Germany auditors are required to maintain sufficient up-to-date experience through carrying out minimum levels of audit work. In the

Netherlands, auditors are allowed to keep their licence when leaving public practice. Hence, it can be concluded that, on this point too, Belgium and Germany have more strict entry requirements than the Netherlands.

With respect to the appointment procedure of statutory auditors, one of the main differences between the three countries is the length of the appointment. In Belgium there is a fixed period of three years, whereas in Germany and the Netherlands there is no regulation on the length of the appointment. Regulations that specify a (long) period of appointment can be expected to impede competition between audit firms, since auditees are not able to change auditors within the specified period. Another regulatory difference affecting the appointment of auditors concerns advertising. Although in all three countries audit firms face restrictions on advertising, the Netherlands seems to have the most liberal regime. In Belgium and Germany all forms of advertising to the public in general are forbidden, although in Belgium advertising on a local scale, if factual and objective, is permitted. In the Netherlands, advertising to the general public is allowed but should be limited to factual and objective information and needs to comply with professional ethics. Restrictions on advertising influence the nature of competition in an audit market since, for example, new entrants to the market will have more difficulty in establishing a reputation and/or a brand name. This will make it more difficult for entrants to compete with incumbent audit firms. Since the Netherlands has the most liberal regime regarding advertising, it can be expected that this will have a positive effect on the level of competition in the Dutch audit market.

An important aspect of regulation regarding auditor independence concerns fee-setting. In general, regulations in this area attempt to prohibit or restrict lowballing. Of the three countries covered, only in Belgium are auditors required to report the number of hours and the fee for an audit to the professional body, which reviews the adequacy of both figures. Although in all three countries auditors are obliged by law or the ethical code to charge a fair and reasonable fee, which may not depend on the result of the audit, the Belgian requirement implies a far stricter enforcement of this general rule. Regulations restricting fee-setting limit the competition for (new) clients on the basis of price. Because the Belgian fee regulation is stricter than in the other two countries it can be expected that its negative effect on competition will be the most profound.

Considering the different regulatory regimes it can be expected that the Dutch audit market should be the most competitive of the three markets. The entry requirements are less, advertising is in general allowed, there is no fixed auditor tenure, and the setting of fees is almost free from restriction. This more liberal set of regulations should be reflected in a number of audit market characteristics. It should be emphasized that ideally the effects of competition should be assessed on the basis of measures of price *and* quality. Both variables are very difficult to measure, however, and we will therefore use only indirect measures of the effects of competition. What follows is taken from national data on the number of auditors admitted to the profession, the total number of auditors, and the qualification age and charge-out ratios of auditors.

FEE (1988) reports for a number of countries the average number of candidates admitted to the profession each year. The results reported are: Belgium 180, Germany 200 and the Netherlands 375. Hence, in absolute terms the entry to the Dutch profession is the highest. In relative terms the same position holds considering that the German economy is much larger than the Dutch economy and the Belgian economy only slightly smaller. FEE (1988) also reports that, of the seventeen countries covered, Germany has the highest qualification age (thirty-five). This is to be expected, considering the German entry requirements.

The effects of entry should be reflected in the total number of auditors active in an audit market. The totals for the three markets in 1990 are given in MARC (1996, p. 120): Belgium 711, Germany 6,625 and the Netherlands 2,770. Of course, these figures should be related to the size of the economy. Morse (1993) has divided the number of auditors active in national markets by the size of the population. His results are: Belgium 0.000069, Germany 0.000096 and the Netherlands 0.000450. Again, these figures confirm the relatively large size of the Dutch audit profession, which is consistent with relatively easy entry.

Ultimately, competition can be expected to affect the prices, or fees, charged by auditors. We therefore provide information on the charge-out ratios of auditors in the three countries. It should be noted that the level of charge-out ratios is also affected by factors other than competition. Preferably, to measure the effects of competition one would also need information on the cost structures of audit firms in the three countries. In combination with fees charged, cost information can give an indication of the economic rents of audit firms. However, data on audit firm fees and cost structures are not readily available.

The data limitations mentioned above should be noted when reading Table 8.1, in which the charge-out ratios of the Big Six firms in Belgium, Germany

Table 8.1 Charge-out ratios of the Big Six audit firms in Belgium, Germany and the Netherlands in 1989

	Total fees* divided by number of professionals* (ECU)	Audit fees* divided by number of auditors† (ECU)
Belgium	72,000	325,000
Germany	99,000	288,000
The Netherlands	65,000	210,000

*Source: NERA (1992)
†Source: Membership lists of the Institut des Reviseurs d'Entreprises/Instituut der Bedrijfsrevisoren, the Wirtschaftsprüferkammer and the Koninklijk Nederlands Instituut van Registeraccountants

and the Netherlands are given. The table contains data on both total fee income and audit fee income. In the Netherlands the total annual fees for each professional amount to 65,000 ECUs and the annual audit fees per auditor to 210,000 ECUs. The results show that for both categories of charge-out ratios the Netherlands has the lowest values. These figures are again consistent with the hypothesis that the Dutch audit market is the most competitive of the three markets.

SUMMARY AND CONCLUSIONS

This chapter has given an analysis of the regulatory regimes governing auditing in Belgium, Germany and the Netherlands. The analysis has emphasized those regulations which can be expected to have the most direct impact on competition in audit markets. Hence, the overview compared the national regulations in the three countries regarding admission to the profession, auditor tenure, advertising, unsolicited offering of services and fee-setting. In addition, information was provided on the liability regimes in the three countries.

On the basis of the regulatory overview it was concluded that the Netherlands is more liberal in terms of audit market regulation than Belgium and Germany. Therefore it can be expected that the Dutch audit market will be more competitive. To illustrate this empirically, some data were provided on entry to the profession, the size of the profession and charge-out rates in the three countries covered in the study. These limited data confirmed that the Dutch audit market appears to be more competitive.

NOTES

1. This section only addresses the regulation of *reviseurs d'entreprises/bedrijfsrevisoren* since they are the only individuals eligible to conduct statutory audits.
2. The Institute of Auditors formulated several other requirements with respect to the traineeship. For example, a candidate is required to spend at least 1,000 hours per year on auditing.
3. These subjects are: bookkeeping, financial accounting and financial statement analysis, management accounting, company law, tax law, civil law, commercial law, labour law and social security law, management information systems, economics, mathematics and statistics, finance, auditing, consolidation, financial reporting law and rules of professional conduct.
4. As at 1 August 1994, approximately 85% of all auditors were members of the Institute of Auditors. Only about 50% of all audit firms are members, but they employ almost 80% of all auditors working for audit firms.
5. Since *Wirtschaftsprüfer* as well as *vereidigte Buchprüfer* are eligible to perform statutory audits, this section addresses the regulation of both types of auditor. To contain the length of this section, however, only the educational programme of *Wirtschaftsprüfer* is considered. The majority of statutory auditors are *Wirtschaftsprüfer*.
6. The only subject not included in the course programme of the Institute of

Auditors is tax law, the reason being that 95% of all candidates are already qualified as tax advisers.

7. The Admittance Committee is a state government body, consisting of a representative of the State Ministry of Economic Affairs, a representative of trade and industry and two auditors.

8. The audit services provided by registered auditors are statutory auditing and contractual auditing. Their non-audit services can be categorized as follows: performing review (*beoordelingsopdrachten*), providing agreed-upon procedures (*specifieke werkzaamheden*), compilation of financial statements (*samenstellingsopdrachten*) and providing consultancy services.

9. In this section the audit market regulation of both registered auditors and certified accountants is discussed. However, to contain the length of the section, we will discuss only the educational programme to become a registered auditor. The majority of statutory auditors are registered auditors.

10. The university courses required for candidates to become eligible to follow the post-doctoral courses need to be approved by the Examination Bureau.

11. The required secondary school level is that of preparatory academic education. Candidates who finished other types of secondary education need to pass an entrance examination at the level of preparatory academic education.

12. Maastricht University offers a post-doctoral programme of one and a half years, whereas the Free University of Amsterdam offers a three-year programme. The length of the post-doctoral programme of a university depends on the subjects candidates were able to pass in the doctoral programme at that university.

13. According to Zeff, van der Wel and Camfferman (1992), this term is almost synonymous with 'business administration with a strong base of economic theory'.

REFERENCES

Beales, J. H. (1980) The economics of regulating the professions, in R. D. Blair and S. Rubin (eds.) *Regulating the Professions*, Lexington Books, Lexington; pp. 125–42.

Benston, G. J. (1985) The market for public accounting services – demand, supply and regulation, *Journal of Accounting and Public Policy*, Vol. 4, pp. 33–80.

Eichenseher, J. W. and Danos, P. (1981) The analysis of industry-specific auditor concentration: towards an explanatory model, *The Accounting Review*, July, pp. 479–92.

FEE (Fédération des Experts Comptables Européens) (1988) *Training for the Profession; A Comparative Study*, FEE, Brussels.

Maijoor, S. J. (1994) Economic effects of accounting regulation for public accountants: evidence from the Netherlands, *Accounting and Business Research*, no. 95, pp. 267–76.

Maijoor, S. J. and van Witteloostuijn, A. (1996) An empirical test of the resource-based theory: strategic regulation in the Dutch audit industry, *Strategic Management Journal*, Vol. 17, pp. 549–69.

MARC (Maastricht Accounting and Auditing Research Center) (1996) *The Role, Position and Liability of the Statutory Auditor within the European Union*, MARC, Maastricht.

Morse, D. (1993) Explaining the international supply of auditors, *International Journal of Accounting*, Vol. 28, pp. 347–55.

NERA (National Economic Research Associates) (1992) *Competition in European Accounting*, Lafferty Publications, Dublin.

Pound, G. D. and Francis, J. R. (1981) The accounting services market: theory and evidence, *Journal of Business Finance and Accounting*, Vol. 8, pp. 353–71.

Sappington, D. E. M. and Stiglitz, J. E. (1987) Information and regulation, in E. E. Bailey (ed.) *Public Regulation*, The MIT Press, Cambridge, pp. 3–43.

Wallace, W. A. (1987) The economic role of the audit in free and regulated markets: a review, in G. J. Previtz (ed.) *Research in Accounting Regulation*, JAI Press, Greenwich, pp. 7–34.

Zeff, S. A., van der Wel, F. and Camfferman, K. (1992) *Company Financial Reporting: A Historical and Comparative Study of the Dutch Regulatory Process*, Elsevier Science Publishers, Amsterdam.

DISCUSSION QUESTIONS

1. What, in your view, are the most important aspects of the relationship between the structure of the audit market and its regulation?
2. What are the major differences between Belgium, Germany and the Netherlands in the role, organization and regulation of audit services? Add to this analysis a comparison with another country you are familiar with.
3. What explanations can be offered for the differences in auditing between Belgium, Germany and the Netherlands?
4. From your knowledge of the regulation of the audit market in one other country, what sort of comparisons would you make between that country and the effects of regulation in Belgium and Germany?
5. How have different countries sought to resolve the difficult auditing issues of auditor independence and liability?

Part II

Forming an Audit Opinion

9

The Auditing Practices Board and Auditing Standards in the UK

Roy Chandler

INTRODUCTION

In the context of UK auditing, much has changed since the last edition of this book. The organizational structure for developing and publishing auditing standards has changed. The Auditing Practices Board (APB), first established in 1991, has taken over from the former Auditing Practices Committee (APC). The APB's auditing standards now appear in a different format and their coverage is more comprehensive than the pronouncements which they replace; this change reflects the increasing extent of regulation over the auditing profession.

The purpose of this chapter is to present an analysis of the standard-setting regime in the UK. The chapter begins with a consideration of the role of professional standards in general; the second section provides a brief review of the history of audit regulation in the UK; the third section reviews the current position of auditing standards; the fourth section compares professional standards with the theoretical notions of auditing as advanced by some academics; and the fifth section looks at the international influences on auditing in the UK.

THE ROLE OF PROFESSIONAL STANDARDS

The development of auditing standards may have been the result of a number of factors. One view is that this development within the accounting profession is closely linked to the raising of public expectations regarding the performance of accountants, especially in their role as auditors. When expectations are unrealized and losses result, there is a tendency to resort to the legal process to seek redress. If dissatisfaction is widespread political pressure may be brought to bear on the profession.

There is clear evidence that the expectations gap is by no means a modern phenomenon. In the nineteenth century during the formative years of the profession, there was much public criticism of auditors. It must be said, however, that at that time there was no requirement for auditors to have professional qualifications. Many, but not all, auditors who found themselves in court were amateurs and not members of professional bodies. As the years passed, the accounting profession acquired a monopoly over company and other audits. During the first eighty years of the twentieth century there were few lawsuits brought against accountants. But public dissatisfaction and litigation came back with a vengeance in the wake of company collapses during the 1970s. This trend has continued to the present day, when audit firms are investigating all avenues to escape or reduce their potential liability for negligent audit work.

The role, or more precisely roles, of auditing standards may be clearly seen against this rather brief sketch of the background to the profession's development:

Quality control

One possible role of the standards of any profession is to narrow the difference in performance of individual practitioners. The existence of standards, if they are followed, means that it is more likely that the profession as a whole will deliver a service of a consistent and acceptable standard.

Practitioner education

Although members of a profession are expected to have reached a minimum level of education and training, these attributes alone may not always be sufficient to enable them to deal with every problem encountered in practice. This is especially true of dynamic professions whose responsibilities and technologies undergo rapid rates of change. In short, there is often a demand from practitioners for guidance as to how to perform their duties. The clearest example of this is the area of audits in the financial services industry which is subject to complex legislation and regulation; the APB has issued a number of detailed Practice Notes to guide auditors in the conduct of such audits.

The disciplinary role

Standards help a professional body establish and maintain acceptable levels of performance. Without such standards, it would be hard for a professional body to determine whether an individual's performance has fallen below a level generally accepted by his or her peers.

The legal role

Similarly, professional standards may be referred to by a court of law in judging whether an individual has exercised reasonable skill and care, the acid-test of a negligence suit. If written standards of conduct exist, these can be used as a benchmark by a court. The APB's (1993) *Scope and Authority of APB Pronouncements* warns auditors that all pronouncements are likely to be taken into account by a court of law considering the adequacy of an auditor's work.

Individual practitioners benefit from having an indication of the minimum level of performance likely to be acceptable to a court and the profession as a whole benefits by avoiding situations where individual courts may make general law (regulating professional conduct) on the facts of a single case. Of course, courts are not bound by a profession's standards. It is possible that a court might find that compliance with professional standards was insufficient where the standards themselves are deemed to be inadequate. To date there have been no such decisions involving auditors in the UK.

The political role

By establishing standards a profession may be able to stave off government interference and maintain its independence. Examples of this form of self-protection can be found on both sides of the Atlantic. In the 1970s in the UK, a boost was given to the audit standard-setting process by the Trade Minister threatening to take action if the profession did not put its house in order. More recently in the USA the profession faced Senate sanctions if it did not respond to concerns regarding the expectations gap: the result was the simultaneous issue of nine expectations gap standards in 1988.

Governments may prefer professions to be self-regulating provided the private interests of the profession's members are not placed before the public interest. Professional bodies are often better able to develop practicable standards which can be updated more speedily than legislation. Furthermore, the costs of the standard-setting and performance-monitoring processes are met from the profession's resources not the public purse.

A BRIEF HISTORY OF UK AUDIT REGULATION

For many years the leaders of the accounting profession were reluctant to issue guidance to practitioners, apparently in the belief that procedural matters were best left to the professional judgement of the individual. An early departure from this position occurred in 1900 when the ICAEW produced a 'standard' audit report following counsel's advice on the implications of the Companies Act 1900, though this was purely advisory rather than compulsory. It was not until 1961 that more guidance started to emerge, again in the form of advisory rather than mandatory statements, known as the U-series statements.

In 1973 the ICAEW set up the forerunner of the APC but little progress was made in setting auditing standards until, in 1976, this committee came under the umbrella of the Consultative Committee of Accountancy Bodies (CCAB), representing all the major professional institutes in the UK. The APC was made up of unpaid members, the majority of whom, under its constitution, were required to be practising auditors. They were assisted by a body of other volunteers who formed project subcommittees to develop draft guidance which was then revised and approved by the APC members. However, before a standard or guideline could be published in final form the APC had to obtain the approval of the Council of each CCAB member body.

The APC issued its first exposure drafts in 1978 and its first full standards and guidelines in 1980. The auditing standards were short, concise statements whose few paragraphs carried mandatory status. The auditing guidelines were lengthier statements, issued in a haphazard fashion dealing with problems as they became topical but organized into categories depending on the nature of their subject matter; for example, there were detailed operational guidelines of general application as well as industry-specific guidelines. The guidelines contained more detail but lacked the authority of the standards. There was some confusion, however, since the guidelines often contained guidance which appeared to be mandatory.

During the late 1980s the climate of the time generally was highly critical of auditors in the light of failures of well-known companies; not for the first time was the profession required to put its house in order to avoid government interference. Furthermore, changes were taking place in the constitution of the APC's sister body, the Accounting Standards Committee, and the subsequent reconstitution of the APC closely, though not entirely, mirrored the changes in the accounting standard-setting process. That time was the start of greater and more detailed regulation over what had previously been a fairly loosely governed professional province. The Companies Act 1989 requires recognized supervisory bodies (the professional bodies) to have rules and practices governing the technical standards to be applied to audits. It was unlikely that the handful of paragraphs of the APC Standards would have satisfied that requirement. A new format for auditing standards was needed and a new framework for issuing these standards was also in demand.

The standard-setting process had become the target of an increasingly hostile and highly politicized campaign which accused the APC of being no more than a front for the large auditing firms, of promoting professional interests rather than the public interest and of acting in an undemocratic and secretive fashion (Sikka, Willmott and Lowe, 1989). Chandler (1991) rebuts many of the largely unfounded claims and Pong and Whittington (1994, p. 173) could find no evidence that APC members 'saw themselves as part of any organization for the defence of the auditing profession'.

Nevertheless, as a result of these various pressures, in 1991 the APB assumed the role of standard-setter and the APC was disbanded. Under the APB's constitution no more than half of its voting members may be practising auditors, the remaining members being drawn from other professions.

Appointments to the APB are made by a selection committee comprising the CCAB presidents, the APB chairman and nominees from the Bank of England and the London Stock Exchange. The aim is to give the standard-setting process some independence from the auditing profession itself and to give wider representation to other interested parties.

Other changes to the constitution and operations of the standard-setting process include the APB's ability to issue standards which the CCAB bodies have undertaken to adopt as applicable to their members. This avoids the time-consuming obstacle of obtaining CCAB Council approval, which delayed much of the APC output. The APB's agenda papers may now be obtained by non-APB members on payment of a small fee; the APB cannot be accused of being secretive although it has yet to experiment with public meetings.

THE APB STANDARDS AND OTHER PRONOUNCEMENTS

The APB issues Statements of Auditing Standards (SASs) containing standards in bold print (often referred to as 'black letter' standards); these are considered to be the basic principles and essential procedures which auditors are expected to follow. The SASs also contain explanatory material which is not prescriptive but is intended to help auditors comply with the SASs. Table 9.1 lists the SASs issued to date.

Relationship between APB and APC pronouncements

The APB's SASs have replaced the APC's Auditing Standards and many of its Auditing Guidelines as indicated in Table 9.2.

A superficial comparison of Tables 9.1 and 9.2 will show that many of the APC's guidelines have been replaced by an APB SAS. However, there are some aspects of the audit process which have for the first time become the subject of authoritative pronouncements, for example the area of illegal acts (SAS 110), knowledge of the business (SAS 210), materiality (SAS 220) and audit sampling (SAS 430).

A number of the APC's guidelines have yet to be replaced; these are mainly the industry-specific guidelines and some of the detailed operational guidelines such as attendance at stocktaking and auditing in a computer environment.

The APB also issues:

(1) Practice Notes: these contain guidance intended to assist auditors in applying SASs in particular circumstances or industries. To date the APB has issued eleven Practice Notes, dealing mainly with aspects of the financial services industry.
(2) Bulletins: these are intended to provide auditors with up-to-date guidance on new or emerging issues; the APB has issued three Bulletins, mainly in the area of reporting on listed company disclosures.

Table 9.1   Statements of Auditing Standards

SAS No.	Title
100	Objective and General Principles Governing an Audit of Financial Statements
110	Fraud and Error
120	Consideration of Law and Regulations
130	The Going Concern Basis in Financial Statements
140	Engagement Letters
150	Subsequent Events
160	Other Information in Documents Containing Audited Financial Statements
200	Planning
210	Knowledge of the Business
220	Materiality and the Audit
230	Working Papers
240	Quality Control for Audit Work
300	Accounting and Internal Control Systems and Audit Risk Assessments
400	Audit Evidence
410	Analytical Procedures
420	Audit of Accounting Estimates
430	Audit Sampling
440	Management Representations
450	Opening Balances and Comparatives
460	Related Parties
470	Overall Review of Financial Statements
500	Considering the Work of Internal Audit
510	The Relationship Between Principal Auditors and other Auditors
520	Using the Work of an Expert
600	Auditors' Reports on Financial Statements
610	Reports to Directors or Management
620	The Auditors' Right and Duty to Report to Regulators in the Financial Sector

(3) Statements of Standards for Reporting Accountants (SSRAs): currently there is only one statement in this category, resulting from the exemptions from statutory audit granted to certain smaller companies.

(4) Discussion Papers: these are intended to promote debate on areas of concern to the auditing profession prior to the development of an exposure draft. Three Discussion Papers are mentioned later in this chapter.

Practice Notes and Bulletins have the same status as the explanatory material in the SASs. The status of the SSRAs is not clear but, since they do contain black letter paragraphs and explanatory material, they are likely to have the same authority as their equivalents in the SASs.

Table 9.2   Auditing Standards and Guidelines – destination to SASs

APC Ref.	Title	Replaced by APB ref.
101	The auditor's operational standard	Various
102	The audit report	SAS 600
201	Planning, controlling and recording	SAS 200 and 230
202	Accounting systems	SAS 300
203	Audit evidence	SAS 400
204	Internal controls	SAS 300
205	Review of financial statements	SAS 470
309	Communications between auditors and regulators under sections 109 and 180(1)(q) of the Financial Services Act 1986	SAS 620 and PN 5
402	Events after the balance sheet date	SAS 150
403	Amounts derived from the preceding financial statements	SAS 430
404	Representations by management	SAS 440
406	Engagement letters	SAS 140
408	Reliance on internal audit	SAS 500
409	Quality control	SAS 240
410	The auditor's considerations in respect of going concern	SAS 130
411	Financial information issued with audited financial statements	SAS 160
413	Reliance on other specialists	SAS 520
414	Reports to management	SAS 610
415	Group financial statements – reliance on the work of other auditors	SAS 510
417	Analytical review	SAS 410
418	The auditor's responsibility in relation to fraud, other irregularities and errors	SAS 110
503	Reports by auditors under company legislation in the United Kingdom (revised) (Practice Note)	PN 8
504	Reports by auditors under company legislation in the Republic of Ireland (Practice Note)	PN 9

PROFESSIONAL GUIDANCE V. ACADEMIC THEORY

For auditing there has not been the same endeavour to develop a conceptual framework as has been seen in the field of accounting or financial reporting. Nevertheless, a number of attempts have been made to develop a theory of auditing. The seminal work of Mautz and Sharaf (1961) may be considered the starting point for this literature; their framework was extended and adapted for the UK context by Lee (1972, 1982 and 1986) and Flint (1988). Ferrier (1991) argues that the professional auditing pronouncements constitute in themselves a conceptual framework.

Audit evidence

According to Mautz and Sharaf (1961), auditing is concerned essentially with the collection and evaluation of evidence to support or refute assertions in the financial statements on which the auditor is required to form an opinion. Audit evidence may take many forms and may be collected using a number of auditing techniques.

Mautz and Sharaf (1961) list nine types of audit evidence and ten auditing techniques of evidence collection. SAS 400, *Audit Evidence*, refers to five types of audit technique with examples of the type of evidence collected:

(1) inspection;
(2) observation;
(3) inquiry;
(4) computation; and
(5) analytical procedures.

Table 9.3 compares the generalized ideas of Mautz and Sharaf on evidence with the contents of the SASs.

Table 9.3   Mautz and Sharaf (1961) and the SASs compared

Mautz and Sharaf – audit evidence	Inclusion in SASs
Audit evidence includes all influences affecting the auditor's judgement	SAS 400, para. 6 lists a wide range of factors affecting audit judgement
The influence of audit evidence varies from being compelling through persuasive to inconclusive	Evidence is usually persuasive rather than conclusive: SAS 400, para. 4
No one method of obtaining audit evidence is always or completely reliable	Auditors often seek evidence from different sources: SAS 400, para. 4
Combining audit evidence of different types increases its persuasiveness	Consistent evidence from different sources is more persuasive: SAS 400, para. 17
Audit evidence must be viewed critically	Auditors apply critical examination and professional scepticism to information: SAS 100, para. 11
The more material an item under consideration, the more persuasive must be the evidence obtained to support it	Materiality is one of the factors affecting judgement on sufficiency of audit evidence: SAS 400, para. 6
The availability of evidence and the time and cost of its collection are principal factors	Auditors consider the cost and value of obtaining evidence: SAS 400, para. 18
The need to resolve apparent inconsistencies between different types of evidence	Auditors consider additional procedures in the event of inconsistent evidence: SAS 400, para. 17

Though the matches in Table 9.3 may not be exact, it is clear that never-theless there is close agreement between standard-setters and the approach of academic theorists such as Mautz and Sharaf. In addition SAS 400 para 16 provides the following generalizations (or presumptions) regarding *reliability*:

(1) evidence from external sources is more reliable than that obtained from the entity's records;
(2) audit evidence from the accounting records is more reliable when the accounting and internal controls are effective;
(3) evidence obtained directly by the auditor is more reliable than evidence obtained by or from the entity;
(4) documentary evidence is more reliable than oral evidence; and
(5) original documents are more reliable than photocopies or faxes.

Due audit care

Much of the discussion in Mautz and Sharaf (1961) on the concept of due audit care is concerned with auditors' responsibility for the detection of irreg-ularities. To counter a situation in which, as it seemed to Mautz and Sharaf at the time (and remains today), society's expectations of auditors were not matched by auditors' performance, they develop the concept of the prudent auditor (see Table 9.4).

Having developed the concept of the prudent auditor, Mautz and Sharaf (1961) then apply it to the auditor's concern with the systems of internal control in an audit client (see Table 9.5).

Fair presentation (or true and fair view)

Mautz and Sharaf (1961) begin their discussion of this important concept by identifying three sub-concepts:

(1) accounting propriety – this is itself composed of three basic ideas: that there exist accounting principles, that these enjoy general agreement and some authoritative support, and that application of these principles results in satisfactory financial reporting;
(2) adequate disclosure – concerned with both the extent and scope of accounting disclosures;
(3) audit obligation – discharged by auditors clearly expressing in their audit reports the nature of their responsibility in relation to the financial state-ments, the extent of the audit work performed and their judgement on the financial statements.

In the UK context, Lee (1986, pp. 145–6) lists a number of issues that audi-tors must address in forming an opinion on truth and fairness:

Table 9.4   The Mautz and Sharaf (1961) prudent auditor concept

Mautz and Sharaf – prudent auditors:	Inclusion in SASs
Obtain readily available knowledge including a thorough review of internal control to assess unreasonable risk to others.	SAS 100.1 requires auditors to obtain evidence to determine if financial statements are materially misstated.
Direct special attention to areas of risk, identified through experience or knowledge of the business.	Auditors' experience and knowledge help identify items having a material effect: SAS 200, para. 7.
Take extra care in planning and performing an audit in the light of unusual circumstances or unfamiliar situations.	SAS 200 requires auditors to plan the audit and subsequently to revise the plan if necessary. SAS 210 requires auditors to obtain knowledge of the business; this is used to identify areas where special considerations apply.
Take appropriate steps to remove doubtful impressions or unanswered questions.	SAS 400 notes the need for additional procedures when evidence from different sources is inconsistent.
Keep abreast of developments in auditing.	This is covered in ethical guidance and audit regulations not auditing standards.
Give clear instructions to audit assistants and review the work performed by those assistants.	SAS 200, para. 5 and SAS 240, para. 6 and SAS 240.2.

(1) Are the accounting policies selected by the audit client recognized and generally acceptable?
(2) Are the accounting policies appropriate and applicable to the type of business of the client?
(3) Are the accounting policies consistently applied?

The principles articulated by Mautz and Sharaf and Lee are recognized by SAS 600, *Auditors' Reports on Financial Statements*, which requires the auditor to include in the audit report a statement that the audit process includes 'considering whether the accounting policies are appropriate to the reporting entity's circumstances, consistently applied and adequately disclosed' (SAS 600.4). In assessing the appropriateness of the accounting policies auditors consider policies commonly adopted in the relevant industry, policies for which there is substantial authoritative support, the need to depart from an

Table 9.5 Application of Mautz and Sharaf's (1961) prudent auditor concept

Mautz and Sharaf – application	Inclusion in SASs
The inherent limitations of an internal control system are recognized.	SAS 300, para. 25 spells out the inherent limitations of internal control systems.
A preliminary review should be performed at the planning stage.	SAS 300.4 requires a preliminary assessment of control risk if auditors intend to rely on systems.
If weaknesses are found it may be necessary to revise the original audit programme.	SAS 300 para 48 explains that revision of control risk assessment leads to changing planned substantive procedures.
Weaknesses which could represent a significant risk to the client should be reported to the management.	SAS 610.2 requires material weaknesses in the accounting and internal control systems to be reported to management.
If sufficiently material, weaknesses should be reflected in the auditors' opinion on the financial statements.	SAS 300, para. 56 suggests that auditors consider the implications for their report when the risk of misstatement is not reduced to an acceptable level.

accounting standard and whether the financial statements reflect the substance of the underlying transactions and not merely their form (SAS 470, para. 5).

Independence and ethics

Mautz and Sharaf (1961, p. 207) develop 'guides or clues indicating whether there has been any infringement on [the auditor's] independence ... Guides such as these should have usefulness to those who find it necessary to evaluate the degree of independence actually enjoyed by a given practitioner under specific conditions. They should be even more useful to practitioners themselves.'

The SASs suffer from a major deficiency: there are no standards of personal qualities. In the UK, the ethical requirements are set out in the ethical guidance of the professional bodies. SAS 100, *Objective and General Principles Governing an Audit of Financial Statements*, states: 'In the conduct of any audit of financial statements auditors should comply with the ethical guidance issued by their relevant professional bodies' (SAS 100.2).

There have been indications that the APB was interested in issuing personal standards: *The Audit Agenda* (APB, 1994, p. 33) proposed that the enduring principles of auditing be incorporated into a revised version of the document, *The Scope and Authority of APB Pronouncements* (APB 1993). In the event this proposal was not adopted. One suspects that the APB, (like its predecessor) was accused of encroaching on the territory of another committee, the Chartered Accountants' Joint Ethics Committee (CAJEC). Instead of personal or ethical *standards*, the APB has issued a discussion paper, *The Auditor's Code* (APB, 1996a), which auditors are expected to follow in complying with the SASs. The Code is in addition to the ethical standards issued by individual professional bodies and embodies the 'enduring principles' of auditing recognized in *The Audit Agenda*.

INTERNATIONAL INFLUENCES

The International Federation of Accountants (IFAC) based in New York has more than a hundred member bodies around the world. The broad objective of the IFAC is to promote the international harmonization of the accounting profession. To achieve this end the IFAC has established standing committees to develop guidance which its member bodies (the professional bodies in different countries) are encouraged to adopt in their national standards. One of these committees is the International Auditing Practices Committee (IAPC), which has thirteen members from different countries and despite a lack of resources has issued more than thirty International Standards on Auditing (ISAs). In a process similar to that of the APB, the IAPC has identified in bold type what it considers to be the basic principles and essential procedures in its ISAs. The APB, in each of its SASs, makes a point of explaining the extent to which its pronouncements comply with the basic principles and essential procedures identified by the IAPC. Table 9.6 gives an indication of how closely the UK's standards follow international practice.

Some of the ISAs have clearly been influential in forming the basis of the UK SASs and in prompting the APB to issue standards on topics not previously covered or only partly covered in previous UK pronouncements: for example, SAS 120, *Consideration of Law and Regulations*, SAS 210, *Knowledge of the Business*, SAS 450, *Opening Balances and Comparatives* and SAS 460, *Related Parties*.

The importance of the ISAs is likely to increase as official recognition of the international standards on accounting and auditing has been promised by the international body of regulators, the International Organization of Securities Commissions (IOSCO). The benefits to IOSCO and its members (and multinational corporations) lie in having a common set of standards which would govern the preparation and audit of financial statements of companies listed on the international stock exchanges, in particular where the same stock is quoted on more than one stock exchange. The benefit to the IAPC is that with IOSCO approval there would be more pressure on national standard-setting bodies to comply with the ISAs – the IAPC itself has neither the ability nor the power to enforce compliance.

The APB by making clear its conformity with the ISAs has taken a

Table 9.6   SASs and ISAs

ISA No.	ISA Title	SAS No.	Extent of differences between the SAS and the ISA
200	Objective and General Principles Governing an Audit of Financial Statements	100	The SAS is less prescriptive on some minor points.
210	Terms of Audit Engagements	140	
220	Quality Control for Audit Work	240	
230	Documentation	230	
240	Fraud and Error	110	
250	Consideration of Laws and Regulations in an Audit of Financial Statements	120	
300	Planning	200	
310	Knowledge of the Business	210	The SAS complies with the ISA when read in conjuction with SAS 470.
320	Audit Materiality	220	The SAS complies with the ISA when read in conjunction with other SASs.
400	Risk Assessments and Internal Control	300	The SAS is less prescriptive on some minor points and part of the ISA is dealt with by SAS 610.
500	Audit Evidence	400	
510	Initial Engagements – Opening Balances	450	The SAS complies with the ISA when read in conjunction with SAS 600. There is no ISA on comparatives.
520	Analytical Procedures	410	
530	Audit Sampling	430	
540	Audit of Accounting Estimates	420	
550	Related Parties	460	Certain minor differences.
560	Subsequent Events	150	The SAS is less prescriptive on one minor point.
570	Going Concern	130	
580	Management Representations	440	
600	Using the Work of Another Auditor	510	The SAS complies with the ISA when read in conjunction with SAS 600.
610	Considering the Work of Internal Auditing	500	SAS 500 does not require a test of internal audit.
620	Using the Work of an Expert	520	
700	The Auditor's Report on Financial Statements	600	
720	Other Information in Documents Containing Audited Financial Statements	160	The SAS is less prescriptive on one minor point.

necessary step in plenty of time if, as seems likely, IOSCO endorses the ISAs by the end of the century. Although some have questioned whether it is either possible or proper for an international body to make rules suitable for the national auditing environment in countries with widely diverse backgrounds, the APB shows no signs of fear that its sovereignty is being usurped by the IAPC. A common criticism is that there is an unhealthy degree of American influence over the content of the international standards which appear to be a mechanism for a form of accounting colonialism. Such an allegation is hard to refute when one takes a close look at the terminology used and the techniques referred to in the standards. However, this development may be unwelcome only if it really does lead to the adoption of auditing standards which are inappropriate to particular national settings. It is therefore likely that there will remain a need to retain national standard-setting bodies even if their agendas are set at the international level. In fact, national standard-setters may find that the IAPC becomes the target for much of the criticism currently levelled against them.

CONCLUSION

A clue to the future may be seen in the APB Discussion Papers, *The Audit Agenda – Next Steps* (APB, 1996b), which represents the third step in developing the audit to meet user needs (this follows *The Future Development of Auditing: a Paper to Promote Public Debate* and *The Audit Agenda* (APB, 1992, 1994)) and *The Audit Research Agenda* (APB, 1996c).

The first paper examines the issues raised in *The Audit Agenda* and how the APB responds to commentators on that paper. Among the issues on which we may expect future developments are auditors' involvement with the interim statements and preliminary announcements of listed companies and the role of auditors in the context of the governance of such companies. At the other end of the spectrum are the specific problems of auditing owner-managed companies, which are the subject of a current APB project. Other projects include fraud, in particular the implications of known cases, and the personal qualities and standards of the audit partner. On other matters in *The Audit Agenda*, the APB recognizes that responsibility for further progress lies with other bodies such as the DTI and the Stock Exchange.

The Audit Research Agenda may be seen as part of the APB's longer-term plan. One main area worthy of research is audit quality within which four key topics are identified: responsibilities for fraud and illegal acts, the audit firm environment, the professional ethos of auditors and auditor liability. For the first time the APB has indicated that it is prepared to fund research though it warns that its resources are very limited.

There is no doubt that auditing has been, is and always will be a continually developing area of professional activity. The duty of the standard-setting process is to attempt to ensure that standards with which practitioners must comply keep pace with what may reasonably be expected of a competent auditor. In a self-regulated profession, standard-setters are given the job of balancing the public and private interests. Standard-setters must live with the fact that public expectations of auditors may never be fully satisfied either because those expectations are unattainable or because those with the expectations are unwilling to pay for their attainment. They must also live with the risk that if they are perceived as caring more for the interests of their profession than for the public interest then some form of government intervention can be expected.

REFERENCES

APB (1992) *The Future Development of Auditing – A Paper to Promote Public Debate* (MacFarlane Report), APB, London.
APB (1993) *The Scope and Authority of APB Pronouncements,* APB, London.
APB (1994) *The Audit Agenda,* APB, London.
APB (1996a) *The Auditor's Code,* APB, London.
APB (1996b) *The Audit Agenda – Next Steps,* APB, London.
APB (1996c) *The Audit Research Agenda,* APB, London.
Chandler, R. (1991) Guardians of knowledge and public interest: a reply, *Accounting, Auditing and Accountability Journal,* Vol. 4, no. 4, pp. 5–13.
Ferrier, R. J. (1991) Auditing standards and guidelines, in M. Sherer and S. Turley (eds.) *Current Issues in Auditing* (2nd edn), Paul Chapman, London.
Flint, D. (1988) *Philosophy and Principles of Auditing – An Introduction,* Macmillan, London.
Lee, T. A. (1972) *Company Auditing: Concepts and Practices,* Gee & Co., London.
Lee, T. A. (1982) *Company Auditing* (2nd edn), Gee & Co., London.
Lee, T. A. (1986) *Company Auditing* (3rd edn), Van Nostrand Reinhold, Wokingham.
Mautz, R. K. and Sharaf, H. A. (1961) *The Philosophy of Auditing,* American Accounting Association, Sarasota, Fl.
Pong, C. and Whittington, G. (1994) The working of the Auditing Practices Committee – three case studies, *Accounting and Business Research,* Vol. 24, no. 94, pp. 157–75.
Sikka, P., Willmott, H. and Lowe, T. (1989) Guardians of knowledge and public interest: evidence and issues of accountability in the UK accountancy profession, *Accounting, Auditing and Accountability Journal,* Vol. 2, no. 2, pp. 47–71.

DISCUSSION QUESTIONS

1. Explain why it has become necessary to have written standards for auditors.
2. In which respects may the current Statements of Auditing Standards be considered to be inadequate?
3. To what extent is the output of the APB the product of a political process?
4. Identify issues which are likely to be of concern to auditing practitioners and standard-setters in the future.
5. To what extent do you believe that the UK standard-setters should be influenced by international developments? If auditing standards can be set by an international body is there any need for a national body such as the APB?
6. 'The standards of the auditing profession have no theoretical basis.' To what extent is this an accurate view of the APB's Statements of Auditing Standards?
7. In what respects do the changes to the APB's constitution and output meet the criticisms of its predecessor, the APC?

10
Audit Reports
David J. Hatherly

INTRODUCTION

Auditors tell each other that an audit report indicates that they have obtained reasonable, though not absolute, assurance that the financial statements are free of a material mis-statement and, further, that the level of reasonable assurance must depend on the preceived risk of the hypothetical mis-statement in question. It would seem useful to inform the readers of this interpretation.

(Anderson, 1977, p. 439)

Anderson (1977) is typical of many who have supported an approach to audit reporting which is informative of what an audit involves and what an audit opinion really means. Given the overriding requirement for informative reporting, this chapter explores the fundamental questions: what the audit report should say and how it should say it. In particular, the chapter identifies ten objectives for the audit report and discusses and analyses the existing UK company audit report by reference to each of these objectives in turn. The chapter concludes by identifying possible future measures which might help to develop still further the information content and usefulness of the audit report.

The auditor's objective to communicate his or her results based on the planning, evaluation and collection of audit evidence is governed in law in the UK by the Companies Act 1985. This requires the audit report to state whether, in the auditor's opinion, the company's balance sheet and profit and loss account have been properly prepared in accordance with the provisions of the Companies Act *and* whether a true and fair view is given of the state of affairs at the year-end and of the profit or loss for the year. Various other reporting duties are also imposed on the auditor by statute and some of these will be discussed in more detail later.

It can be argued that these statutory requirements should be extended to bring company auditing more in line with auditing in the public sector. For example, the auditor could be given a statutory duty to report on whether the company has procedures to prevent fraud, bribery or other illegal activity and whether it has procedures to ensure the economical, efficient and effective use of company resources. Some such extensions may come in time, but if they do they are likely, as is currently the case in the public sector, to be the subject of one or more separate reports distinct from the report on the financial statements. This chapter limits its ambition to a discussion of the reporting problems that arise from the company auditor's present statutory responsibilities in respect of the company's financial statements. However, it should be noted that there is already a legal requirement in respect of regulated businesses (investment businesses, banks, insurance companies, building societies and friendly societies) for the auditor to report to the regulator in certain circumstances. Auditors have a duty to report breaches of statutory or regulatory requirements encountered during the audit and of material significance to the regulator. Such breaches are likely (APB, 1994a, App. 1) to relate to regulations about the maintenance of adequate financial resources, the conduct of the business in a sound and prudent manner or the 'fit and proper' status of directors and senior management.

WHAT SHOULD THE REPORT SAY?

Prior to the introduction of SAS 600 (APB, 1993), which required the current 'expanded' audit report for September 1993 year-ends onwards, the UK was using the following 'short form' report:

Auditor's report to the members of XYZ Limited.

We have audited the financial statements on pages . . . to . . . in accordance with Auditing Standards.

In our opinion the financial statements give a true and fair view of the state of the company's affairs at 31 December 19— and of its profit and source and application of funds for the year then ended and have been properly prepared in accordance with the Companies Act 1985.

In a previous edition of this book, Hatherly and Skuse (1991, p. 116) argued that an audit report should:

1. identify for whom the audit report is written;
2. explain that the financial statements are prepared by the directors and that the main purpose of the audit is to provide an independent opinion on the reliability of those financial statements;

3. identify the financial statements to which the audit report relates and explain the nature of any auditor responsibility for information in the annual report but outside the financial statements;

4. explain the limits of the auditor's responsibility for detecting fraud and irregularity;

5. give an indication of the fact that evidence available to support any audit opinion is persuasive rather than conclusive;

6. describe the audit work performed on the financial statements and in particular the role of internal control;

7. positively state all audit opinions;

8. as regards the true and fair view opinion, indicate the basis on which the true and fair view is judged;

9. make clear that the true and fair opinion relates to the financial statements as a whole rather than to individual figures within those financial statements;

10. clearly explain the nature of, reasons for, and effect of, any qualified audit opinion.

The Auditing Practices Board (APB) has issued auditing standards and guidelines which, among other things, explain the nature of the audit. An audit report incorporating all the ten elements above would be largely 'free-standing' of the standards and guidelines since the report would itself go much of the way to explaining the responsibilities of the auditor and the nature of the audit. In the free-standing approach, therefore, there is no assumption that the audit report reader is familiar with, or even has access to, the standards and guidelines or other explanatory documents. The audit report itself is taken as the principal means of communication of the auditing profession with the 'financial public'.

In May 1993 the APB (APB,1993) issued a standard, *Auditors' Reports on Financial Statements*, which introduced an expanded audit report covering many of the ten requirements.[1] For instance, para. 14 on the basic elements of the auditors' report states:

Auditors' reports on financial statements should include the following matters:

(a) a title identifying the person or persons to whom the report is addressed;

(b) an introductory paragraph identifying the financial statements audited;

(c) separate sections, appropriately headed, dealing with
(i) respective responsibilities of directors (or equivalent persons) and auditors,
(ii) the basis of the auditors' opinion,
(iii) the auditors' opinion on the financial statements;

(d) the manuscript or printed signature of the auditors; and

(e) the date of the auditor's report. (SAS 600.2)

Paragraph 24 on the basis of opinion states:

Auditors should explain the basis of their opinion by including in their report:

(a)   a statement as to their compliance or otherwise with Auditing Standards, together with the reasons for any departure therefrom;

(b)   a statement that the audit process includes

    (i)   examining, on a test basis, evidence relevant to the amounts and disclosures in the financial statements,

    (ii)   assessing the significant estimates and judgments made by the reporting entity's directors in preparing the financial statements,

    (iii)   considering whether the accounting policies are appropriate to the reporting entity's circumstances, consistently applied and adequately disclosed;

(c)   a statement that they planned and performed the audit so as to obtain reasonable assurance that the financial statements are free from material misstatement, whether caused by fraud or other irregularity or error, and that they have evaluated the overall presentation of the financial statements.   (SAS 600.4)

The current position in the UK

The introduction of SAS 600: *Auditors' Reports on Financial Statements* means that the current unqualified audit report in the UK for a company without subsidiaries typically reads as follows:

UNQUALIFIED REPORT – SAS 600

AUDITORS' REPORT TO THE SHAREHOLDERS OF XYZ PLC
We have audited the financial statements on pages . . . to . . . which have been prepared under the historical cost convention (as modified by the revaluation of certain fixed assets) and the accounting policies set out on page . . .

Respective responsibilities of directors and auditors
As described on page . . . the company's directors are responsible for the preparation of financial statements. It is our responsibility to form an independent opinion, based on our audit, on those statements and to report our opinion to you.

Basis of opinion
We conducted our audit in accordance with Auditing Standards issued by the Auditing Practices Board. An audit includes examination, on a test basis, of evidence relevant to the amounts and disclosures in the financial statements. It also includes an assessment of the significant estimates and judgments made by the directors in the preparation of the financial statements, and of whether the accounting policies are appropriate to the company's circumstances, consistently applied and adequately disclosed.

We planned and performed our audit so as to obtain all the information and explanations which we considered necessary in order to provide us with sufficient evidence to give reasonable assurance that the financial statements are free from material misstatement whether caused by fraud or other irregularity or error. In forming our opinion we also evaluated the overall adequacy of the presentation of information in the financial statements.

Opinion

In our opinion the financial statements give a true and fair view of the state of the company's affairs as at 31 December 19— and of its profit (loss) for the year then ended and have been properly prepared in accordance with the Companies Act 1985.

Registered auditors   *Address*
Date

A later section of this chapter discusses this report in detail by reference to each of the ten elements previously suggested for inclusion in a free-standing audit report. It thus examines how well the standard (SAS 600) meets the ten requirements.

HOW SHOULD IT SAY IT?

The Department of Trade Inspectors (1979, p. 156) in the Peachey Property case, accused the auditors of reporting in 'hieratic' language, which they defined as 'language which is neither comprehensible as ordinary speech nor adequately defined to a specialist'.

Audit reports may not need to be understood by every person who 'travels on the Clapham omnibus', but they should be comprehensible to the vast majority of individuals who buy and sell shares, to bank managers, tax inspectors, those in business who give credit, to companies, and to the financial journalist. The potential 'user' or 'reader' of audit reports may not have received any formal accountancy or audit training but it can be hypothesized that such a person has had a sound general education, has some knowledge of the way business works and can accordingly be defined as a 'reasonably competent' reader.

To be comprehensible, therefore, either the audit report must use language in its natural sense or, if it uses technical language, that language must itself be capable of clear definition in non-technical terms to the reasonably competent reader. The use of natural language is consistent with the free-standing philosophy referred to earlier, in the sense that the language used in the report should be readily comprehensible and need no further explanation for the reasonably competent reader. A report that uses brief technical terms – specialized symbols serving as coded messages – should use definitions which are widely available to reasonably competent readers. Examples of coded messages are the use of the 'except for' wording in qualified audit reports and the use of expressions such as 'limitation of scope' and 'disclaimer of opinion'. These are explained in the relevant audit standard – paras. 67 and 69 of SAS 600 (APB, 1993).

Particular problems exist with respect to phrases such as 'true and fair view', 'profit' and 'state of affairs' which the Companies Acts require to be used in the auditor's opinion. By their nature such concepts are not capable of easy definition. As used in the audit opinion the term 'profit' does not just mean the accounting profit but a broader concept of financial performance embracing accounting profit, cash flow and recognized gains and losses. On the other hand, 'state of affairs' is usually interpreted more narrowly than its natural meaning, so as to be the state of *financial* affairs or *financial* position. It is often identified with the balance sheet and relevant notes. Most difficult of all is an understanding of the term 'true and fair view'. Its meaning is discussed later in this chapter.

ELEMENTS OF A FREE-STANDING REPORT

Element 1 Identify for whom the audit report is written

The UK reporting standard (APB, 1993, para. 14) expressly requires the auditor to identify those to whom the report is addressed. The effect of this requirement is that, in the UK, the audit report is addressed to the shareholders. The US auditing profession also recognized the need for the report to be addressed to someone, and para. 9 of SAS 58 (AICPA, 1988) states: 'The report may be addressed to the company whose financial statements are being audited or to its board of directors or stockholders.' However, it is important to remember that in both countries the identification of the addressees of the report does not of itself limit the extent of the auditor's liability to third parties for negligent work. For further discussions of this topic, see Chapter 6.

Element 2 Explain that the financial statements are prepared by the directors and that the main purpose of the audit is to provide an independent opinion on the reliability of those financial statements

It is a fundamental auditing concept that the auditor is independent of the persons responsible for the preparation of the financial statements. In the UK audit report there is an express reference to the fact that the financial statements were prepared by the directors. At the same time as pointing out that the auditor does not prepare the financial statements, the audit report explains what the auditor does do, i.e. provides an independent opinion on the financial statements.

Element 3 Identify the financial statements to which the audit report relates and explain the nature of any auditor responsibility for information in the annual report but outside the financial statements

The UK reporting standard (APB, 1993, para. 14) expressly requires the auditor to identify the financial statements to which the audit relates, and this is done by use of the phrase 'the financial statements on pages . . . to . . . '. The Companies Act 1985 recognizes the need for the directors' report to be consistent with the financial statements and imposes an obligation on the auditor to comment if this is not so. The problem is that the annual report may contain, as well as the financial statements and directors' report, further information such as a chairman's report, an operating and financial review, value-added reports and reports to employees. Much of this information is expressed in financial terms. In most cases the auditor will, as a matter of good practice, review this unaudited information in the annual report for consistency with the financial statements. It might be helpful for the audit report to explain the nature of the work performed by the auditor in respect of the directors' report and, where appropriate, any other 'unaudited' information. This is not done in the current audit report. *The Audit Agenda* (APB, 1994b) recognizes this as a weakness. It argues (p. 7) that audits should provide assurance to shareholders on the consistency of all textual information accompanying the financial statements with the view portrayed by the financial statements.

Element 4 Explain the limits of the auditor's responsibility for detecting fraud and irregularity

Responsibility for fraud detection is a highly sensitive topic. The professional accountancy bodies' interpretation of the current legal requirement is some way from the 'popular' view of the auditor as someone whose job it is to track down fraud. The UK profession's view, expressed in the standard audit report, is that auditors should design their tests to give 'reasonable assurance that the financial statements are free from material misstatement whether caused by fraud or other irregularity or error'. It sounds as though the auditor does not make a distinction between the levels of assurance required in respect of fraud and other errors. However, paras. 21 and 22 of SAS 110 (APB, 1995a) indicate that what is 'reasonable' assurance in the context of fraud is likely to be regarded by the profession as less than what is 'reasonable' in respect of non-fraudulent errors. The concept of 'reasonable assurance' remains a difficult area of understanding for both the giver and receiver of the audit report. The implication of the 'popular' view might be that auditors should work with a higher level of assurance (a stricter materiality concept and/or a higher standard of care) in respect of errors caused by fraud or irregularity than for other errors. It was suggested by Jack (1983), at least in respect of frauds or irregularities perpetrated by company officials, that the present statutory position following the Companies Act 1980 (since consolidated into the Companies Act

1985) is closer to the 'popular' view than it is to the profession's interpretation. Such a suggestion is consistent with current concerns over corporate governance and the accountability of directors.

Element 5 Give an indication of the fact that evidence available to support any audit opinion is persuasive rather than conclusive

According to a study by Arthur Andersen (1974), a substantial minority of shareholders (37 per cent) erroneously thought that the auditor determines the accuracy of financial statements by going through all financial records. This study was conducted some time ago but its implication is that audit report readers can gain an exaggerated impression of the quality of the evidence which can realistically be obtained by the auditor. In reality, the evidence available to the auditor can be only persuasive, rather than conclusive, for a number of reasons, especially the need to sample the financial records and the subjective nature of any evaluation of the system of internal control. The way of indicating the persuasive nature of audit evidence is through the words 'An audit includes examination on a test basis' as well as the reference to 'reasonable assurance' in the opinion paragraph of the audit report.

Element 6 Describe the audit work performed on the financial statements and in particular the role of internal control

The present audit report refers to the audit being conducted in accordance with auditing standards and goes on to explain some of the key points contained in those standards. However, the role of internal control is not explicitly addressed. This issue is brought into focus by looking at the example engagements letter included as an appendix to SAS 140 (APB, 1995b). This says that '[the auditor] shall obtain an understanding of the accounting and internal control systems in order to assess their adequacy as a basis for the preparation of the financial statements' (para. 2.1). It also says (para. 2.2) that 'the nature and extent of our [the auditor's] procedures will vary according to our assessment of the company's accounting system and, where we wish to place reliance on it, the internal control system'.

The question arises that, if such a description is included in the engagement letter to help directors understand the audit process, why then should it not be included in the audit report to help the shareholders and others understand the audit process? Of course, if such a description were included it might lead to demands to know what kind of an evaluation of the internal controls had been carried out and the results. The auditor could not divulge the results of any internal control evaluation in a public report without a formally recognized change to include evaluation of internal control as a specific objective of the audit. However, this was one of the recommendations of the Cadbury Committee (CFACG, 1992), and consequently there has been much discussion as to whether the auditor can give shareholders an explicit report on the company's internal control and, if so, how this report would be worded.

Element 7 Positively state all audit opinions

Positive reporting can be contrasted with reporting by exception, in which the auditor includes his or her opinion in the audit report only if that opinion is unfavourable. For example, section 237 of the Companies Act 1985 requires that, if the auditors are of the opinion that proper accounting records have *not* been kept, or that proper returns have *not* been received from branches not visited by the auditors, or if the balance sheet and profit and loss account are *not* in agreement with the accounting records, they shall state that fact in their report. Similarly, if the auditors *fail* to obtain all the information and explanations necessary for the purposes of the audit, they are to state that fact in their report, and, as previously mentioned, if the auditor is of the opinion that any of the information in the directors' report is inconsistent with the financial statements that too must be stated. Unlike reporting by exception, positive reporting requires the auditor to express his or her opinion in the audit report, whether the opinion is favourable or unfavourable.

Positive reporting can also be contrasted with negative reporting, in which an auditor is prepared to say that he or she has no reason to believe there is anything wrong, but never positively states that he or she believes things to be *right*. There is no statutory requirement or authority for the auditor to use negative reporting in connection with the annual statutory audit of a limited company's financial statements. Section 173(5) of the Companies Act 1985 does, however, require a negatively worded report from the auditor in special circumstances where a company purchases its own shares. The problem with negative reporting is that the less work the auditor does, the more confidently can he or she voice an opinion that he or she 'knows of no reason'. This contrasts with positive reporting where, generally, the more work the auditor does, the more confidently the opinion can be given.

It is reasonable to assert that positive reporting provides less potential for misunderstanding than either reporting by exception or negative reporting.

Element 8 As regards the true and fair view opinion, indicate the basis on which the true and fair view is judged

The Companies Act 1985 sets out statutory accounting principles, but it also provides that these principles and the format and disclosure requirements of the Act should be overridden, if necessary, in order to provide a true and fair view, if, owing to special circumstances in the case of any company, the balance sheet or profit and loss account would not otherwise show a true and fair view (s. 226(5)). The Act also requires (s. 226(4)) that, if compliance with the provisions of the Act is insufficient to give a true and fair view, the necessary additional information shall be given.

Thus, the Act appears to link the 'true and fair view' with both the sufficiency of the information provided by the presentation and disclosure of the financial statements and the appropriateness of the accounting principles to the particular circumstances of the business.

Skerratt (1982) has drawn attention to the fact that the phrase 'true and fair' is inappropriate for audit reporting unless the purposes for which the accounts will be used are specified. Although it may not be practical at the present time to state the assumed purposes of the accounts in the audit report (possibly they should be stated in the accounts?), the fact remains that any judgement regarding a true and fair view is linked to an assumed purpose or set of purposes for the financial statements.

On the basis of these discussions the following definition of a true and fair view might be ventured (Hatherly and Skuse, 1991, p. 124):

> Financial statements of an enterprise give a true and fair view if they, together with related notes, are sufficiently informative of matters that affect their use, understanding and interpretation by those for whom they are intended, and they are prepared in accordance with accounting principles appropriate to the circumstances of the business.

Such a definition gives at least some guidance as to the basis on which the true and fair view should be judged.

In considering the use of the words 'true and fair view' in UK audit reports, the question needs to be asked whether the words constitute natural language, readily understandable to the reader without further definition. It seems plausible that the phrase 'fair view' might be more natural language than 'true and fair view' since truth in accounting is conditioned by a concept of materiality and so is very different from the non-expert's concept of truth. However, the basis of opinion paragraph in the current UK report does give some indication of the meaning of a true and fair view. In particular, this paragraph explains that the auditor evaluates the overall adequacy of the presentation of the information in the financial statements, and conducts an assessment of whether the accounting policies are appropriate to the company's circumstances.

The opening paragraph of the current report has an optional reference to the financial statements having been prepared under the historical cost convention (as modified by revaluations). Clearly historical costs may not be entirely appropriate to the circumstances of the business if the business is experiencing rapid price changes in its markets. The reference to the historical cost convention is really code for the fact that the financial statements do not attempt to reflect the impact of changing price levels upon the financial performance and position of the company. Where price changes are an issue it would be clearer to state this explicitly rather than rely on a reference to the historical cost convention.

Element 9 Make clear that the true and fair view opinion relates to the financial statements taken as a whole rather than to individual figures therein

Present practice in the UK is to report on whether 'the financial statements give, in our opinion, a true and fair view of the state of affairs, and profit for the year'. It might be more helpful to stress that the true and fair opinion does not relate to individual figures in the financial statements by reporting whether 'the financial statements, taken as a whole, give, in our opinion, a true and fair view of . . .'.

In this connection, it is interesting to note that the US Reporting Standard (AICPA, 1988, p. 6) states: 'the report shall contain an expression of opinion regarding the financial statements, taken as a whole'. The UK has not followed the US lead in this regard.

Element 10 Clearly explain the nature of, reasons for, and effect of, any qualified audit opinion

Under SAS 600 (APB, 1993, para. 33) only limitation of scope and disagreements on accounting treatment or disclosure are valid reasons for a qualified audit opinion. The reporting standard requires different forms of qualified report as follows:

Nature of circumstances	Material but not fundamental	Fundamental
Scope limitation	'Except for'	Disclaimer
Disagreement	'Except for'	Adverse

The rows represent two different categories of circumstance, either of which might *cause* a qualification. The columns represent two possibilities for the extent to which the underlying problem *affects*, or potentially affects, the view given by the financial statements. Thus, each of the four possible permutations represents a different cause/effect combination.

The end product is a coding system, but because two of the underlying combinations are coded using the same 'except for' language the 'except for' code can only be read in the context of the report as a whole. If readers are unfamiliar with the qualifying propensity of the individual auditor, the efficiency of any code depends partly upon the extent to which different auditors, faced with exactly the same set of circumstances and the same actual or potential effect on the financial statements, would apply the same coded message to communicate their qualified opinion. There is some evidence (Dillard, Murdock and Shank, 1978) that such coding schemes may not in this sense be effective. Only 53 per cent of the CPAs participating in the Dillard study agreed with the disclosure and opinion form used by other CPAs in a selected set of cases. The effectiveness of the code is also conditional upon it being understood by the reader of audit reports, who would also have to understand the meaning of words such as 'material' and 'fundamental'. Doubts about the code make it doubly necessary to support the opinion paragraph with a 'reservation' paragraph explaining both the circumstances and the effect on the financial statements. Readers are thus allowed to draw their own conclusions as to the extent to which the true and fair view is impaired. In this way the reader of the report receives both a coded message, which places the particular problem in one of the broad categories, plus a paragraph explaining the situation in more detail.

The treatment of uncertainty

Under SAS 600.6 (APB, 1993, para. 54), if uncertainties are properly accounted for and disclosed, then their existence does not preclude the presentation of a true and fair view. This is consistent with the Companies Act presumption that a true and fair view can always be given. With an uncertainty the issue is whether the auditors agree with how it has been accounted for and disclosed. If there is disagreement then an 'except for' qualification or an adverse report follows. If there is agreement then there is no qualification. However, if the uncertainty is a fundamental uncertainty (for example, major litigation pending and/or serious going concern problems), a separate paragraph headed 'fundamental uncertainty' within the basis of opinion section of the report highlights the uncertainty. This is not a qualification. Its purpose is to highlight the auditor's attention to this matter during the auditor's opinion formation.

FUTURE DIRECTIONS

Future developments in audit reporting will be necessary in respect of new and emerging audit services such as reporting on internal control, major business risks and information included in the annual report but outside the financial statements. Auditors' reports are being developed in respect of internal control but at the time of writing they require further refinement.

This chapter discusses two possible interrelated developments for the future of the traditional reporting function in the financial statements. These developments are, firstly, the adoption of 'free-form' reporting and, secondly, the recognition of the audit opinion as a professional judgement. By way of introduction it is helpful to consider the advantages and disadvantages of the current expanded report.

Unlike the current expanded report, the previous short-form report made no attempt to be a 'free-standing' report. If the reader wanted to know more of the basis for the audit opinion it was necessary to consult auditing standards and guidelines. To date, academic research into the use of the expanded audit report (e.g. Hatherly, Innes and Brown, 1991) supports the view that the expanded report changes the reader's understanding of the auditor's responsibilities, the audit process and the nature of the audit opinion. It also enhances the reader's perception of the usefulness and credibility of the audited financial statements.

Perhaps for these reasons the expansion of the audit report has largely been accepted by the professional and commercial communities. However, it is not above criticism. First there is the argument that users of financial statements care little for the technicalities of the audit and simply want to know whether or not the financial statements are 'OK'. This is similar to the view (Epstein, 1976) that the auditor's report is a code or symbol, providing a seal of approval. If so, then whether or not the report is qualified can be seen quickly from the old 'short-form' report, which therefore is a neater, more digestible piece of code.

A second line of criticism maintains that the change to an expanded audit report follows from the profession's desire to 'educate' users into greater understanding and acceptance of the present audit as a substitute for addressing the need for a wider range of audit responsibilities, a more rigorous audit process and a more informative audit report than is presently provided. The 'free-form' report attempts to address the last of these concerns. Although the expanded audit report is much longer than the short-form report it mostly retains standard wording. The main innovation of the expanded audit report was the inclusion of a section headed 'Basis of opinion'. However, only the description of any fundamental uncertainty, or the explanation for a qualification, varies from audit to audit. Most of the wording is 'boilerplate'.

Free-form reporting

Estes (1982, p. 93) was among the first to argue against standardized wording. He states: 'All standardized wording should be dropped; the auditor's report should be composed anew, 'from scratch', for each audit.' Free-form reporting is an approach which allows and encourages the auditor to explain the circumstances of each individual audit opinion in terms of the difficulties and experiences of the particular audit.

The free-form approach avoids investor conditioning which Estes (1982, p. 91) describes in the following terms:

> The hypothesis of investor conditioning is based on the standardization of audit report wording and format. The wording of the standard unqualified audit report is prescribed by the American Institute of CPAs and most CPA firms follow this wording precisely. Even qualified reports are made as uniform as possible. By standardizing the audit report, the accounting profession may have insured that it will be uninteresting. The reader has apparently been conditioned to expect no surprises and so does not read the audit report.

It is likely that any future move to free-form reporting would have to retain some specified framework around which the free-form report would be written. In a recent study Hatherly, Innes and Brown (1996) experimented with a free-form report based on a style of report already offered by a 'big six' firm to boards of directors on a private basis. This report was structured around a framework of (1) constructive recommendations (management letter points), (2) adjustments to the financial statements as a result of the audit, and (3) difficult issues of judgement arising during the audit and their resolution. It was found that, compared to an SAS 600 report, such a 'free-form' report does significantly change the users' perceptions of the audit process and audit product. In essence the process is perceived as more rigorous and the product as more useful in a number of key respects.

Much of the potential of free-form reporting lies in its ability to provide insights into the 'quality' of the audit conducted in terms of both the evidence gathering and the opinion formation. This might generate competition between auditing firms on the basis of quality. At present audit quality is not visible to the investing community except when an audit goes badly wrong. Thus competition tends to take place on the dimensions of the firm's brand name and cost rather than quality *per se* (Moizer, 1993).

The audit opinion as a professional judgement

A further current issue with respect to audit reporting is whether or not the audit report should carry the name of the engagement partner and possibly a brief description of the engagement partner's role. This is really part of a much deeper debate about the nature of an audit opinion and the extent to which it represents the engagement partner's judgement (or a collective judgement by a group within the firm) rather than due completion of an audit firm's process. Judgement in crucial areas such as inherent risk, control risk, analytical review and the true and fair view is unlikely to lead to high levels of consensus between individual (or even group) judgements. If this is so, then the argument goes that the name of the judge(s) should be shown in the audit report to allow the track record to be observable. As with free-form reporting, greater disclosure provides for market competition, this time around the reputation of the judge. Those who support this proposition argue that the value added of an audit comes from the quality of the professional judgement(s) rather than due compliance with process, which in many areas may be virtually indistinguishable from one audit firm to the next.

CONCLUSION

This chapter has focused on the company auditor's current style of audit report in accordance with SAS 600. This report is evaluated as a 'free-standing' report which can be read and understood by the reasonably competent reader without knowledge of technical terms or knowledge of the auditing standards and guidelines. The current audit report is found to meet many of the criteria for such a free-standing report.

The chapter also contrasts the current audit report with the short-form report which was used prior to 1993 and with proposals for a 'free-form' audit report which does not use 'boilerplate' language but which explains the difficulties involved in forming the audit opinion in the particular circumstances of each individual audit. Finally, the chapter acknowledges the merit of the individual audit engagement partner signing the audit report in his or her name alongside the name of the audit firm.

NOTE

1. The author was a member of the APB working party which developed this standard.

REFERENCES

AICPA (1988) *Reports on Audited Financial Statements*, Statement on Auditing Standards 58, American Institute of Certified Public Accountants, New York.

Anderson, R. J. (1977) *The External Audit*, Pitman, London.

APB (1993) *Auditors' Reports on Financial Statements* (SAS 600), Auditing Practices Board, London.

APB (1994a) *The Auditors' Right and Duty to Report to Regulators in the Financial Sector* (SAS 620), Auditing Practices Board, London.

APB (1994b) *The Audit Agenda*, Auditing Practices Board, London.

APB (1995a) *Fraud and Error* (SAS 110), Auditing Practices Board, London.

APB (1995b) *Engagement Letters* (SAS 140), Auditing Practices Board, London.

Arthur Andersen & Co. (1974) *Public Accounting in Transition: American Shareholders View the Role of Independent Accountants and the Corporate Reporting Controversy*, Arthur Andersen, Chicago.

CFACG (1992) *Report of the Committee on the Financial Aspects of Corporate Governance* (Cadbury Committee), Gee, London.

Department of Trade Inspectors (1979) *Inspectors' Report on Peachey Property Corporation Limited*, HMSO, London.

Dillard, J. F., Murdock, R. J. and Shank, J. K. (1978) CPAs' attitudes toward 'subject to' opinions, *The CPA Journal*, August, pp. 43–7.

Epstein, M. J. (1976) The corporate shareholder's view of the auditor's report: conclusions and recommendations, reported in AICPA (1978) *Appendix B of the Commission on Auditors' Responsibilities: Report, Conclusions and Recommendations*, AICPA, New York.

Estes, R. (1982) *The Auditor's Report and Investor Behavior*, Lexington Books, Lexington, Mass.

Hatherly, D. and Skuse, P. (1991) Audit reports, in M. Sherer and S. Turley, *Current Issues in Auditing* (2nd edn), Paul Chapman, London, pp. 115–30.

Hatherly, D., Innes, J. and Brown, T. (1991) The expanded audit report – an empirical investigation, *Accounting and Business Research*, Autumn, pp. 311–16.

Hatherly, D., Innes, J. and Brown, T. (1996) The power of free form reporting, unpublished working paper, University of Edinburgh.

Jack, R. B. (1983) Shareholder protection and the auditor, *Symposium on Auditing Research 1982*, University of Glasgow Press.

Moizer, P. (1993) Audit quality and auditor reputation: a theoretical and empirical investigation, unpublished Ph.D. thesis, University of Manchester.

Skerratt, L. (1982) Auditing in the corporate sector: a survey, in A. G. Hopwood, M. Bromwich and J. Shaw (eds.) (1982) *Auditing Research: Issues and Opportunities*, Pitman, London, pp. 69–79.

DISCUSSION QUESTIONS

1. 'The audit report should be of great interest to investors, but it is not. It appears instead to be widely ignored' (Ralph Estes, 1982, p. 90).
   (a) Why should the audit report be of great interest to investors?
   (b) If Estes's and others' research results are correct and the audit report is largely ignored by investors, what could be the reasons for the lack of interest?
2. Discuss the advantages and disadvantages of the audit report consisting of a series of short coded messages. How much of the current UK unqualified audit report do you consider to consist of coded messages?
3. Consider the following audit report wording:

AUDITOR'S REPORT TO THE MEMBERS OF AB LTD

Scope of audit
We have audited the financial statements on pages ... to ... in accordance with approved Auditing Standards and have obtained all the information and explanations we considered necessary in the circumstances. In accordance with company law, the overall responsibility for the preparation of the financial statements is that of the directors. The audit is an independent examination of, and expression of opinion on, these financial statements.

The audit process
Auditing Standards require:
(1) that we obtain an understanding of the accounting system in order to assess its adequacy as a basis for the preparation of the financial statements, and that we
(2) vary the nature and extent of our tests according to our assessment of the accounting system, and where appropriate, our assessment of the system of internal control, so as
(3) to obtain relevant and reliable evidence sufficient to enable us to draw reasonable conclusions therefrom.

Unqualified opinion
We have obtained reasonable assurance that in our opinion the financial statements, referred to above, taken as a whole:
(1) give a fair view of the financial position of AB Limited at ... 19— and of the results of its operations and cash flow for the year then ended, based upon the sufficient presentation and disclosure of the information contained in the financial statements in accordance with accounting principles appropriate to the circumstances of the business;
(2) comply with the Companies Act 1985.

(a) Does the above report comply with the present UK Companies Act reporting requirements?
(b) In what way does it differ from the present style of audit report used in the UK, and do you consider it to be an improvement?
(c) To what extent does the report fail to take up all ten suggestions made in the chapter as regards the content of a 'free-standing' audit report?
4. Discuss the advantages and disadvantages to the large auditing firms of any proposal for
   (a) free-form reporting;
   (b) the audit engagement partner to sign the audit report.

11

Developments in Audit Approaches: From Audit Efficiency to Audit Effectiveness?

Andrew Higson

INTRODUCTION

In relation to the external audit, perhaps the only constant thing is change. During the 1970s and 1980s auditors made enormous alterations to, and developments in, their audit methodologies. However, what has happened since then? Though the repercussions of the auditor's work are seldom out of the business news, there is very little publicly available information regarding the way that individual practices of registered auditors conduct their audits. Large firms' audit methodologies have been examined in the past (e.g. Cushing and Leobbecke, 1986; Higson, 1987; Turley and Cooper, 1991), but there is very little about what has been happening in the 1990s. In order to shed some light on this situation, a number of interviews were conducted with senior audit practitioners. Therefore, the objective of this chapter is to try to give an appreciation of the debates which are taking place regarding the conduct of the external audit. The results which are presented may be impressionistic but they should give a good insight into the current issues relating to external auditors' approaches to the conduct of their work.

In the 1980s audit efficiency was probably the major driving force behind audit developments (e.g. Burton and Fairfield, 1982). Accountancy firms were quite open about this, and Turley and Cooper (1991, p. 23), following their interviews with senior auditors, were able to conclude: 'The most important

Andrew Higson is a Lecturer at Loughborough University Business School.

criterion for making the choice of [audit] strategy is the notion of efficiency.' Whilst there is no doubt that auditors are still very much concerned with efficiency, there is now evidence, both public (Davis, 1996) and from the interviews undertaken for this chapter, that things may be starting to change. Given the current litigious atmosphere, auditors are starting to reassess the objective of the audit and, consequently, how this should be accomplished. So, rather than simply concentrating on how to do their work more efficiently (by trying to carry out existing procedures more cost effectively), they are now starting to question what, as auditors, they are trying to achieve and, thus, what sort of work this requires. Therefore, there appears to have been a move by some firms to reconsider the overall effectiveness of their audit approaches in the light of a re-evaluation of the risks (both audit and commercial) that they face – hence the title of this chapter. The nature of the changes implemented by some firms is such that the developments could almost be classified as an example of 'process re-engineering'. This is likely to have a dramatic impact on what people consider auditing is all about, and could indicate a need for the reassessment of the external auditor's function.

BACKGROUND

The external audit has evolved in line with changes in the auditor's role, the auditing environment and auditing technology. The role of the auditor has changed over time (e.g. Brown, 1962; Bird, 1970; Flint, 1971; Beck, 1973; Carmichael and Whittington, 1984; Lee, 1986), is still changing, and will probably continue to change (McInnes, 1993; APB, 1994). Auditing approaches have therefore been forced to adapt in order that a commercially viable service could survive. An examination of the auditing literature shows that there have been very few recent attempts to examine individual accountancy firms' auditing practices. Indeed, generally there has been very little information about how actual audits are conducted (Gwilliam, 1987). In the past, due to the then confidential nature of the audit process, there was a debate as to the similarity, or otherwise, of accountancy firms' audit practices. For instance, Stevens (1984, p. 74) considered that the large firms went about their work in much the same way, and that the distinctions they make were more a matter of marketing tactics than substantive technical procedure, whereas Jones (1985, p. 243), for example, was of the view that it seemed to be a point of honour among the large firms that they each interpret the audit process in a different way. Cushing and Loebbecke (1986, p. 32) concluded that 'There are significant differences [between firms] in the degree of structure of audit processes.' However, this debate seems to have arisen because there was very little information about how auditors actually conduct their work. Certainly until the 1980s, many firms considered their auditing methods to be strictly confidential. During the 1980s details of individual firms' audit approaches started to appear in the academic literature (e.g. Elliott, 1983; Mock and Willingham, 1983; Grobstein and Craig, 1984; Walker and Pierce, 1988). More recent papers include the discussion by Felix *et al.* (1990) of Arthur Andersen's monetary unit sampling approach, a description by Graham, Damens and Van Ness (1991) of the development of Coopers & Lybrand's expert system for risk identification, and Gillett's (1993) description of Grant Thornton's development of ADAPT (an audit automation expert system tool for assisting in tailoring audit programmes). Currently, only one firm in the UK has a long history of publishing a version of its audit manual, namely, Coopers & Lybrand (its fifth edition was published in 1992 – the first edition in 1966). Grant Thornton published the fourth edition of its audit manual in 1990 (as Thornton Baker it published its manual for the first time in 1981). Other publicly available audit manuals include that of Robson Rhodes (1994), one produced by Sterling Professional Services (1995) 'for the use by partners and staff of Haines Watts' (p. 1) and the manual edited by Woolf (1992), which relates to Kingston Smith. A general audit manual was edited by Harris (1995). However, even these publications do not really give an insight into the debates which exist regarding the way the external audit should be conducted. It is only occasionally that these debates, which auditors are constantly engaged in, are made public.

In a recent article Davis (1996, p. 6) discussed Coopers & Lybrand's audit philosophy – describing the firm's approach as 'the fourth generation audit'. Davis considered that the first-generation audit could be described as 'verifying transactions in the books'. In relation to the audits of large companies, the first generation of audits probably ended during the late 1960s; however, the attempted verification of transactions probably continued in relation to the audit of very small companies until the abolition of their statutory audit requirement in 1994. The second-generation audit was described as 'relying on systems'. This approach involved the auditor ascertaining and documenting the accounting system, with particular regard to information flows and the identification of internal controls. It required the evaluation of the usefulness to the auditor of these controls, and then compliance tests were required if the auditor wished to rely on them. If this work showed that the controls were effective, this would enable a reduction in the level of detailed substantive testing (although in the early days this was not always the case, and thus there was a concern about 'overauditing'). Though the 1970s were the high point of the systems-based approach to auditing, this was never really appropriate for the audit of small companies. This was due to the lack of controls necessary to give audit assurance to external auditors. The early 1980s saw a readjustment in auditors' approaches. The assessment of systems was an expensive process, and so auditors began to cut back their systems work and make greater use of analytical procedures (see Higson, 1987). Linked with this was the development during the mid-1980s of risk-based auditing (see Turley and Cooper, 1991), which Davis (1996) has termed the third-generation audit. The significance of the application of the concept of risk to the audit approach 'is that its concern is not with the choice of a particular strategy for collecting evidence *per se*, but rather with providing a criterion for making that choice and determining the overall direction of audit work' (Turley and Cooper, 1991, p. 15). Though risk-based auditing may have dominated auditors' approaches during the first half of the 1990s, Davis considered that it was now time for the evolution of the fourth generation audit, namely, 'the investigatory audit'. He described it as follows (1996, p. 6):

> It means audit people making judgements about audited people. With integrated business and accounting systems, most system failures in larger companies are now detected long before the audit. Things go wrong from human abuse of the systems and of trust. The motives are usually personal protection in seeking to conceal poor profits, or personal gain through theft. The whites of the eyes test is worth hundreds of words in an audit programme.

This approach appears to be moving the auditor's focus further away from the detail of the entries in the accounting system and on to the people who manage the business. This is almost a recognition that external auditing could be regarded as the audit of motivations (Higson, 1991). After all, as one provision could wipe out the profit from a million transactions, it is important for auditors to recognize the impact that management motivations could have on the presentation and content of a set of financial statements. Though the Accounting Standards Board (ASB) has made great efforts to limit management's discretion regarding the preparation and presentation of their financial statements, it must be recognized that the production of any set of financial statements requires the employment of judgement. Therefore, the honesty and motivations of management are important. However, there is a debate as to how much audit emphasis should be placed on these things rather than on the detail of the accounting records.

Another public example of one of the debates that auditors are engaged in relates to the impact of information technology (IT) on the audit process (e.g. Dresser, 1995). During the last decade most firms have been considering how to harness the forces of information technology in their audit approaches. All firms are considering how to make the best use of IT, and Dresser cites Coopers & Lybrand's development of 'Class', Price Waterhouse's 'Comet', and that Neville Russell has persuaded the ASB to put all its financial reporting standards on its 'Folio View' software. The leading edge of IT development involves the design of expert systems to assist the auditor's evaluations and judgement. Dresser highlights the debate as to how far the 'heavy investment in information technology' can go. One partner was reported as stating that he 'distrusted any over-automated approach to audit, because the human input was so valuable' (1995, p. 18). This does raise the question as to how much of the audit process can be automated and how much must be leg work, discussion and judgement.

A major recent development has been the replacement of the *Auditing Standards and Guidelines* (which were first issued in 1980 (APC)) by the Statements of Auditing Standards (APB, 1995) (discussed in Chapter 9). The Statements of Auditing Standards (SASs) contain the basic principles and essential procedures with which auditors are required to comply. The objective of an audit of financial statements was defined by SAS 100 as being 'to enable auditors to give an opinion on those financial statements taken as a whole and thereby to provide reasonable assurance that the financial statements give a true and fair view (where relevant) and have been prepared in accordance with relevant accounting or other requirements' (APB, 1995, p. 115). SAS 100 then sets out the auditor's responsibilities in relation to the conduct of an audit. Auditors are required to:

a) carry out procedures designed to obtain sufficient appropriate audit evidence, in accordance with Auditing Standards contained in SASs, to determine with reasonable confidence whether the financial statements are free from material misstatement;

b) evaluate the overall presentation of the financial statements, in order to ascertain whether they have been prepared in accordance with relevant legislation and accounting standards; and

c) issue a report containing a clear expression of their opinion on the financial statements.   (paragraph 2)

SAS 210 adds to this: 'Auditors should have or obtain a knowledge of the business of the entity to be audited which is sufficient to enable them to identify and understand the events, transactions and practices that may have a significant effect on the financial statements or the audit thereof' (APB, 1995, p. 123). This can be derived from knowledge of the industry in which a client operates and the legislation which relates to it. Knowledge of a specific client can be obtained through past experience with it, recent discussions with management and visits to the sites of the client's operations. The findings need to be related back to what is known about the industry. This knowledge can then be used to assist in the assessment of risk. SAS 300 requires the auditor to 'use professional judgement to assess the components of audit risk and to design audit procedures to ensure it is reduced to an acceptably low level'. It defines audit risk as being composed of three components: inherent risk, control risk and detection risk. In developing an audit approach an auditor must assess the likelihood of inherent risk ('the susceptibility of an account balance or class of transactions to material misstatement, either individually or when aggregated with misstatements in other balances or classes, irrespective of related internal controls' (APB, 1995, p. 128)). Therefore, inherent risk would include the integrity of the directors and management (and pressures on them), the nature of the business and the industry in which it operates. Lower down the organizational structure, inherent risk would include the quality of the accounting system, the complexity of transactions, adjustments involving a high degree of estimation and unusual transactions. A control risk is the risk that a material error or misstatement may go undetected by an accounting or internal control system (N.B. 'inherent risk and control risk are highly interrelated' (APB 1995, p. 129) because, in situations where high inherent risk is likely to exist, management often counter this by their accounting and internal control systems), whereas detection risk is the risk that auditors' substantive procedures will not detect a material mis-statement. SAS 300 defines the internal control system as 'the control envi-ronment and control procedures' (1995, p. 128) – thus highlighting the distinction between the two. The control environment is the overall philos-ophy and operating style of the directors and management in relation to their company's internal controls, while control procedures relates to specific poli-cies and procedures. This distinction is quite crucial when it comes to under-standing the developments in this area.

The SASs contain a lot more detail than the very general auditing stan-dards and guidelines which applied previously, and to that extent they may result in greater conformity in the way that external audits will be conducted. In view of the very limited amount of information about auditors' approaches to their audits, however, the question has to be raised as to what are the cur-rent issues in this area. In order to go some of the way to answering this question, eighteen interviews (including one pilot interview) were conducted (between November 1995 and February 1996) with audit partners and man-agers. These people were predominantly based in the 'top 30' accountancy firms and located mostly in London. Consequently the findings probably tend to reflect recent audit developments in larger firms and on larger audits, but they do illustrate issues which are of concern to many auditors.

THE AUDIT ENVIRONMENT

The auditor is first and foremost an entrepreneur – trying to make a suc-cessful living by providing a service. As with any other type of business, this involves having to survive in a competitive market. Audit approaches have developed over time – trying to balance commercial risk against the constant needs for efficiency and effectiveness. Therefore, auditing has evolved in response to changes in society's needs, market pressure and technological developments. During the 1980s auditors were concerned about the threat of litigation; the 1990s, however, appear to have brought about the threat of financial destruction – hence auditors' actions to cap their potential lia-bilities. The litigation pressures have translated into a greater awareness of risks – in the real sense of risks to the audit firm. A major driving force has been the need to protect their practices. The moves by some auditors to base their head offices in the Channel Islands, or to incorporate their audit prac-tices, indicate an increased perception of risk. Though only a few interviewees mentioned the litigation threat, this possibly illustrates the old adage that actions speak louder than words.

Competition in the audit market

Just about all those interviewed were concerned about increased competition and constrained audit fees – 'fee pressure has continued unabated' was one view. Although company directors have long complained about the levels of their audit fees, the late 1980s and early 1990s have seen an increasing willingness for them to put their audits out for tender. Thus, there has been increased competition in the market which is fairly stagnant. Another problem for auditors has been that 'people are questioning the value of the audit' and some regard it as 'a statutory evil'. The employment of better qualified staff and the general improvement in accounting systems mean that 'accounting errors are not happening' and the relevance of the audit is being questioned. Auditing is an unusual service, in that the people with whom the auditor has most dealings (the directors and the audit committees) are not the primary intended beneficiaries of the audit process. It is also very difficult for these people to measure audit quality. Consequently, there has been an increasing tendency for auditors to try to differentiate their services. As a result some auditors 'are far more likely to share their audit approach with clients and audit committees'. Another way has been to try to add value to the audit (e.g. Steen, 1989), in order to ensure that management receive something of tangible benefit. Increasingly, some auditors are using the notion of value added to give themselves a competitive edge and to try to differentiate their service from that of others – 'everyone's published report is the same – we must do something to differentiate ourselves'. The vast majority of those interviewed considered that value added was an important part of the auditor's function, a number thought it was 'fundamental' and that it 'was important from the commercial point of view'. One person stated that 'you don't keep clients if you don't come up with support for management'. Examples of 'adding value' cited by the interviewees included benchmarking, keeping management informed about what was happening in their business sector, and advice regarding foreign currency management, treasury issues and stock management. This does raise a question regarding independence (e.g. see Hatherly, 1989) – whether there may be a conflict between an independent examination of the financial statements of a business and giving formal advice regarding the running of that business. However, one view was that auditors were now simply formalizing what had happened in the past, but now they were making sure that clients appreciated what they were doing. Some reservations were expressed about the notion of 'value added'. One person considered that it was a 'buzz phrase' and that it was very difficult to undertake given the fee pressures, whilst another stated that 'audit is a commodity, what you do not do is try to add value'. The dominant view, however, was 'though, strictly speaking, it is not part of the audit, it is part of the client relationship'.

Information technology

All firms were constantly considering how to make the most of information technology, though limiting factors for some firms were development and implementation costs, as well as problems in seeing potential improvements in audit efficiency. One person considered that it was 'difficult to perceive bottom-line benefits'. All firms were using word processing, spreadsheets and packages for accounts preparation to some extent. Some firms had software for producing their audit programme (e.g. based on Lotus notes), thus enabling them to be easily tailored to individual clients. Less common was the development of software containing things like the audit manual, Financial Reporting Standards (FRSs) and the company accounts checklist. As can be seen from the above, most of these developments relate to assisting in the administration of the audit. Audit work conducted with the assistance of IT included analytical review and sample selection. A very few firms were working on the development of expert systems. Computer-assisted audit techniques (CAATs) tended to be used only on the very largest clients when there was no other practical way of conducting the audit; however, the use of sophisticated CAATs seems to be fairly limited. In general the audit team was expected to be able to deal with clients with standard software packages, and computer specialists were used only when the client's computer is 'mission critical'. The change can be summarized as follows: 'There was a time when clients with computer systems presented a problem [to the auditor], now without a computer the auditor has got a problem.' One person did express a concern that 'general auditors don't have the depth of experience' and, therefore, computer specialists were necessary in order to enable the transfer of skills. However, the general tendency appears to be to audit the controls around the computer system and then analyse the output, rather than auditing through the computer. So, two aspects to the use of IT can be discerned: first, its role in assisting in the administration of the audit and, second, its influence on the actual conduct of the audit. Many of the recent developments relate to the first of these two categories, and whilst some firms are pushing forwards and making greater use of IT in this area, a number are concerned that they have achieved 'not as much as we would like'. In relation to the second aspect, which could be described as the 'automation' of the audit, many of these developments have tended to be very much dependent on the nature and size of the audit clients.

Regulation

Another aspect to the audit environment has been the increase in regulation. The implementation of the Statements of Auditing Standards (which are more specific about what an auditor should do in the conduct of an audit) has already been mentioned, but in addition to this there has been the establishment of the Joint Monitoring Unit (JMU), which has resulted in the external scrutiny of firms' audit approaches and audit files. All this has led to an impression that 'more people are looking over your shoulder'. There was a general consensus that 'there was nothing fundamentally new' about the SASs, and that they were simply 'a codification of best practice'. As the SASs had stronger force than the previous auditing standards and guidelines, firms had taken steps to 'remind our people that the new standards had been brought in'. Some adjustments had been necessary to firms' audit manuals, but overall the impact of the SASs was considered to be fairly minimal. One view was that as a result the firm was 'a little more careful about the basics, e.g. planning'. It was also considered that SAS 230 on working papers, and SAS 240 on quality control for audit work, had created greater 'pressures to improve documentation' and had emphasized the importance of personal records of work done and questions asked. As to the impact of the JMU, the general views were that it had 'concentrated the mind', but that on audit approaches it had 'no real effect at all'.

In 1987 an audit partner was reported as stating that audit practices had developed 'on the battlefield' (Higson, 1987, p. 298). However, in the light of the fee pressure, competition, greater regulation, 'adding value' and the threat of financial destruction, it can be seen that not only is the war continuing but it appears to be becoming even more intense. So, given all these factors, what has been the impact on the conduct of the external audit?

SIGNIFICANT DEVELOPMENTS IN AUDIT APPROACHES

Risk-based auditing

Most firms moved towards a risk-based audit approach in the late 1980s. Since then there have been a number of developments, though most of these may be described as 'incremental' – building on what was already there. One person considered that, over the last decade, the increased emphasis on risk has been 'out of all proportion' to the way it was used when risk-based auditing first came in. A number of the larger firms do appear to have made significant alterations to their audit approaches. These approaches now place much greater emphasis on risk – particularly the risk to the auditors themselves, i.e. not just audit risk (the risk of a wrong opinion) but also commercial risk (the adverse consequences of an audit failure). This has led to a reassessment of the fundamentals of the audit: 'Do we need to do all this work? What are the risks?' Therefore, there is evidence that audit effectiveness is being questioned. Effectiveness could be defined as an assessment of whether the auditor's approach is achieving its objective (as opposed to efficiency, which relates inputs to outputs). Therefore, 'audit effectiveness' leads the auditor to question whether something really needs to be done in order to formulate an audit opinion, whereas it could be argued that 'audit efficiency' (in the literal sense of the phrase) is about whether an existing procedure can be done in a more cost-effective manner. Consequently, some auditors are placing considerably greater emphasis on high-level risk – concentrating much more on the individuals who comprise the management team. There has been a greater emphasis on understanding management's control of business risk and their overall control of the information systems. This has involved examining management's attitude to controls and the strength of their control environment (i.e. controls over the detection of errors and controls aimed at preventing fraud and manipulation). A couple of the interviewees stated that it was now their firms' policies to resign or refuse reappointment as auditors if they had doubts about the integrity of any of their clients.

A number of interviewees (speaking about other firms' approaches) were concerned about this emphasis and reliance on high-level risks and controls. One person stated that, as part of the risk assessment, the audit staff would look at management, but this interviewee perceived a problem: 'I don't think we have enough information about the individual people.' Another person considered that: 'The Big 6 can risk away with impunity.' Therefore, it can be seen that a debate exists regarding how much assurance auditors should be seeking from their assessment of the levels of risk. SAS 400 requires that 'Auditors should obtain sufficient appropriate audit evidence to be able to draw reasonable conclusions on which to base the audit opinion' (APB, 1995, p. 131) and, as one person stated: 'It all comes back to judgement at the end of the day.'

Planning

Central to the conduct of an audit is the development of a strategy aimed at achieving the audit objective, followed by a specific plan to implement the strategy. Auditors are required to 'obtain an understanding of the accounting and internal control systems sufficient to plan the audit and develop an effective audit approach' (APB, 1995, p. 128). It is a requirement of SAS 200 that auditors should plan their work and then document it. Thus the overall plan should describe the expected scope and conduct of the audit. All those interviewed considered that the time spent on these parts of the audit had increased – with some admitting to a significant increase. The planning stage was seen as an opportunity for auditors to consolidate their knowledge of the client, and 'enables the identification of problem areas at the start of the audit, and not at the end'. However, other factors appear to have been the JMU visits as well as the new SAS on planning.

Audit committees

The 1990s have seen a growth in the number of companies (particularly larger companies) with audit committees. As a consequence this has started to have an impact on external auditors. In the early days, one person stated, audit committees 'didn't understand and didn't care'; however, as a result of recent collapses, and the Cadbury Report (1992), this person considered that they now 'take the job more seriously'. It is now useful for the auditor to have a meeting with the audit committee before the commencement of the audit. The objective of such a meeting is seen as being to discuss the audit strategy with the committee. The auditor will also have at least one other meeting before the financial statements are approved. It is considered that the audit committee has improved the auditor's ability to communicate with clients, but at a price. These meetings have resulted in more work for the auditor, as more effort is required to produce more documentation. Therefore, audit committees could be said to have put up the costs of the audit, but they appear to have had very little impact on audit procedures.

Systems of internal control

During the 1970s auditors had placed greater emphasis on their clients' internal controls. One reason for this was due to improvements in the accounting procedures. The increasing complexity of accounting systems had required the implementation by management of a greater number of internal accounting controls. Another change had been the increase in the number of qualified accountants working in industry, resulting in generally improved standards in accounts departments. During the early 1980s auditors started to reduce their emphasis and reliance on internal controls. At the time, however, it was reported (Higson, 1987, p. 305) that at least one firm realized that it was possible to take some comfort from the existence of good management controls. These were the controls which came about due to the close involvement of management in the day-to-day running of a business. It was stated that previously management controls were not regarded as being of much benefit to the auditor, from the point of view of deciding upon the level of substantive testing to be undertaken. The US branch of this partnership had adopted a policy of observation and inquiry regarding management controls, and it was anticipated that this procedure would also be implemented in the UK. It appears that this approach has now caught on and has been adopted by quite a number of other firms, because it was certainly evident from the interviews that in the 1990s the focus of the auditor's work has changed – now concentrating (as already mentioned) on the control environment as opposed to the control procedures. Previously the emphasis had been on flowcharting the information and documentation flows, i.e. this was on low-level controls (e.g. authorization of invoices, segregation of duties, etc.) and so involved looking at and testing the detailed entries in an accounting system. Some auditors' approaches now tended to emphasize the overview of the flows and 'the top level controls are more and more important'. Therefore, auditors are now interested in 'how managers manage the business', or as another person described it, 'a top down' approach to controls – 'historically, people worked up from the bottom (e.g. transactions controls and compliance)'. As a consequence, there has been 'far less compliance testing by low-level junior staff'. It was considered that recent auditing disasters had illustrated the threats posed by things going wrong at the top of the organization. Another reason given for this switch from concentrating on the low-level detailed controls was the change in the nature of the clients' systems. One person stated that auditors 'hardly ever find controls work picking up errors'. The greater use of IT by clients was cited as being particularly important in this respect. Thirty years ago most systems were clerical-based, whereas now IT predominates, and consequently the auditor needs to obtain a different type of evidence. Management's use of IT means that auditors are now encountering much fewer clerical errors – 'there has been a drastic reduction in the number of errors found'. Therefore, auditors tend to consider that the client's use of standard software packages has contributed to a reduction in control risk. They obviously need to review the individual environments and the potential for any unauthorized adjustments to the systems, but generally it was considered that 'the vast majority of companies do not have people with the necessary expertise'. This person stated that 'fraud in a computerized environment is not extensive – big frauds do not happen as a result of a manipulation of software', and as a consequence this interviewee considered that 'computerized systems were less risky than manual systems'. It appears that auditors are most concerned when management make alterations to their systems – one person stated that 'change equals risk'. A few types of audits are of necessity systems-based (e.g. in the financial sector), but in general one can now report the 'death' of the old systems-based audit (i.e. the second-generation audit). One person considered that the move away from systems work was 'a shame because of a loss of quality in what we can provide', and consequently the auditor's comments were not as helpful to management. In view of the emphasis on 'adding value' this is an interesting opinion.

It was suggested that the systems audit can often be done by internal audit, and then the external auditors can review this work. The existence of an internal audit function does depend very much on the nature and size of the company being audited. It still tends to be the largest companies which make extensive use of them. As a result of the Cadbury Report (1992) more companies were reassessing their use of the internal audit function. A development has been the out-sourcing of this function – some companies have started to use the Big Six firms for internal audit work rather than set up their own departments. Though external auditors try to make as much use as possible of the internal auditor's work, its value to them is often limited – because of its varied nature. It is just as likely to relate to operational issues (such as economy, efficiency and effectiveness) as opposed to the operation of the financial controls. Where possible, more use was being made of internal audit departments. A number of auditors made favourable comments regarding the quality of the people in such departments and the clarification of their reporting lines. Generally, the auditors' views of internal audit departments appeared to be a lot more positive than in the mid-1980s. However, one person made it clear that he did not want to comment on the usefulness of the few internal audit departments that he had encountered.

Analytical review

The early 1980s saw the rise of analytical auditing procedures. In general, auditors have continued to make greater use of analytical review, and it is seen as an extremely important part of the audit. As one person stated, 'the whole thing is about reducing [detailed] substantive testing – justifiably'. Another person stated: 'If you want reduced costs but the same coverage, analytical review is the answer.' Analytical review was regarded as 'very important . . . and very powerful'. The main perceived advantages were that it enabled the reduction in other types of work, it was relatively cheap to perform, it should force the auditor to think about the implications of the results and it focused the auditor on problem areas. Though analytical review is mandatory at the planning and review stages of an audit (SAS 410), one person considered that it was 'nonsense in relation to the beginning of the audit – if analytical review is an attempt to predict an account balance'. Though the intention in using it at the start of the audit is to identify unusual variations and subsequently direct audit attention to them, this person was concerned that at the commencement of an audit it was often very difficult to attempt to make a prediction of what the relationship should be. Another person was concerned about the lack of management accounting information available to auditors in some businesses. This person considered that the limited use of management accounting was 'one of the most disappointing things about British business'. Thus, there was a concern that the data necessary for an analytical review may not be available. Other drawbacks were stated as being the difficulty of interpreting the results and determining when something was unusual. One interviewee considered that analytical review was 'strong regarding completeness . . . [but] there is a question as to how effective it is'. Another person considered that 'in many cases the quality of analytical review leaves much to be desired . . . the quality has improved and it needed to!' The general view was that analytical review was now of a better quality and performed more thoughtfully than in the past. It was considered that auditors were now better trained in its use. However, one view was that 'it was a constant struggle to use more analytical review' and that 'slow progress' was being made, because 'it was difficult to get people to relate it intelligently to the audit'. Therefore, concerns still exist regarding the effectiveness of analytical review and there is a question regarding the amount of assurance which should be obtained from it.

Substantive testing

Perhaps the key thing to come out of the interviews is how greatly the detailed substantive testing of transactions appears to have declined. The early 1980s saw a swing away from reliance on internal controls towards more substantive testing (analytical review and testing of transactions). This was because partners required a heavy level of detailed substantive testing in order to feel comfortable about forming the audit opinion. An examination of audit manuals in the mid-1980s (Higson, 1987, pp. 254–5) found that a number of firms then considered that '[s]ubstantive tests of detail are the most reliable source of evidence' and at least one considered that 'Direct substantive testing of transactions and balances can provide high, easily measurable, levels of assurance and in many cases the bulk of our evidence will derive from this source.' It can be seen that detailed substantive testing used to be a fundamental type of audit procedure. However, there was a perception at the time that overauditing was taking place, and hence the subsequent reduction in the reliance on internal controls. The rise of analytical auditing procedures during the 1980s also resulted in a justification for reductions in detailed

substantive testing. The implementation of risk-analysis approaches continued to reduce the volume of detailed substantive testing. This trend has continued. From the interviews it was clear that in recent years less and less
audit assurance was being sought from detailed substantive testing. All firms
were developing their audit approaches so as to be able to justify reductions
in detailed substantive testing – 'we have moved a long way from gaining
assurance from detailed substantive assurance'. Another person described the
trend as 'a waning of heaving substantive tests'. The risk evaluation
approaches adopted by some of the larger firms have had the impact of eliminating a number of areas of work. The justification was that if a company
had good internal controls and there was a good analytical review, then the
auditor 'may not do any tests of detail in many cases'. Clients' use of IT was
also considered to have contributed to the decline in detailed substantive testing. Reliance on this has enabled auditors to concentrate on analysing what
is produced – to the extent that 'the need to check transactions is much
reduced – if not eliminated'. The effect of these developments is such that,
in some firms, one can almost pronounce the demise of detailed substantive
testing, as, increasingly, 'sampling is a test of last resort'. The changes identified here are profound and it can be concluded that the nature of some
audits (particularly those of large companies) has been completely revolu-
tionized. In the light of this development, one wonders whether the 'basis of
opinion' paragraph in the current unqualified audit opinion really reflects the
work which underpins the formulation of the auditor's view. This paragraph
states: 'An audit includes examination, on a test basis, of evidence relevant
to the amounts and disclosures in the financial statements' (APB, 1993, p.
112). Given the swing away from testing, and the additional emphasis being
given to the assessment of risks and high-level controls, it may now be appropriate to revise the above wording.

Not everyone is in agreement with the extent to which some of these devel-
opments have been taken. One person considered that 'transactions are key.
If you ignore transactions you are getting away from your responsibilities.
This is taking risk too far, which is what we are not prepared to do.'

It is clear that each firm has had to formulate its own view for deriving
an audit strategy to obtain sufficient appropriate audit evidence, and that
there is still a debate within the profession regarding the nature and extent
of the audit evidence required by the auditor.

Statistical sampling

The decrease in the reliance on detailed substantive testing also has implications in relation to statistical sampling. The 1970s saw the growth in statistical sampling and statistical approaches to auditing – recent developments
mean that these have now almost been eliminated. Even with the reductions
in sample sizes which occurred in the 1980s, firms would claim that there
was an underlying statistical basis for their work. Now with most firms there
is little pretence at a statistical approach to auditing. One person whose

firm did use 'an essentially statistical method' considered that they 'tend to find statistical theory more helpful in planning sample sizes and choosing the sample, rather than in the evaluation process . . . [as] you do need judgement for this'. Even this person considered that 'statistical evaluation was not that useful at the end of the day'. The main advantages of a statistical approach were seen as 'ensuring comparability across the firm' and that it 'makes some people think about what they should be thinking about when selecting a sample'. Another person stated: '*If* we resort to sampling it is only on a statistical basis.' However, this 'was relatively infrequently used. Often enough confidence comes from the controls and analytical review.' When samples were conducted, most interviewees considered that efforts were made to ensure that they were representative of the whole population – though this did not necessarily mean that they were selected on a statistical basis. In general, there appears to have been a swing away from quantitative approaches to auditing. Without a statistical basis, it would now be very difficult for auditors to try to specify any sort of confidence levels to underpin their opinions – this may be reflecting the essentially judgemental nature of the external audit; that in one person's view, 'auditing is an art form'. Another reason for abandoning a claim to a statistical approach could be due to the current litigious atmosphere. After all, if under scrutiny a 'statistical' approach were found to be faulty, it would obviously damage an auditor's defence.

Directional testing

The original concept of directional testing comes from the principles of double-entry bookkeeping. Provided that the accounting records are in balance, for every debit there is a corresponding credit. So, if a debit entry has been overstated, either a credit entry will also have been overstated or another debit will have been understated. Therefore, by properly structuring the direction of audit tests it is possible for one test to provide evidence for more than one audit area (for example, testing debtors (an asset) for overstatement will give some comfort regarding the overstatement of income (a credit) and, conversely, testing income for understatement will give some comfort regarding the understatement of debtors). In the mid-1980s directional testing appeared to be a concept which was not too widely used. However, a majority of the interviewees stated that their firms now used this concept. One person considered that the term 'directional testing' has two meanings, the first being the one described above (giving audit assurance in another area). This person stated that this approach would only work if there was a totally comprehensive audit. If auditors simply tested areas which were susceptible to error, it would mean that other areas would go untested and so the complementary under- or overstatement would be missed. Therefore, this firm did not make a claim to using it. The second meaning was stated as being the checking from the financial statements to the underlying records. This was obviously a more general use of the term but, given the substantial cutbacks in detailed substantive testing, it may be a more appropriate reflection of its current operational meaning.

CONCLUSION

Overall, it can be seen that a number of fundamental changes have been identified as having occurred in recent years. Underlying all this has been a growing sense of crisis, and perhaps there is now a need for a reassessment of the auditor's role. The ever present pressures on auditors have meant, in the words of one interviewee, that 'developments have been accelerated by market forces driving auditors into more and more desperate ways of increasing efficiency'. Another person expressed his unease as follows: 'My biggest concern is whether an audit, as currently designed, is appropriate . . . the big problem with audit is, unlike other services, it is not for the benefit of the directors . . . therefore, a cost-benefit analysis can never be done properly.' This comment was reinforced by another person who posed the question: 'Does the independent audit have a future?'

This chapter set out to explore the current issues which relate to audit approaches. Though it has probably raised more questions than it has answered, it does give an insight into the problems faced by the external auditor. The extent of the developments in auditors' approaches over the last decade cannot be overstated. This chapter has attempted to view the developments in terms of 'audit effectiveness'. Due to the pressure that auditors face, it appears that they have been reassessing what the audit is trying to achieve, and this has resulted in an extensive questioning of how it should be done. Therefore, it is suggested that it may be possible to view developments in terms of a change from audit efficiency to audit effectiveness. There has been a resurgence in the emphasis on judgement – judgement regarding the assessment of risks and controls, judgement regarding the interpretation of analytical review and judgement in relation to any (limited) testing. The focus, by some firms, on the higher-level risks and controls, together with the justification of very limited amounts of detailed substantive testing based on their risk analyses and analytical reviews, has completely altered previous conceptions of the external audit. The extent of these changes is such that the wording of the current unqualified audit report may need revising – to give a fairer reflection of the approaches being adopted by auditors. It is clear that external auditors are going through a period of immense uncertainty; whether this is a terminal crisis, only time will tell.

REFERENCES

APB (1993) SAS 600: *Auditors' Reports on Financial Statements, Accountancy*, June, pp. 106–16.

APB (1994) *The Audit Agenda*, Auditing Practices Board, London.

APB (1995) Statements of Auditing Standards (SAS 100: *Objective and General Principles Governing an Audit of Financial Statements*; SAS 200: *Planning*; SAS 210-: *Knowledge of the Business*; SAS 230: *Working Papers*; SAS 240: *Quality Control for Audit Work*; SAS 300: *Accounting and Internal Control Systems and Audit Risks Assessments*; SAS 400: *Audit Evidence*; SAS 410: *Analytical Procedures*), *Accountancy*, April pp. 115–50.

APC (1980) *Auditing Standards and Guidelines*, Auditing Practices Committee, London.

Beck, G. W. (1973) The role of the auditor in modern society: an empirical appraisal, *Accounting and Business Research*, Spring, pp. 117–22.

Bird, P. (1970) The scope of the company audit, *Accounting and Business Research*, Winter, pp. 44–9.

Brown, R. G. (1962) Changing audit objectives and techniques, *Accounting Review*, Vol. 37, no. 4, pp. 692–703.

Burton, J. C. and Fairfield, P. (1982) Auditing evolution in a changing environment, *Auditing: A Journal of Practice & Theory*, Vol. 1, no. 2, Winter, pp. 1–22.

Cadbury Report, The (1992) *Report of the Committee on The Financial Aspects of Corporate Governance*, Gee & Co., London.

Carmichael, D. R. and Whittington, R. (1984) The auditor's changing role in financial reporting, *Journal of Accounting and Finance*, Vol. 7, Summer, pp. 347–61.

Coopers & Lybrand (1992) *Manual of Auditing* (5th edn), Gee & Co., London.

Cushing, B. E. and Loebbecke, J. K. (1986) *Comparison of Audit Methodologies of Large Accounting Firms*, Studies in Accounting Research, American Accounting Association, Sarasota.

Davis, R. (1996) Serving the public interest, *True & Fair*, December 1995/January 1996, p.6.

Dresser, G. (1995) Does IT deliver a better audit?, *Accountancy Age,* 7 December, pp. 18–19.

Elliott, R. K. (1983) Unique audit methods: Peat Marwick International, *Auditing: A Journal of Practice & Theory*, Vol. 2, no. 2, Spring, pp. 1–12.

Felix, W. L., Jr, Grimlund, R. A., Koster, F. J. and Roussey, R. S. (1990) Arthur Andersen's new monetary unit sampling approach, *Auditing: A Journal of Practice & Theory*, Vol. 9, no. 3, Fall, pp. 1–16.

Flint, D. (1971) The role of the auditor in modern society: an explanatory essay, *Accounting and Business Research*, Autumn, pp. 133–51.

Gillett, P. (1993) Automated dynamic audit programme tailoring: an expert system approach, *Auditing: A Journal of Practice & Theory*, Vol. 12, Supplement, pp. 173–89.

Graham, L. E., Damens, J. and Van Ness, G. (1991) Developing Risk Advisor[sm]: an expert system for risk evaluation, *Auditing: A Journal of Practice & Theory*, Vol. 10, no. 1, Spring, pp. 69–96.

Grant Thornton (1990) *Audit Manual* (4th edn), Longman Group, London.

Grobstein, M. and Craig, P. W. (1984) A risk analysis approach to auditing, *Auditing: A Journal of Practice & Theory*, Vol. 3, no. 2, Spring, pp. 1–16.

Gwilliam, D. (1987) *A Survey of Auditing Research*, Prentice-Hall International/ICAEW, London.

Harris, S. (ed.) (1995) *The Auditing Manual* (2nd edn), Gee, London.

Hatherly, D. J. (1989) Discussion: adding value to the audit, *Auditing and the Future: Proceedings of an Auditing Research Conference*, ICAEW/ICAS, Edinburgh.

Higson, A. W. (1987) *An empirical investigation of the external audit process*, unpublished Ph.D. thesis, University of Bradford.

Higson, A. W. (1991) *Communication Through the Audit Report: What Is the Auditor Trying to Say?*, Loughborough University Management Research Series, November.

Jones, M. E. (1985) Auditing: a subject with ever-widening horizons, in D. Kent, M. Sherer and S. Turley (eds.) *Current Issues in Auditing*, Harper & Row, London.

Lee, T. A. (1986) *Company Auditing* (3rd edn), Van Nostrand Reinhold, London.

McInnes, W. M. (ed.) (1993) *Auditing into the Twenty-First Century*, ICAS, Edinburgh.

Mock, T. J. and Willingham, J. J. (1983) An improved method of documenting and evaluating a system of internal accounting controls, *Auditing: A Journal of Practice & Theory*, Vol. 2, no. 2, Spring, pp. 91–9.

Robson Rhodes (1994) *Audit Manual, Vol. 1: The Robson Rhodes Audit*, Robson Rhodes, London.

Steen, D. M. C. E. (1989) Adding value to the audit, *Auditing and the Future: Proceedings of an Auditing Research Conference*, ICAEW/ICAS, Edinburgh.

Sterling Professional Services (1995) *Audit Manual* (2nd edn), Sterling Professional Services, Nottingham.

Stevens, M. (1984), *The Big Eight*, Macmillan, New York.

Thornton Baker (1981) *Audit Manual*, Nova Communications, London.

Turley, S. and Cooper, M. (1991) *Auditing in the United Kingdom*, Prentice-Hall/ICAEW, Hemel Hempstead.

Walker, N. R. and Pierce, L. T. (1988) The Price Waterhouse audit: a state of the art approach, *Auditing: A Journal of Practice & Theory*, Vol. 8, no. 1, Fall, pp. 1–22,

Woolf, E. (ed.) (1992–) *Audit Manual and System* (updated to August 1995), CCH, Bicester.

DISCUSSION QUESTIONS

1. Can an auditor ever be fully confident of having done enough work to support an unqualified audit opinion?
2. To what extent would you agree with the view that external auditing could be regarded as the audit of motivations?
3. Does 'adding value' to the external audit threaten the auditor's independence?
4. By 'adding value' to the external audit, is the auditor trying to do too much within the time available?
5. Is there a future for the external audit in its present format?

12

The Audit Process in Practice

Mike Woodrow

INTRODUCTION

The purpose of this chapter is to provide an overview of the structure and stages the auditor goes through when carrying out an audit for an individual organization. Other chapters have discussed many general issues about the role of auditing, and areas of debate as to how the auditor's responsibilities should be executed, for example the need for auditor independence and the nature of audit reporting. While these debates are of critical importance for the credibility and development of auditing, in practice the current objectives for a specific audit assignment must be derived from the legislation or other regulations under which the audit is required. Typically, financial audits start and end with the financial statements of an organization (for example, in a company, the profit and loss account, balance sheet, notes to the accounts and directors' report). The end product of an audit is an opinion on the financial statements that have been presented by the organization to the auditor. It is the management's responsibility to prepare these accounts and the auditor's duty is to express an opinion on them. This is an important division of responsibilities.

In order to arrive at an audit opinion the auditor must undertake a process of collecting and evaluating evidence. Evidence is critical to the rationality and purpose of auditing. Without evidence the audit opinion can have little, if any, validity. This chapter is about how the evidence collection process is structured in a modern large audit firm. For ease of exposition, the discus-

Mike Woodrow is honorary Senior lecturer at Lancaster, where he teaches auditing. He is an HR Director at KPMG in the North, but the views he expresses are his own and the process described is similar to that used by many firms, and is not that used by KPMG.

sion refers primarily to the audit of a limited liability company, as required by the Companies Act 1985 and subject to the relevant regulations contained in auditing standards. Although financial audits in other types of organization might involve particular different responsibilities, the broad framework and approach to evidence collection will be very similar. The precise terminology and approach adopted by individual audit firms, and the emphasis placed on different parts of the evidence collection process, will vary. The framework described in this chapter sets out a broad structure covering the main components commonly found in the audit approaches of major firms.

The detailed testing and other work the auditor carries out in an individual audit will vary as a consequence of what is contained in the financial statements. A manufacturing company will have physical stocks and work-in-progress as a major part of its balance sheet but a finance company will have very little equivalent stock or work-in-progress. The audit work and time spent on these areas of the accounts will therefore differ considerably between the two companies. The best guidance to an auditor on which areas of the financial statements attention should be concentrated upon will come from the previous year's accounts and the organization's management accounts (if there are any). The auditor must always start the audit process before the current year's accounts are finalized.

Auditors have no statutory duty to detect fraud although, as discussed elsewhere in this volume, recent surveys indicate that the public believe that they do check for fraud. However, a material fraud is likely to affect the accounts and would therefore prevent the auditor from confirming that they show a true and fair view. Hence, the auditor must design the audit approach to have a reasonable chance of detecting material fraud which, if undetected, would lead to accounts being published which did not show a true and fair view of the organization's performance and position.

Against the background of these general points, the framework within which evidence collection to support an audit opinion is carried out can be described by recognizing four main stages to an audit: strategy and planning, systems evaluation and testing, balances verification and profit and loss account review, and completion. What is involved in each of these stages of an audit is described in turn below.

STRATEGY AND PLANNING

Strategy

People are a key resource to an audit firm. Staff are highly trained and it is important that their time is used effectively and efficiently. The audit firm's concern is to avoid a clean audit opinion being given on financial statements that contain a material error. Consequently, audit effort is concentrated on those sections of the accounts that may contain such errors – what can be referred to as 'critical audit areas'. These will differ from company to company and industry to industry. Equally, some companies are affected more by general economic conditions than others and a downturn in the economy will make some balance sheet captions more likely to contain material misstatements, not through deliberate manipulation but because the directors are more bullish about, say, the net realizable values of stocks than is prudent.

Audit strategy is the process that sets the direction of the audit and links the auditor's understanding of the client's business to the focus of the audit work. A good audit strategy requires a sound understanding of the business, the environment in which it operates and the way in which it is managed. This understanding provides the context within which the financial statements can be viewed, and drives an appreciation of the risks affecting the organization, management controls that address these risks and the identification of areas of high audit risk. These factors then provide a basis for the early specification of critical audit objectives and an outline of the audit approach in those areas.

Strategy is a partner-led activity. The engagement partner should be responsible for developing the audit strategy and communicating it to the audit team, although the partner may delegate certain elements and seek advice from colleagues and specialists. The audit strategy should be based on information obtained from management, as well as prior year experience and ideas arising from the previous year's debriefing. Consideration must be given to the key business and financial reporting issues affecting the organization and their effect on the current year's audit, and factors must be identified that are important to the success of the audit, both for developing a programme of work to support the audit opinion and for providing other professional services agreed with the company management.

Audit strategy covers the overall approach to management controls. The auditor should consider how the management runs the business, the information they use and the controls (both at a high level and within the key systems) which ensure its reliability. This naturally extends to information technology (IT), which is an integral feature of control for most organizations which rely on computer-based systems. By placing reliance on these controls, the auditor can develop a cost-effective approach to the routine systems, which meets management expectations and which enables much of the audit work to be carried out at a time of year which is most suitable for both the auditor and the organization's management.

Discussions with management, past experience of working with the organization and initiatives identified in the previous year's debriefing provide the context within which the auditor can identify client service needs and plan an approach to meet them. It is also necessary to determine what specialist skills are needed to conduct the audit effectively and to plan for the appropriate input.

Audit strategy should be documented in a manner which reflects the specific audit circumstances, summarizes the matters addressed by the engagement partner when developing strategy and communicates the result to the audit team. The engagement partner and manager usually brief the audit team at a meeting about key issues and their implications. Through understanding the company's business, a tailored approach to the audit can be developed which focuses on critical audit objectives as well as matters of concern to management. In this way the auditor can obtain audit evidence efficiently, avoid unnecessary audit work and provide a valued service.

Experience has shown that there a number of conditions that, if present, heighten the auditor's awareness of the potential for fraud or error, and these should be considered when setting strategy. These conditions can be recognized by evaluating existing knowledge of the organization and current up-to-date information about changes affecting the business and industry. Table 12.1 shows some examples of the kind of information that may provide certain signals to the auditor.

Table 12.1 Examples of information that may signal risk of error

Existing knowledge of the client	Changes affecting the client's business
• Weak internal control	• Major changes in products or businesses
• Ineffective board – same CEO and chairman	• Major expansion or explosive growth
• Ineffective corporate governance	• Acquisition orientation
• High turnover of key staff	• Attractive acquisition target
• Unusual related-party transactions	• Problems with regulators
• Significant adjustments in prior years	*Industry and general economy*
• Low quality accounting records	• Distressed industry
• Frequent changes in auditors/legal advisers	• Intense competition
• Several audit firms involved	• Rapidly changing industry

Where any of these conditions are present, the auditor should consider the implications for the organization being audited and the possible effect on the financial statements. If it appears that the effect is likely to be material, appropriate modified or additional audit procedures should be planned. It should also be recognized that fraud is often difficult to detect as steps are normally taken to conceal it. The audit procedures that are planned should therefore take into account the difficulty of obtaining audit evidence. Plans may be made to obtain more persuasive audit evidence, such as corroborative evidence from several sources and evidence from external sources rather than that generated internally or by related parties. Substantive tests may also be performed later in the year rather than earlier.

Planning

Audit strategy sets the broad direction for the audit and links the auditor's understanding of the business being audited to the focus of the audit work. Audit planning expands on this strategy, providing instructions to guide the audit team through the audit. It defines the most efficient way of obtaining effective audit evidence. The main components of the planning process can be considered under the following three headings: technical, logistical and client service.

Technical planning

Technical planning covers the selection of audit procedures based on an understanding of the company's business, analysis of the financial information and assessments of the risks of significant misstatements. It includes the auditor's planned approach to critical audit objectives and internal controls. Procedures followed during the technical stage of planning could include:

(1) Performing analytical procedures, for example by analysing available relevant information contained in management reports and in data prepared routinely in the company to manage the business and current and prior period financial data; other sources of data that might be used include non-financial information (production volumes, sales and market share), publicly available information, with particular attention to benchmark data and the reported results for competitors, and the company's budgets and forecasts.

(2) Discussion of results with management, to improve the auditor's understanding of the business and to confirm interpretation of the results of the analytical procedures: such discussion can increase awareness of, for example, business issues and accounting developments, the client's financial position, and recent trends, variations and future developments. For example, if the audit is planned on the assumption that a particular division is to be sold part way during the year, confirmation may be sought that the sale is proceeding as originally intended.

(3) Understanding the system of internal controls.

(4) Understanding the internal audit function.

Once the above steps have been carried out the auditor will be able to determine the planned approach to each critical audit objective, decide whether a systems-based approach or a substantive approach would be best suited to the particular company being audited and determine the audit procedures. These procedures are then documented on audit programmes which act as checklists of tests to be performed.

Logistical planning

Logistical planning is the management of the audit as a project. It covers important elements such as the allocation of tasks and the timing of the work, preparing a timetable and a budget, identifying which of the business's computer files are needed for the audit and agreeing a timetable for tasks to be completed by company staff and the audit team. Procedures could include:

(1) establishing the staffing and other resources required for the engagement, including specialists;
(2) co-ordinating the provision of other services to the client, such as preparation of tax computations, pension scheme audit, etc.;
(3) determining involvement of other offices of the audit firm and any other auditors, for example for subsidiary companies within a group;
(4) planning use of computer-assisted audit techniques;
(5) deciding the location and planned timing of the audit work;
(6) preparing of cost and time budgets;
(7) planning timing of clearance matters (for example the final audit meeting, submission of reports and signing of accounts);
(8) co-ordinating the schedules and information to be prepared by client staff.

Client service planning

Client service planning refers to the auditor's desire to ensure that the individual service requirements of the company are identified and met. This could involve performing additional work of a checking nature but which is not part of the auditor's legal obligation, or carrying out some internal audit work or checking one particular aspect of the accounting systems in detail. Alternatively, it could mean co-ordinating audit work with some non-audit service company management requires which the audit firm can provide.

The audit risk model

For effective planning, a framework is needed which links the evidence procedures to be undertaken to the auditor's objective in assessing the financial statements. The audit risk model provides such a framework. Audit risk is the risk that the auditor issues an unqualified or otherwise inappropriate audit opinion on a set of accounts that are materially misstated. Audit risk is a combination of the risk that a material misstatement occurs in the first place, the risk that the company fails to detect it and the risk that audit procedures fail to pick up the error.

The risk of a material error being there in the first place is called *inherent risk*. The risk that the company's internal controls fail to discover a material error is called *control risk*. The risk that audit procedures fail to detect material error is called *detection risk*.

The risk model matches the auditor's assessment of inherent risk and control risk and indicates the amount of detection risk that can be tolerated in substantive audit procedures and still arrive at a satisfactory audit conclusion. The level of detection risk dictates the substantive audit evidence required. If the combined inherent and control risk is high a significantly higher amount of substantive work must be performed than if it is low.

The auditor would expect that management monitor, control and therefore reduce the inherent risk and would look to obtain evidence that the risks influencing the financial statements are effectively controlled. Similarly, the quality of the controls on the capture and accurate processing of financial information will be assessed. The assessment of inherent risk starts at the planning and strategy stage and continues throughout the audit. A preliminary evaluation of the strength of internal controls is also made at the planning and strategy level but this is investigated primarily at the second main stage of the audit – systems evaluation and testing.

SYSTEMS EVALUATION AND TESTING

In order to understand the value of systems evaluation and testing it will be helpful to outline the components of control which are of interest to the auditor before going on to describe how these can be incorporated into the audit process.

The components of a system of internal controls

A system of internal controls consists of the following components:

(1) the management's risk assessment;
(2) the control environment;
(3) general control activities;
(4) the information and communication systems (which includes the design of the system and efficiency of data capture).

Each of these four components must be considered by the auditor before the appropriateness of using a systems-based audit approach can be assessed. The auditor's overall assessment of controls should be recorded on a control overview document. Briefly, the four components comprise the following.

Management's risk assessment

Management sets both entity-level objectives and activity-level objectives. All entities, regardless of size, structure, nature or industry, are subject to business risks. All entities should therefore have processes in place to identify those risks and to assess their effect on the achievement of objectives.

Control environment

The control environment consists of four factors that influence the control consciousness of people in an entity:

(1) management integrity, operating style and the use of independent review;
(2) organization structure;
(3) responsibility and authority levels;
(4) personnel policies.

General control activities

General control activities are the policies and procedures that help provide assurance that management's directives are carried out. They provide assurance that necessary actions are taken to address risks to the achievement of the entity's objectives. These controls contribute to or support many financial statement assertions.

Information and communication systems

Information systems produce reports containing information that make it possible for management to run and control the business. Typically this information can relate to operational, financial or compliance matters or a combination of these. Once reports are produced they must be communicated to the people who need to act upon the information contained within them. The information communicated should be accurate, timely and appropriate.

The systems-based audit approach

In a systems-based audit approach as much audit evidence as possible is obtained from the client's accounting system. Management should have built controls into their systems for recording financial information that ensure that data are correctly captured, valued and processed. The control system can act as a source of evidence because, if the auditor can confirm that adequate controls are in place and that these are operating effectively, it is possible to have confidence about the quality of information output produced by the system. In other words, the proper operation of controls allows the auditor to make inferences about balances generated by an accounting system.

As an example, in a sales system when a sales order is received there must be procedures that ensure it is fulfilled and not lost. So a register of all sales orders would be kept. This is control one. Control two would be that this register is regularly reviewed and orders not yet delivered investigated. The next key stage in a sales system is when goods are dispatched. There must be controls in place to ensure that all goods dispatched are invoiced. At this stage the documents contain information about quantities and a subsequent control will be that these are correctly priced. At the final stage of a sales system invoices are posted to a sales ledger account and there must be controls to ensure that debtors are regularly followed up for payment.

A systems-based audit approach would first evaluate the strengths and appropriateness of the controls in place and would then test them through a process called compliance testing. The auditor would always seek to identify high-level controls, that is, the overall supervisory controls which are generally operated by management who are outside the day-to-day routine of the systems and which are the means by which management satisfy themselves that the financial information produced by the accounting system is largely free from error. The most efficient way to identify high-level controls is to ask management how they ensure that the information they use to manage the business is free of errors and/or omissions. If high-level controls are missing then this is a problem for the organization itself (not just for the auditor) and the attention of management would be drawn to such control weaknesses in a management report.

A fundamental assumption of a systems-based audit approach is that if management rely on their systems it is also appropriate for the auditor to do so. Reviewing the high-level controls provides an opportunity to identify, at an early stage, risks affecting the business which are not subject to satisfactory control. Regardless of the size of the organization, there should normally be some high-level controls which provide senior management with the assurance that they require. A failure to identify and evaluate high-level controls may result in too much attention being paid to detailed controls and lead to overauditing. Examples of high-level controls are: comparison with information from third parties, such as customers (credit control), suppliers (statement reconciliations) and bankers (reconciliations to statements); comparisons to physical assets, for example perpetual stock checks, fixed asset counts, and checks of deeds and securities; and comparisons to predicted amounts such as budgeted figures.

It should be emphasized that the audit evidence obtained from tests of controls does not eliminate entirely the need for substantive audit procedures. However, reliance on control systems may enable the auditor to reduce significantly the extent of planned substantive audit procedures, or to modify the nature of the planned substantive audit procedures (for example, more reliance may be placed on analytical procedures rather than tests of details). In addition, the auditor may be able to modify the timing of the planned substantive audit procedures (for example, performing substantive audit procedures before the year-end).

A systems-based approach provides a number of potential benefits for the auditor. Audit work need not be restricted to the year-end. By performing more audit work in 'off peak' periods, better use can be made of audit staff. Less detailed testing work at the final audit means that pressure at the year-end is reduced, making deadlines easier to achieve. The pressure on client staff at the year-end is also reduced. Further, a systems-based approach provides the opportunity for more constructive reporting to management well before the year-end. Companies typically expect their auditors to review and comment on the systems of control and a systems-based approach facilitates this. It will also help the audit team to understand the client's business in more detail.

BALANCES VERIFICATION AND PROFIT AND LOSS ACCOUNT REVIEW

Ultimately the audit report contains an opinion about the figures reported in the financial statements and the auditor must have confidence about these balances. When auditing assets – fixed assets, stock, debtors, etc. – the auditor looks to ensure that the asset is not overstated in either quantity or value. If assets are overvalued and have to be reduced the corresponding entry is to reduce profit. Equally, if liabilities – creditors, overdrafts, etc. – are undervalued the correcting entry is again to reduce profit. In constructing tests to examine individual balances, there are a number of key attributes or assertions implied in the balance and these provide the objectives against which the auditor is seeking verification.

The auditor must collect evidence to satisfy six objectives. These are:

(1) *Completeness*, which concerns whether the account balance in the financial statements represents all of the underlying assets, liabilities, income or expense, e.g. are all the fixed assets owned by the client recorded in the financial statements?

(2) *Existence*, which concerns whether the account balance represents real assets or liabilities and whether any items have been duplicated, e.g. does the account balance represent fixed assets that physically exist?

(3) *Accuracy*, which refers to whether the item has been correctly recorded with respect to party, price, date, description and quantity, e.g. looking at the underlying entries for the account, has the clerk pressed the correct buttons on the calculator or the correct keys on the keyboard, or has the depreciation charge been correctly calculated?

(4) *Valuation*, which concerns whether the account balance is valued at the appropriate amount, e.g. has the correct depreciation rate been used, is that rate appropriate and is the fixed asset worth the amount at which it is recorded?

(5) *Ownership*, which relates to a question of title – whether the asset is the property of the company, e.g. is the fixed asset owned by the company, or is there evidence that a third party such as a leasing company has an interest, or has the company bought assets which are subject to 'reservation of title' clauses?

(6) *Presentation*, which relates to the manner of presentation of an account balance in the financial statements, e.g. whether creditors have been correctly split between short- and long-term creditors.

Auditors make use of two main categories of audit procedures to test individual account balances in order to confirm objectives on the above attributes for individual balances – tests of detail and analytical procedures.

Tests of detail

There are seven types of audit technique that can be used at any stage of the audit. Two of these, *observation* and *inquiry*, are most commonly used at the systems evaluation stage of the audit. A combination of five other procedures are used at the balance sheet verification and profit and loss review stage of the audit. These generic types of audit procedures are:

(1) *comparison*, for example comparing the company staff's and auditor's own inventory counts for quantity differences;
(2) *computation*, for example verifying the accuracy of inventory costs by computing price multiplied by quantity;
(3) *confirmation*, for example writing directly to third parties, requesting that they confirm inventory quantities held by them on behalf of the company;
(4) *inspection*, for example reading purchase invoices to verify inventory price;
(5) *physical examination*, for example verifying the existence of inventory by physically examining raw materials and finished goods held by the company.

Vouching is a term often used to refer to a test of details using a combination of comparison, computation and inspection techniques.

Selection and sampling

The auditor may apply a test of detail to every item in the population or to a selection of the items. If tests of detail are applied to fewer than every item in an account, the auditor must accept some uncertainty in the audit evidence obtained. Indeed, even if the auditor checked all the individual items in a population, there may still remain some uncertainty, or risk of error. The remaining risk can be accepted because the auditor's objectives can be satisfied with persuasive rather than conclusive audit evidence. By combining audit evidence from more than one source and by performing analytical procedures in addition to the tests of details, the risk of undetected error can be minimized.

When fewer than all items from an account are selected for testing, two main approaches are used for the selection of individual items. First, the auditor may choose to test what are considered to be *key items*. This involves reading through documents and files of transactions or balances and selecting items that the auditor believes to be prone to misstatement because they are unusual, unexpected or in excess of a designated monetary amount. As these items are selected because they are in some way unique or unusual, audit procedures applied to them provide little or no audit evidence about the remaining portion of the population. The second method of selection is *representative sampling*, where items are chosen to be representative of the population as a whole. When testing a representative sample, the auditor relies on inference about the full population from the results for the sample. Sometimes the auditor's investigation of a particular balance may include a combination of both methods, for example selecting items over a predetermined amount and a representative sample from the remainder of a population.

In deciding whether to select key items for further investigation or whether to apply representative sampling, the following general factors may affect which method is appropriate. Selecting key items is likely to be more effective when the auditor has obtained evidence from tests of control and analytical procedures and therefore requires relatively little substantive audit evidence from the test of details, and where the population contains a small number of individually significant items, as testing a relatively small number of key items efficiently addresses a relatively high proportion of the account. Key item testing will also be appropriate where the population contains mainly non-routine transactions or accounting estimates, as in this circumstance the account is unlikely to consist of similar items that could be sampled in a representative manner, i.e. the population is not homogeneous.

In contrast, representative sampling is likely to be more effective when the auditor has obtained little or no audit evidence from tests of control and analytical procedures, and therefore requires relatively more substantive audit evidence over the whole account from the test of details, and when the population contains a large number of individually insignificant items, such that testing a relatively large number of key items would be required to address a significant proportion of the account balance. A population that contains mainly routine transactions will also be appropriate for representative sampling as the account is likely to consist of similar items that may be efficiently sampled.

When performing a test of details, the auditor applies audit procedures to the population from which individual items are selected to obtain audit evidence that the data reconcile to the financial statements. For example, the additions of the account listing may be checked and the total compared with the recorded amount in the financial statements.

Analytical procedures

The analytical procedures used by the auditor when testing balances can be divided into three main types: reasonableness tests, trend analysis and ratio analysis.

Reasonableness tests

Reasonableness tests comprise computations involving estimation of an account balance. The auditor develops a model, computes a prediction of the account balance or class of transactions through the use of relevant financial and operating data and compares the prediction with the recorded amount. Models range from simple mathematical formulae to complex regression techniques. For example, payroll may be predicted using the number of employees, the average wage rate and the average number of hours worked. One model would be simply to multiply these variables together. Sales of a retail store could be predicted from a more complex model using certain operating data, local economic data and descriptions of each store and its location. These variables have no simple mathematical relationship to sales and so regression techniques would be more appropriate.

Trend analysis

Trend analysis refers to the analysis of the changes in a given account balance or class of transactions between the current and prior periods or over several accounting periods. This contrasts with a reasonableness test, which involves an analysis of the changes within one accounting period. The auditor obtains an understanding of what causes the trend in the account balance and class of transactions. Using this knowledge an estimate of what the current year's amount should be is computed, based upon the past trend and the auditor's knowledge of the company's current transactions. The auditor then compares this prediction with the recorded amount. In this way potential problems may be identified where there is little or no change in the current balance from the prior period but where there should have been a significant change.

Again the basis of estimation may range from simple calculations of a single variable based on the trend in annual data to more complex analyses using many variables. Examples of the kind of predictions the auditor might make are: sales, based on the trend of historical annual sales; investment income, based on the trend in the value of investments; and the gross profit margin, based on the trends in the sales mix. For the last item, an analysis of the trend in monthly gross margins is unlikely to provide audit evidence unless it is performed by product or group of products. The changes in the sales mix and the consequent effect on the gross margin may be difficult to identify in sufficient detail to identify potential misstatements.

An important requirement for the auditor when using trend analysis is that there should be a clear understanding of why it is believed that a trend will be predictable, since data sometimes appear to be related when they are not. For example, there may be no causal relationship between expenditure on legal fees in one year and in the next.

Ratio analysis

Ratio analysis is a term often used to refer to the analysis of the ratio of:

(1) An account balance to another account balance. For example, when examining debtors the auditor may analyse the ratio of credit sales to average net receivables; for stock the ratio of cost of goods sold to average inventory may be reviewed; and for revenue and expense accounts the auditor may analyse the ratios of investment income to investments, depreciation expense to gross assets subject to depreciation, and the repairs and maintenance expense to related property, plant and equipment.

(2) A class of transactions to an account balance. Examples would include analysis of the ratio of sales returns and sales discounts to total sales, and the ratio of cost of goods sold to total sales, by individual product line.

(3) Financial data to operating data. Analysis could be undertaken of the

ratio of total sales to selling space in a retail company, of the ratio of payroll expense to average employee numbers and of the changes in ratios within the entity over time or the ratios of different entities or different segments within the entity. For example, the ratio of revenue to number of units sold as a series could be analysed: over time for an individual product range, over different sales centres for an individual product range and over different products for an individual sales centre. Such procedures may be a valuable source of audit evidence as, when auditing completeness of transactions, the cost of examining all items, especially routine transactions, is generally uneconomical.

Computer-assisted audit techniques (CAATs)

CAATs is a term used to describe the use of audit software to examine data produced by a computer. At their most basic, CAATs can remove some of the mechanical routine of audit work, but they may also enable the performance of tests that auditors cannot do themselves. Data interrogation can allow the auditor to undertake tests in ways that are not really feasible manually. It can also allow more thorough, and therefore more effective, testing to be carried out.

In many situations the auditor will test data by running the computer audit programs against a file obtained before the year-end. In this way the development and documentation work can be undertaken at a point in the audit that is less pressured than the final audit visit and the benefits of a working program can be obtained in its first year of use. Increasingly, the developments in information technology mean that files of data for interrogation or other testing can be downloaded or transferred to a portable computer easily and cheaply. If data acquisition is more costly, then overall savings are most likely where data interrogation replaces one or more time-consuming manual procedures.

Individual audit firms all have available their own customized computer programs and packages which are designed in a manner which is consistent with the firm's overall audit methodology. The use of CAATs can always be considered where the organization's accounting system is computerized and some examples of the areas of audit work in which they can make a contribution are:

(1) producing special reports for the auditor, e.g. a report of unallocated cash on the sales ledger;
(2) selecting individual items for inspection or confirmation, based on formal criteria such as size or age, e.g. select all customer accounts over a certain monetary value for individual confirmation;
(3) reperforming calculations such as bank interest and depreciation;
(4) providing an aged analysis of a data file, e.g. age the detailed debtors listing, using appropriate bands;
(5) summation or other checks on an entire data file;

(6) scanning through an entire data file to highlight gaps or duplications, e.g. scan through the sales ledger to identify missing or duplicate sales invoices;

(7) combining the information contained within two or more data files to produce new analyses, e.g. combine the stock and sales data to produce a usage report, highlighting stock lines which have not moved in a specified period;

(8) comparing the information contained within two or more data files to highlight differences, e.g. match the dates on dispatch notes to appropriate invoices to highlight cut-off discrepancies.

COMPLETION

After all the systems have been evaluated, and evidence collected and tested as set out in the audit programmes decided at the planning stage, the final stage of the audit comprises the completion procedures, which lead ultimately to the decision on the audit opinion to accompany the financial statements. There are three main aspects to the completion of an audit:

(1) an overall pulling together of the work done and a consideration of all errors found and adjustments agreed with management where necessary – this stage will normally involve a review of the audit work done by an independent person, such as an audit manager or partner;

(2) confirmation that the accounts comply with the Companies Acts;

(3) consideration of the impact on the financial statements of Financial Reporting Standards (FRSs) and Statements of Standard Accounting Practice (SSAPs), or of other specific regulations applicable to the organization being audited.

Review

Audits take place under fairly tight time constraints. The company's staff themselves have to produce draft financial statements shortly after the year-end and the auditors have to complete their work within a short time thereafter. It is difficult to convey the dynamic and sometimes frantic activity of an audit unless you have experienced it. It is important, therefore, that somebody who knows the company and industry but who has not been involved in the 'hurly burly' is able to look at the final accounts from a more detached perspective than those involved in the detailed audit work. In a large firm of chartered accountants this will be a two-stage operation: a manager review followed, once the manager's points have been cleared, by a partner review.

Companies Act requirements

The financial statements produced by the company will have to adopt one of the permitted formats for presentation of accounts and also comply with information that the Companies Act dictates must be included and shown. The auditor will often use a detailed checklist to carry out this review.

Financial Reporting Standards (FRSs) and Statements of Standard Accounting Practice (SSAPs)

Ensuring that the accounting policies applied by the company do, in fact, conform with FRSs and SSAPs (or other equivalent regulations) is an important part of the audit. As students doing financial accounting courses will know, this is not an easy area. Just take the thorny problem of off-balance sheet finance and the treatment of leases. An auditor often has to use considerable judgement as the spirit of SSAP 21 is to have a consistent treatment so that operating leases which are more akin to rental agreements or hire purchase can be accounted for in the profit and loss account but finance leases where, to all intents and purposes, the company owns the asset should be shown in the balance sheet. An auditor will have to review the legal documents and then, by applying judgement and the criteria within the standard, will have to decide on the appropriate method of accounting that should be used.

Audit report

If the auditor is satisfied that the accounts are materially correct a 'clean' audit report will be given saying that the accounts show a true and fair view and comply with the relevant statutes. For audits carried out under the Companies Acts, a 'clean' report also implies that proper books have been kept by the company and that they agree with the underlying records and that FRSs and SSAPs have been applied properly.

If the auditor is not satisfied that the financial statements meet these criteria, a qualified audit report will be issued. Such a report will set out the reservations that the auditor has. It may be that a particular FRS has not been applied, but subject to that the auditor can give a true and fair view opinion. In other cases the auditor may not have been able to check or substantiate items in the accounts that are so significant that the auditor does not believe that the accounts show a true and fair view. The qualified audit report should state circumstances and the amounts involved so that the readers of the accounts are left in no doubt as to the implications of such a report. Many audit firms have technical departments which have experience of all types of qualified reports and the circumstances behind them and they are likely to be consulted by, and provide advice to, the audit team at the client.

Probably the most common audit qualification is that of going concern, i.e. whether the company is able to continue in operational existence for the foreseeable future. With the high number of company liquidations in the past ten years many companies are under financial pressure at their year-end and the auditor has to decide if this is likely to affect their ability to continue as a going concern. It would obviously be extremely embarrassing if the accounts were issued with a clean audit report and within a short period of time the company went into liquidation owing money to creditors and other users of the accounts.

Post-balance sheet events

Part of the completion process is the need to review the activities of the company during the period from the end of the audit until the directors actually sign and date the accounts. This review is necessary because events may occur during that period which will affect the accounts and potentially make them misleading to the users and the readers. If it were a condition existing at the balance sheet date, SSAP 17: *Accounting for Post Balance Sheet Events* defines what sort of events would warrant an adjustment to the accounts (such as a large debtor becoming insolvent). The standard also defines those events which need only to be mentioned in the notes (for example, the closing down of a large subsidiary or factory where this was not anticipated before the year-end). SSAP 18: *Accounting for Contingencies* also defines which contingent liabilities should be accounted for and which should form part of the notes to the accounts. At the end of this post-balance sheet period, just before the directors are to sign the accounts, the auditor should revisit the company or at least make contact by telephone. Ideally, the auditor should review board minutes and the cash book since the year-end and have discussions with senior management on potential problems.

SUMMARY

This chapter has presented a framework structure of stages and steps which comprise the audit evidence process in a normal limited company. It is important for the auditor to follow a suitable framework in order to ensure that audit effort is properly directed and assists with meeting the audit objectives. In conclusion, some general points about the character of the audit process should be reiterated.

First, effective auditing depends on the auditor having an appropriate understanding of the business being audited. This is a critical condition for good planning. Second, it is important to recognize that much of the evidence an auditor will collect is persuasive rather than conclusive. Indeed, the use of evidence frequently involves inference, for example from the strength of a control system to the quality of output it will produce, from the results of a sample to the value of an entire population and from the estimates generated in analytical procedures to the actual balances recorded by the company. Third, although the evidence process involves many detailed procedures and schedules of tests, it is primarily a judgemental rather than a purely procedural or mechanical activity. The quality of the audit work depends crucially on judgements by the auditor, for example about the risks affecting the financial statements, the choice of tests to undertake, the interpretation of evidence and its sufficiency. By recognizing these general characteristics, the auditor can ensure that the audit process is properly designed to support an audit opinion.

FURTHER READING

Further details of the steps and procedures involved in the audit process, particularly the type of work that may be undertaken to audit particular areas of the financial statements, can be found in many auditing textbooks. For example:

Dunn, J. (1991) *Auditing: Theory and Practice*, Prentice-Hall International, Hemel Hempstead.

Gray, I. and Manson, S. (1989) *The Audit Process: Principles, Practices and Cases*, Chapman & Hall, London.

Porter, B., Simon, J. and Hatherley D. (1996) *Principles of External Auditing*, John Wiley, Chichester.

Woolf, E. (1997) *Auditing Today* (5th edn) (1997), Prentice-Hall, London.

DISCUSSION QUESTIONS

1. Outline the main issues that an auditor should consider at the planning stage of an audit.

2. If effective planning requires a good understanding of the business being audited, how can an auditor develop such an understanding?

3. (a) Describe the role that systems-based auditing has in the overall audit process.

   (b) What are the risks to the auditor of following a systems-based approach?

4. Outline the role that professional judgement plays in the audit evidence process and identify five key areas of judgement that will affect the conduct of an audit and the formulation of an audit opinion.

5. Identify the main objectives the auditor is testing when confirming an account balance and the main types of procedure that may be used in audit tests. Devise examples of actual tests for specific account balances (e.g. stocks, debtors, tangible fixed assets, sales turnover, payroll expenditure) and how they would meet desired audit objectives.

13
Audit Risk and Sampling
Stuart Manson

INTRODUCTION

The word risk seems omnipresent in all aspects of commercial life in the 1990s. It would appear that no discussion of financial matters would be complete without a discussion of the risks involved. It has reached the stage where Turley (1989, p. 113) notes that it has become a 'buzz word', an important signifier of modernity. It is thus no surprise that the term should now be an accepted part of discourse in auditing.

Audit risk is defined in SAS 300: *Accounting and Internal Control Systems and Audit Risk Assessments* (APB, 1995a, para. 3) as the risk of the auditor giving 'an inappropriate audit opinion on financial statements'. Although defined in terms of giving an inappropriate opinion, audit risk is often discussed and conceptualized as a form of approach that auditors use when undertaking an audit. When discussed in the above sense the audit risk approach is seen as a successor to the vouching audit and systems approach to auditing. To a certain extent the audit risk approach can be viewed as evolving from previous audit approaches, the evolutionary process consisting of modification and refinement rather than revolutionary change.

It is pertinent at this stage to consider why the audit risk-based approach has emerged in the 1990s as the dominant audit approach used by audit firms. It is generally considered that the risk-based approach is both an effective and efficient way of performing an audit. Its emergence came about as audit firms were coming under increasing pressure to curb increases in fee levels charged to clients. This was prompted by the increasing attention paid by clients to audit fees when selecting their auditors and the increasing number of clients putting their audits out for tender. The pressure on audit fees undoubtedly caused audit firms to examine the way in which they performed audits to determine if they could be made more efficient (Turley and Cooper, 1991; Porter, 1993; Fischer, 1996). A form of constraint exists, however, in that auditors have been increasingly criticized for the quality of their audit work. Thus, any changes to the audit approach had to be coupled with maintaining or indeed improving the quality of audit work. It is within the context of these two pressures that audit firms have developed the risk-based approach.

As the name of the approach implies it requires auditors specifically to consider the risks that they face. In particular, there are two important risks with which auditors are concerned. These are the risk of giving a qualified opinion when a clean opinion should be given and the risk of giving a clean opinion when a qualified opinion should have been given. Of these two risks it is the latter that is of more concern to auditors. This is because it is this risk that could lead the auditor to being sued for negligence with the consequent costly implications for him or her. The auditor is therefore concerned with minimizing the risk of giving a clean opinion on financial statements which are materially[1] misstated.

THE AUDIT RISK MODEL

The risk of the financial statements being misstated, that is, audit risk, can be broken down into three components: inherent risk, control risk and detection risk. These are defined in SAS 300 (APB, 1995a, paras. 4, 5 and 6) as follows:

[Inherent risk] is the susceptibility of an account balance or class of transactions to material misstatement, either individually or when aggregated with misstatements in other balances or classes, irrespective of related internal controls.

[Control risk] is the risk that a misstatement that could occur in an account balance or class of transactions and that could be material, either individually or when aggregated with misstatements in other balances or classes, would not be prevented, or detected and corrected on a timely basis, by the accounting and internal control systems.

[Detection risk] is the risk that auditors' substantive procedures (tests of details of transactions and balances or analytical procedures) do not detect a misstatement that exists in an account balance or class of transactions that could be material, either individually or when aggregated with misstatements in other balances or classes.

In terms of the audit risk model these three components are commonly related to audit risk in the following way:

$$AR = IR \times CR \times DR$$

where:

$$AR = \text{audit risk}$$
$$IR = \text{inherent risk}$$
$$CR = \text{control risk}$$
$$DR = \text{detection risk}$$

Detection risk is sometimes subdivided into tests of detail risk (TD) and analytical review risk (ARR). Thus:

$$DR = ARR \times TD$$

In operationalizing the audit risk model the first decision auditors have to make is the level of audit risk they are willing to bear. Subsequent to this they assess the level of inherent risk and control risk. Having determined three of the constituents of the audit risk model auditors can then, by suitably rearranging the equation above, calculate the remaining constituent, detection risk. Thus:

$$DR = \frac{AR}{IR \times CR}$$

By expressing detection risk in terms of audit risk, inherent risk and control risk the auditors can calculate the level of confidence, being 100 per cent minus the detection risk calculated, they need to achieve when performing their substantive procedures. This provides a guide for them when determining the extent of substantive procedures they must perform if they are to achieve the identified level of audit risk.

This can be illustrated as follows. If the auditor is willing to accept an audit risk of 5 per cent, that is, he or she is operating at a 95 per cent confidence level, and has assessed inherent risk and control risk as 75 and 50 per cent respectively, then the detection risk will be:

$$DR = \frac{0.05}{0.75 \times 0.5} = 0.133, \text{ or } 13.3\%$$

What this means is that the auditor has to determine the amount of substantive procedures required to reduce detection risk to 13.3 per cent and hence achieve the desired audit risk of 5 per cent or, in terms of its corollary, give a confidence level of 95 per cent in his or her audit opinion. With the audit risk model expressed in this form it is clear that detection risk, as the residual component, is important because it is the factor which determines the extent of an auditor's substantive procedures. In the example above, if audit risk had been set at 1 per cent, detection risk would be 2.67 per cent, or, stated alternatively, the auditor would need to perform sufficient substantive procedures to provide him or her with a confidence level of 97.33 per cent. We can see that there is an inverse relationship between audit risk and the amount of substantive procedures an auditor has to perform to achieve the desired audit risk level. The less audit risk the auditor is willing to bear, for given amounts of inherent and control risk, the greater the amount of substantive procedures will have to be performed to achieve the derived detection risk level. Similarly, if either or both inherent risk or control risk are increased the auditor will have to perform a greater amount of substantive procedures to meet the desired audit risk level. In Porter's (1993) terms, detection risk is controllable by the auditor whereas the risk of errors occurring and not being corrected is not. Auditors can of course indirectly influence control risk by advising their clients how internal controls can be improved. In the next section the three components of audit risk – inherent, control and detection risk – will be discussed in detail.

Inherent risk

The risk-based approach can be seen as an extension of the systems-based audit. The main difference between the two approaches is that the risk-based approach specifically recognizes and requires the auditor to assess inherent risk. This is not to say that when auditors performed systems-based audits they were completely oblivious to inherent risk (see Elliott and Jacobsen, 1987; Dirsmith and Haskins, 1991) but merely that there tended to be no formal evaluation of inherent risk. The evaluation of inherent risk takes place at the planning stage of the audit. Because of the evaluation of inherent risk greater importance is now attached and more audit time is spent on the planning stage of audits (Humphrey and Moizer, 1990). When assessing inherent risk the auditor is concerned with assessing the susceptibility of errors or misstatements occurring in account balances or transactions. Consequently, the auditor needs to consider the factors which are likely to influence the occurrence of errors or misstatements. It is common practice for the factors to be classified into two types: factors affecting the likelihood of errors or misstatements occurring in the financial statements in general (termed entity level factors in SAS 300); and factors affecting the likelihood of errors or misstatements occurring in specific account balances or class of transactions.

SAS 300 lists the following factors which may influence inherent risk at the entity level (APB, 1995a, para. 15):

(1) unusual pressures on directors or management;
(2) the integrity of directors and management;
(3) management experience and knowledge and changes in management during the period;
(4) the nature of the entity's business;
(5) factors affecting the industry in which the entity operates.

The first two factors are related to the susceptibility of management deliberately to misstate the financial statements. The first is concerned with the environment in which the company operates and its particular circumstances which may provide incentives for management to misstate the financial statements. The second factor is effectively asking auditors to consider the extent to which they trust the directors or management. The more trustworthy the auditors consider the directors and management to be the less likely they are to succumb to unusual pressures. The assessment of these factors, which may be interrelated, is left to the professional judgement of the auditors. It is likely that some of the influences on the factors lend themselves to identification; if a company is close to infringing its debt covenants, for example, this may lead to pressure on the directors and management deliberately to misstate the financial statements. The integrity of directors and management is a factor which is difficult to judge and is likely to require auditors to use their past experience and knowledge of the individuals concerned to come to some judgement as to their trustworthiness. They may use certain evidence to support that judgement, such as the extent to which the directors have been truthful in the past and their personality traits, for example the extent of their apparent desire to demonstrate to the stock market their effectiveness as directors.

The final two factors relate essentially to the entity and the environment in which it operates. These factors recognize that certain industries are more volatile and subject to change than others. For example, firms operating in the fashion industry are subject to sudden and unexpected changes in taste which may affect the demand for their products. Similarly, for the final factor, economic conditions such as interest, exchange and inflation rates may have particular relevance to the prospects and security of a company. Assessment of the above factors assists the auditor in coming to some overall conclusion about the inherent risks faced in a particular audit. They help the auditor decide if the audit has low, medium or high inherent risk. This assessment will help the auditor determine the overall amount of audit work that requires to be carried out.

Similarly, SAS 300 lists a number of factors which may influence inherent risk at the account balance and class of transactions level. These factors are (APB, 1995a, para. 15):

(1) financial statement accounts likely to be susceptible to misstatement, for example, accounts involving a high degree of estimation;
(2) the complexity of underlying transactions;
(3) the degree of judgement involved in determining account balances;
(4) the susceptibility of assets to loss or misappropriation (an example of an asset which has a high risk of susceptibility to loss would be cash);
(5) the quality of the accounting systems;
(6) the completion of unusual and complex transactions;
(7) transactions not subjected to ordinary processing.

These factors direct the auditors' attention to the account balances and transactions where they will need to focus their audit effort and audit tests. In particular, they assist auditors in determining the nature and scope of their audit testing. For example, if the client is a construction company with a number of long-term contracts the auditor will be particularly concerned with these because of their complexity and the likelihood of them involving managerial judgement. The auditor will thus direct audit effort to obtaining audit evidence to substantiate the figures in the accounts relating to long-term contracts. To assess the factors listed above requires the auditor to have considerable knowledge of the client and sufficient experience. Because of this, the task of assessing inherent risk is likely to be performed by a senior member of the audit team, such as the audit manager. The assessment of inherent risk by the auditor will usually be documented in some form of planning document, for example, the audit planning memoranda.

Control risk

As part of normal audit procedures the auditor will document and assess the internal control systems of an entity. The documentation procedures are likely to include the use of narrative notes and flowcharts. The auditor's assessment of internal control will usually be assisted by using internal control questionnaires and internal control evaluation questionnaires. In addition to the specific internal controls operated by it the auditor will also be concerned with the general control environment in the company. The control environment encompasses aspects such as the attitude the directors and management have towards internal controls. If the directors place an appropriate level of importance on internal controls and appear to have sufficient experience and knowledge to implement appropriate systems, this will provide the auditor with some assurance of the likelihood of the company having an appropriate system of internal control.

As a result of this evaluation the auditor will make a preliminary assessment of control risk. This assessment is based on the auditor's judgement as to the effectiveness of the internal controls. If, after this initial assessment, the auditor comes to the conclusion that some reliance can be placed on those controls the next step will be to perform tests on those controls. If the auditor believes that the internal controls cannot be relied upon, that is, the control risk is high, then all the necessary audit evidence will have to be obtained by performing substantive procedures. After performing tests on the internal controls the auditor has to decide if the initial evaluation of inherent risk is appropriate. If the auditor's tests of controls are as expected, in terms of the number of errors detected, it would be perceived as evidence supporting the initial judgement of control risk. Conversely, if the number of errors detected exceeded expectations, or the nature of the errors detected caused the auditor some concern, the level of control risk may have to be reassessed.

It has been observed in the auditing literature (see, for example, SAS 300, para. 32) that there is often an interrelationship between inherent risk and control risk. For example, some of the factors which influence inherent risk, such as management's integrity, may also affect their attitude towards the internal controls and hence influence control risk. Where auditors believe there is a strong interrelationship between the two types of risk SAS 300 (APB, 1995a, para. 32) suggests that 'the effects of inherent and control risk may be more appropriately determined by making a combined assessment'.

Detection risk

After having assessed inherent and control risk the auditor has to determine the amount and nature of substantive procedures it is necessary to perform in order to reduce audit risk to the desired level. The substantive procedures the auditor performs are likely to include analytical review, proof in total, selection of key items, 100 per cent testing and sample testing. The extent of these must be sufficient to reduce detection risk to the amount commensurate with the acceptable level of audit risk. The split of substantive procedures between tests of detail and analytical review will be determined by the auditor's assessment of the level of assurance each type of test produces and the cost of performing the tests. Analytical review procedures are considered one of the least costly forms of testing to perform but there is some evidence that auditors do not consider them particularly effective and therefore tend to rely more on tests of detail to provide them with the necessary assurance (Turley and Cooper, 1991). In view of this it may be considered somewhat surprising that SAS 300 (para. 54) notes that the substantive procedures may consist solely of analytical procedures where they provide the auditor with sufficient appropriate evidence. Finally, it is interesting that SAS 300 states that, whatever the assessed level of inherent and control risk, the auditor should always perform some substantive procedures. This appears to reflect a conviction that no matter how low the inherent and control risks an auditor always needs to perform some 'direct' tests on transactions or balances.

SAMPLING

Although today it is generally accepted that, in arriving at an opinion, the auditor will have carried out only test checks, this was not always the case. Lee (1986) notes that the movement, in the 1930s and 1940s, from detailed checking and vouching of transactions to test checking transactions was prompted by the emergence of larger companies and a change in the role of the auditor. Prior to this time it was the consensus that one of the prime functions of the audit, and hence of the substantial checking done, was to detect fraud and error. As it became accepted that company management was responsible for this the need for the auditor to carry out detailed checking was reduced. Similarly, the increase in size of businesses had the consequence that the only way an audit could be completed in a reasonable time, and hence at a reasonable cost, was by test checking. In both instances the underlying motive was undoubtedly the fact that the benefit to be gained by continuing with detailed checking was outweighed by the costs.[2] The importance of sampling has been recognized by the Auditing Practices Board, which issued an auditing standard, SAS 430: *Audit Sampling*, in March 1995.

Audit strategy

Having decided on a particular audit strategy which contains some amount of sampling the auditor has to determine whether to use statistical or non-statistical sampling. The Draft Audit Brief, *Audit Sampling* (APC, 1987), lists three benefits of statistical sampling:

(1) it imposes on the auditor a more formal discipline as regards planning the audit of a population;
(2) the required sample size is determined objectively;
(3) the evaluation of test results is made more precisely and the sampling risk is quantified.

Against these advantages may be set a number of disadvantages. It is usually more time consuming to carry out statistical sampling, and this will lead to higher audit costs. In order to perform statistical sampling each individual item (the sampling unit) in the population must be capable of being identified in some unique way. The ability to do this may depend on the form in which the audit client maintain its records, it being generally recognized that statistical sampling is more likely to be feasible when the records are computerized. It can also be argued that statistical sampling leads to a mechanistic audit approach and thus loses out in the use of the auditor's experience and 'gut' feeling about the likely location of errors in the company's records or when there are most likely to be problems. Audit firms may also be reluctant to implement statistical sampling because of its complexity.

Sample selection

The auditor selects and evaluates a sample with a view to making inferences about the population from which it has been drawn. For these inferences to be justified certain conditions must be met.

A representative sample

The sample selected must be representative of the underlying population; only if this is the case can the auditor validly reach conclusions about the population based on the sample. The ideal of obtaining a representative sample does not apply just in cases of statistical sampling, it should also be an objective in non-statistical sampling. Various methods can be used to select a representative sample. The basic objective is the same in all methods, that is, the desire to select a random sample. A random sample is a sample where each item in the population has an equal chance of being selected for examination. One way in which an auditor can obtain a random sample is by using random number tables to select it. Methods of selection such as block sampling do not ensure that every item has an equal chance of being selected and thus do not conform to a basic requirement of statistical sampling.

Is the population homogeneous?

Prior to selecting a sample the auditor has to ensure that the population is homogeneous.[3] For instance, if the auditor is checking that invoices have been properly authorized prior to payment, it is a requirement that all the invoices be subject to the same control procedure. If there were two individuals who signed or initialled invoices as authorized, one of them authorizing payments greater than, say, £50 and the other payments for lesser amounts, then, effectively, we have two populations of invoices and the auditor should carry out tests on both populations. If this is not done any inferences the auditor makes based on the sample could be in error.

Sample size determination

Statistical sampling, which is based on sampling theory,[4] enables the auditor to determine the appropriate sample size for any given population size. To do this the auditor must determine the confidence level to be used and decide on the tolerable error. The confidence level or degree of assurance required by the auditor is simply a quantitative assessment of the reliability that can be placed on the sample results; tolerable error refers to the maximum error or deviation rate the auditor is willing to accept in the underlying population. Thus, on the basis of the sample results, the auditor can state, for a given level of confidence, that the error rate in the population lies within certain bounds. The extrapolation from a sample means that the auditor can never be 100 per cent certain. This would be possible only if every single item in the population was examined,[5] which would defeat the whole purpose of test checking. The converse of the confidence level is the risk the auditor is taking that any statement concerning the population may be incorrect. Thus, when the auditor is operating at a 95 per cent confidence level there is a risk, detection risk, of (100–95) 5 per cent that the inferences made about the population may be incorrect.

Attribute sampling

Attribute sampling is typically applied in compliance testing, where the auditor is concerned to establish whether or not a particular characteristic is present. In compliance testing the characteristic is usually whether a particular internal control has been properly applied. Attribute sampling may also be used in substantive testing when the population does not contain monetary values or it is not in a form suitable for using other forms of statistical testing. The prime aim of compliance testing is to enable the auditor to form some estimate of the reliability of the internal controls and use that either to support or to modify his or her initial evaluation of control risk.

In attribute sampling the auditor is required to determine a confidence level for the particular control procedure being tested. The level chosen will to some extent reflect the importance of the particular control procedure that is being tested and the assurance either gained or expected to be gained from other audit procedures (e.g. substantive procedures) which are related to the control procedure. The tolerable error is defined in SAS 430 (APB, 1995b, para. 18) as 'the maximum rate of deviation from a prescribed procedure that auditors are willing to accept in the population and still conclude that the preliminary assessment of control risk is valid'.

The confidence level and the tolerable error, together with the auditor's estimate of the expected error rate in the population (which is likely to be influenced by past experience), are used in conjunction with suitable statistical tables to calculate the sample size.

When evaluating the sample results and extrapolating these to the population the auditor is concerned with determining, at the confidence level being used, if the expected upper error or deviation rate of the population exceeds the tolerable error. If this is the case the auditor may have to revise the amount of reliance that was going to be placed on the internal control systems, that is, reassess the original estimate of control risk. If, on the other hand, after carrying out the tests the auditor finds the upper error rate is less than the tolerable error rate, this confirms the appropriateness of the initial assessment of control risk.[6]

Monetary unit sampling

In monetary unit sampling[7] the auditor attempts to come to some conclusion about the amount of monetary error in a population. This can generally be accomplished only if the population is specified in terms of £1 monetary amounts and a cumulative total of these amounts can be calculated. Thus, if the auditor is concerned with selecting debtors for circularization purposes, a monetary cumulative running total of the amounts owed will be required, and within that total the allocation of specific monetary units to particular debtor accounts. Since the population is in £1 units the sample selected will consist of specific £1 units from the population. These £1 units are, however, only a hook for the individual debtor accounts that are to be audited. Based on the specific £1 units selected the auditor obtains a sample of debtors to be circularized. The determination of the sample size proceeds as follows.

The auditor, first, must specify the confidence level and the tolerable error – the amount of error in the account being audited which when combined with errors in other accounts would lead to the financial statements being misleading. Using the specified confidence level, the tolerable error and an estimate of the likely error together with suitable statistical sampling tables the auditor can determine the appropriate sample size.

When evaluating the sample results the auditor first calculates a point estimate corresponding to the most likely error in the population. This is supplemented by calculating an estimate of the upper error limit in the population. Using these the auditor is able to make a statement of the most likely error and, at the confidence level being used, the upper error limit in the population. If the upper error limit is less than the tolerable error the auditor can accept the population. If the opposite is the case the auditor may adjust the upper error limit for any errors found – assuming the client agrees to the adjustment – to determine whether that reduces the upper error limit to below the tolerable error. If the upper error limit remains above the tolerable error the auditor should carry out such procedures as are laid down by the audit firm to deal with this situation.

PROBLEMS IN APPLYING THE AUDIT RISK APPROACH

Thus far in this chapter there has been no mention of the limitations or complexities involved in applying a risk-based approach. A number of authors, however, have recognized that the description of the audit risk model, such as in the AICPA Auditing Standards SAS 39 and 47 (1991, 1993), are a simplification of reality (Cushing and Loebbecke, 1983; Colbert, 1987). In this section a number of the limitations and complexities in the audit risk approach will be discussed.

The aggregation problem

The definition of audit risk given earlier was expressed in terms of the auditor attempting to reduce to an acceptable level the audit risk relating to the financial statements as a whole. In reality the auditor does not actually substantiate the financial statements in the aggregate but instead gathers evidence to support specific assertions. An example of an assertion the auditor attempts to substantiate is that the finished goods stock is correctly valued. Substantiation of this within a risk-based framework requires the auditor first to evaluate the inherent and control risk relating to the finished goods stock. Some of the factors influencing the inherent risk of finished goods stock are relatively obvious, for example the competence of the staff involved in the stock function within the client company and the degree of estimation involved in valuing the stock. It is less obvious how the auditor evaluates the extent to which the environmental or entity-level factors discussed earlier influence the inherent risk of stock. This is obviously a process which requires the auditor to exercise considerable judgement. Having arrived at some estimate of inherent risk the auditor would then estimate the control risk for finished goods stock. In determining this the auditor is likely to depend on the standard control evaluation procedures, such as internal control evaluation questionnaires and, where appropriate, compliance testing. The next stage in the substantiation of finished goods stock is the identification of an appropriate level of audit risk. Using this and the estimates of inherent and control risk the auditor can then derive the amount of detection risk. The auditor then has to decide upon an appropriate mix and scope of substantive procedures to perform to achieve this derived detection risk. The final stage in this process is the aggregation of the audit risk for all the various audit assertions to determine the overall audit risk. There is, however, no one agreed or definitive procedure in the professional auditing literature which suggests how this aggregation process should be achieved. The complexity and severity of the aggregation problem led Cushing and Loebbecke (1983, p. 29) to conclude: 'it is unclear how appropriate the audit risk analysis model is as the foundation for an auditing methodology which is useful in practice'.

The aggregation problem is also pertinent to the evaluation of the individual components of audit risk: inherent, control and detection risk. In arriving at an evaluation of each of these components the auditor will usually have to consider a number of factors. For example, in determining the inherent risk of a particular account balance the auditor will have identified a number of factors which may influence its inherent risk. The auditor has to combine these factors to arrive at some overall view of the level of inherent risk of the specific account balance. This requires the auditor to assess the importance of each of the factors and consider any interdependencies that exist between them. This process is further complicated because the weight which an auditor attaches to any one factor is not necessarily constant but may vary from audit to audit depending on the particular circumstances. There is very little guidance or discussion in the auditing literature of how auditors should combine the various relevant factors to arrive at an overall assessment of the audit risk components. In general, any guidance on how auditors should address the aggregation process is usually couched in the ubiquitous phrase that it is an area where auditors must exercise their professional judgement.

Independence of components

An assumption of formal risk models, such as that advocated by SAS 39 (AICPA, 1981), is that the individual risk components are independent. It is, however, widely recognized that the components of the audit risk model may not be independent. The interrelationship which is most often discussed in the auditing literature is that between inherent risk and control risk. Where the internal controls of a company are weak, that is, control risk is high, this may have implications for inherent risk. For example, employees recognizing that the internal controls are weak may be more inclined to commit fraud or may be less inclined to perform their work diligently. This would lead to the inherent risk being higher than would be the case if the internal control system was strong, and illustrates the potential interrelationship between the two risk components. A possible solution to the interdependence problem would be for the auditor to consider both aspects of risk together and have a combined assessment for inherent and control risk. Another example of a possible interdependence is between control risk and analytical review risk. Analytical review procedures are often based on the relationship between two or more accounting numbers, the most obvious example of this being in the calculation of accounting ratios. A correct interpretation of, for example, the trend in the ratios calculated depends, among other things, upon the validity of the accounting numbers forming the ratios. The accounting numbers are more likely to be correct if the company has a good system of internal control. This is an example of where control risk affects the effectiveness of analytical review procedures which are part of the substantive procedures used by auditors to reduce detection risk to an acceptable level. To assess detection risk correctly in this example would require the auditor to take into account the impact of the internal control system, and hence control risk, on the effectiveness of the substantive procedures.

Non-sampling risk

In the formulation outlined earlier in this chapter the audit risk model assumes that the only relevant form of risk is sampling risk. This is implicit in the discussion contained in SAS 300 (APB, 1995a, para. 50) of detection risk, where it is stated that detection risk is 'primarily the consequence of the fact that auditors do not, and cannot, examine all available audit evidence'. This ignores the non-sampling risk arising from auditor error. This error can arise from sources such as the failure to evaluate correctly the test results, failure to perform appropriate audit tests or misapplying audit tests. If auditors fail to evaluate certain substantive procedures correctly their assessment of detection risk may be understated. Audit firms will normally attempt to minimize non-sampling risk by instigating quality control procedures such as training and review procedures.

Audit outcome space

A number of papers have been published which criticize the audit risk model approach in the US standards SAS 39 and 47 because of its failure to measure audit risk correctly (Kinney, 1989; Sennetti, 1990; Skerratt and Woodhead, 1992). In particular, these criticisms have emphasized that the risk model as presented in the professional standards relates to *planned* audit risk and fails to take into consideration events which may arise during an audit. Skerratt and Woodhead (1992, p. 121), whilst accepting that planning is important in an audit, emphasize that 'it is essential that the risk model should be able to contribute to the formation of the audit opinion *after* the conduct of the audit tests'. Thus, the studies cited above consider that the auditor needs to be concerned with posterior risk, that is, the probability that material misstatements remain in the accounts after the auditors have completed their audit tests. The difference between planned audit risk and posterior risk is discussed below.

We saw above that the audit risk model is normally represented as follows:

$$AR = IR \times CR \times ARR \times TD$$

Skerratt and Woodhead (1992) use a simplified example to show that the posterior risk would be: the probability that a material misstatement exists but is not detected by audit tests divided by all the possible outcomes that lead to acceptance by the auditor that there is not a material misstatement. The latter consists of both the incorrect acceptance and correct acceptance of there being no material misstatement in the assertion being tested. This is shown in Figure 13.1.

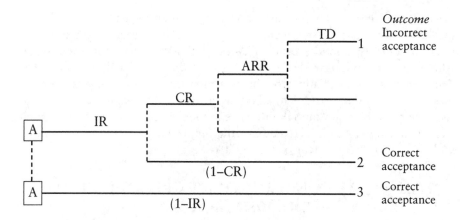

A = Assertion in the financial statements being tested.

Note: In outcome 2 a material misstatement has occurred but has been corrected by the internal controls. The auditor, however, is not aware of the detection and correction of the material misstatement.

Figure 13.1 Planned and posterior risk
Source: Adapted from Skerratt and Woodhead, (1992)

Figure 13.1 shows that there are two outcomes where the auditor correctly accepts the assertion that there is not a material misstatement. The first of these outcomes (outcome 2) is when a material misstatement does exist but is corrected by the client's internal control system. The second outcome is when there is no material misstatement at the outset (outcome 3). At the conclusion of the audit, however, the auditor knows only that he or she has found no material misstatement. This could be because there is no material misstatement or because one does exist but has not been detected. The posterior risk is given by the probability of the latter divided by the combined probabilities of all the acceptance outcomes.

In terms of the components of audit risk the planned audit risk is IR × CR × ARR × TD, whereas the posterior risk is given by:

$$\frac{IR \times CR \times ARR \times TD}{\underset{\text{(Outcome 1)}}{IR \times CR \times ARR \times TD} + \underset{\text{(Outcome 2)}}{[IR \times (1 - CR)]} + \underset{\text{(Outcome 3)}}{(1 - IR)}}$$

It can be seen that the two forms of audit risk differ and that because of the nature of the denominator the posterior risk, in all practical situations, will be greater than the planned audit risk.

The example above, involving only three possible outcomes, may appear rather simplified when compared to the number of possible outcomes that may occur in an actual audit. Skerratt and Woodhead (1992, p. 132) show, however, that more generally audit risk can be expressed as a function of three events: the probability that material misstatement remains undetected; the probability that misstatement has arisen but has been corrected by the internal controls; and the probability that misstatement has not occurred. Although it may appear that these criticisms are likely to be of only academic interest Skerratt and Woodhead demonstrate, using numerical examples, that depending on the numbers attached to the various categories of risk, there can be a substantial difference in the assessment of audit risk when using planned audit risk (derived from the simple audit risk model) compared with a posterior assessment of the audit risk.

THE SOCIAL CONSTRUCTIVIST CRITIQUE OF THE AUDIT RISK APPROACH

As outlined above, the audit risk model has been subject to a number of criticisms. These, however, tend to accept the general rhetoric about the value of and reasons why the audit risk approach was introduced. Most of the criticisms are of a technical nature, concerned with highlighting deficiencies in the audit risk model and, in some instances, identifying how it can be improved. More recently, however, the audit risk approach has been subject to a different form of critique. This critique has been concerned less with technical deficiencies in the audit risk approach but has instead emphasized the social nature of, and discourse surrounding, the approach (Humphrey and Moizer, 1990; Power, 1995; Fischer, 1996).

A typical example of this form of critique is Humphrey and Moizer (1990), who first of all note that one of the features of the risk-based approach is the greater emphasis it places on audit planning. They argue that the increased emphasis on audit planning commensurate with a risk-based approach 'serves both significant ideological and marketing functions (the former designed to legitimize the choice and extent of audit work, and the latter designed to maintain and if possible increase the fee income from the client)' (p. 217). This study highlights that the motivation for audit firms introducing and using the audit risk-based approach may have been influenced by issues other than improving the efficiency and effectiveness of the audit process.

Fischer's (1996) study was concerned with investigating what influences audit firms achieving efficiency gains when new technologies are introduced into the audit process. Of particular relevance to this chapter is Fischer's finding (1996, p. 223) that what constitutes a 'quality' audit 'is difficult, if not impossible, to answer conclusively. In the absence of directly observable measures, audit practitioners appear to rely on proxies of audit quality.' This would seem to suggest that the assumption in the audit literature that the implementation of a risk-based approach will reduce the costs of an audit whilst maintaining or improving audit quality is a feature that needs to be investigated rather than taken for granted. Fischer also notes that in his study one factor influencing changes in the approaches taken by audit firms was the issuing of specific auditing standards which served to endorse the new approaches. While the issuing of SAS 300 in the UK may simply be seen as codifying best practice and, perhaps, encouraging the adoption of a risk-based approach, the views expressed by one of the interviewees[8] in the Fischer study (1996, p. 226), admittedly in a US context, concerning the role of General Accepted Auditing Standards (GAASs) in improving the quality of auditing is rather worrying:

> 'what happened was that the firms had competed down the price of audits to the point where you could no longer make money doing all that work, so that GAAS had to be changed to allow for less work. So we put ... [an auditing standard] out there that said, you know where we used to do this expensive stuff called substantive testing? Hah! Look at a few ratios, that's just as good. And you know where we used to look at internal control and test it? Hah! Just look at superior controls and just look at them every three to four years to make sure that management has the right attitude. It's all a way of institutionalizing less work under GAAS.'

This would seem to suggest that the motivations of the individual members of the Auditing Practices Board for introducing the specific auditing standard, SAS 300, on audit risk assessments, is worthy of further investigation.

Power (1995) advocates that audit research needs to go beyond the consideration of audit processes and practices as technical phenomena and that there is a need for a 'sociology of audit technique' approach. This alternative perspective, he states, 'demands an approach to professionally familiar procedures of audit in which claims to instrumental efficacy are bracketed and in which the technicality of the audit process is regarded as a *product* of social processes rather than as a neutral medium' (1995, p. 330). In contrast to most discussions on audit risk, which are couched in terms of efficiency and effectiveness, Power contends that audit risk functions in a number of other different ways. First, he asserts that the audit risk model serves to promote a 'scientifically rational image' of the audit process. In this sense Power contends (1995, p. 331) that 'the audit risk model replaces and subsumes the role formerly played by statistical sampling'. Secondly, the emergence of a hitherto hidden source of audit assurance, that is the assignment of less than 100 per cent to the component inherent risk, provides a justification for the auditor to reduce the amount of detailed audit testing performed and hence reduce audit costs. Finally, he believes that terms like audit risk provide a way of perceiving and talking about auditing which can be used to justify 'operational decisions' to colleagues, other audit firms and, perhaps, in a court of law. Power argues that the adoption and use of the risk-based approach cannot be explained entirely in technical terms but instead we need to consider the other functions it serves as outlined above and in particular its role in 'symbolizing a new efficiency', as a 'cultural artefact' and in constituting the auditor as a 'risk expert' (p. 322).

EMPIRICAL EVIDENCE ON THE AUDIT RISK APPROACH

As might be expected, there have been numerous and varied empirical studies concerned with investigating the risk-based approach. In this chapter there is space only to outline a few of these studies.

Turley and Cooper (1991) reviewed the audit methodologies of twenty-one UK audit firms and found that fifteen included some explicit consideration of the application of risk in auditing. Ten of the fifteen firms referred to the audit risk model as contained in the US standard SAS 47 (AICPA, 1983). It is, however, interesting that of the firms which mentioned the audit risk model a majority presented the model in descriptive terms rather than mathematical terms. In general, they found that firms appeared to prefer a judgemental approach to risk assessment. This is consistent with expressing risk in qualitative terms such as low, moderate or high rather than in mathematical terms. The overall impression gained from this study is that the audit risk approach has been accepted and implemented by the larger audit firms in the UK.

In the light of the criticisms discussed earlier relating to the realism of simple audit risk models it is pertinent to determine the extent to which the application of the models is consistent with the assessment of total audit risk by audit staff. Using a case study involving debtors, Daniel (1988) asked a sample of thirty-three audit managers to specify their assessment of the total audit risk and the individual risk components involved in the audit assignment. She found that, although total risk in isolation was commonly assessed at 5 per cent, the estimate of this provided by using three risk models was generally less than 5 per cent. There were a number of managers who estimated audit risk at 5 per cent, who gained some assurance from the system of control and the analytical review, yet who nevertheless used 5 per cent (i.e. 95 per cent confidence level) in their substantive tests of detail. This would seem to imply that the auditors were overauditing in their substantive tests and needlessly increasing the costs of the audit.[9]

It has previously been stated that a major innovation of the audit risk approach is the consideration of inherent risk by audit practitioners. Given this, it is interesting to determine the extent to which audit staff are able to identify correctly factors likely to influence inherent risk. A study of this nature was performed in the UK by Helliar et al. (1996). They investigated a sample of audit practitioners' perceptions of the importance of a number of factors which may influence inherent risk. They found that the practitioners were competent in identifying inherent risk factors but had 'some difficulty in differentiating between control risk factors and inherent risk factors' (1996, p. 66). An interesting result from their study was that the subjects placed little importance on low inherent risk factors. If this result holds in actual audit practice it could lead to overauditing of low-risk areas.

CONCLUSION

The audit risk approach has gained general acceptance as the most effective and efficient way of performing an audit. It developed as a response by auditing firms to how they could make their audit work more cost effective whilst still maintaining audit quality. It is likely that audit firms will continue to seek out ways in which audit work can be improved. This may be achieved by further developing the risk-based approach, perhaps by identifying ways in which auditors' judgement of inherent and control risks can become more accurate and consistent. Alternatively, auditors may rely to a greater extent, more so than even at present, on the reliability and effectiveness of internal controls and the evidence provided by analytical review procedures. At this stage, however, it is difficult to envisage any quantum leap in the audit risk approach. For example, it is unlikely that any of the more sophisticated mathematical modelling associated with audit risk discussed in academic journals (e.g. Shibano, 1990) will find general acceptance in audit practice.

The increased use of the audit risk approach has also led to a change in emphasis on the form of substantive procedures performed by auditors. There is greater focus on the investigation of individual significant transactions and analytical review and less emphasis on audit sampling. In particular, as Loebbecke (1995, p. 189) notes, the use of statistical sampling 'in practice appears to have greatly diminished'. Even though the use of sampling may have diminished it still remains an important part of auditors' substantive procedures and one they wish to ensure is efficient and effective.

NOTES

1. Materiality is defined in the Auditing Practices Board's glossary of terms (APB, 1995c) as follows: 'a matter is material if its omission or misstatement would reasonably influence the decisions of an addressee of the auditors' report'.
2. Two interesting articles on the development of audit sampling are Power (1992) and Carpenter and Dirsmith (1993).
3. Items in a population are homogeneous if they all possess the same characteristics, such as being subject to the same control procedures or for similar amounts. Where populations are not homogeneous it is possible – by dividing the population into sections, where each section is effectively a sub-population having similar characteristics – to improve homogeneity. This process of division is commonly referred to as stratification.
4. Typically the sampling theory is based on the hypergeometric distribution or its approximations, the binomial and Poisson distribution.
5. Even if the auditor did test the complete population the possibility of non-sampling risk (see page 246) would prevent the auditor from reaching a conclusion with 100 per cent certainty.
6. SAS 430: *Audit Sampling* states that auditors also need to consider qualitative aspects such as the nature and cause of the errors they have detected.
7. There are many variants of, and different names for, monetary unit sampling, including combined attributes-variables sampling (CAV), probability proportionate

to size sampling (PPS), cumulative monetary amount sampling (CMA) and dollar unit sampling (DUS).
8. Fischer (1996) states the interviewee concerned was a senior national audit partner in a Big 6 audit firm, who was a former member of the Auditing Standards Board in the US.
9. Skerratt and Woodhead (1992) suggest that the results obtained by Daniel (1988) are consistent with differences between planned audit risk and posterior audit risk.

REFERENCES

American Institute of Certified Public Accountants (1981) Statement on Auditing Standards no. 39, *Audit Sampling*, AICPA, New York.

American Institute of Certified Public Accountants (1983) Statement on Auditing Standards no. 47, *Audit Risk and Materiality in Conducting an Audit*, AICPA, New York.

Auditing Practices Board (1995a) Statement of Auditing Standards 300: *Accounting and Internal Control Systems and Audit Risk Assessments*, APB, London.

Auditing Practices Board (1995b) Statement of Auditing Standards 430: *Audit Sampling*, APB, London.

Auditing Practices Board (1995c) *Glossary of Terms*, APB, London.

Auditing Practices Committee (1987) *Draft Audit Brief: Audit Sampling*, APC, London.

Carpenter, B. and Dirsmith, M. (1993) Sampling and the abstraction of knowledge in the auditing profession: an extended institutional theory perspective, *Accounting, Organizations and Society*, Vol. 18, no. 1, pp. 41–63.

Colbert, J. L. (1987) Audit risk – tracing the evolution, *Accounting Horizons*, September, pp. 49–57.

Cushing, B. E. and Loebbecke, J. K. (1983) Analytical approaches to audit risk: a survey and analysis, *Auditing: A Journal of Practice & Theory*, Vol. 3, no. 1, pp. 23–41.

Daniel, S. J. (1988) Some empirical evidence about the assessment of audit risk in practice, *Auditing: A Journal of Practice & Theory*, Vol. 7, no. 2, pp. 174–81.

Dirsmith, M. and Haskins, M. (1991) Inherent risk assessment and audit firm technology: a contrast in world theories, *Accounting, Organization, and Society*, Vol. 16, no. 1, pp. 61–92.

Elliott, R. K. and Jacobsen, P. D. (1987) Audit technology: a heritage and a promise, *The Journal of Accountancy*, May, pp. 198–218.

Elliot, R. K. and Rogers, J. R. (1972) Relating statistical sampling to audit objectives, *The Journal of Accountancy*, July, pp. 46–55.

Fischer, M. J. (1996) 'Real-izing' the benefits of new technologies as a source of audit evidence: an interpretive field study, *Accounting, Organization, and Society*, Vol. 21, no. 2/3, pp. 219–42.

Helliar, C., Lyon, B., Monroe, G. S., Ng, J. and Woodliff, D. R. (1996) UK auditors' perceptions of inherent risk, *British Accounting Review*, Vol. 28, no. 1, pp. 45–72.

Humphrey, C. and Moizer, P. (1990) From techniques to ideologies: an alternative perspective on the audit function, *Critical Perspectives on Accounting*, Vol. 1, no. 3, pp. 217–38.

Johnson, R. N. (1984) Sampling? use your professional judgement, *Accountancy*, January, pp. 70–3.

Kinney, W. R., Jr (1989) Achieved audit risk and the audit outcome space, *Auditing:*

A Journal of Practice & Theory, Vol. 8, Supplement, pp. 67–84.

Lee, T. (1986) *Company Auditing* (3rd edn), Van Nostrand Reinhold, Wokingham.

Loebbecke, J. K. (1995) On the use of Bayesian statistics in the audit process, *Auditing: A Journal of Practice & Theory*, Vol. 14, no. 2, pp. 188–92.

Porter, B. (1993) *Principles of External Auditing in New Zealand*, Dunmore Press, Palmerston North, New Zealand.

Power, M. (1992) From common sense to expertise: reflections on the prehistory of audit sampling, *Accounting, Organizations and Society*, Vol. 17, no. 1, pp. 37–62.

Power, M. (1995) Auditing, expertise and the sociology of technique, *Critical Perspectives on Accounting*, Vol. 6, no. 4, pp. 317–33.

Sennetti, J. T. (1990) Towards a more consistent model for audit risk, *Auditing: A Journal of Practice & Theory*, Vol. 9, no. 2, pp. 103–12.

Shibano, T. (1990) Assessing audit risk from errors and irregularities, *Journal of Accounting Research*, Vol. 28, Supplement, pp. 110–40.

Skerratt, L. C. L. and Woodhead, A. (1992) Modelling audit risk, *British Accounting Review*, Vol. 24, no. 2, pp. 119–37.

Turley, S. (1989) Concepts and values in the audit methodologies of large accounting firms, in *The Future of the Audit*, ICAS/ICAEW, Edinburgh.

Turley, S. and Cooper, M. (1991) *Auditing in the United Kingdom*, Prentice-Hall/ICAEW, Hemel Hempstead.

DISCUSSION QUESTIONS

1. Outline the main factors which are likely to be considered as important by auditors when assessing the inherent risk of long-term contracts for a UK construction company which earns 85 per cent of its revenues from long-term contracts both in the UK and overseas.

2. Critically evaluate the appropriateness of using formal audit risk models in auditing.

3. Some major firms use 'conventional' attribute statistical sampling, some use monetary unit sampling and some use only judgemental sampling. To what extent do you believe this knowledge should influence your interpretation of the reliability of these firms' respective audit reports?

4. Discuss the extent to which you believe auditors can rely on a client's internal control system to ensure the reliability of the figures in the accounts. Outline the problems one is likely to encounter when determining the control risk in a particular client.

5. Discuss the usefulness of Power's (1995) sociology of audit technique approach in investigating audit practices and processes.

14
Audit Automation: Improving Quality or Keeping up Appearances?

Stuart Manson, Sean McCartney and Michael Sherer

INTRODUCTION

A basic definition of audit automation is provided by Williamson (1994, p. 1): 'The process of applying any information technology based system to assist auditors in the planning, performance, control, completion and administration of audit work.'

The ways in which auditors can apply information technology to assist in the above functions include such aspects as the preparation of audit working papers, building up a library of standard pro forma documents and templates, and documentation of audit work (O'Kane, 1990). Whilst accepting this basic definition, for the purposes of this chapter we have operationalized the above definition of audit automation as 'the use of information technology in planning, controlling and recording audit work'. It should be noted that the use of information technology in the administration of the audit is different from the use of information technology to audit clients' computerized systems.[1]

The purposes ascribed to audit automation in the literature include: 'to improve efficiency and reduce costs, to improve quality and reduce audit risk, to improve response time and to push down (or deskill) work so that more junior staff can perform work currently done by more expensive senior staff' (O'Kane, 1990, p. 4). An illustration of the potential benefits of audit

Stuart Manson is Senior Lecturer in Accounting, Sean McCartney is Lecturer in Accounting and Michael Sherer is Royal London Professor of Finance, all at the Department of Accounting, Finance and Management, University of Essex.

automation is the suggestion by Ebbage (1993) that a significant amount of audit time could be saved by adapting automated working papers from the previous year instead of preparing them from scratch. Indeed, he suggests that overall there could be a 10 per cent saving of audit time if audit firms implemented audit automation. The practitioner journals also contain a number of articles discussing examples of the applications of audit automation within specific audit firms. The increasing implementation of information technology by a number of audit firms over the last few years and their increasing experience in its use facilitates the exploration of whether the expected objectives are being achieved. In addition, it is clear that the increased use of information technology may have wider implications in terms of the nature of audit work and the structure of the profession. For example, the nature and qualification of the personnel employed and the work they undertake within audit firms may be changing as a consequence of audit automation.

Audit automation represents an additional use of information technology by audit firms which had previously used information technology in the auditing of client firms' systems. The widespread use of computer-assisted audit techniques would seem to suggest that audit firms had the expertise to utilize information technology for audit automation. It may seem, therefore, somewhat paradoxical that such an obvious extension of the use of information technology into audit automation should lag behind its use as an audit technique by a number of years. It might be thought that it was the lack of availability of PCs at reasonable cost which inhibited the introduction of audit automation by audit firms. However, PCs have been available at reasonable cost since the early 1980s but it is only in the 1990s that we have witnessed a high level of interest in audit automation, as evidenced by the publication of an Accounting Digest on the subject in 1992 (Bones, 1992) and the establishment of the journal *aud*IT in 1990.

To understand why the use of information technology for audit automation purposes has been developed only recently it is necessary to locate this use within a wider context. One reason for this delay may be the fact that audit automation is seen as being somewhat peripheral to the main purpose of the audit. It may be argued that audit firms see the essence of the audit as consisting of a body of techniques to perform the audit, and in particular audit tests, as effectively and efficiently as possible. Within this context it is no surprise that changes in audit testing, such as the introduction of audit sampling and the move from systems-based auditing to risk-based auditing, have occurred. These changes deal with aspects which are located within the auditor's central area of concern. They are, in effect, part of the constituents of auditing. The use of information technology in the audit process arose partly as a result of expediency. Increasingly, audit clients were using computers to process their data and auditors were no longer able to audit those systems efficiently and effectively unless they themselves employed similar technology.

On the other hand, it could be argued that the increasing use of information technology in the audit process was a direct consequence of the constant downward pressure on audit fees in the 1980s and 1990s. Audit firms were motivated to search for further ways to improve the efficiency and effectiveness of their audit work. There did not appear to be any significant changes in the audit techniques themselves which could achieve the sought-after gains and, therefore, there was now a systematic attempt to utilize information technology within the existing auditing framework. Thus, audit firms, particularly the larger ones, introduced information technology to replace and supplement at least some of the audit tasks performed manually, for example Companies Act and accounting standards checklists, the use of templates for analytical review and the preparation of standard documentation.

It can also be argued that audit firms have made increasing use of information technology for other reasons. Audit firms are conscious that clients regard the annual audit as a routine task with little to differentiate the work of one firm from another (Goldman and Barlev, 1974). There is a concern to make the quality of the audit visible to the client in some way. Examples of this visibility include the management letter prepared by the auditor for the directors of the company (Manson, McCartney and Sherer, 1994) and the stress on 'input-criteria' such as 'the attire of audit staff' (Humphrey and Moizer, 1990, p. 231) as giving a 'better indication of how the audit has gone than the actual working papers [which] the client does not see'. The highly visible use of computers by audit staff can be seen as an additional way in which audit firms can enhance their prestige and reputation.

EXTENT OF AUDIT AUTOMATION

Most audit firms have allocated the overall responsibility for the development and implementation of information technology in the audit process to an audit partner. This probably reflects a desire on the part of the audit firms to ensure that any new audit automation developments are firmly based in the needs of the audit (Turley and Cooper, 1991). In many cases audit automation applications simply replaced the manual technique without in any way changing the audit task itself.

The fact that many of the people in the IT units within audit firms have an audit background or indeed have been seconded from the auditing side of the firm also helps to ensure that IT developments are always influenced by audit practice. In the past, a number of earlier audit automation applications, such as regression analysis, never gained general acceptance because they were not regarded as useful or helpful, for example because the application was too complicated or involved a lot of set-up time. Partly because of these earlier failures audit firms now recognize the importance of basing any audit automation application on audit practice.

The discussion in the remainder of this chapter is based largely on a mail survey of the forty largest audit firms in the UK and extensive interviews conducted in four of the firms. The survey and the interviews were carried out in 1993 and 1994. For the purposes of the research the forty firms were classified into three groups:

(1) Big Six: firms ranked 1–6 by fee income;[2]
(2) medium-sized: firms ranked 7–20 by fee income;
(3) small: firms ranked 21–40 by fee income.

From this survey it is clear that the Big Six audit firms use information technology more extensively than the other firms. As an illustration, in these firms a portable or laptop computer is taken out on all audits other than very small ones. Medium-sized firms also generally use information technology for most of their audit clients. For the small firms the experiences are more varied with a majority of firms using computers in only a limited number of audits. Consistent with these observations is the finding that the smaller the audit firm the higher the ratio of audit staff to computers.

In many ways these findings are not surprising. Large audit firms tend to have a higher proportion of large clients where the use of information technology in the audit is likely to be more appropriate and cost effective. Consequently, large audit firms will have an incentive to invest in audit automation in order to conduct the audits of large clients efficiently. Having made this investment and acquired the expertise of implementing audit automation in their work, the large audit firms are more likely to use information technology in the audits of all their clients. For smaller audit firms there may be two factors inhibiting the extensive use of information technology. First, the cost not only of computer hardware and software but also of staff training may discourage small audit firms from making a significant investment in information technology. Secondly, for smaller audit clients the marginal benefit to be gained from using information technology will be less than for larger audit clients. Therefore, since smaller audit firms have a higher proportion of smaller audit clients the total marginal benefit to the firm will be less than it will be for larger audit firms.

Audit automation is used for a variety of planning, controlling and recording tasks within the audit process. The main types of tasks under the three headings are shown in Table 14.1.

For some tasks, such as allocation of staff to functions, recording and monitoring time spent and costs incurred on audit tasks, and preparation of standard documentation, there is little difference in the extent of use between Big Six, medium-sized and small audit firms. There are, however, marked differences between the groups of audit firms in the extent of usage of a small number of applications. For example, under the heading of 'Planning tasks' more use is made of information technology for the preparation of planning memoranda and tailored audit programmes by the Big Six firms than the other two groups of audit firms. Under the heading of 'Controlling tasks' the calculation of time and cost variance from budget is used by the Big Six and medium-sized firms more than by the small firms. Finally, under the heading of 'Recording tasks' the preparation of the summary of results for partner review, flowcharting and documentation of accounting systems are used more

Table 14.1. The main audit tasks which can be automated

Planning tasks	Controlling tasks	Recording tasks
Creation of time budgets	Recording and monitoring of time spent on audit tasks	Preparation of standard documentation, e.g. letters of representation
Allocation of staff to functions	Recording and monitoring of costs incurred on audit tasks	Summary of results for partner review
Preparation of planning memoranda	Calculation of time variance from budget	Drafting of management letters
Calculation of appropriate financial ratios and statistics for analytical review	Calculation of cost variance from budget	Flowcharting
Risk assessment	Record of manager/partner review	Documentation of accounting system
Preparation of tailored audit programmes		Preparation of lead schedules
Calculation of sample sizes		Maintenance/update of permanent audit file details
Database of (changes in) accounting standards/ auditing guidelines/ relevant legislation		

extensively by the Big Six than either the medium-sized or small groups of audit firms. These results are consistent with the nature of the client base for each group of audit firms; we would not expect smaller audit firms with fewer and smaller clients to make use of information technology for the preparation of tailored audit programmes. As a corollary, for larger audit firms, which tend to have a more 'appropriate' client base, it is worthwhile investing time and effort in developing and introducing more audit automation in their audit work.

There is generally more use of computers for activities such as preparation of standard documentation and management letters. It is likely that these tasks will be accomplished using standard word-processing packages available to both audit and secretarial staff across all audit firms. For the more specialized recording tasks the Big Six make more extensive use of information technology than other firms. Once again, for many of the tasks there is a positive relationship between the size of audit firm and the extent to which information technology is used.

The Big Six audit firms are spending considerable amounts on the development and implementation of information technology. Specifically, Manson, McCartney and Sherer (1997) found that three of the Big Six audit firms have budgets in excess of £1 million per annum. Although most of the medium-sized firms spent less than the Big Six, two of them had budgets between £500,000 and £1 million per annum. The size of the budgets for information technology is consistent with the evidence discussed above which suggested that the Big Six firms used information technology more extensively than any of the other firms. It is, however, acknowledged that since the Big Six are by definition the largest firms one would expect them to spend more.

TYPE OF SOFTWARE USED

The majority of the use of information technology in planning, controlling and recording audit work involves the use of general-purpose packages such as spreadsheets and word-processing programs. Small audit firms almost invariably use general-purpose packages rather than specialist auditing programs. With these packages they have the ability to undertake tasks such as creating standard letters, for example engagement letters and letters of representation.

Most of the Big Six firms have developed internally some auditing software, for example Companies Act checklists and audit programme generators. In contrast, medium-sized firms undertake very little development of software, preferring instead to buy in auditing application packages and auditing software developed by specialist firms.

Because the Big Six firms have the resources to develop software internally it might be thought that they would have a competitive advantage in the use of information technology in the audit process. Thus, if these firms identify a potential use for information technology in the audit they would be able to develop the appropriate software whereas smaller firms would probably have to wait until that application is generally available through commercial software houses. However, one of the Big Six firms believes that internal development is probably not cost effective, and that increasingly the firm will rely on cheaper standard packages in the future. As the manager responsible for introducing information technology in this firm put it:

> interestingly, things like Companies Act checklists are also available as packages in the market place and the general sceptical view is that it takes so long to write an application yourself you are much better off buying packages if you can . . . the mass market in software means you can buy enormously sophisticated tools . . . at knock-down prices, £50 per user, £20 per user, and therefore small firms can buy in over that technological barrier.   (Manson, McCartney and Sherer, 1997, p. 25)

In the early days of audit automation the use of information technology involved primarily the application of individual programs and packages where the audit firm had identified suitable tasks. It may be argued, therefore, that the initial development of information technology uses in the audit process was somewhat *ad hoc* without a clear strategy for integrating it fully into the audit. Recently, more thought has been devoted by the Big Six firms in particular to the possibilities of using information technology to move towards a fully integrated automated audit.

At least one of the Big Six firms has been piloting such an integrated audit automation approach. This integrated audit automation system consists of an integrated set of third-party software and the audit firm's own internally developed software. Each audit staff member at the client's premises needs to have his or her own laptop for recording all his or her audit work. These PCs are networked so that information can be shared by all staff. Thus, work prepared by one staff member can be copied at regular intervals to other members of the audit team. This integrated system helps to plan and complete the audit by providing a means to record, organize and share audit information. It also enables an electronic audit file to be created for each engagement within which working papers can be created, filed and retrieved. Other features of the system include the ability to:

(1) bring forward prior year audit work relevant to the current year;
(2) devise and record the audit strategy, including the identification of inherent risks and the creation of tailored audit programmes for each audit area;
(3) incorporate spreadsheet and word-processing files into the current audit working papers;
(4) record in a database those issues which need to be brought to the attention of managers or carried forward to next year;
(5) share audit information and the contents of the audit file so that each member of the audit team has an up-to-date version of the audit work carried out by the rest of the team;
(6) 'tag' each working paper according to its current status, e.g. in progress, completed, reviewed by manager, etc.

One of the main effects of using this type of integrated audit automation package is that members of the audit team are obliged to adopt the practices laid down by the firm. This occurs in two ways: first, there are inbuilt disciplines embedded into the software, and, secondly, the facility for information sharing enables managers and partners to monitor the work of staff more expeditiously. This more disciplined and structured approach to the audit has obvious appeal for partners.

An auditor at the client can access databases held on the audit firm's computer, and has easier access to the partner through e-mail, whilst a manager or partner can access the audit file (which exists in electronic form, and is shared by the audit team), review schedules, see what is going on, and leave comments and suggestions. Partners can be much more closely involved in what the audit team is doing, even updating themselves on the work being undertaken on an audit while it is in progress. The use of e-mail and modems has enabled managers and partners to monitor more closely the work carried out by seniors and assistants at clients' premises. This obviously has the potential to change relationships between seniors and assistants on the one hand and managers and partners on the other.

A less costly alternative than the integrated audit automation package involves using a 'toolbox' approach. Here specific tasks suitable for audit automation are identified, and the appropriate software purchased if available, or developed internally where there is something distinctive in the firm's approach.

BENEFITS OF AUDIT AUTOMATION

The general benefits from audit automation are identified in a semi-official publication published by the ICAEW: 'The use of computers in the management, planning, performance and completion of audits to eliminate or reduce time spent on computational or clerical tasks, to improve the quality of audit judgements, and to ensure consistent audit quality' (ICAEW, 1993, p. 5). In this section we consider the evidence from our study for each of these supposed benefits together with some additional ones identified in Williamson (1994).

Improve audit quality and audit judgement

The main benefit firms perceive they gain from using information technology is an increase in audit quality. Although this finding was confirmed in our interviews it is notable that a number of interviewees had difficulty in identifying specific areas in which quality had been improved. Their responses tended to be vague and couched in general terms, for example that it would improve the quality of audit staff thinking or the quality of the presentation of the audit files. Overall, although there may be benefits in terms of improving the quality of audit work from using information technology, the difficulty some of our interviewees had in articulating these improvements would seem to suggest that they are not dramatic or immediately apparent.

Firms might also believe that such improvements in audit quality and audit judgement arising from increasing audit automation might reduce the probability that they would be successfully sued for negligence. If an audit firm is sued for negligence the use of information technology may be regarded by the courts as best audit practice and this may reduce the chances of the courts finding against the audit firm.

The ICAEW's IT Briefing No. 4, *Audit Automation* (ICAEW, 1993, p. 5), suggests that audit automation can improve the quality of audit judgements 'by structuring audit decision processes, and ensuring that staff address the right questions at the right time, and are aware of the possible answers and their implications'. Examples of this would include the use of information technology for analytical review and audit review checklists. Auditors also believe that audit automation enhances audit quality because it ensures completeness and accuracy of work done. One example of this is the use of templates to ensure a consistent quality of audit work by all audit staff.

Some auditors even suggested to us that the notion of quality extends to the perceptions that clients have about the quality of service given to them. The use of IT is regarded as helpful in promoting this perception of quality because it is associated with what is thought to be modern and up to date. By this is meant that IT, by its very nature, is a symbol for all that is progressive, advanced, efficient and reliable, and it is therefore not surprising that audit firms wish to embrace the aura of audit automation. In contrast to the popular belief that the use of IT leads to a mechanistic approach to auditing, many auditors believe that audit automation may produce better thinking because of its disciplinary nature. '[Audit automation] will improve the quality of the thinking that our staff will be forced into; if it is nothing else it is a discipline on the team' (Manson, McCartney and Sherer, 1997, p. 34).

Although most of the interviewees in our study readily accepted that audit automation would improve audit quality it was noticeable that few of them could point to specific instances where quality improvements had been made. Furthermore, none of the interviewees suggested how these improvements in audit quality might be measured in any objective way.

Improve efficiency and reduce audit costs

The existing literature, in evaluating the benefits of audit automation, places great emphasis on the saving in audit time and costs. For example, the ICAEW's IT Briefing states:

> For many auditors, the ultimate objective of automating audit tasks is to improve audit cost-effectiveness, either in the short or in the medium term . . . Auditors who have adopted audit automation have often found that elimination or reduction of audit time has allowed additional work to be carried out without increasing costs, audit fees to be controlled or reduced, or the profitability of particular audits to be increased
>
> (ICAEW, 1993, p. 5)

Although the literature stresses that cost reductions are the main motivation for introducing audit automation the results of our survey show this as clearly second to improving audit quality. Furthermore, although most audit firms indicated that they undertook some form of cost–benefit analysis there is little evidence of any attempt to quantify the cost reductions that had been achieved by audit automation. Indeed, given the number of other changes that have taken place (e.g. the move to a risk-based audit approach), it is probably impossible to isolate the impact of audit automation as such. The interviewees we spoke to were unsure whether the introduction of audit automation had resulted in any substantial cost savings. It is possible, however, that although the introduction of an individual audit automation application may be perceived by audit staff as saving relatively little time, the cumulative effect of a number of applications may result in noticeable savings in time and hence cost. This belief would appear to be reflected in the responses of some of our interviewees who suggested that firms adopting audit automation will achieve major cost reductions in the long run. The ability to achieve cost savings should be a focus of attention for those firms, such as the Big Six, which are committing substantial resources to IT developments. It may be of lesser importance to those firms whose commitment is very small. Thus, it is important that any firm planning to commit significant resources to audit automation be aware that cost savings are neither easy to achieve nor easy to measure.

None of the interviewees was able to put a precise figure on the efficiency gain or cost reduction attributable to audit automation. Nevertheless, attempts have been made to put a figure on the kind of savings that might be available from audit automation. For example, Ebbage (1993, p. 3) estimated that there could be significant savings in audit time:

> I have now come across several pilot implementations in both internal and external audit to automate all detailed audit working papers using a spreadsheet and word processing software. The results indicate that audit time can be reduced by up to 15 per cent in years two and three. On the other hand, audit costs could rise by 10 per cent in the first year.

Our interviewees indicated that the identification and quantification of savings are more problematic than might appear from the above. There is considerable scepticism among those responsible for implementing information technology over the question of quantifying the savings, if in fact they existed. One Big Six audit partner saw cost reduction as something still to be achieved: 'it ought to be more efficient once we've got everybody trained up and got the particular system that we're going to use bedded down in the practice . . . I think there should ultimately be a significant saving in audit time.' An audit partner from another Big Six firm stated that real quantification of costs and benefits was impossible: 'I think there's a great act of faith needed. I don't think you can just do a conventional cost benefit analysis for the investment. Partly because you can't value quality . . . really to make it work you've got to believe in it and then get the [support] of the organization.'

The overall conclusion about the efficiency gains and cost savings to be achieved from audit automation is that very little has been achieved thus far. This may be because there have not been any cost savings, or because of the difficulty of measuring any savings which have been made. Indeed, most respondents are anticipating that cost savings will be made in the future. But the problem of quantifying the cost savings still remains. Apart from anything else, it is virtually impossible to separate the impact of IT from that of other changes in auditing, which may also have contributed to general cost savings.

Ensure consistent quality of audit work and documentation

Audit firms have for many years tried to ensure a consistency of audit work via the use of work programmes, standard letters and prescribed procedures. The use of information technology further enhances the consistency of audit work by providing a number of tools and aids. For example, in the case of standardized letters, such as letters of representation, audit staff can have available on their PCs a template which can be tailored to specific client needs. Another example is the availability of a computerized company accounts compliance checklist which enforces a more disciplined, and hence consistent, approach to audit work.

One of the interviewees from a Big Six firm thought that the use of audit automation helps to ensure that the audit will be conducted in line with the firm's approach. Hence, audit automation creates a uniformity of behaviour on the part of seniors and assistants which helps to promote and reinforce the audit methodology of the firm. However, in order to achieve the major improvements in the consistency of audit work which are desired and expected it may be necessary for audit firms to adopt the fully integrated audit automation approach described above, rather than a piecemeal approach in which only certain audit tasks are automated.

Improve competitive edge

Big Six partners and managers we interviewed emphasized the need to maintain a competitive edge, by which they meant keeping up with other Big Six firms rather then simply maintaining a lead over smaller firms.

One audit manager clearly saw the development of audit automation as important in gaining a competitive edge over other Big Six firms: 'My perception is that, along with many other firms, we are striving to gain and maintain and reach some sort of competitive edge. And that has been attempted in the past through similar methods in the accounting practices' (Manson, McCartney and Sherer, 1997, p. 36). This interviewee clearly saw the development of automation as just another marketing tool in the firm's quest to remain competitive with its rivals.

This concern with being competitive was echoed by one of the medium-sized firm's managers interviewed. When asked if it was necessary for his firm to do more in the IT field he responded:

> I don't think we can afford to be left behind. I think the way the market is, that people generally are using IT more in their auditing techniques, I think we need to be amongst it. I don't think at the moment there is really too much constraint budget-wise. I think computers can demonstrate that they are useful and then they will have them.
>
> (Manson, McCartney and Sherer, 1997, p. 36)

This quotation also makes it clear that audit firms are likely to react to audit automation developments taking place in other firms. Audit firms do not wish to appear to be lagging behind their competitors in the introduction of information technology into the audit process.

There is also some suggestion that audit automation might have some beneficial effects on the pattern of work in audit firms, for example by enabling more junior staff, perhaps even non-audit staff, to perform more significant audit work. Audit automation may also improve the motivation, job satisfaction and performance of staff. This may be because audit automation can eliminate or reduce the time spent by professional audit staff on computational or clerical tasks or simply because employees actually get enjoyment from 'playing' with computers (Starbuck and Webster, 1994). Some of these human resource aspects of audit automation are explored further below.

COSTS AND PROBLEMS OF AUDIT AUTOMATION

Table 14.2 contains the main costs of audit automation identified in the literature (see, for example, Ebbage, 1993) and the importance attached to each of them by the respondents in our survey.

Table 14.2 Principal costs of audit automation

	Ranking in order of decreasing costs
Cost of learning time	1
Cost of additional staff training	2
Cost of developing software	3
Cost of hardware	4
Cost of purchasing software	5

For all sizes of audit firms the major costs of introducing information technology are the time required by users to learn the new application and the associated additional training required. In response to a separate question most audit firms stated that the overall training time, and hence cost, had been increased as a consequence of introducing information technology into the audit process. An IT manager in one of the Big Six audit firms described the type and amount of information technology training in the following terms: 'When we update people they go on a 2–3 day Windows course. At a minimum people will have three days training, which is absolutely mandatory plus they would have spent at least three days training on networking office systems' (Manson, McCartney and Sherer, 1997, p. 38).

In contrast, one of the audit managers in a medium-sized firm believed that on-the-job training was more effective than formal classroom teaching:

I've long been an advocate of [on-the-job training]; I have never liked training courses. When people come clamouring to me for Lotus training I say, 'You don't need it, go away and use it'. To a large extent I believe that people who want to use it can pick it up straight away and the people who are coming up asking to be trained are not using it for other reasons, and they're using their lack of training as an excuse.'

(Manson, McCartney and Sherer, 1997, p. 38)

This negative reaction to formal training in information technology is somewhat surprising given that the amount of training being talked about, perhaps six or seven days for audit fieldworkers, does not seem an excessive additional burden, given the amount of training that audit firms provide for their staff. Nevertheless, there is some evidence that formal training will become less important as applications become more user-friendly: 'A lot of software we have used in the past hasn't been user-friendly, it is not very approachable. With Lotus I don't think training is such a big issue, people can learn a lot of basics themselves just by using it' (Manson, McCartney and Sherer, 1997, p. 39).

We also identified the main problems audit firms have to deal with when introducing audit automation. The results set out in Table 14.3 rank the problems in terms of significance as perceived by audit firms.

Table 14.3   Main problems of introducing audit automation

	Rank
Lack of familiarity/understanding of IT by senior staff and partners	1
Quantifying the benefits/costs of IT	2
Maintenance of security over sensitive information held on computer files	3
Lack of enthusiasm for IT by audit fieldworkers	4
Difficulties in applying software in real situations	5
Increased staff turnover	6

From the table it can be seen that the main problems identified by the audit firms when seeking to extend the automation of the audit are the lack of familiarity and understanding of at least some of the senior staff and partners and the difficulty of quantifying the benefits and costs. There is some concern about security of information held on computer on the part of Big Six firms but this is not seen to be a major problem for the other firms. One of our interviewees gave the following example of partner resistance to information technology: 'It's the more established staff that have difficulty in changing. There will be some who will never do it [use a PC], they will have their secretaries printing [their e-mail] off so they've got a piece of paper and can read it' (IT manager, Big Six audit firm). Other problems mentioned to us in our interviews were that not all staff had access to a PC whenever they wanted one and the limited amount of formal training given to staff. It is evident, however, that junior staff, audit assistants and audit seniors do not lack any enthusiasm for using information technology; indeed, most of the junior staff we interviewed had a very positive attitude to audit automation.

Overall, then, our respondents and interviewees did not perceive there to be any major problems involved in implementing information technology in the audit process. They did, however, recognize that cost was a barrier to achieving the full potential of audit automation.

IMPACT ON AUDIT AND NON-AUDIT STAFF

In this final section we consider some of the consequences for audit and non-audit staff of the increasing use of information technology in the audit process. As noted above, some of the perceived benefits of introducing audit automation come about through changing the nature of work, and particularly who does what task in the audit firm. One area of debate is whether audit work is being de-skilled as tasks become more routinized through audit automation.

The de-skilling debate

The argument here is that information technology is facilitating and accelerating an already existing tendency for accounting work in general to become increasingly formalized, that is, characterized by procedures and rules. Consequently, the skills of qualified/professional accountants are under-used. As a result, the professional accountant is degraded to a technician, or he or she is replaced by less skilled labour (see Roslender, Glover and Kelly (1991) for an extreme version of this argument). The counter-argument to this might be that there is, on the contrary, a process of 'up-skilling': the auditor now needs information technology skills in addition to those previously required. Either way, such trends would show up in changes in the recruitment policies of firms but there is no evidence that these have changed significantly as a consequence of audit automation. The vast majority of trainees are still graduates, with the most important attributes being the quality of their degree and their inter-personal skills. There does not appear to an increase in trainees with computer-orientated degrees nor is computer literacy a specific requirement, although it should be noted that most graduates acquire at least some computer skills during their university studies.

There has been a small increase in the number of accounting technicians employed by the Big Six but little change for the other two categories of firms. Similarly, there does not appear to have been much substitution of non-professional for professional staff in any of the groups of audit firms. It is also worthy of note that there has been an increase in the use of information technology specialists in both the medium-sized and small groups of firms. One explanation for this might be that the smaller audit firms are now catching up with the larger firms, having made relatively little investment in information technology until quite recently. In contrast, the larger firms have invested quite heavily in information technology from the very beginning of its application to accounting and audit. From our study, therefore, there appears to be very little evidence of de-skilling in the sense of less qualified staff replacing more qualified staff as a result of increasing the use of information technology in the audit.

Is the technology taking over?

Another issue is whether the increasing use of information technology leads auditing into a situation where the 'machine takes over' and auditors simply follow the instructions of the software and the answer, for example the risk assessment, is provided by the computer. For example, Dillard and Bricker (1992, p. 205) refer to the 'encroachment of technical consciousness' where the decision of the expert system replaces the judgement of the human auditor.

All respondents were clear on this and had no intention of 'going down this road'. They were insistent, and in the case of partners, often in terms which suggested that this issue had been the subject of some discussion, that this was being consciously rejected. The information technology tools were regarded as precisely that:

> We do not use the computer to weight our decisions on risk priorities in any way whatsoever. You use your brain to do that. . . . The determination of risk is a manual intellectual process. And it tends to be iterative, involving the partner, the manager, the in-charge, and probably the client.
>
> (Manson, McCartney and Sherer, 1997, p. 47)

Similarly most auditors would argue that computers can never replace judgement and indeed that in the last few years, with the emphasis on a risk-based approach, auditing has become more, rather than less, judgmental.

We then investigated whether there is a tendency for audit staff to use PCs simply because they are available rather than ensuring that they are using them efficiently to accomplish a particular audit task. A number of audit partners we interviewed recognized that there might be a danger that staff who were most enthusiastic about using information technology would do so without considering whether it was the most efficient way of performing the task.

Audit firms believe the increasing use of information technology in the audit process has allowed experienced staff to spend more time on non-routine, technical issues which are more directly relevant to conducting an efficient audit. This is particularly the case for the Big Six firms.

Related to this finding is the perception that job satisfaction and morale of audit staff have improved with the increasing use of information technology. The interviews provided evidence to support the view that audit staff (particularly audit assistants and seniors) find using IT enjoyable. Job satisfaction is of course difficult to measure but the survey and the interviews with partners indicate a conviction in the firms that information technology is improving the 'lot of the audit fieldworker', especially the more junior, by automating boring and repetitive tasks.

One significant point here is that those involved in the implementation of information technology stressed the voluntary nature of the tools they had developed: the use of information technology is, to some extent, at the discretion of the auditor. There is evidence that where accountants have discretion over the amount of use they make of PCs, it is the perceived ease of use rather than the perceived usefulness of the PC which determines how much use is actually made (Ferguson, 1994). The clear impression from the interviews, at all levels, is that it is the more junior employees who are keenest to use information technology.

Impact on non-audit staff

Another issue we investigated in our study was the impact of audit automation on secretarial and clerical staff in audit firms. It would appear that because auditors are preparing their own memos and sending out their own letters to clients the nature of the work of the secretarial and clerical staff is changing or would need to change in the near future.

This is an example of an unintended consequence of audit automation which has not been identified in much previous research in this area. It is not so much that secretarial and clerical staff have been de-skilled by information technology; rather that some of their traditional skills, especially typing letters and reports, have been taken away from them by professional staff. The response of managers and partners may vary, with some just accepting it: 'I would say that the days of the typical secretary in this organization are numbered' (Manson, McCartney and Sherer, 1997, p. 45), and other partners and managers seeing it as an opportunity to employ secretaries more effectively in other ways: 'What I have found is, because there are certain tasks which the audit team are doing which traditionally the secretaries had done, it means that I can give my secretary some of my administration work, because she has more time available' (Manson, McCartney and Sherer 1997, p. 46).

It is clear that audit firms are only beginning to consider the implications of audit automation for non-professional staff such as secretaries. It may be necessary for audit firms to develop human resources policies which encompass the potential audit automation has for affecting the division of work tasks between audit and secretarial staff.

CONCLUSIONS

This chapter has been concerned with audit automation, which is the use of information technology in the planning, controlling and recording of audit work. Although audit firms were relatively slow to introduce information technology into their work the pace has quickened significantly in the last four or five years. The increased interest in audit automation may be attributed in part to the falling real cost of personal computers and the improved quality of general purpose applications packages for word processing and financial analysis. It is also likely, however, that the larger audit firms especially have been motivated by a desire to improve the consistency, and hence the overall quality, of their audit work as well as a hope that investment in audit automation will lead to efficiencies and cost savings.

The Big Six firms, and at least some of the medium-sized firms, are making extensive use of audit automation, as evidenced by the very large sums committed to this activity in their annual budgets. Although in many firms the range of applications is limited to templates for standard letters, spreadsheets for analytical review and the preparation of time and cost budgets, a small number of firms has extended audit automation across most areas of the audit process. For example, some firms have created computerized versions of Companies Act and accounting standards checklists and can generate detailed audit programmes from given information about the client and the level of audit risk. At least one of the Big Six firms has gone so far as to design a fully integrated audit automation system which allows remote review of audit files by partners and managers.

At this stage in the development of audit automation it is difficult to assess the extent to which there have been improvements in audit quality and reductions in audit cost. First, there is the conceptual problem of trying to identify separately any change in quality or cost which can be attributable solely to the advent of audit automation. Secondly, there is the practical difficulty of measuring something as intangible as audit quality. It is not surprising, therefore, that while many audit firms agree that any investment in audit automation should be subject to a cost–benefit analysis very few firms have successfully implemented this evaluation.

Although it may be difficult to assess the effect of audit automation on audit quality and audit costs there are other effects which may be easier to observe. For example, audit staff need to acquire a certain level of computer literacy very quickly and must ensure that they update their skills on a regular basis. Fortunately, almost all new entrants into the profession already have some familiarity with information technology and most are usually keen to make use of the computer in their audit work. The same cannot always be said for partners and managers and in some firms this can even spill over into a resistance to audit automation itself. This resistance usually reflects a concern that information technology should be subservient to professional judgement and not the other way round. Audit firms have tried to ensure, therefore, that developments in audit automation are led by, and are consistent with, the audit methodology employed by the firm.

Finally, audit automation is having an impact on work patterns and behaviour in audit firms. Increasingly, communication between staff is via e-mail, which facilitates speedier and more effective interaction between partners and managers in the office and audit staff at the client. Clearly, audit staff are spending much more time on their PCs, often doing tasks such as word processing which were previously done by secretarial and clerical staff. There is very little evidence that this has resulted in any actual or even perceived de-skilling of audit staff. Indeed, in many cases, audit staff have welcomed the increasing use of information technology in providing them with new skills and giving them more time to think and exercise professional judgement. On the other hand, however, the increasing use of audit automation has affected the work patterns of secretarial and clerical staff, and audit firms will need to give serious consideration to the way such staff are employed in the future.

ACKNOWLEDGEMENTS

Much of the discussion in this chapter is based on research undertaken for the Institute of Chartered Accountants of Scotland and published in a report by Manson, McCartney and Sherer (1997). The authors gratefully acknowledge the financial support given to this research by the Research Committee of the Institute of Chartered Accountants of Scotland.

NOTES

1. Although they both involve the use of information technology audit automation should not be confused with computer auditing. Audit automation refers to the use of information technology in the planning, controlling and recording of audit work whilst computer auditing is the use of information technology to audit clients' computerized systems.
2. The ranking of firms by fee ranking was prepared by The Centre for Interfirm Comparisons (ICC), published in *Accountancy Age*, 20 May 1993.

REFERENCES

Bones, S. R. (1992) *Audit Automation*, Accountants Digest No. 292, ICAEW, Autumn.

Dillard, J. F. and Bricker, R. (1992) A critique of knowledge-based systems in auditing: the systemic encroachment of technical consciousness, *Critical Perspectives on Accounting*, Vol. 3, no. 3, pp. 205–24.

Ebbage, K. (1993) Audit automation: benefits or just costs?', *aud*IT, no. 15, pp. 3–6.

Ferguson, C. (1994) The use of microcomputers by accountants, unpublished Ph.D. thesis, Deakin University, Australia.

Goldman, A. and Barlev, B. (1974) The auditor–firm conflict of interests: its implications for independence, *The Accounting Review*, Vol. 49, no. 4, pp. 707–18.

Humphrey, C. and Moizer, P. (1990) From techniques to ideologies: an alternative perspective on the audit function, *Critical Perspectives on Accounting*, Vol. 1, no. 3, pp. 217–38.

Institute of Chartered Accountants in England and Wales (ICAEW) (1993) *Audit Automation*, IT Briefing Number 4, London, Chartech Books.

Manson, S., McCartney, S. and Sherer, M. (1994) *The Usefulness of Management Letters*, Research Report No. 38, The Chartered Association of Certified Accountants, London.

Manson, S., McCartney, S. and Sherer, M. (1997) *Audit Automation: The Use of Information Technology in the Planning, Controlling and Recording of Audit Work*, Research Report, ICAS, Edinburgh.

O'Kane, B. (1990) What is audit automation?, *aud*IT, no. 1, September, pp. 4–7.

Roslender, R., Glover, I. and Kelly, M. (1991) *Future Imperfect? The Uncertain*

Prospects of the British Accountant, University of Stirling, Department of Accountancy and Finance working paper.

Starbuck, William H. and Webster, Jane (1994) When is play productive, *Accounting, Management and Information Technology*, Vol. 4, no. 1, pp. 71–90,

Turley, S. and Cooper, M. (1991) *Auditing in the United Kingdom*, Prentice-Hall/ICAEW, Hemel Hempstead.

Williamson, A. L. (1994) *Audit Automation*, Accountants Digest No. 318, ICAEW, London.

DISCUSSION QUESTIONS

1. Discuss the extent to which developments in audit automation are helping further to fracture the auditing profession into two distinct groups: a small number of firms which audit almost all the large companies and the rest.

2. What are the main differences between an 'integrated approach' and a 'toolkit approach' to audit automation? Why might audit firms opt for one approach over the other?

3. Evaluate the argument that the increasing use of audit automation is de-skilling the work of professional audit staff.

4. The main benefits of audit automation are perceived to be improvements in audit quality and reductions in audit costs. Are these two benefits compatible and how might they be assessed in practice?

5. To what extent do you think that increasing audit automation is responsible for a more scientific and structured audit approach at the expense of the traditional subjective and judgemental audit approach?

Part III

Special Contexts

15

The Auditor and the Smaller Company

Michael Page

INTRODUCTION

There are two broad questions to be discussed in this chapter: Should small companies be required to have their accounts audited? And: if an audit is required by the operation of company law or otherwise, what special problems do auditors of a small company face and how should they resolve them? The first question is a matter of public policy and in practice needs to be answered by government; the second question is about the conduct of auditing engagements and is a matter upon which members of the accounting and auditing professions need to form a view.

Recent moves to reduce the burden of administrative requirements on small businesses have, paradoxically, made the position more complicated, as the next section will show. For the rest of this chapter the term 'small company' will be used to refer to a small company as defined in the Companies Act 1985 (the Act) as subsequently amended. The essence of the definition is that a small company satisfies two of the following criteria:

(1) turnover – not exceeding £2.8 million;
(2) total assets before deducting current liabilities (balance sheet total) – not exceeding £1.4 million;
(3) number of employees – not exceeding fifty.

The definition is derived from a permissible rounding-up of the criteria provided by the European Union (EU) Fourth Directive on Company Law; the monetary totals are updated for inflation from time to time.

DO SMALL COMPANIES NEED AN AUDIT?

The UK is unusual in requiring small companies to prepare full audited accounts. In nearly all other countries small companies are not required to disclose comprehensive accounts to the public and only in a few countries (for example Belgium, Denmark, Sweden and Switzerland) are small companies required to have an audit. Compare the difference between the situations in the UK and in the USA.

In the UK all companies with a turnover of more than £350,000 are required to prepare full audited accounts complying with the Act. Because the Act requires the accounts to show a true and fair view, they need also to comply with UK accounting standards, if the auditors are not to qualify their report.

Small companies need not file full accounts with the Registrar of Companies; instead they can submit so-called 'modified' or 'abbreviated' accounts which contain much less information than the full accounts. Modified accounts comprise a balance sheet in abbreviated form, a statement of accounting policies and little else.

As from August 1995 the smallest companies do not need an audit report. Companies with a turnover of up to £90,000 need not have an audit. A company with a turnover of more than £90,000 but not more than £350,000 does not need an audit but is required to file an audit exemption report (AER) signed by a qualified accountant.[1] For the purposes of this chapter, a company with a turnover of up to £90,000 will be called a micro-company and one with a turnover of between £90,000 and 350,000 a mini-company.

In the USA only public companies are required to disclose audited financial statements which 'fairly present' a view of the enterprise in accordance with 'generally accepted accounting principles'. Non-public companies need neither disclose information to the world at large nor, unless they so choose, have their accounts audited. This means they are free to prepare accounts other than in accordance with generally accepted accounting principles; they can omit items which they feel it would not be cost-beneficial to report to the users of the accounts; and they can measure the items which they recognize in the accounts in ways which they think are more appropriate to their business. As an alternative to an audit, non-public companies can choose either to have a 'review' of their accounts or, if a public accountant prepares the statements and does no other work on them, he or she can issue a 'compilation report' which states that no audit or review has been carried out.

Thus in the UK the concessions which apply to small companies for auditing and reporting fail to give them the freedom of reporting enjoyed by similar companies in the USA (and many other countries). This is because UK small companies are still required to produce true and fair accounts and to have them audited (unless turnover is less than £350,000); they cannot produce accounts which do not comply with the recognition, measurement and disclosure criteria of the generally accepted accounting conventions, the disclosure requirements of the Companies Acts and accounting standards, which are the ingredients of the true and fair view. There have been some moves to exempt small companies from the onerous requirements of some accounting standards, but not from the whole framework of reporting. The ASB (1996) has published (CCAB, 1995) a draft standard which would attempt to replace the whole body of existing standards to which small companies are subject. The paper is based on responses to previous consultative documents (CCAB, 1994, 1995) which showed a clear consensus that accounting standards were a burden to small companies. However, the exposure draft proposes to adopt all the measurement rules inherent in existing accounting standards so that the only simplifications which would be available would be reduced disclosures, although more extensive simplifications would be considered in the future. (See also Carsberg *et al.* (1985) and Ernst and Young (1994, pp. 21–4) for more on this topic.)

Table 15.1 summarizes the audit and accounting exemptions available to small companies[2].

Table 15.1   Exemptions available to small companies

Size of company	Audit requirement	Filing of accounts requirement
Turnover not exceeding £90,000 (micro-company)	No audit, no exemption report	Abbreviated accounts
Turnover exceeding £90,000 but not exceeding £350,000 (mini-company,	No audit, exemption report	Abbreviated accounts
Small companies with turnover exceeding £350,000	Compulsory audit	Abbreviated accounts
Medium-sized companies	Compulsory audit	Some exemptions
Large companies	Compulsory audit	Full accounts

Whether audits should be necessary for small companies must depend upon the nature of the companies and the uses and users of their accounts. The company – a corporate person with a separate legal identity – is a much more popular form of business vehicle in Britain than in other countries and the number of companies has been growing steadily for 150 years. As at 31 March 1994 there were 945,000 private companies and 12,000 public companies (DTI, 1994). Not all these companies are active and independent; many are subsidiaries of other companies, dormant companies or companies too recently formed to have filed accounts. Probably about 40 per cent of unlisted companies can be thought of as active, independent and subject to reporting regulations at any time. Of these companies, a very large proportion will be regarded as small under any reasonable definition. Analysis of filed accounts of companies suggests that over 90 per cent of active independent companies are likely to come within the terms of the Companies Act definition. Statistics which show that 308,000 companies, being 40 per cent of active companies, filed abbreviated accounts (DTI, 1994, App. C) corroborate these estimates. Adoption of a different basis of definition, or different thresholds, might alter the companies falling into the category at the margin, but the bulk of companies would continue to be regarded as small under any definition which is likely to be widely acceptable.

Similarly, analysis of the filed accounts of small companies shows that directors control the majority of shares in over 90 per cent of companies; in two-thirds of small companies the directors own all the shares. These statistics give little support to the formal view of financial reporting for small companies in which directors report to shareholders and auditors check that the shareholders are not being misled.

The origin of the current position was more historical accident than design. The Companies Act 1900 demanded an audit for all companies (including unlimited companies), a provision which has remained in force until the limited exemption for micro- and mini-companies was introduced in 1995. However, the 1900 Act predated the development requirements about the contents of accounts and the distinction between public and private limited companies. Subsequent development of detailed requirements for the contents of accounts seems to have been designed mainly for public companies, but was applied to the information reported to private company shareholders without much consideration of the cost or need for audit. The Companies Act 1967, however, abolished the exemption from public filing enjoyed by most private companies and so left the private company exposed to the full rigour of reporting requirements. Thereafter the rapid expansion of accounting standards and the codification and elaboration of auditing procedures continually increased the cost of financial reporting.

The promulgation of the EU Fourth Directive on Company Law in 1978 provided an opportunity to reassess the position. The Directive enforced minimum disclosure standards on companies in all countries of the EU; it also made an audit compulsory for large and medium-sized companies, but allowed small companies to be exempted.

There then ensued a debate about whether small companies needed an audit. The Auditing Practices Committee (APC) had begun the codification of best auditing practice and it became clear that if the same standards of verification were to apply to small companies as were needed for large companies auditing costs would increase. Discussion papers from the DTI (1979 – 'the Green Paper') and from the APC (1979) sought opinion on whether the audit should remain compulsory. The Green Paper put forward three possibilities for discussion:

(1) small companies should continue to be audited;
(2) instead of an audit, a lower level of attestation called a 'review' should be introduced;
(3) there should be no audit requirement.

The Green Paper clearly favoured the first possibility, but offered the suggestion that: 'the adoption of the three-tier classification of companies in law might be used as a basis for developing further standards setting out the different approach and methods appropriate to the circumstances of smaller companies' (Department of Trade, 1979, Ch. 2, para. 14). This passed the buck neatly to the accountancy profession.

The APC's (1979) discussion paper, *Small Companies: The Need for Audit*, recognized that, unless there were some concessions in law or auditing standards, many small companies would receive qualified audit reports. There ensued a vigorous debate in the professional press. The logically prior question of what small companies' accounts should contain received little attention, and it is possible that the outcome of legislation would have been different if this had not been the case. The government decided, after receiving responses to the Green Paper, to retain the audit because there was no strong consensus for its abolition. The debate did not die down, however, and has continued throughout the ensuing years in response to various government reports and White Papers.

In 1985 the DTI published a scrutiny (DTI, 1985a) of the main burdens imposed on small businesses by central and local government. The scrutiny team suggested, *inter alia*, considering whether to 'eliminate the present statutory audit of accounts for "shareholder-managed" small businesses', together with simplification of reporting requirements (DTI, 1985a, p. 7). In response, the DTI published a further discussion paper (DTI, 1985b) setting out what it saw as the main arguments for and against the small company audit and requesting comment about whether the audit requirement should be abolished for small companies, all of whose shareholders were directors; a subset of very small companies; or for all small companies at the option of shareholders. The discussion paper was clearly more favourable towards abolition than the Green Paper had been. There followed a vigorous debate in which the various accountancy bodies were unable to present a united front. The Association of Certified Accountants came down in favour of retention of the audit, but the Institute of Chartered Accountants in England and Wales (ICAEW) reversed the view it held in 1979 and argued for allowing small companies to opt out of audits, provided all shareholders agreed. The ICAEW also wanted a simplified set of accounts for the use of shareholders and for filing at the Companies Registry (ICAEW, 1985). The 1989 Companies Act introduced provisions which allow listed public companies to send summary financial statements to shareholders who wish to receive them.

Concurrently with the debate about small company financial reporting, audit regulation was becoming an issue. The EU Eighth Directive committed the government to some form of audit regulation and, although a process of registration of auditors would have been adequate for the purposes of the Directive, the government went further and, with the co-operation of the accounting bodies, implemented a system of rules and monitoring of compliance. Audit regulation was enacted in the Companies Act 1989 and came into effect on 1 October 1991. The three institutes of chartered accountants, keen to be recognized by the government as self-regulating bodies for this purpose, set up a common code of demanding rules together with a Joint Monitoring Unit to visit firms of accountants. Non-compliance with the rules could lead to removal from the audit register and disciplinary proceedings. The effect of audit regulation was to increase sharply the cost of small audits. Fearnley and Page (1992, 1993) indicate the scale of these costs. Practitioners had faced considerable costs in implementing audit regulation and, despite recession, were seeking to pass on these costs to their clients. Many very small companies, such as companies formed by individuals so that their employers could avoid employment legislation and management companies for blocks of flats, found themselves facing sharply increased audit fees. The political pressure brought to bear was sufficient to tip the balance in favour of some form of audit relaxation. A consultative document was issued by the DTI (1993). At first the government proposed only that companies with a turnover below the VAT registration limit (about £37,600 at the time) should benefit from exemption, possibly subject to a compilation report. However, under pressure to be seen to be increasing deregulation and to favour small business, the much greater exemption limit of £350,000 was announced by the Chancellor of the Exchequer in his budget of November 1993. The move was widely welcomed; however, the form of report to be provided by a qualified accountant became controversial. The APC took on the responsibility of formulating guidance and its initial attempt was viewed as requiring too much work by the reporting accountant (who need not be a registered auditor) and being insufficiently distinguished from an audit. Subsequently, with some adjustment to the proposed wording of the legislation, the compilation report became the 'audit exemption report' (AER - APB, 1994). AERs require opinion to be expressed on three matters:

(1) the accounts are in agreement with the accounting records kept by the company;
(2) the accounts are drawn up in a manner consistent with the accounting requirements of the Companies Act;
(3) the company satisfies the conditions for exemption from audit.

Note that the reporting accountant does not express an opinion on the appropriateness of the companies accounting policies or the credibility of the accounts.

It is expected that accountants who prepare small companies' accounts will obtain most of the information they need for the report by preparing the accounts; not all small practitioners agree, however. Writing in relation to proposals to extend audit exemption Marshall (1995, p. 82) states:

> the exemption report represents a pathetic replacement for the audit, cutting little of the cost but most of the value. The report gives no assurance to the accounts user that either the system of accounting records the company uses, or its accounting policies, are appropriate to its size and operation.

Marshall goes on to point out that for most small companies the original documents (e.g. invoices and delivery notes) form part of the company's accounting records required by the Act so that the reporting accountant should logically check the original documents, thus performing much of the work of an audit. However, the Statement of Standards for Audit Exemption Reports issued by the APB in October 1994 suggests that these procedures are not necessary. Marshall concludes that the AER could be converted into a more useful report with little more work, thus effectively becoming a 'review'.

At first sight it is surprising that the ICAEW should have campaigned vigorously for audit exemption, given that its members were responsible for the majority of small company audits. However, the difficulty of framing appropriate auditing standards for large companies within the constraint that they needed to be applied to small companies was hindering the work of the APC. Such evidence as was available showed that the ICAEW's smaller practitioner members had no shortage of work and that a majority felt that they could spend time more profitably in advising clients rather than auditing their accounts. Subsequent research confirms that, post-audit regulation, practitioners were strongly in favour of audit exemption (Fearnley and Page, 1992, 1993).

Within the accounting profession, commentators on various proposals have divided among the three possibilities put forward in the original Green Paper: favouring abolition of the audit requirement; proponents of some form of limited assurance (a review); and retentionists.

Abolition

The case made for abolition rests on three points. First, the audit report of small companies should generally be qualified. This is 'not because there is a lack of controls, but because of a lack of independent evidence as to their operation and the completeness of the records' (Davison, 1980, p. 42).

Secondly, the economic benefits of the audit are not held to justify the cost. For example, Briston and Perks (1977) estimated (very much on a rule of thumb basis) the annual cost of auditing unlisted companies at £90 million and concluded that the possible benefits of the audit could not merit such a cost. Barker (1985, p. 14) suggested that the value of one of the benefits – information for suppliers – was low because of filing delays: 'normal trade creditors ... would be ill-advised to rely on accounts likely to be at least nine months out of date'. And, as Rutteman (1985) points out, creditors may have access only to modified accounts which contain little information. Creditors have found other ways to protect themselves. He concluded (1985, p. 12): 'The crux of the issue is whether the cost of the audit, albeit small in itself, is disproportionate to the benefits it brings as far as small companies are concerned.'

Thirdly, comparison with other countries where audit (and frequently disclosure) is not required suggests that no real harm will result if the requirement is abolished.

Review

The case for review accepts most of the abolitionist argument, but makes the observation that a small company's accounts are almost invariably prepared by the professional accountant who subsequently audits them. In the process of preparation the accountant gains considerable insight into the state of the business, and does much to update and correct the company's records. The argument runs that the insight thus gained should enable the accountant to 'review' the accounts and attest to their 'reasonableness' without going on to obtain independent evidence of the truth and fairness of the final accounts. Gemmell (1977) developed a framework for the review, consisting primarily of 'enquiry, comparison and discussion of [the] financial statements, and of the information and explanations supplied' by analogy with existing procedures in the USA and Canada. *Small Companies: The Need for Audit* (APC, 1979) provided a similar formulation.

The advantages of a review are its relative cheapness, since it involves little, if any, extra work by the accountant, and its avoidance of the problem of auditing businesses with rudimentary systems of internal control. In addition, those who take a monolithic approach to unified auditing standards for all businesses hold that progress in improving the audit function for listed companies is retarded by the need to have similar standards for small companies (e.g. Davison, 1978). Opponents of review, starting from the same premise of monolithic auditing standards, however, argued that the review would not be sufficiently distanced from the audit to avoid danger of confusion. Shaw (1978, p. 79) argues: 'Because a significant part of the total work of the accountancy profession in the UK has been involved in audit and the expression of opinion, there has developed an expectation that the public accountant validates by association.' And, further, that attempts to remedy this are futile: 'The proposed review procedure requires the reviewer to make manifestly clear by unambiguous disclaimer that his review was to all intents and purposes worthless' (1978, p. 80).

As Marshall's (1995) comments suggest, the AER, as a limited form of attestation, has some characteristics of a review and the arguments put forward in 1978 are still applicable.

Retention

The argument for retention of the audit for small companies is based either on the premise that the audit is the 'price of limited liability', that is, that only by offering reliable accounts to the public may potential creditors be safeguarded (e.g. White, 1985; DTI 1994), or on grounds of equity – because many small companies would continue to have their accounts audited to satisfy the requirements of banks or to facilitate acceptance of tax computations, they should all do so.

As a compromise between the retention of the audit and a review is the suggestion made in the Green Paper (Department of Trade, 1979, pp. 3–4) that the accounting profession should develop separate auditing standards for small companies. This suggestion was opposed in a number of articles in the accounting press and elsewhere, mainly on the grounds that the audit of large companies to existing standards might thereby be jeopardized, at least in the opinion of the public. This is also a position which has been rejected by the APB (1996).

WHAT PROBLEMS DO AUDITORS OF A SMALL COMPANY FACE, AND HOW SHOULD THEY RESOLVE THEM?

The preceding section suggested that there may be inherent contradictions in requiring directors of small companies to pay for an audit of information which in most cases is addressed, at least formally, to themselves. Nevertheless, in the UK the accounts of small companies must be audited. This section deals with the way in which the auditor can go about the task, and what advice auditing standards and guidelines give. There are two essential problems which face the auditor.

First, there are economies of scale in auditing; it does not cost twice as much to audit a company which is twice as big as another. This means that it is relatively more expensive to carry out similar audit procedures on small companies than on large ones. The reasons for the existence of economies are numerous, but two important reasons are that the sizes of samples for use in statistical tests do not depend to any great extent on the size of the population being sampled, and that there is an element of fixed costs in many audit procedures (such as checking compliance with the Companies Act and accounting standards, audit planning, audit review).

Secondly, auditing is more difficult in small companies, because they neither possess nor require the elaborate systems of internal control upon which the auditor can rely when auditing a large company.

There seem to be three possible reactions by auditors to these problems:

(1) they can audit small companies in the same way as they audit big companies, adapting procedures as necessary;
(2) they can adopt different auditing standards of evidential support;
(3) they can qualify their audit reports.

Audit in the same way as big companies

Treating small companies in the same way as large companies enables an auditor to take a purist view of the nature of the audit, but involves placing a very heavy burden on the companies concerned. As previously mentioned, auditors have often expressed this by saying that an audit is 'the price of limited liability' (and ignoring the fact that unlimited companies must have an audit as well). Implicitly, to adopt this attitude is to say that most small limited companies should never have been incorporated in the first place. Indeed, making disincorporation easier, or introducing a new business vehicle for small companies, is often suggested as a means of alleviating burdens on small companies (e.g. Barker, 1985; DTI, 1994). The Auditing Practices Board (APB, 1996) has issued a consultation draft of a practice note, *The Audit of Small Business*, which takes a strong universalist view: 'The Board considers that the "universal" applicability of SASs to all audits, with no concessions on the grounds of size, is a consequence of the basic concept of audit' (APB, 1996, p. 117).

But to say that small companies should be audited in the same way as large companies is not to say that audit procedures should be identical. Because there is little evidence of the operation of controls in small companies, and because of the danger of management override, auditors tend not to rely on controls and to do much more substantive testing, but these sorts of tests are also used in large company audits. A report of the Canadian Institute of Chartered Accountants (CICA, 1988) concluded that substantive testing of balances and analytical review were the most useful techniques in auditing small business. Similar conclusions were reached by Raiborn, Guy and Zulinski (1983).

Level of evidential support

The second possible strategy for auditors is to adopt lower standards of evidential support for their opinion. Auditors may be willing to give a true and fair opinion on small companies' accounts at less cost, if they are willing to countenance a higher relative degree of inaccuracy in the numbers in small companies' accounts, i.e. if they are willing to use a wider confidence limit for the figures in the accounts. Two ways in which the auditor can justify such a position are by looking to the nature of the 'true and fair view' and to the nature of the auditors' concept of materiality.

When the Companies Act requires companies to prepare accounts showing a true and fair view, no mention is made of the costs of obtaining that view; on the face of it the requirement is absolute. Can the cost of attaining a true and fair view be explicitly considered by preparers and auditors of accounts? An analogous question confronted the Accounting Standards Committee, which took counsel's opinion (ASC, 1983) on the nature of the true and fair view and whether the ratio of costs to benefit could be considered in framing requirements for accounting compliance with the true and fair view.

Counsel's view was that cost–benefit considerations were a factor in defining the true and fair view. Auditors who accept this position could decide that the cost of forming an opinion on the truth and fairness of accounts should be limited by the potential benefits which users of the small companies' accounts are likely to be able to obtain. Recognizing the cost–benefit consideration would allow auditors to reduce the scope of their audits and to simplify auditing procedures. However, this might well conflict with auditing standards and guidelines, which make no explicit concessions to a simplification of audit procedures for small companies.

As an alternative to cost–benefit considerations, auditors can look to the meaning of materiality in small companies' accounts in order to reduce the cost of their procedures. Like a 'true and fair view', 'materiality' is an undefined term in accounting and auditing. Its meaning does not seem to be susceptible to definition without introducing new, undefined terms, although it is possible to discuss its meaning using generally understood concepts. Perhaps the most widely used characterization of the meaning of 'material' is the idea that something is material if knowledge of it is 'big enough to make a difference' to decisions made by the users of a small company's accounts. Then auditors can look to the probable use of those accounts and determine how great they believe an error in the accounts would need to be to make a difference to potential users. Such considerations can give auditors good reason to increase the percentage of error which they would be prepared to accept in the financial statements under review. For example, an auditor might well be prepared to accept an error of 10 per cent in the value of stock in a small company where the total value was only, say, £2,000 and the principal users of the accounts were the directors; but he or she might find an error of 5 per cent too high if the company were listed on the Stock Exchange, there was a substantial body of investors relying on the accounts and the total value was, say, £20 million.

In discussing materiality the APB (1996, para. 58) does not take the opportunity to use the concept to reduce audit costs. In particular, it refers only to the relative size of amounts in relation to pre-tax profit rather than to absolute amounts, and does not refer to the characteristics of the users of the accounts. Similarly, in relation to audit risk the APB (1996, para. 23) refers only to the possibility of material error rather than looking at the absolute amount of possible losses. The APB does suggest that where the auditor also prepares the accounts he or she will use a lower level of acceptable error than would be appropriate for auditing purposes, reducing the probability of finding material error in the audit phase of the engagement.

Small company qualification

Another option for the auditor in auditing small companies' accounts is to qualify the audit report. At first sight, qualification of the audit report would not seem an attractive route to adopt: because the Companies Act requires the auditor to form an opinion, there is a professional bias toward using qualification of the audit report sparingly to preserve its effectiveness, and clients would be expected to resist it. Nevertheless, a special form of audit report was the solution preferred by the APC between 1980 and 1989. The report which was Example 6 in Auditing Guideline 501 was as follows:

> We have audited the financial statements on pages ... to ... Our audit was conducted in accordance with approved Auditing Standards having

regard to the matters referred to in the following paragraph.

In common with many businesses of similar size and organization the company's system of control is dependent upon the close involvement of the directors/managing director, who are major shareholders. Where independent confirmation of the completeness of the accounting records was therefore not available we have accepted assurances from the directors/managing director that all the company's transactions have been reflected in the records.

Subject to the foregoing, in our opinion the financial statements, which have been prepared under the historical cost convention, give a true and fair view of the state of the company's affairs at 31st December 19 . . and of its profit and source and application of funds for the year then ended and comply with the Companies Acts 1948 and 1967.

(APC, 1980, p. 122)

Keasey, Watson and Wynarczyk (1988) found that in the period from 1980 to 1982 about a quarter of small company reports had the small company qualification and the proportion rose thereafter. The companies most likely to receive the qualification were those which had been audited by a large firm of accountants, had few directors and non-director shareholders, had secured loans or had a long lag between the end of the financial year and the signing of the audited accounts.

The APC changed its mind about the small company qualification and withdrew the Example 6 report. The stated reasons were: the wording was inconsistent – if auditors believed the management assurances the 'subject to' qualification should be unnecessary; the report was too general – it did not specify in which areas management assurances had been relied upon; and its use had become so widespread that it was being used where it was not needed, so its meaning had become impaired (APC, 1989).

CONCLUSION

The special problems which arise in auditing small companies have their origin, as do many other auditing problems, in an accounting problem: the requirement for small companies to produce full, 'true and fair' accounts complying with the Companies Act and accounting standards. Once the decision was taken the government had the option of requiring an audit, a limited form of attestation such as a review or having no requirement. After nearly two decades of debate, it has chosen all three options: micro-companies need no audit, mini-companies need an exemption report and other small companies need a full audit. The original Green Paper suggested that the profession should develop special standards taking into account the characteristics of small companies, but the current response is that audit standards are 'universal'.

NOTE

1. The other conditions for audit exemption are that the company does not have a balance sheet total of more than £1.4 million and that at no time in the year was it a public company, a parent or subsidiary company and that it is not a banking or insurance company or a member of certain classes of financial services company.
2. In March 1997 the government announced the audit exemption threshold was to be raised from £90,000 to £350,000, effectively removing the need for AERs except for incorporated charities, for which the old limit will remain.

REFERENCES

AICPA (American Institute of Certified Public Accountants) (1979) *Compilation and Review of Financial Statements*, AICPA, New York.

APB (Auditing Practices Board) (1994) *Statement of Standards for Reporting Accountants – Audit Exemption Reports*, APB, London.

APB (1996) *The Audit of Small Business*, APB, London (reprinted in *Accountancy*, May 1996, pp. 117–28)

APC (Auditing Practices Committee) (1979) *Small Companies: The Need for Audit*, APC, London.

APC (Auditing Practices Committee) (1980) *Auditing Standards and Guidelines*, ICAEW, London.

APC (1989) The old 'example 6' form of audit report and the new reporting standard, *Accountancy*, May, p. 163.

ASC (Accounting Standards Committee) (1983) Legal opinion on 'true and fair', *Accountancy*, November, pp. 154–6.

ASC (1996) Financial Reporting Standard for Smaller Entities (Exposure Draft) *Accountancy*, February, 1997, pp. 111–137.

Barker, B. (1985) Why small businesses need no audit, *The Accountant*, 30 November, pp. 14–15.

Briston, R. J. and Perks, R. (1977) The external auditor: his role and cost to society, *Accountancy*, November, pp. 48–52.

Carsberg, B. V., Page, M. J., Sindall, A. J. and Waring, I. D. (1985) *Small Company Financial Reporting*, Prentice-Hall International/ICAEW, London.

CCAB (1994) *Exemptions from Standards on Grounds of Size or Public Interest*, CCAB, London.

CCAB (1994) *Designed to Fit – A Financial Reporting Standard for Smaller Entities*, CCAB, London.

CICA (1988) *Audit of Small Business*, CICA, Toronto.

Davison, I. H. (1978) Do auditors give value for money?, *Accountancy*, January, pp. 91–4.

Davison, I. H. (1980) Small companies – why a review is not the answer. *Accountancy*, March, pp. 42–6.

Department of Trade (1979) *Company Accounting and Disclosure*, Cmnd 7654, HMSO, London.

DTI (Department of Trade and Industry) (1985a) *Burdens on Business*, HMSO, London.

DTI (1985b) *Accountancy and Audit Requirements for Small Firms*, DTI, London.

DTI (1989) *EC Directive Amending the Fourth Company Law Directive: A*

Consultative Document, February, DTI, London.

DTI (1993) *Auditing and Accounting Requirements for Very Small Companies*, DTI, London.

DTI (1994) *Company Law Review: The Law Applicable to Private Companies*, DTI, London.

Ernst and Young (1994) *UK GAAP* (4th edn), Macmillan, London.

Fearnley, S. and Page, M. (1992) Counting the cost of audit regulation, *Accountancy*, January, pp. 21–2.

Fearnley, S. and Page, M. (1993) Audit regulation one year on, *Accountancy*, January, pp. 59–60.

Gemmell, J. (1977) Audit problems ahead with small companies, *Accountancy*, July, pp. 48–50.

ICAEW (Institute of Chartered Accountants in England and Wales) (1980) *Small Companies – The Need for Audit?: Memorandum to the Department of Trade*, TR377, ICAEW, London.

ICAEW (1985) *Response to 'Accounting and Audit Requirements of Small Firms'*, TR592, ICAEW, London.

Keasey, K., Watson, R. and Wynarczyk, P. (1988) The small company audit qualification: a preliminary investigation, *Accounting and Business Research*, Winter, pp. 323–33.

Marshall, T (1995) Gone but not forgotten, *Accountancy*, December, pp. 82–3.

Page, M. J. (1984) Corporate financial reporting and the small independent company, *Accounting and Business Research*, Summer, pp. 271–82.

Raiborn, D. D., Guy, D. M. and Zulinski, M. (1983) Solving audit problems in small business engagements, *Journal of Accountancy*, April, pp. 50–8.

Rutteman, P. (1985) Abolishing small audits: the pros (of change), *Accountancy*, June, p. 12.

Shaw, J. (1978) Why a review simply won't do, *Accountancy*, March, pp. 79–81.

White, R. (1985) (Abolishing small audits) the cons of change, *Accountancy*, June, p. 13.

FURTHER READING

Recommended for further reading are APB, 1996, APC (1979), Carsberg *et al.* (1985), Davison (1980) and Raiborn, Guy and Zulinski (1983).

DISCUSSION QUESTIONS

1. Why audit small companies? Why not?
2. The characteristics of the users of the accounts of a large, listed company are different from those of the users of the accounts of a small, private company. Discuss the implications of this observation for the individual auditor.
3. Is the law asking for the impossible by requiring the auditor to form an opinion on the truth and fairness of the accounts of a small company?
4. Why can auditors not put much reliance on the system of internal control in many small companies?
5. 'The audit is the price of limited liability.' Discuss.
6. Why not have dual auditing standards for large public companies and small private companies?

16
Auditing in the Financial Services Sector
John Tattersall

THE BACKGROUND

The financial services sector has been dogged by company failures and unexpected losses in recent years: the collapses of Drexel Burnham Lambert and BCCI, the large losses and subsequent disappearance of Kidder Peabody, unexpected losses at Metalgesellschaft and Salomon Brothers, huge bad debts at Crédit Lyonnais and Deutsche Bank and, most recently, the failure of Barings and enormous losses at Daiwa Bank make it appear to be a very risky sector. In the UK alone, the Investors' Compensation Scheme has had to fund investors' losses on 182 failed investment firms between 1988 and 1995.

In all these crises, it has been tempting for those who have suffered loss to turn to the auditor for some recompense, whether or not the auditor was at fault. In many instances the auditor is the only 'deep pocket' left to pursue and therefore, not surprisingly, in many of the above examples legal actions have been commenced and pursued against auditors.

The auditor's traditional responsibility, however, is to the proprietors of a company and not to its customers: it is to the proprietors (shareholders,

John H. Tattersall MA FCA is a partner in Coopers & Lybrand, chartered accountants and management consultants, and specializes in the financial services sector. He is Chairman of the firm's Financial Services Specialist Team and of its Banking and Capital Markets Technical Committee, and is also a member of the Capital Committee of the Securities and Futures Authority and of the Banking Sub-Committee of the Institute of Chartered Accountants in England and Wales. The views and opinions expressed in this chapter are those of the author and do not necessarily reflect those of Coopers & Lybrand.

members, partners, etc.) that his or her report is addressed, and it is to them that the auditor has responsibilities enshrined in company law. However, those who suffer from the collapse of a business in the financial services sector are far more likely to be customers, depositors or clients of those businesses, and it is in this capacity that they would normally wish to seek recompense. It is difficult for them to do so under company law.

The 1980s and 1990s have, accordingly, seen changes in the obligations imposed upon, and public expectations of, auditors, embodied in new legislation, going far beyond those in company law, and giving the auditor new responsibilities to the regulator or supervisor. It is those regulators and supervisors who themselves have the job of looking after the interests of customers, depositors and clients and ensuring that financial markets remain stable.

The financial services sector may be distinguished from other sectors by the extent to which the businesses within it hold or take responsibility for their customers' assets. Frequently, that responsibility is actually represented by physical possession: stockbrokers often hold their clients' money while they effect transactions and securities, bankers hold their customers' cash as deposits to fund the loans that they make in order to generate an adequate return, and fund managers hold and manage their customers' investments. Even those financial services institutions which never physically deal with their customers' funds, such as investment advisers, have considerable responsibility to their customers to advise them when to effect changes in their portfolios, when to change their strategy and when to make various elections. It is therefore appropriate that auditors of stockbrokers, bankers, fund managers and advisers should monitor the ways in which those businesses dispose of their assets and ensure that those businesses are in a position to continue their roles and repay their deposits on demand or at maturity.

The financial services sector is wide: it traditionally covers banks, building societies, stockbrokers and other securities houses, investment managers, investment brokers, futures and commodity brokers, insurance companies, insurance brokers and agents, and professional firms which undertake investment business as part of their services. In the UK the enactment of the Financial Services Act 1986 introduced the concept of 'investment business', essentially covering the dealing in, management of and advice upon investments. It initiated a regulated system for such business in an environment where regulation had previously been piecemeal and, in many aspects, nonexistent. The Building Societies Act 1986 further developed the regulations affecting building societies, and the Banking Act 1987 updated the arrangements for authorization and regulation of deposit takers, including banks. The Insurance Companies Act 1982 consolidated much previous legislation governing the writing of insurance, though the marketing of life insurance products is covered by the Financial Services Act. The Friendly Societies Act 1992 extended this to cover friendly societies. All these Acts now include some concept of regulatory reporting by auditors in addition to their responsibility to the proprietors of the businesses that they serve.

Internationally, many regulators have been equally demanding of auditors though, particularly within the banking sector, regulators and supervisors have been more inclined to rely on visits by their own personnel than reports from auditors. The convergence of regulation, particularly in Europe, by means of various directives such as the Banking Coordination Directives, the Investment Services Directive and various insurance directives, has inevitably provided a focus for harmonizing the reporting requirements imposed on auditors. Directive 95/26/EC, colloquially known as the BCCI Directive, provides for auditors to provide information to regulators without breaching their duties of confidentiality, thus transferring the additional responsibilities referred to above on to a cross-Europe basis.

THE ROLE OF THE AUDITOR REDEFINED

The responsibilities of the auditor of a financial services business under company legislation have not been redefined: although disclosures in the financial statements of many financial services businesses are more extensive, as a result of the significant disclosure requirements in respect of off-balance-sheet commitments and other financial instruments, as well as fiduciary roles, the basic responsibility to shareholders remains the same. The major redefinition of the auditor's role is in respect of reports to regulators or supervisors, or in certain cases of reports issued to clients for onward transmission to regulators and supervisors. These include reports:

(1) on what is colloquially described as an 'ad hoc' basis, on matters of which the auditor has become aware in his or her capacity as auditor and of which the regulator or supervisor should be made aware;
(2) on accounting records and systems of internal control, particularly where those records and systems relate to the assets of the business's clients;
(3) on statistical or prudential returns in respect of the business's affairs, normally at a year or period end, but also including returns submitted during the year and on 'interim' profits so that such profits can be taken into account for regulatory capital purposes;
(4) on the disposition of clients' assets; and
(5) on the adequacy of the financial resources of the business, as defined in various rules and regulations.

The statutory nature of many of these duties, particularly the requirement to report directly to regulators and supervisors, is one which could well create a further liability for the auditor to depositors and customers, although the legal situation is far from clear: if an auditor fails to report a matter on a timely basis, those who suffer as a result of his or her failure to report in this way may well be able to claim against the auditor. As far as the regulators and supervisors themselves are concerned, at least in the UK, their own immunity from most forms of litigation, provided they act in good faith, means that they themselves are unlikely to pursue the auditor.

Nevertheless, the auditor should not undertake responsibilities in respect of a financial services business lightly.

APPROACHING THE AUDIT

Regulators and supervisors have carefully addressed the question of whether or not any registered auditor, properly authorized to carry out the audit of a company in the UK, should be allowed to audit businesses within the financial services sector, or whether an additional experience requirement should be imposed to ensure that those charged with reporting to regulators actually understand the principles and issues involved. While the decision has been made to impose only the formal qualification requirement of the registered auditor, in line with that for appointment as auditor under the Companies Act 1985, regulators have to approve the appointment of auditors to financial services businesses, thus giving them the right to disqualify auditors who do not have sufficient experience or, indeed, whose performance has not matched up to expectations. In addition, regulators have the right to appoint a second auditor to re-audit the books of a bank or investment business where the regulator believes that there is good reason to do so.

The auditor must therefore ensure that all those responsible for managing and performing the audit of a client within the financial services sector have appropriate levels of experience and are aware of their responsibilities to regulators and supervisors as well as to proprietors. There are many specific considerations which the auditor must take into account:

(1) Does the audit team have access to the relevant rulebooks issued by regulators and supervisors?
(2) Are there adequate training courses for the auditor's staff or alternative means of training (by means, for example, of self-study packs or even multi-media interactive programmes)?
(3) Do his or her staff understand the arrangements set out to protect customers' assets and deposits, in particular by segregating them from the assets belonging to the investment business itself?
(4) Has he or she monitored carefully to ensure that each individual taking a responsible position on the audit team has appropriate experience, as well as training?

While qualifications do not extend beyond those of registered auditor, regulators do, in general, require that the specific additional responsibilities imposed upon auditors are clearly set out in the letter of engagement, which must be available to them: accordingly, auditors must give appropriate attention to their engagement letter, ensuring that it contains details of all of the responsibilities imposed on them and, in particular, on the requirement on them to report direct to regulators on matters of which they believe the regulators and supervisors should be aware. There may well, in addition, be specific independence issues which they require to address: for example, the auditor of an investment business may not also be an appointed representative (or tied agent) of that business. In the case of auditors of banks, it would generally be regarded as unacceptable for the auditing firm to bank with the relevant institution and, indeed, for the firm's partners and staff to have arrangements with that bank outside the ordinary course of business. While it is not normally necessary for audit staff to be prevented from having conventional accounts with a banking client, it would be considered a conflict of interest for the bank to make loans to partners to finance their capital in the auditing firm.

THE RELATIONSHIPS OF THE AUDITOR WITH HIS OR HER CLIENT AND THE REGULATOR

Ad hoc reporting

The Financial Services Act 1986, the Building Societies Act 1986, the Banking Act 1987, a section inserted in the Insurance Companies Act 1982 by the Financial Services Act, and the Friendly Societies Act 1992, all made a fundamental change to the auditor's duty of confidentiality to his or her client. Previously, the auditor was precluded from giving any client information to third parties without the client's consent, except in the very restricted circumstances detailed in the Institute of Chartered Accountants' ethics guide.

Section 109(1) of the Financial Services Act states:

> No duty to which an auditor of an authorized person may be subject should be regarded as contravened by reason of his communicating in good faith to the Secretary of State, whether or not in response to a request from him, any information or opinion on a matter of which the auditor has become aware in his capacity as auditor of that person and which is relevant to any function of the Secretary of State under this Act.

This section is matched by similar sections in the other legislation. The statutory right thus created was made into a professional *duty* by an auditing guideline issued by the Auditing Practices Board (APB) in 1990: Ad hoc *Communications between Auditors and Regulators*.

It took the collapse of BCCI and Lord Justice Bingham's report into the circumstances of that collapse to reopen the issue of the duty of auditors to report to regulators. Although Lord Justice Bingham did not lay the blame for the collapse of BCCI on any failure by the auditors to report a matter to the regulators (in that instance, the Bank of England), he did indicate that the statutory right, albeit a professional duty as well, should be made into a statutory duty, and the legislation was therefore amended to require the auditor to communicate with the regulator in circumstances where:

> The auditor has reasonable cause to believe that the matter is, or is likely to be, of material significance in determining either:
> (a) whether a person is a fit and proper person to carry on investment business; or
> (b) whether disciplinary action should be taken or powers of intervention exercised, in order to protect investors against significant risk of loss.

The equivalent legislation for banks, building societies, insurance companies and friendly societies is worded differently, but the intent is the same.

The guidance which had been issued by the profession to auditors had to be rewritten: the main guidance on *ad hoc* reporting is now contained within a Statement of Auditing Standards (SAS 620) issued by the Auditing Practices Board (APB, 1994a): *The Auditors' Right and Duty to Report to Regulators in the Financial Sector*. This SAS is supported by practice notes for each of the financial sectors, as follows:

Practice Note 3: *The Auditors' Right and Duty to Report to the Bank of England* (APB, 1995a).

Practice Note 4: *The Auditors' Right and Duty to Report to the Building Societies Commission* (APB, 1994b).

Practice Note 5: *The Auditors' Right and Duty to Report to SIB and Other Regulators of Investment Businesses* (APB, 1994c).

Practice Note 6: *The Auditors' Right and Duty to Report to the DTI in Relation to Insurers Authorized under the Insurance Companies Act 1982* (APB, 1994d).

Practice Note 7: The Auditors' Right and Duty to Report to the Friendly Societies Commission (APB, 1994e).

However, the essence of the duty is contained in SAS 620 itself (APB, 1994a, para. 2):

> Auditors of regulated entities should bring information of which they have become aware in the ordinary course of performing work undertaken to fulfil their audit responsibilities to the attention of the appropriate regulator without delay when:
> (a) they conclude that it is relevant to the regulators' functions, having regard to such matters as may be specified in statute or any related regulation; and
> (b) in their opinion there is reasonable cause to believe it is or may be of material significance to the regulator.

The SAS goes on to spell out the manner in which this report should be delivered (1994a, para. 50):

> When the auditors conclude, after appropriate discussion and investigations, that a matter which has come to their attention gives rise to a statutory duty to make a report, they should bring the matter to the attention of the regulator without undue delay in a formal manner which will facilitate appropriate action by the regulator. When the initial report is made orally, the auditor should make a contemporaneous written record of the oral report and should confirm the matter in writing to the regulator.

Auditors are permitted to reach agreement with the directors on the circumstances giving rise to this report, but they still have to make the report even if they are satisfied that the matter has already been referred to the regulator. Nevertheless, in certain circumstances they are required to report direct, without notifying the directors (APB, 1994a, para. 54):

> When the matter giving rise to a statutory duty to make a report direct
> to a regulator casts doubt on the integrity of the directors or their com-
> petence to conduct the business at the regulated entity, the auditors should
> make their report to the regulator without delay and without informing
> the directors in advance.

The professional duty to report, however, remained in addition to the statutory duty and SAS 620 indicates how to handle this (para. 58):

> When a matter comes to the auditors' attention which they conclude does
> not give rise to a statutory duty to report but nevertheless may be rele-
> vant to the regulator's exercise of its functions, they should:
> (a) consider whether the matter should be brought to the attention of the
>   regulator under the terms of the appropriate legal provisions enabling
>   auditors to report direct to the regulator; and if so
> (b) advise the directors that in their opinion the matter should be drawn
>   to the regulators' attention.

Where the auditors are unable to obtain, within a reasonable period, adequate evidence that the directors have properly informed the regulator of the
matter, they should make a report direct to the regulator without undue delay.
Matters to which the statutory duty would not apply but which might be
covered by a professional duty could include matters in respect of holding,
subsidiary or associated companies of the firm being reported upon.

The Practice Notes give further guidance on how to apply these requirements in practice. The main elements are as follows:

(1) To enable the auditor to be protected from an accusation of breach of
    confidentiality, his or her action must be in good faith and not malicious:
    in theory the legal profession could provide many interpretations of what
    the term 'good faith' means, and there are areas where legal advice may
    be necessary, but the need for swift action if investors' or customers'
    assets are to be protected requires the auditor to make his or her own
    mind up, speedily, as to whether a matter requires to be reported.
(2) The right and duty to report apply regardless of the source of the infor-
    mation to be reported, provided that the auditor becomes aware of the
    matters reported in his or her capacity as auditor or reporting accoun-
    tant of the specific business concern.
(3) This *ad hoc* reporting line does not replace the normal primary sources
    of information for the regulator which come directly from the business's'
    management and directors.
(4) The obligation imposed in practice does not require extra work by audi-
    tors but only extra vigilance to report those matters of which they
    become aware in the ordinary course of their audit work or reporting
    accountants' examination.
(5) The obligation applies only in respect of matters coming directly to the

attention of the audit team during the course of their audit work, and SAS 620 (APB, 1994a, para. 2) specifically refers to 'information of which they become aware in the ordinary course of performing work undertaken to fulfil their audit responsibilities'. Where an accounting firm provides other services, which could include investigation work, work done by a taxation team or by management consultants, reports arising from that work should be made available to the audit partner so that he or she may consider the results of such work as part of the planning and conduct of the audit. It is incumbent on an accounting firm to ensure that such information is transferable and, indeed, that the audit partner is aware of other relationships between his or her client and the accounting firm.

The critical guidance for auditors is on when to report. The guidance requires them to take the initiative in the following circumstances:

(1) when there has been an adverse occurrence or a change in the auditor's perception of an existing situation, that may include an adverse change in the circumstance of the business;
(2) where the above situation has given rise to a material loss or to loss of control over the assets or records, where it indicates with a reasonable probability that such a material loss may arise or where there is evidence of dishonesty, serious incompetence or serious failure to observe rules or regulations for the conduct of a regulated business; and
(3) where the position is such that, because of a significant risk which is material to the collective interest of investors or depositors, their interests might be better safeguarded if the matter were reported to the regulator.

There can be no doubt that this reporting requirement imposes an additional strain on traditional auditor–client relationships in the financial services sector. The auditor must ensure that his or her client is aware of the *ad hoc* reporting requirement, by including appropriate statements in the letter of engagement.

In practice, if the actual relationship between auditor and client, critical to the successful conduct of an audit in any event, is to be preserved, quite apart from his or her duty of confidentiality, the auditor's first duty on discovering something which might jeopardize customers' interests should be to encourage the client to report the matter in almost all circumstances: failing the chief accountant, financial controller or financial director, then chief executives, chairmen or non-executive directors need to be approached. The auditor may then make his report to the regulator jointly with the investment business, bank, building society, insurance company or friendly society. It is only when all these routes fail (which must be unlikely, given the implications for those individuals if the auditor's concerns prove to be right), or when the need for urgent action does not allow them all to be pursued, that the auditor must go direct to the regulator.

It is, of course, a matter for the auditor's judgement whether he or she has lost confidence in the integrity of the client's directors or senior management or believes that they have committed or are about to commit a fraud or other irregularity, forcing him or her to report directly without consulting them. However, auditors should seek to build up proper relationships with their clients, in the first instance, which should involve openness and frankness: in such circumstances, an auditor should already have been aware that the relationship had broken down and the decision to report directly should be an obvious one.

Regular reporting to regulators

The responsibility of auditors in reporting to regulators in the financial services sector, in addition to their reports on the financial statements, is to provide assurance to the regulator on the financial information provided by the investment business to the regulator, and on the accounting records and control systems operated by the business during the period covered by the report and, of particular importance, on the investment business's stewardship of client assets.

The precise matters on which auditors are required to report vary according to the regulator and the nature of their client's business. A typical report to an investment business regulator will cover the following matters:

(1) confirmation that the auditors have obtained all the information and explanations considered necessary for their audit;
(2) whether the financial statements present a true and fair view and have been properly prepared in accordance with the regulations concerned;
(3) whether the statements of actual and required financial resources have been properly prepared and whether the requirements were met on the balance sheet date;
(4) whether the accounting records and specified systems were adequate to meet the regulator's requirements throughout the period; and
(5) whether the investment business complied with the client assets rules at all relevant dates.

The requirements in respect of accounting records and specified systems permit the auditor to satisfy the regulator that systems are in place to protect customers' assets from loss from unauthorized use or disposition, that risks are properly monitored and evaluated and that transactions are executed in accordance with established procedures and recorded properly.

The Bank of England's approach has been to commission reports from auditors (referred to under the Bank of England guidelines as 'reporting accountants') on any aspect of a bank's systems and controls which it chooses, and in many cases on all of the systems and controls in use. The Bank of England's powers to commission reports on systems and controls are not limited to a bank's UK operations and, where it believes that it is desirable in the interests of depositors or potential depositors of the bank, it can commission reports under section 39 of the Banking Act 1987 on any current or former parent, subsidiary, fellow subsidiary or associated undertaking of the bank. The Bank of England's (1994b) requirements are based on its own published guidance notes on reporting accountants' reports on accounting and other records and internal control systems, and reports prepared for the use of the Bank of England are required to have regard to whether or not the institution has met the requirements set out in the Bank of England's guidelines.

Reports on systems and controls commissioned by the Bank of England are, in practice, addressed to banks themselves and are passed on to the Bank of England. This has the advantage for the Bank of England of concentrating the auditor's responsibility directly on to the bank itself, and giving the bank the responsibility to pay for that report. The Bank of England requires such reports to be supported by appendices covering:

(1) the key risks faced by the bank, the key controls in place and the reporting accountant's overall assessment of the control environment for each business area examined;
(2) an outline of the organizational structure of the bank and a brief description of the nature and approximate volume of transactions entered into in the areas examined;
(3) a summary of the procedures followed by the reporting accountant in carrying out the assignment; and
(4) the exceptions to which the reporting accountant's report is subject (i.e. those aspects of the controls and systems which do not meet the Bank of England's guidelines), prioritized as to importance.

This regular reporting should not present such a strain on auditor–client relationships as does the *ad hoc* requirement: particularly in the case of reporting accountants' reports commissioned by the Bank of England, the client has the opportunity to discuss the areas of coverage by the reporting accountant, and indeed can select as reporting accountant a firm which is not also the bank's auditor. The object of this approach is to ensure that the areas covered by the reporting accountant are of use both to the Bank of England and to the bank which is the subject of such reports. Reports on prudential returns, essentially covering the extraction of those reports from a bank's records (though also, on occasions, covering the accuracy of the information provided in those returns) may on the face of it be of less value to a client, though the responsibility of officials of each bank for such returns must mean that they should take comfort from investigations to be processed by the reporting accountants. The report by the Board of Banking Supervision (1995) into the circumstances of the collapse of Barings in 1995 suggested that responsibility for the accuracy of such returns should be placed at a senior level in each bank, to avoid approval of such returns only by a junior official who did not have a full understanding of all of the activities of the bank concerned.

MEETINGS WITH THE REGULATORS

The requirement on auditors and reporting accountants of authorized deposit-taking institutions (i.e. banks) to attend joint meetings involving the regulator, client and auditor or reporting accountant also represents a source of potential strain on client relationships. This approach has not been followed to the same extent by regulators of other elements of the financial services sector although regulators do have the power to require attendance at such meetings. Nevertheless, tripartite meetings have the advantage of ensuring that both regulator and auditor are aware of each other's understanding of the circumstances of the client, without the need to embarrass clients in any way by following matters through between auditor and regulator directly. In particular, they provide the opportunity for the regulator to inquire of the auditor whether there are any additional matters which should be brought to the attention of the regulator and to understand what matters required specific focus during the auditor's task. They also provide an opportunity for the auditor to inquire of the Bank of England whether there is anything that the Bank should bring to the auditor's attention to enable him or her to carry out the audit. The reciprocity of this information flow has been an important matter in the agreement of additional responsibilities for auditors, although there are still particular difficulties in providing reciprocal information from the DTI to auditors of insurance companies, because of drafting of the relevant insurance legislation.

Experience of such meetings over a number of years has suggested that they can be conducted without undue strain on relations between auditor and client, though they will obviously be more effective if regulator and auditor feel able to speak frankly. Not unnaturally, clients will expect to have some advance notice of what the auditor will raise but the auditor should not allow his or her independence to be compromised by being told what he or she is allowed to raise! The Bank of England is, to an increasing extent, pressing for these meetings to be complemented by bilateral meetings with the reporting accountant, particularly where there are concerns about the institution.

Caveats

When reporting to regulators was first established in the 1980s, the auditing profession sought to spell out various caveats to the regulator, indicating the limitations on the value which should be placed on the auditors' work. The issue of Practice Note 1: *Investment Businesses* by the Auditing Practices Board in 1992 provided an alternative means of spelling out this limitation: the Practice Note sets out quite clearly (APB, 1992, para. 7):

> The objective of accounting systems and controls is to provide a high level of assurance that assets are safeguarded against loss from unauthorised use or disposition, that risks are properly monitored and evaluated and

that transactions are excluded in accordance with established procedures and are recorded properly. Accounting systems and controls also assist management in conducting the business in a prudent manner. In considering the adequacy of control systems required by the client assets and accounting records rules, auditors and regulators must recognise the inherent limitations in such systems. . . . . These limitations mean errors or irregularities may nevertheless occur and not be detected. Also projection of any evaluation of the systems to future periods is subject to the risk that management information and control procedures may become inadequate because of changes in conditions or the risk that the degree of compliance with those procedures may deteriorate.

Paragraph 20 spells this out in more detail:

It is the responsibility of an investment business's management to design, establish and maintain adequate records and control systems. All control systems have inherent limitations and cannot guarantee the totally effective operation of systems, nor the completeness and accuracy of the records. Also they cannot be proof against fraudulent collusion, especially on the part of those holding positions of authority or trust. Authorisation controls can be abused by the person or persons in whom authority is vested and management is frequently in a position to override controls. Whilst the competence and integrity of the personnel operating the controls may be aided by careful selection and training, pressures can be exerted from both within and outside the business. Furthermore, human error due to errors in judgement or misunderstanding, carelessness, fatigue or distraction will undermine the effective operation of systems and controls.

With these caveats, auditors feel emboldened to issue reports to regulators, though are generally cautious in allowing such reports to be seen by third parties, who may not be aware of the caveats, even though reports to regulators specifically refer to Practice Note 1. In this era of increased litigation against auditors whenever third parties have suffered loss, it is hardly surprising that auditors are cautious about the wide circulation of their opinions.

Money laundering

In the UK the law relating to money laundering is contained in various different Acts, principally the Drug Trafficking Act 1994, the Prevention of Terrorism (Temporary Provisions) Act 1989 and various Criminal Justice Acts, most recently the Criminal Justice Act 1993. This last Act implements the Money Laundering Regulations, which provide greater detail on the anti-money laundering measures to be taken by a range of financial services businesses, reflecting the requirements of the Money Laundering Directive.

This wealth of legislation provides an additional burden for auditors: it becomes an offence to provide assistance to those involved in money laundering and, in the case of the laundering of the proceeds of drug trafficking or terrorist activity, an offence not to report suspicions of money laundering to the appropriate authorities, usually the National Criminal Intelligence Service. It is also an offence to prejudice further investigations by tipping off those involved that a report has been made.

Financial sector businesses are required to meet certain requirements in the following areas:

(1) establishment and maintenance of policies, procedures and controls to deter and to recognize and report money laundering activities;
(2) evidence of customer identification;
(3) retention of customer identification and transaction records for use as evidence in future investigation;
(4) education and training of staff.

The detailed requirements for financial sector businesses are spelt out in a number of detailed guidance notes issued by the Joint Money Laundering Steering Group (1995) in four documents covering:

(1) mainstream banking, lending and deposit-taking activities;
(2) wholesale, institutional and private client investment business;
(3) insurance and retail investment products;
(4) receiving bankers.

Auditors have, in addition to considering whether their client has complied with the law in relation to money laundering, to consider their own reporting responsibilities if they develop any suspicions that their client has been involved, either knowingly or otherwise, in money laundering transactions. In this instance, the responsibility is a different one from that spelt out under SAS 620: they have to be aware of the prohibition on tipping off when considering whether to discuss their suspicions with client management.

THE SCOPE OF THE AUDIT

The systems-based audit

The main impact of the requirements spelt out above is to extend the scope of the audit to enable the auditor to give opinions on systems and controls. Whereas many auditors have for many years based their audit approach on an understanding of and testing of systems of internal control, many smaller audits have consisted largely of substantive tests of year-end balances and transactions, particularly where systems of internal control were not deemed to be sufficiently reliable. That approach is now no longer acceptable for companies which hold client money or other assets, or which accept deposits from customers. The audit has to be structured in such a way as to enable the auditor to assess whether or not sufficient controls have been in place throughout the period under audit. Almost inevitably, this raises further the experience level and ability expected of audit staff.

The extension of the report to cover the financial resources of the institution and whether it meets the regulator's financial resource requirements also demands a detailed knowledge of precisely what the business did during the year, in order to assess what category of membership or which set of requirements applied. The extension of such financial resource requirements to meet the Capital Adequacy Directive with effect from 1996 onwards have imposed far greater burdens on auditors in this respect, and will extend to the use of 'risk management models' by clients to determine financial resource requirements in particularly complex trading activities.

More difficult is the question of whether or not an investment firm has or has not held client money during the year: this could cause it to be in a substantially different category depending on whether or not it did hold client money or assets. It falls to the auditor to be satisfied that the business did not hold client money before he or she can accept that reduced financial resource requirements apply. Under Practice Note 1 (APB, 1992), auditors are encouraged to rely on representations from their clients to the effect that they have not held client money or assets, though they must also carry out appropriate review procedures to corroborate such representations before basing their reports to the regulators on such representations.

The compliance function

A further area which has demanded increased attention from auditors is that of the compliance function: all investment businesses are required to appoint a compliance officer who is responsible, *inter alia*, for confirming to the regulator at least annually that the business has complied with the relevant regulations. The issue of SAS 120: *Consideration of Law and Regulations* in 1995 focuses the attention of auditors on the risk that non-compliance by an entity with law or regulations may materially affect the financial statements. Although the auditors' report is limited to accounting records, internal controls, financial resources and controls over client property and assets, the penalties which could be imposed upon an investment business that failed to comply with all the other regulations, particularly the Conduct of Business Rules governing relationships with clients and customers generally, could have a significant impact on the future of that investment business. SAS 120 (APB, 1995b, para. 2) states: 'Auditors should plan and perform their audit procedures and evaluate and report on the results thereof, recognising that non-compliance by the entity with law or regulations may materially affect the financial statements.' In paragraph 22 it goes on to state: 'The auditors should obtain sufficient appropriate audit evidence about compliance with those laws and regulations which relate directly to the preparation of, or the inclusion or disclosure of specific items in, the financial statements.'

More generally, it sets out what they should do which does not directly affect the financial statements:

The auditors should perform procedures to help identify possible or actual instances of non-compliance with those laws and regulations which provide a legal framework within which the entity conducts its business and which are central to the entity's ability to conduct its business and hence to its financial statements, by:

(a) obtaining a general understanding of the legal and regulatory framework applicable to the entity and the industry, and of the procedures followed to ensure compliance with that framework;

(b) inspecting correspondence with relevant licensing or regulatory authorities;

(c) enquiring of the directors as to whether they are on notice of any such possible instances of non-compliance with law or regulations, and

(d) obtaining written confirmation from the directors that they have disclosed to the auditors all those events of which they are aware which involve possible non-compliance, together with the actual or contingent consequences which may arise therefrom.

(APB, 1995b, para. 28)

In the case of financial services businesses, this is particularly significant. The auditor must therefore extend the review of the business's affairs in order to be satisfied that adequate compliance procedures are in place including, for example, reviewing the tests carried out not by the compliance officer but by someone delegated by him or her to ensure that regulations are being followed. The auditor should extend this review to the personnel department to deal with the question of whether or not adequate checks are made on those employees who will deal with clients before they are employed. Investment businesses themselves take responsibility for ensuring that their employees are fit and proper and for notifying the regulatory authorities accordingly, and any failure to follow proper practices could also have severe consequences.

Client assets

The underlying principle behind client asset protection is that money held or securities of any sort held by investment businesses on behalf of their clients should be protected from the claims of those businesses' creditors and from rights of set-off which might be established by their bankers. A further principle, effectively amplifying what was already contained in the law of agency, is that investment businesses should be required to seek the best return available for their clients on money which they hold from time to time, taking into account also the risk and inconvenience involved, and to pass on such return to those clients unless they have specifically (and not under duress) agreed otherwise.

For banks, the application of such rules is rather different, given that the opening of a specific account for a customer in a bank means that such an account is itself protected by the Banking Act 1987 and the Deposit

Protection Fund established under the Act. Accordingly, most of the specific requirements which relate to clients' money are waived where the businesses are also authorized deposit-taking institutions, provided that client funds are immediately credited to an account opened in the name of the client concerned rather than being left in a general suspense account.

The main areas of attention in respect of client assets for auditors become:

(1) making sure that client money or other assets received are immediately identified and channelled into appropriate accounts or classifications;

(2) checking that such accounts or classifications thereafter remain separate and satisfy the regulations which protect such assets from claims by creditors or bankers: this extends to the titles of client money accounts, undertakings required of the banks at which such accounts are held and the arrangements with custodians that physically hold client securities for another investment business;

(3) reviewing the regular carrying out of reconciliations between statements from third parties (banks or custodians) and summary accounting records and the detailed underlying accounting records;

(4) testing procedures to ensure that interest is paid at appropriate intervals on clients' funds held; and

(5) testing procedures governing the withdrawal of client funds and assets and restricting such withdrawals to appropriately authorized officers and circumstances.

While the rules for the protection of client assets sometimes appear simple to administer, this is the area of greatest temptation for the unscrupulous manager of an investment business: clients' money or assets become particularly tempting when the business itself is under financial strain. The trust placed with such managers could be easily abused by fraudsters. Accordingly, this is a specific area which auditors ignore at their peril.

Custodian arrangements

A trend which has become apparent more recently is the increasing concern expressed by auditors of investing institutions (investment trusts, pension funds and other investment funds) as to the quality of custodial arrangements and, indeed, investment management services provided by investment businesses. The publication of a statement from the Institute of Chartered Accountants in England and Wales in 1994 (FRAG 21) provides guidance to auditors of custodians, in particular on the form of reporting that they should adopt to enable auditors of their client's own customers to take comfort from their client's controls and procedures. The essence of FRAG 21 is that the responsibility for controls within a custodian rests with management, and it is therefore management that should make a statement of the control objectives set for their activities and the policies and procedures which they adopt to meet those objectives. The custodian's auditors should then prepare a report, subject to appropriate caveats, indicating whether in their opinion the policies and procedures set out in management's statement have been in place throughout the period and whether they are sufficient to meet the control objectives stated. In this way, visits by auditors of investing institutions to the custodians to check the controls and, indeed, the existence of their clients' securities, should be avoided.

CONCLUSION

The scope of auditing within the financial services sector has been redefined over the past decade by the implementation of new legislation, itself triggered by the major banking and commodity losses of the 1970s and further refined by the financial sector collapses and losses of the late 1980s and 1990s. The burden created by such legislation for the auditor of a financial sector institution is considerable, and one which places considerable strain on his or her relations with clients. The auditor must be able to show that the staff he or she fields for such audits have the requisite knowledge and have had access to necessary technical material. They must also be sufficiently competent to cope with the rigours of auditing complex institutions.

The increasing regulatory expectations of auditors and their increasing prominence have inevitably placed yet more pressure on them, as has the willingness of the press and investors to blame auditors for losses arising from the collapse of investment businesses for which they themselves were not responsible. Auditors must take care to ensure that they do not conduct audits in the financial services sector or, indeed, provide letters of comfort or statements about their audit clients which will create unnecessary liability for them. When it comes to additional reporting for their clients, such as those under FRAG 21, they must seek to limit their liability whenever they can. However, no careful phraseology or legal limitation of liability is as effective a protection for the auditor as properly trained and competent staff, and proper supervision of the work that they do by an appropriately experienced audit partner.

REFERENCES AND FURTHER READING

Auditing Practices Board (1992) Practice Note 1: *Investment Businesses*, APB, London.

Auditing Practices Board (1994a) SAS 620: *The Auditors' Right and Duty to Report to Regulators in the Financial Sector*, APB, London.

Auditing Practices Board (1994b) Practice Note 4: *The Auditors' Right and Duty to Report to the Building Societies Commission*, APB, London.

Auditing Practices Board (1994c) Practice Note 5: *The Auditors' Right and Duty to Report to SIB and Other Regulators of Investment Businesses*, APB, London.

Auditing Practices Board (1994d) Practice Note 6: *The Auditors' Right and Duty to Report to the DTI in Relation to Insurers Authorised under the Insurance Companies Act 1982*, APB, London.

Auditing Practices Board (1994e) Practice Note 7: *The Auditors' Right and Duty to Report to the Friendly Societies Commission*, APB, London.

Auditing Practices Board (1995a) Practice Note 3: *The Auditors' Right and Duty to Report to the Bank of England*, APB, London.

Auditing Practices Board (1995b) Statements of Auditing Standards 120: *Consideration of Law and Regulations*, APB, London.

Auditing Practices Committee (1982, revised 1989) Auditing Guideline: *Building Societies in the United Kingdom*, APB, London.

Auditing Practices Committee (1989) Auditing Guideline: *Banks in the United Kingdom*, APC London.

Bank of England (1996c) *Guidance Notes on Reporting Accountants' Reports on Bank of England Returns Used for Prudential Purposes (S&S/1996/7, April)*, Bank of England, London.

Bank of England (1992) *Verification of Interim Profits in the Context of the Own Funds Directive (BSD/1992/5, August, amended (S&S/1995/5) December 1995)*, Bank of England, London.

Bank of England (1996a) *The Bank of England's Relationship with Auditors and Reporting Accountants* (S&S/1996/5, April), Bank of England, London.

Bank of England (1996b) *Guidance Notes on Reporting Accountants' Reports on Accounting and Other Records and Internal Control Systems* (S&S/1996/6, April, March), Bank of England, London.

Banking Act 1987, HMSO, London.

Board of Banking Supervision (1995) *Inquiry into the Circumstances of the Collapse of Barings*, HMSO, London.

Building Societies Act 1986, HMSO, London.

Coopers & Lybrand (1996) *Generally Accepted Risk Principles*, Coopers & Lybrand, London.

Financial Institutions (Prudential Supervision) Regulations 1996 (Statutory Instrument 1996/1669) HMSO, London.

Friendly Societies Act 1992, HMSO, London.

Hitchins, Hogg and Mallett (1996), *Banking – An Industry Accounting and Auditing Guide*, Accountancy Books .

Inquiry into the Supervision of the Bank of Credit and Commercial International (1992), HMSO, London.

Insurance Companies Act 1982, HMSO, London.

Institute of Chartered Accountants in England and Wales (1994) FRAG 21, ICAEW, London.

Investment Management Regulatory Organisation Limited (1988) *Rules* (regularly updated), IMRO, London.

Joint Money Laundering Steering Group (1995) *Guidance Notes*, JMLSG, London.

Morgan, C. and Patient, M. (1989) *Auditing Investment Businesses*, Butterworths, London.

Penn, G. (1989) *Banking Supervision – Regulation of the UK Banking Sector under the Banking Act 1987*, Butterworths, London.

Personal Investment Authority (1995) *Rules* (regularly updated), PIA, London.

Securities and Futures Authority (1996 most recent updated) *Rulebook*, SFA, London.

Securities and Investments Board (1988) *Rules* (including guidance notes, regularly updated), SIB, London.

DISCUSSION QUESTIONS

1. What sort of experience should be expected of audit staff responsible for the audits of businesses within the financial services sector?
2. What sort of consideration should be given by an auditor before reporting directly to a self-regulating organisation, the Bank of England or the Building Societies Commission on matters concerning a client?
3. How does an auditor decide what constitutes 'good faith'?
4. What sort of work should an auditor do to establish whether or not a client has accepted 'client money' or 'client assets' during the year?
5. What work might an auditor be expected to do to establish whether or not an investment business client has complied with Conduct of Business Rules during the period under audit or, indeed, the period between the year-end and the date on which the auditor signed the audit opinion?
6. If an auditor suspects a client of involvement in money laundering, but is uncertain of the facts, should he or she approach the client, even at a senior level, and risk being accused of 'tipping off' the client under the Criminal Justice Act 1993, or should the auditor go direct to the National Criminal Intelligence Service and make a report, even if he or she is not sure of the facts?

17

The Audit Commission

Vanessa Couchman

A BRIEF HISTORY

Ever since the first local rates were levied in England in the early seventeenth century, the principle has been accepted that any money raised for local government purposes should have the accompanying safeguard of an external check on how that money is spent. In the early days, various bodies – centred mostly on the local justices – were established to check that no unlawful use was being made of public funds. A more organized method was introduced in 1846, when the District Audit Service was founded to examine the accounts for districts of the Poor Law Unions, the forerunners of the present system of local government in England and Wales.

Once appointed, auditors were required by law to act entirely independently of influence by politicians or others with an interest in the bodies being audited. This important principle remains true today.

In 1972 Parliament allowed local authorities to choose whether their accounts were audited by a private firm of accountants or by the district auditors. Then, in 1982, the government brought local authority auditing in England and Wales under the control of a single, independent body which, together with the auditors, was given the additional task of examining the overall management of local government (Local Government Finance Act 1982). That body was the Audit Commission; it began work in April 1983. In 1990 its role was extended further – to include National Health Service authorities, trusts and other bodies (NHS and Community Care Act 1990). In 1992 the Audit Commission was given additional responsibilities – including a duty to direct local authorities to publish comparative indicators of performance annually (Local Government Act 1992).

The Commission is required to be self-financing year on year. Its income derives almost entirely from fees charged to the local authority and NHS bodies for audit work. It receives no government grant or subsidy. The Commission operates independently of the government. It is a non-departmental public body sponsored by the Department of the Environment and the Department of Health and the Welsh Office. The Commission has up to twenty members drawn from – but not representing – a range of backgrounds including industry, health services, local government, trade unions and accountancy.

A small central staff carries out national value-for-money studies and provides support for auditors. About 40 per cent of the Commission's work, including 30 per cent of the audits, is carried out by external accountancy firms. District Audit, the Commission's own auditing agency, has offices across England and Wales.

Today the Audit Commission's remit covers more than 10,000 local government and health authorities in England and Wales which between them spend about £90 billion a year of public money on vital services – from street cleaning to housing, from education to public work and from hospitals to care in the community.

THE ROLE OF THE AUDIT COMMISSION

The Audit Commission has three principal duties, described below.

Appointment of auditors

The Commission appoints auditors to all local authorities, health authorities and NHS Trusts, in England and Wales. Once appointed, auditors must observe the requirements of the Commission's Code of Audit Practice and ensure that audited bodies are spending money and reporting their financial situation in accordance with the law, and that there are proper safeguards against fraud and corruption. They must also help audited bodies to improve their performance by showing how services can be provided as cost effectively as possible.

Carrying out 'value-for-money' studies

The Commission has a duty to promote 'best practice' in local government and NHS bodies, encouraging economy, efficiency and effectiveness in both the management and the delivery of services.

In partnership with public service providers themselves and other experts, as well as with the auditors, the Commission carries out a number of detailed national studies on particular services each year. These studies compare performance of local authorities or NHS bodies, identify what works well and recommend ways in which service providers can learn from one another (see 'Value for money' below).

Reporting on the impact of government policy

The Audit Commission also has a duty to investigate and report on the impact of legislation or government action or advice *for local authorities only*. Some Commission studies focus exclusively on central government action – for example, the Commission's study of central government funding of local government, *Passing the Bucks* (Audit Commission, 1994b). All local government national studies also consider the impact of government measures.

THE PRINCIPLES OF PUBLIC SECTOR AUDIT

The Commission believes that certain principles of public sector audit should apply to bodies which provide public services, rely upon public money and make social policy choices. It is the Commission's view that for those bodies:

(1) external auditors should be entirely independent of the bodies under audit;
(2) audits must include value-for-money studies to ensure funds are used effectively and efficiently, as well as correctly and honestly;
(3) auditors should be entitled to publish reports about significant problems, if they believe it is in the public interest to do so.

To uphold these principles, the Commission believes that a body independent of those being audited should appoint auditors and determine their fees, regulate and control the quality of audits and identify and promulgate good practice through value-for-money studies. The Audit Commission fulfils these functions for services delivered in England and Wales by local government and the National Health Service.

THE AUDIT PROCESS

At the local level, auditors carry out the formal audits of the accounts of local government and NHS bodies, produce the value-for-money reports on the individual audited bodies and work in partnership with colleagues in local government and the NHS to help them improve their services. This role is broader than that carried out under private sector audits and places particular duties and responsibilities on the auditors. The way auditors fulfil their duties is governed by the Commission's Code of Audit Practice (Audit Commission, 1995).

Appointing auditors

The complexities of local government and the NHS require a special audit knowledge. The Audit Commission takes this into account when deciding on the appointment of auditors to any local authority or NHS body. The Commission currently appoints District Audit to about 70 per cent of audits while the remaining 30 per cent are carried out by private accountancy firms which have developed the necessary expertise.

Appointments are made after consultation with the audited bodies concerned. District Audit, or the appointed firm, then nominates individuals to carry out the duties of auditors. Appointments run for a period of five years and an auditor's performance is carefully monitored by the Commission through its programme of quality control reviews.

District Audit

The Commission employs its own auditors in a separate auditing service, called District Audit. District Audit is organized into five regions. The staffing of each region depends on the nature of the workload, but all regional offices have a regional director, several district auditors and a number of teams of auditors, as well as back-up personnel. The teams are based at convenient locations throughout each region, often on the premises of major local authorities.

In addition, each region is supported by an Added Value Unit composed of value-for-money and computer audit specialists who provide assistance to audit teams.

Private accountancy firms

The accountancy firms which carry out audits on behalf of the Commission are among the foremost in the country. Eight firms were appointed as auditors for 1995/96. Appointed auditors have exactly the same powers and status as district auditors.

Auditors' responsibilities

Auditors must carry out their duties strictly in accordance with the Audit Commission's Code of Audit Practice. This is regularly updated by the Commission and carries the full weight of approval by Parliament. The contents of the Code, its revisions and new requirements, are discussed with relevant government departments, the accountancy bodies and local authority and NHS associations before being put before Parliament. The Code is guided by the principle, however, that auditors are independent of the Commission and the authorities they audit, as well as of central government.

The contents of the Code embody the best professional practice in terms of standards, procedures and techniques. It sets out the general duties of auditors and tells them how they should conduct the audit, given their special responsibilities regarding proper accounting, fraud, corruption, value for money and legislation. It also sets out how they should report the results of the audit, in the form of the audit opinion, management letters and public interest reports.

Financial accounts

The auditor is required to give an opinion as to whether an audited body's annual accounts 'represent fairly' its financial position. This opinion work involves a review of accounting systems such as payroll, payments and income, and a detailed examination of the final accounts including cash/bank balances, debtors, stocks and creditors.

Fraud and corruption

The primary responsibility for safeguarding against fraud and corruption rests with local authorities and health bodies themselves. The auditor, however, is required to ascertain whether each audited body has taken reasonable steps in meeting that responsibility – such as setting up adequate internal control systems which segregate duties, proper authorization procedures and an effective internal audit function. Where they suspect fraud or corruption, auditors will pursue their investigations in collaboration with the authority concerned and, where necessary, with the police.

Legality

Checking the legality of an audited body's spending is a further responsibility of the auditors. They must be satisfied that it is complying with statutory requirements and, in the case of NHS bodies, with Department of Health policies.

Value-for-money – optimum use of resources

It remains the fundamental task of the audit to check that public funds are being used properly for the correct purposes. However, a substantial effort is now focused on how to make the best use of resources, 'adding value' to local services. (This work is discussed in detail in 'Value for money', below.)

Auditors' powers

Appointed auditors have legal powers in certain areas. For example, they are legally entitled to obtain any information they feel is necessary to fulfil their audit duties, although they are bound to treat this information in confidence.

Auditors have powers to issue reports to draw attention to important matters. For local government and NHS bodies, the auditors can report publicly on the matter if they consider it to be in the public interest. In the case of an NHS body, the auditors can also refer the issue by special report to the Secretary of State (Health or Wales).

Auditors are ultimately answerable to the courts in exercising their powers, but will usually seek to resolve issues without resorting to the law. If auditors find that an audited body has taken, is taking, or is about to take, illegal action, they will where possible first discuss the matter with the authority itself. If they feel it is necessary, they can apply to the High Court for a declaration that a past action is illegal or, in the case of a future action, issue a prohibition order.

If, in the case of local authorities, auditors find that there is a loss due to wilful misconduct or failure to account for money or goods, they can themselves order those concerned to repay the money. There is, however, a right to appeal against the order to the High Court.

Reporting the audit

Auditors report on the statutory audit of accounts and value-for-money work in three main ways. These reports provide a snapshot of an audited body's financial standing and chart its current and potential progress towards greater economy, efficiency and effectiveness.

Audit opinions

Each year auditors are required to give an opinion on the accounts of the bodies they audit, stating whether or not they are satisfied that the accounts fairly present their financial position. If they are not satisfied, the audit opinion will state the reasons.

Project reports

Auditors report on each of their local reviews of value-for-money. These summarize the audit findings and conclusions, make recommendations for improved value for money and provide an agreed basis for action by the audited body. It is up to that body to decide whether to make these documents public.

Management letters

Auditors also write a 'management letter' to all the members of the audited body (councillors in local government, board members of NHS bodies) summarizing the main matters which have arisen from the audit and the benefits anticipated from the implementation of agreed action. The letter also provides a brief account of all the audit work undertaken for the year. It includes a review of progress on earlier recommendations, any comments arising from the review of the body's management systems and a reference to audit work planned for the future.

Members have the chance to discuss and ask questions about the letter at a meeting with the auditors. The audited body can decide whether to publicize the letter except that, in the case of local authorities, an auditor can require an authority to respond publicly to specific recommendations which it contains.

There are two further reports which auditors are empowered or may be required to make in exceptional circumstances: reports in the public interest and extraordinary audit.

Reports in the public interest

Auditors may discover issues at any time which raise particular concerns. If they consider it to be in the public interest, they can publish a report on those matters. The audited body concerned must publicize locally the fact that such a report has been issued and, briefly, what it covers and consider the report at a public meeting.

Extraordinary audits

Auditors can be required by the Commission or the relevant Secretary of State (Environment or Wales) to hold an extraordinary audit. This is an extremely rare occurrence and applies only to local authorities. The implications behind the holding of an extraordinary audit are serious but it confers no extra powers on the auditors. Its main purpose is to enable the public to be given immediate rights to lodge an objection to part or all of the audited body's accounts.

Rights of the public

Local government law gives the public important rights in the audit framework. These rights allow members of the public to inspect local authorities' accounts and question the auditor on specific items in those accounts, and give them the opportunity to object to the accounts.

These statutory rights do not apply to the audit of NHS bodies. However, a member of the public is entitled to give information at any time to the auditors of NHS bodies – and of local authorities – who will usually inform him or her of the general outcome of any possible investigations of the matters raised.

VALUE FOR MONEY

Promoting value for money is a major responsibility for the Audit Commission and auditors. Appointed auditors have a duty to satisfy themselves that each audited body has made visible and appropriate arrangements to secure economy, efficiency and effectiveness in the use of its resources.

With several thousand bodies spending about £90 billion each year on very diverse activities, there are inevitably significant opportunities for improvement. But with such diversity there are also a great many examples of innovation and efficiency from which others can learn. Much of the Commission's effort is concerned with discovering and communicating these examples of 'best practice' to every provider of local services and encouraging them to implement improvements. For example, *A Prescription for Improvement: Towards More Rational Prescribing in General Practice* (Audit Commission, 1994a) found that national opportunities of £400 million could be achieved if all GPs prescribed following best practice achieved by 20 per cent of general practices.

Financial savings, although important, are not the only benefits that auditors and the Commission seek. They also place great emphasis on identifying ways in which an audited body can improve the quality and management of its services, as well as the delivery of those services to the people who need them. The Commission's report, *Remote Control: The National Administration of Housing Benefit* (Audit Commission, 1993), said that priority should be given to improving the quality of service and that this should be achieved before seeking financial savings.

National studies

The Commission selects its programme of national studies carefully each year, taking into account a number of factors:

(1) coverage: over a period, the Commission aims to cover all major areas of activity;
(2) importance: there is particular value in concentrating national studies on issues or services which influence the effectiveness of large items of expenditure;
(3) variability: where it is possible to identify significantly different levels of performance from one place to another, there is greater likelihood that 'best practice' recommendations will add value locally;
(4) change: national studies focus on those areas where change is needed and audited bodies are likely to be receptive to good ideas.

Before starting a national study, the Commission consults every audited body for its views. It also consults widely with government departments, local authority and NHS associations, other interested parties and with those trade unions concerned. It seeks their views on whether a topic selected is a suitable one.

As soon as the decision is made to go ahead, a small team is formed to carry out necessary research and analysis. Depending on the subject matter, this team could include auditors, health service or local government officers seconded to the Commission for the period of the study, or staff from outside consultancy firms, together with members of the Commission's own staff.

By analysing the way particular activities are tackled in a number of local service providers, the study team distils the elements of good management practice and identifies performance indicators which will help point the way towards improvements.

Preliminary findings are first tested on a wide range of the bodies concerned. National reports and an audit guide are then produced. National reports summarize the results of the research and identify opportunities for improving the activity examined.

Local value-for-money reports

The Commission helps auditors in their value-for-money work with audit guides based on the results of the studies into individual services. The audit guides enable auditors to apply expert national research to subjects they examine locally. The audit staff are given comprehensive training in the approach to the topic and support is provided by the central study team.

The subsequent local value-for-money reports are a vital part of the Commission's overall impact. Local auditors apply the centrally researched project to varying local circumstances, helping managers identify and implement improvements at local level. Implementation is helped by including specific recommendations in the auditor's report which are tailored to local needs. These can then be agreed with local managers and followed up at subsequent audits to ensure appropriate action has been taken.

Auditors also carry out value-for-money projects to meet specific local needs. Subjects are chosen in conjunction with local managers so they have regard to local circumstances, the potential for improvement and the relevance to the audited body. These account for over one third of all the value-for-money projects undertaken.

Since the Commission was set up in 1983, auditors have carried out over 11,000 value-for-money projects. Two or three major exercises of this kind are conducted at each audited body every year.

Management

The Commission's work towards achieving greater value for every pound spent extends into examination of management systems, structures and responsibilities.

As well as being part of most national studies and audit guides, this has been done most visibly in the publication of a series of management papers. They cover topics ranging from the role of the local authority chief executive to the development of an appropriate information technology strategy. Auditors have also been given a variety of tools to help them assess the effectiveness of management arrangements in the bodies they audit.

Investigating effects of government action on local authorities

Alongside national and local value-for-money studies, the Audit Commission has specific responsibilities to carry out detailed evaluation of the impact on local government of legislation or central government action or advice.

Occasionally the Commission publishes a study which focuses exclusively on central government action – for example, its report on standard spending assessments (Audit Commission, 1994b). More usually, however, the Commission includes consideration of the impact of government measures in its value-for-money studies.

The Commission's investigations aim to show what initiatives might be taken by central – rather than local – government to help authorities improve their management performance. As well as being discussed with relevant government departments, the results are sent to the National Audit Office, the public auditor of central government.

THE CITIZEN'S CHARTER – PERFORMANCE INDICATORS

Indicators which compare the performance of one body over time, or of similar bodies at the same time, can be a powerful spur to improvement.

Local authorities

Under one of the first initiatives inspired by the Citizen's Charter, the Audit Commission was given a legal duty to draw up a list of indicators for measuring the performance of local government services (Local Government Act, 1992). Councils are obliged to measure and report their own performance against these indicators. They must publish the results in a local paper within the nine months following the end of the relevant financial year and the Commission will then publish the results nationally.

The first list was issued in December 1992. It covered performance in 1993/94 for the results to be published early in 1995. In subsequent years, the publication of year-on-year comparisons enables the public to see what improvements their authority has achieved across a range of services. Further indicators continue to be developed.

Performance indicators can help local authorities improve the standards of services they provide and communicate more effectively with the public. The Audit Commission has programmes in place to share best practice and to assist them to achieve their aims.

For the NHS

For the Patient's Charter, which grew out of the Citizen's Charter, the Department of Health sets the performance indicators and is responsible for their publication. However, auditors appointed by the Commission have been involved in evaluating the systems for collecting the data, to help determine whether the results are valid.

THE ROLE OF THE AUDIT COMMISSION:
THE WIDER DEBATE

An independent, external review of the Audit Commission was carried out in 1995. That review drew attention to two potentially conflicting roles of the Commission and its auditors:

> The Commission considers that its mission requires it to adopt two main roles. The first is to act as a watchdog on behalf of the public, providing assurance that its money is properly accounted for and spent on services which provide value for money. The second is to help those responsible for public services to improve them, a facilitation role which is akin to that of a management consultant.
>
> The two roles have a synergy; the research and data needed for the watchdog role help the Commission and auditors to fulfil the consultant role. But they can also be in conflict. Watchdogs must operate in the public eye and audited bodies will often defend themselves against public criticism. Consultants work best in private. They are usually brought in because management already recognises the need for change. They recommend what it should be, bringing insights which encourage ownership by managers, and then they often work in partnership with management to help them implement it. On the other hand, auditors identify the need for change and make recommendations on how to achieve it. They do not implement it. . . . There is no simple answer to the conflict between these twin roles.   (Butler, 1995, pp. 6–7)

Continuing to strike a balance between these two roles presents the Commission and its auditors with a challenge. They must ensure that the regularity and probity of public expenditure are on a firm foundation. But public services have become increasingly complex. Changes have been introduced to the way in which services are provided, for example through purchaser/provider splits and the devolution of responsibility for budgets to a large number of smaller bodies. Consultants can help public services to face the challenges that these changes present. The task for the Audit Commission in assuming both roles is to maximize the synergy between them whilst reconciling the potential contradictions.

REFERENCES

Audit Commission (1993) *Remote Control: The National Administration of Housing Benefit*, HMSO, London.

Audit Commission (1994a) *A Prescription for Improvement: Towards More Rational Prescribing in General Practice*, HMSO, London.

Audit Commission (1994b) *Passing the Bucks: The Impact of Standard Spending Assessments on Economy, Efficiency and Effectiveness*, 2 vols., HMSO, London.

Audit Commission (1995) *Code of Audit Practice for Local Authorities and the NHS in England and Wales*, Audit Commission, London.

Butler, P. J. (1995) *Review of the Audit Commission*, privately published.

Local Government Act 1992.
Local Government Finance Act 1982.
NHS and Community Care Act 1990.

DISCUSSION QUESTIONS

1. What are the advantages of having a national body to appoint and over-see the work of external auditors in the public sector?
2. What is the role of the auditor in respect of policy decisions made by audited bodies?
3. In what ways could value-for-money auditing be applied to the private sector?
4. How can the auditor combine the roles of watchdog and consultant?
5. 'The public should be entitled to receive information on the performance of local authorities.' Discuss.

18

The Audit of Central Government

David Dewar

INTRODUCTION

Audit in central Government has much in common with audit elsewhere. A key objective is to express an opinion on the accuracy of annual accounts and financial statements, based on sufficient, relevant and reliable evidence. Audit risk and the coverage of the examination need to be carefully planned and the work carried out accurately and thoroughly. The staff involved are qualified members of one of the professional accountancy bodies, working to published standards. Independence is a primary requirement.

But the use of public funds and resources imposes further special demands. Accountability to Parliament and the public needs to be to the highest standards, with full public reporting of the results and conclusions of the audit. Special importance attaches to the requirements of legality, regularity, propriety and the proper conduct of public business. The auditor's responsibilities extend beyond the accounts into wide-ranging examinations of the economic, efficient and effective use of resources of all kinds.

The audit is also being carried out against a background of continuing change in the organization and delivery of Government services, and the objectives, approach and priorities adopted. These include efforts to reduce public expenditure and to direct resources more closely; the transfer of operational responsibilities to agencies and wider contracting-out of service delivery; and a closer focus on 'customers' and 'clients' for the various programmes concerned.

ROLE OF THE NATIONAL AUDIT OFFICE

These developments present both risks and opportunities. Maintaining accountability, safeguarding public funds and improving performance are primarily the responsibilities of the government departments and agencies involved, but audit has a positive role to play in monitoring the work being done and reporting the results. The responsibility here lies with the National Audit Office (NAO) as the statutory auditor for all central government expenditure and for many of the agencies and other bodies concerned.

The NAO was established in 1984 to take over the responsibilities of the Exchequer and Audit Department following the passing of the National Audit Act (1983). Much of the work continued to be carried out under previous legislation, but the 1983 Act introduced some important changes. Under the Act the conduct of the NAO's work is independent of both the executive (an obvious safeguard) and Parliament; its budget is approved directly by Parliament and does not come under the control of the Treasury; and the head of the NAO, the Comptroller and Auditor General (C&AG), is an Officer of the House of Commons, is appointed by the Sovereign and can be removed from office only by an address presented to the Sovereign by both Houses of Parliament. This independence is crucial, and extends also to such matters as staffing, pay and conditions of service. A key feature of the NAO's powers is that it reports directly to the House of Commons on the results of its work; and that when presented these reports are followed up by the Committee of Public Accounts (PAC).

The NAO's statutory responsibilities cover both financial audit and value-for-money examinations.

Financial audit

Financial audit is conducted mainly under the Exchequer and Audit Departments Acts 1866 and 1921 but also under a number of other statutes and by agreement. The scope of the work covers *certification audit* of the accounts and accounting systems to establish whether the annual financial statements are accurate or present a true and fair view, together with *regularity audit* to confirm that expenditure and receipts conform with statutory provisions and with parliamentary and other authority. The work also includes propriety audit to examine how public business is conducted, especially in accordance with parliamentary and PAC expectations. On the appropriation accounts which cover central government expenditure a key task is to ensure that funds have been spent only on those services for which Parliament voted the relevant grants, and not diverted elsewhere.

As the appointed external auditor for all government departments and a wide range of other bodies, the C&AG provides a separate audit opinion on some 550 annual accounts from over 300 organizations, covering total expenditure of around £200 billion. These include the main departmental appropriation accounts, cash accounts for a number of other bodies of different sizes, and a range of commercial and other accounts prepared on an accruals basis. The C&AG also audits the annual revenue accounts of the Inland Revenue, Customs and Excise and other bodies, involving the collection of around £250 billion a year.

Much of the work on the various elements of financial audit has remained broadly the same for a number of years, though there have, of course, been changes in audit methods and techniques. But changes are taking place in such areas as the examination of regularity and the proper conduct of public business, and in the form of accounts, and these will have an increasingly significant impact on the scope and conduct of the audit. These developments are referred to further below.

Value for money

The National Audit 1983 Act gave the C&AG statutory authority to carry out examinations of economy, efficiency and effectiveness in the use of resources, supported by direct access to documents, records and other information and with the vital power to report results directly to the House of Commons throughout the year. Such 'value-for-money' examinations are carried out not only in those departments and agencies and other bodies for which the C&AG is the appointed auditor but also in hundreds of other bodies receiving public funds to which the C&AG has rights of inspection and access. For example, under the terms of the Education Reform Act 1993 the C&AG has inspection rights to all grant maintained schools, and is required to give an annual report to the House of Commons on the results of his examination.

There are a few significant exclusions to this wide-ranging remit, such as the activities of local Government (covered by the Audit Commission for England and Wales and the Accounts Commission for Scotland) and the work of the nationalized industries and public corporations. Nevertheless, the total expenditure and revenue subject to the NAO's value-for-money audit is around £500 billion a year, as too are incalculable capital assets and other resources.

The National Audit Act 1983 is framed in powerful terms. In particular, it provides for direct examination of the effectiveness of projects and programmes, which is limited only to the extent that it does not entitle the C&AG 'to question the merits of policy objectives'. (It should be noted that this is not, as is sometimes assumed, a barrier to examining and reporting upon the implementation of policy and the results achieved.) In this respect the 1983 Act goes significantly further than equivalent audit statutes in Canada, Australia and a number of other countries which, in one way or another, restrict the power to carry out direct examinations of effectiveness or prohibit them entirely as getting too close to policy issues which lie at the heart of government.

Despite the strength of its provisions, and the fact that it provided the first statutory framework for value-for-money work, the 1983 Act did not mark the introduction of economy, efficiency and effectiveness examinations. Such work had in practice been carried out by the former Exchequer and Audit Department over many years, without statutory authority but with the strong and active support of the PAC. Waste, extravagance and poor value for money were exposed and criticized from the earliest days of public sector audit, and such work developed extensively in the period between 1946 and 1983 as a consequence of the massive growth in public expenditure. During that period the Exchequer and Audit Department published more than a thousand reports on a wide range of value-for-money issues, to be followed up by the PAC. Such work became a dominant feature of the Department's priorities, often using the best staff. The results produced were not, however, always presented to best effect, since they were often drafted in a rather flat and factual manner and were attached to the massive volumes of accounts which were published only once a year. Nevertheless, the overall success of the work, and the results achieved, prompted a chairman of the PAC during this period to point out that the Committee's effectiveness 'depended on the fact that it had the C&AG's reports as a starting point'.

Major subjects pursued under the pre-1983 arrangement included defence procurement; contract control and pricing; project management in such areas as weapons systems, civil works, roads and hospitals; the use of grants and subsidies; National Health Service programmes; agricultural schemes and projects; and assistance to industry. The range of this work makes it clear that when some – who should know better – suggest that the staff of the former Exchequer and Audit Department were 'not much more than bookkeepers' they do so with an inadequate grasp of the facts. Many of these staff were also prominent in developing the work under the new legislation.

But although the 1983 Act was not quite the watershed sometimes assumed, it was the starting point for major improvements in the planning, content and presentation of economy, efficiency and effectiveness examinations. By providing statutory authority for such work it put the NAO in a stronger position *vis-à-vis* the departments and other audited bodies. The legislation enabled the publication of separate in-depth reports throughout the year, with more penetrating analysis of increasingly complex issues. Reports were published hard on the heels of examinations and not bundled with the annual accounts, and their early publication gave immediacy and impact.

The need for more detailed planning and closer discussions with the audited bodies – though sometimes a slowing-down factor – also fitted in well with the developments in the NAO's own strategic planning and improved audit methods which had been set in hand a few years before. These developments included the introduction of a range of specialisms to complement the basic audit thrust of the NAO's approach and to provide the wider expertise to support the complex evaluations now being carried out. The premium placed on this work by the 1983 Act, and the expectations it generated, therefore lifted the conduct of economy, efficiency and effectiveness examinations into areas and subjects that would not have been tackled without it, and thus pushed out the boundaries of the audit.

The NAO publishes around forty free-standing reports a year on the results of its main value-for-money examinations. The balance and thrust of the programme of examinations vary from year to year; the aim is to pursue cycles of coverage based on the materiality of the expenditures and resources involved, the assessed risks to value for money, the demands of parliamentary accountability and the views of the PAC, and the opportunities to secure improvements in systems, controls and results. The pattern of reports includes:

(1) a concentration on systems designed to secure good value for money rather than reporting examples of bad value for money – but avoiding a 'top down' approach which becomes too rarefied and continuing to report individual cases from which there are important lessons to be learned;

(2) examinations of how departments determine aims, objectives and targets for programmes and projects, monitor progress, report results, and take remedial action;

(3) more examinations dealing specifically with effectiveness issues, and with efficiency rather than economy in expenditure – i.e. spending well on the right things rather than simply spending less;

(4) continuing efforts in familiar areas where massive resources are still involved – such as defence procurement, the National Health Service, social security, employment, and education;

(5) early coverage of new or emerging issues in such areas as the accountability of agencies, contracting-out of services and privatization;

(6) examinations of environmental issues, either directly in their own right or where environmental factors are important elements in other projects or programmes.

The basic purpose of the reports is not simply to criticize past mistakes but to encourage better value for money and help to identify worthwhile improvements in systems and controls. Hard evidence of past weaknesses has an important part to play, of course, but there is also close working with the audited bodies to learn lessons and introduce necessary changes. Pursuing such longer-term benefits means that monitoring recommendations in the reports and following up implementation are standard practice, both by using the PAC and by liaising directly with the audited bodies and, where appropriate, the Treasury. Properly handled, such liaison does not prejudice the NAO's independence. Following up in this way means that promised improvements are not simply taken on trust, but progress and results are reviewed in considering future audit coverage and subsequent examinations.

Nothing stands still, and the work of the NAO is continually developing, but the position outlined above remains the framework of its responsibilities on both financial audit and economy, efficiency and effectiveness examinations. This, therefore, is the context within which current developments, and potential opportunities and threats, fall to be considered. Accountability to Parliament and the public remains the cornerstone of the NAO's work but audit in central government must remain flexible and ready to adapt to the changes taking place within the environment in which it operates, and within audit itself. Some of these emerging issues are considered further below.

CHANGES IN ORGANIZATION, MANAGEMENT AND DELIVERY OF SERVICES

The Thatcherite programme of 'rolling back the boundaries of the state' has in many areas broken the mould of government business under which an increasing range of programmes and services continued to be planned, managed and delivered by major central government departments. Efforts to contain or reduce public expenditure – successful or otherwise – have been accompanied by measures to privatize, hive off or contract out what were previously public functions. Under the 1988 'Next Steps' initiative (HMSO, 1988) a wide range of agencies has been set up to plan and manage the delivery of services, with a range of relationships with the government department responsible for policy in the area concerned. This was not intended to be simply a change in organization; the aim was to bring in the methods and approach of the private sector which were perceived as more likely to be efficient than traditional public sector methods. The belief in more 'commercial' approaches has also subsequently been linked with an emphasis on the 'customer' for public services and developments in customer and citizen 'charters'.

Though these and related changes in organization and approach have been in place for some time, they are still to some extent in a state of flux. Some agencies have been more successful than others; some have secured substantial freedom of action and independence from their parent policy departments within a clear 'framework document' intended to set out objectives, targets and operating parameters, but there is continuing confusion elsewhere; some departments have been better than others in allowing agencies and similar bodies the freedom to manage with minimal departmental intervention; and some of the boundary lines – though robust on paper – have not withstood the pressure of unexpected events.

These developments have had – and are continuing to have – a significant impact on the NAO's work, both in those bodies where C&AG is the appointed auditor and in those where he has rights of inspection and access. The main areas of interest can be summarized as:

(1) audit access;
(2) accountability;
(3) contracting out;
(4) annual reports;
(5) accepting risk.

Audit access

Where the C&AG is the appointed auditor of an agency or other body, the NAO obviously needs all necessary access to accounting systems, records, documents and other relevant information. And under the 1983 Act there is also the automatic power to conduct examinations of economy, efficiency and effectiveness. At the other end of the spectrum, if a government activity is fully privatized, it ceases to be a public function and public funds and resources are no longer involved, then the NAO's involvement normally ends. But in between the question of continuing NAO access depends on a variety of factors, since the C&AG does not have the automatic right 'to follow public money wherever it goes'. The most important consideration is the extent to which a body's income comes directly or indirectly from public funds, with a strong presumption of NAO access when a major or significant proportion of the income is so derived.

But access in such cases is by agreement and has to be negotiated for individual bodies or groups of bodies, sometimes also involving discussions with the sponsor departments and the Treasury. This can be awkward and time consuming; although all those involved accept the need for parliamentary and public accountability, the NAO's examinations and published reports, and PAC follow up, can prove difficult and embarrassing – and turkeys are not renowned for voting for Christmas! Nevertheless, since 1983 access rights have been agreed and exercised for hundreds of organizations of many kinds, to generally acceptable timescales.

But the continuing changes taking place in the organization and delivery of services, the dispersal of responsibility and the several levels of operations mean that the NAO has to remain vigilant and vigorous in maintaining and extending its access rights. Where public funds and resources continue to be involved, however channelled or filtered, the presumption should be for NAO to be given full access in support of parliamentary and public accountability; and where appropriate access cannot be negotiated, or is unduly delayed or hedged around with constraints, the NAO has the right – indeed the duty – to report the facts to Parliament so that the departments and others involved can be required to explain and justify the position before the PAC. (For later developments on access issues see below.)

Accountability

Notwithstanding the changes taking place in the organization, management and delivery of public services, it can be argued that the broad overall position remains that ministers and their departments are responsible for policy, and agencies and other bodies for operational management and delivery. In principle this may still be so, but in practice there are ambiguities and confusion which make it increasingly difficult to allocate clear accountability and responsibility, particularly when difficulties and the unexpected arise, and things go wrong. Reasons for this include the following:

(1) There is not – nor indeed would it be healthy if there were – a clear separation between 'policy' and 'administration/execution'. Good policy is not formulated *in vacuo* but with close regard to how it is to be carried

through; and administration/execution shapes policy where it matters – on the ground – and informs future policy options and developments. This interchange is emphasized by the freedoms and flexibilities deliberately given to agencies and other bodies in carrying out their functions.

(2) Ministers and departments may well intervene – for a variety of reasons, good and bad – in the operational running of agencies. Where things work out well there is generally little reluctance to claim credit for such intervention, but if they go wrong the position and consequent responsibilities for decisions often become clouded. It might seem obvious and reasonable that accountability and responsibility should lie with whoever takes decisions – of any kind – in practice, rather than according to some abstract organizational framework, but it doesn't always work out like that.

(3) There are sometimes attempts to draw distinctions between accountability and responsibility, and to accept one but not the other. But if not exactly two sides of the same coin, the two concepts are inextricably entwined and lose their cutting edge if artificially separated, particularly if the exercise is motivated mainly by the desire to find a ministerial bolt-hole in times of trouble. Perhaps it would help if there were more recognition of the further concept of 'culpability'; for example, it may well be that a minister or the department is accountable for a service but not responsible (i.e. culpable) for mistakes in day-to-day execution by an agency or other body; but they surely remain responsible for reviewing the consequences and ensuring that prompt and effective action is taken to put things right.

These three sources of potential confusion often go hand in hand. A particularly telling example of this kind involved the circumstances surrounding the dismissal by the Home Secretary of the Head of the Prison Service following security lapses at Parkhurst Prison. Without taking sides on the complex issues raised, and the claims and counter-claims, it emerged strongly that further clarification is needed to deal with the gaps and weaknesses revealed in both the accountabilities and responsibilities of ministers and departments on the one hand, and those of agency accounting officers on the other. It is not the responsibility of the NAO to supply such guidance – though it may have a contribution to make – but confusion over the boundaries of accountability certainly adds to the difficulties of the audit, particularly when strong criticisms emerge.

Contracting out

The changes in the organization and delivery of services, particularly those following the 1991 'Competing for Quality' initiative (HMSO, 1991) and associated market testing, mean that an increasing number of activities and functions, previously carried out in-house, are now contracted out to private sector firms and other bodies. Where this involves straightforward functions

– for example, building maintenance or secretarial and similar administrative tasks – no significant difficulties arise on accountability or on audit access; they can be examined in the same way as previous contracts for supplies and services, using departmental records and information.

But important issues arise where contracting out extends to more fundamental services to the public, involving wider rights and obligation. For example, special considerations arise on services involving physical powers over individuals – such as law and order, prisons, security, etc. – or which involve financial sanctions, such as taxation, customs, claims, benefits or grants. This is not the place to argue whether such services should indeed be contracted out at all, given their 'public service' characteristics and the difficulties of infusing contract arrangements with the priorities and ethos on which their proper and effective performance often depends;[1] but it is relevant to consider how far the NAO remains unequivocally in a position to examine the proper conduct of business under contracted-out arrangements, and the economic, efficient and effective performance of the services concerned.

The answer is mixed. A very good example of how things ought to work is the contract for the management of the first 'privatized' prison, the Wolds. Here the Home Office commendably wrote clear provisions for NAO access into the terms of the contract, the contractor co-operated willingly with the NAO on an early examination of the new arrangements, and a full published report to Parliament in 1994 set out findings and conclusions.

This is not the only case of this kind, but the fact remains that it is not the norm for departments automatically to provide for NAO access to contracted-out services, particularly to carry out examinations of economy, efficiency and effectiveness. The onus normally is on the NAO to identify the need for access, including essential access for certification and regularity purposes, to justify the case and to negotiate with departments accordingly.

This position is difficult to justify given the nature of many of the services concerned and the fact that securing effective parliamentary accountability for contracted-out services depends even more strongly on direct NAO 'on the ground' examinations than it does for direct departmental and agency, etc., services. There is no credible case for suggesting that NAO access and examination are inherently inappropriate for 'commercial' activities carried out under contract; and in any case there are well-established arrangements for protecting commercially sensitive information when publishing reports and when these are being followed up by the PAC. Limiting accountability by limiting NAO access is presumably not – surely not? – a persuasive factor when departments are considering the case for contracting-out; and it seems odd that if market testing results in functions continuing in-house then NAO access remains automatic, but if the decision is to go outside the presumption seems to be against NAO access.

At the end of the day, of course, the action to resolve any problems in this area remains as it does for the access difficulties referred to earlier.

The NAO has the power and the duty to report the matter to Parliament for follow up by the PAC with the department concerned, and with the Treasury where appropriate.

Annual reports

The strong focus of agencies and other new bodies towards service delivery, and towards meeting the needs of their 'customers' and 'clients', makes it reasonable to expect them to report clearly and fairly on their results and performance in the main areas of their operations. Many indeed produce annual reports on such matters. But there is a risk that such reports may be seen as a vehicle for favourable publicity rather than a means of reliable accountability. Independent audit scrutiny and validation, would therefore provide valuable underpinning of the facts and figures quoted and how fairly the body's activities and performance are reported. The sort of questions that might be considered include: Do reports consistently cover the most important functions/activities as set out in approved plans and programmes? Do reports clearly identify the key measures/indicators against which performance is to be judged? Do they set out the original targets/forecasts against which delivery can be compared? Are data quantified and costed wherever practicable? Are consistent measures/indicators used from year to year, to enable patterns/trends to be identified? Are failures/shortcomings/ adverse results properly disclosed – or are the reports 'good news only'? Are reports readily available, at reasonable cost?

The NAO uses the published annual reports of agencies and other bodies when planning its programme of work and preparing for specific examinations; and it has scrutinized and reported on published departmental performance measures in individual cases. But hitherto it has not regularly or systematically examined the reports on the lines indicated above, as a clear and specific part of its wider work in support of parliamentary and public accountability. Here again, however, the position is still developing, with the possibility of a wider NAO role being agreed for independent scrutiny of key performance data to be published under resource accounting arrangements.

Accepting risk

One of the purposes of moving the delivery of public services out to agencies and other bodies was to encourage a more adventurous and entrepreneurial approach: to foster a positive and 'can do' attitude; to concentrate on results not process; and generally to act more 'commercially'. It was not intended to create 'departments in exile' and to transfer bureaucratic methods. Auditors need to recognize such developments when carrying out examinations; this may mean accepting a greater degree of risk where this is commensurate with the freedoms and flexibilities which the new arrangements were designed to provide. This is, of course, a question of balance; it does not signal a bonfire of tried and tested controls or a Gadarene rush towards new or streamlined procedures without carefully assessing potential consequences and necessary safeguards. The need to maintain the proper conduct of public business – see below – applies at a least as much to the activities of agencies and other bodies as it does to the continuing mainstream work of departments.

PROPER CONDUCT OF PUBLIC BUSINESS

Formal regularity of expenditure has always been an important element in the audit of central government, as reflected in the provision of the 1921 Exchequer and Audit Departments Act that expenditure must 'conform to the authority that governs it'. Regularity, in terms of compliance with statute and accompanying rules and regulations, also merges into questions of propriety and the broader concerns surrounding the proper conduct of public business. 'The proper conduct of public business' is a useful catch-all term which encompasses a wide range of factors, with flexible boundaries. It covers straightforward and obviously sensible safeguards such as the requirement for competitive tendering for supplies and services, provisions to avoid potential conflicts of interest and codes of staff conduct. Even more obvious – and a repeated concern of the PAC – is the need to pursue and root out questions of fraud or corruption. Error, carelessness, inadequate financial controls and poor stewardship of public money and assets were also identified by the PAC in its 1994 review of the proper conduct of public business in various departments and agencies (Committee of Public Accounts, 1993-4).

In some cases the criteria for what constitutes proper conduct may be less clear-cut, and matters may have to be looked at with an innate feel for the proper and reasonable use of public funds in differing circumstances, rather than the application of established rules and procedures. Expenditure may be perfectly regular within existing provisions yet open to question under this more subtle yardstick. Prominent cases of this kind reported to and pursued by the PAC in recent years include the payment of legal expenses on behalf of the Chancellor of the Exchequer and other ministers; special salary arrangements or redundancy payments negotiated for senior staff in agencies and other bodies; and concerns over payments for travel on behalf of the Director of the National Lottery.

Nolan Committee

In a number of ways the re-emphasis in the NAO's audit towards the proper conduct of public business links up with wider concerns over standards in public life, in Parliament and elsewhere. Looking forward, developments in such work will therefore be significantly influenced by the ongoing work of the Nolan Committee[2] and the changes this is producing in identifying the key elements in proper and acceptable behaviour for public servants, and translating these into codes of practice. Such developments clearly impact on many of the issues identified above, and tracking and examining their implementation will be an important part of the NAO's future work. This work will be strengthened by the greater codification of standards now taking place, since this will provide a firmer audit base in what has, until now, been in some respects a shadowy and judgemental area.

As already noted, attention surrounding the first Nolan Report focused largely on the recommendations concerning the personal conduct of MPs and others in public life.[3] However, it also covered the governance and audit arrangements for public bodies. The C&AG and the Chairman of PAC gave oral evidence to the Nolan Committee during the course of its work and stressed their concern about limitations on the extent to which the NAO, and subsequently Parliament, could follow public money wherever it goes. The Nolan Report noted a lack of consistency in the audit arrangements for public bodies whereby the C&AG audited some but had only inspection rights to others. The Committee saw merit in granting the C&AG inspection rights over all public expenditure but did not make specific recommendations on this. They recommended instead that the Government review the framework governing accountability and propriety in public bodies.

This review was carried out by the Treasury and the Office for Public Service, also taking account of recommendations in the Second Nolan Report on Local Spending Bodies such as universities, colleges and housing associations. NAO staff met the review team frequently and the Chairmen of the PAC and the Parliamentery Accounts Commission submitted evidence to the review. The Chairmen called for the C&AG to audit all non-departmental public bodies (contracting-out much of the work to the private sector) and guaranteed to have inspection rights to follow public funds.

The Government published its initial findings in a consultation paper 'Spending Public Money – Governance and Audit Issues'. The NAO published a joint response to this paper with the Audit and Accounts Commission, and the C&AG also submitted comments on the proposals.

The consultation paper was extremely encouraging for the NAO. For instance, the Government acknowledged the important role audit could play in examining issues of propriety and corporate governance and was generally positive. The paper set out principles for public audit covering structure, scope and using the results:

Scope – that public audit should include a greater emphasis on regularity than is common in the private sector, including how well funds are used; the value for money achieved; the extent to which contractual obligations are met; and compliance with codes of conduct. This was a welcome recognition that the scope of public audit is broader than that required in the private sector.

Structure – that public audit should meet the needs of both the auditee and the funding body; that auditing standards and practice should be determined by an independent body; that audit arrangements should avoid duplication and utilize private sector skills where appropriate; and that audit requirements should not cause distortion of effort to meet them. The

NAO response was supportive, whilst underlining that the needs of Parliament are paramount and that auditors should be free to determine best audit practice. Duplication was already minimized by NAO placing reliance where possible on other auditors.

Using the results – that Parliament should be able to scrutinize the use of public funds by bodies accountable to it; that reports should be addressed outside the audited body on major issues; and that effective follow up is required. These were welcome recommendations, particularly since they recognize the importance of Parliament's role, with the PAC providing a powerful and public means of follow up.

However, the consultation paper did not propose to alter the current audit arrangements for public bodies, leaving the appointment for many such bodies to the Government. The Government also proposed a review of the terms of the 1992 agreement between the Treasury and the C&AG on audit access to public bodies, particularly to ensure that NAO inspections are directed at key areas. The NAO, whilst willing to cooperate with any review, has re-emphasized the need for the C&AG alone to determine where, when and how he makes his inspections.

However, the NAO has welcomed other proposals: that the C&AG's inspection rights at bodies should extend to companies owned by them; that his reports should be distributed to sponsor departments; that there is scope for more work to be specifically agreed with departments; and that value for money studies should extend to comparative performance studies across a range of bodies.

The Government has agreed that the NAO needs to have access to contractors in most situations where services are contracted-out. But this will have a statutory basis and so decisions on access rights will continue to rest on negotiations with departments on a case-by-case basis.

Finally the Government proposed that the C&AG should consider, with the PAC, the possibility that accountancy firms could compete with the NAO for certain audits. In response the NAO pointed to the significant and increasing amount of work currently contracted out and that the C&AG already employed private sector skills where appropriate.

Early indications are that the proposed White Paper is unlikely to differ greatly from the consultation paper and the Government will not be proposing sweeping change to NAO powers or workload.

In carrying such work forward there is, however, one important area where specific attention will need to be given as developments based on Nolan work their way into departmental operations. So far, attention has, rightly, been concentrated upon the personal attributes or characteristics which exemplify the proper behaviour of those in the public service, particularly perhaps at more senior levels. Whilst this will no doubt spread more widely in due course, it will also be important to review operational systems and procedures to ensure that these too are conducive to the proper conduct of routine business along Nolan lines. The nature of departmental or agency work, particularly in day-to-day activities dealing with members of the public, is inevitably procedure driven and there is often limited scope for procedures to be modified, even in the interest of equity, by staff on the ground; so unless key operational procedures are ethically sound then the benefits of higher personal standards could start to slip away under the pressures of routine business. And how will Nolan principles be applied and monitored, if at all, to contracted-out public services, where the need is at least as great? Though high personal standards have a vital part to play, they are the means to an end; the aim is to secure the highest standards in the delivery of public services, however organized.

The importance of fostering ethical performance, in all its aspects, at day-to-day operating level cannot be over-emphasized. It is unfortunately a feature of many views of the civil service from Northcote-Trevelyan to Fulton and a host of other commentators, that the 'real' civil service – certainly the important one – comprises the thin layer of senior officers concerned with policy issues and advising Ministers, rather than the vast bulk of these officers actually delivering programmes and services on the ground. But to the overwhelming majority of people, the most important public servant in the country is not the head of the civil service or anyone like him or her; it is instead the person across the counter in the social security office, or in the housing department, or checking their tax return. It is the actions and attitudes of individual staff at working level that have the most immediate and significant impact on matters of day-to-day concern to most ordinary people; and ensuring high standards of ethical conduct and integrity and performance at that level are therefore crucial. And the need to get it right in day-to-day operations gains added importance as developments in public administration push decision-making further down the line to middle and lower levels and outwards to a wider range of bodies.

WIDER ETHICAL ISSUES

NAO and PAC examinations into the proper conduct of public business are clearly concerned with a number of ethical issues, particularly in terms of their financial impacts. But the work does not extend to a full 'ethical audit' which would require a far wider-ranging examination of ethical and related factors in the planning, delivering and accountability of government programmes and services. Such work might address such matters as equity and equality in targeting and delivering particular services in education, housing, unemployment and similar 'social' areas; fairness in the administration of benefits and effective arrangements for complaint and redress; consultation, communication and responsiveness in the operation of programmes and services with a high personal impact, such as services for the disabled; and the degree of openness and disclosure in dealing with the public. Such work could be considered part of the audit of effectiveness, widely conceived, but at present it lies outside the main thrust of the NAO's activities in this area.

Clearly an 'ethical audit' of this wider kind would pose special difficulties. There would be a shortage of agreed and accepted measures or indicators of performance; many factors are highly judgemental; there is a significant risk of involvement with policy and/or political issues; hard evidence and firm data are difficult to come by; and some of the 'softer' or 'grey' factors could be difficult to pursue successfully at the PAC. Nevertheless, the re-emergence of ethics as an important issue in public business, and the firmer base for audit inquiry that should result from the greater codification of standards and higher expectation under the Nolan developments, suggest that this is an area of central government audit with challenging prospects and the potential for valuable results. In particular, it would emphasize the importance of ethical programmes by departments, and not just ethical standards for individuals – it would emphasize 'ethics in action.'

SERVICE TO OTHER PARLIAMENTARY COMMITTEES

The NAO reports to and serves the House of Commons as a whole, not the PAC. Nevertheless, the long-standing special relationship with the PAC, which is recognized in the provisions of the National Audit Act 1983, means that in practice the NAO's work is considered only by the PAC and is not normally covered by other Select Committees. This has caused those committees some concern since they too would like to profit from the results of the NAO's direct audit access to departmental papers and other information; this concern is particularly relevant to the work of various departmental Select Committees examining performance and expenditure in their designated areas. It has therefore been suggested that better arrangements are needed to channel selected NAO reports to the relevant departmental committee, and that those committees, like the PAC, should have an input into the planning of the NAO's future work.

There are a number of difficulties to be overcome before such a development could take place on a consistent or regular basis.

(1) The NAO's access rights are based entirely on its audit duties in respect of past expenditure and use of resources. It cannot operate as a conduit of information and analysis to Parliament on any wider basis, and it does not examine future spending plans and programmes with which other Select Committees are frequently concerned. Changing the NAO's role would require legislation.

(2) It is one of the strengths of the NAO's and PAC's work that they do not consider the merits of policy objectives, whereas policy issues are firmly on the agenda of the other committees.

(3) Similarly, the strongly bipartisan approach of the PAC, supported by the fact that it takes evidence only from the Accounting Officer and other officials, is not repeated in the work of other committees, which frequently take evidence from ministers. The party political risks involved in the latter would inevitably wash back into the handling of the NAO's

work and reports within departments.

(4) Care would be needed to avoid putting strains on the NAO's existing relationship with the PAC, which would remain the main customer for the NAO's reports and has an important part to play in planning the NAO's forward programme and in advising on its budget.

Despite these difficulties, there is scope for a widening of the NAO's relationships with other Select Committees, with the support of the PAC. Individual NAO reports of particular interest to one of the other Select Committees could be followed up by them rather than the PAC, by mutual agreement. The possibility of progress on a wider front could then be reviewed in the light of the results of such examinations, taking also into account the views of departments and the Treasury. Such a cautious 'suck it and see' approach is, I believe, necessary to protect the key benefits to financial accountability which flow from the existing long-established relationships. And if other Select Committees were to restrict their pursuit of NAO reports to issues of financial management then the way forward would be easier.

CHANGES IN FORMS OF ACCOUNT

This final issue brings the spotlight back to the NAO's original basic function – the financial audit and certification of the annual departmental appropriation accounts. These accounts have from the outset been prepared on a strictly cash basis in accordance with Parliament's voting of supply on a year-to-year cycle. Criticisms of the narrowness and limitations of the cash basis of accounting, and of the strict annuality rules which can lead to a rush of spending at the year-end, have been repeated periodically for at least the last seventy-five years.[4] But the advocates of an accruals basis of accounting, with appropriate separation of capital and current spending and a relaxation of the annuality rules, have not, until recently, persuaded the Treasury that any change was necessary. The simplicity and brute strength of the cash basis of accounting has fitted in well with the Treasury's concerns to maintain a fierce grip on departmental spending on a year-by-year basis, underlined for many years by the system of control by cash limits. Accruals-based accounts and cost accounts were adopted for specific trading or manufacturing activities within departments but not for their main appropriation accounts.

But the position is now changing and arrangements are in hand, and trials being carried out, to move to a system of resource accounting which is designed to apply the key principles of accruals and the separation of capital and revenue spending, in a parliamentary context. This is a major undertaking which will take some time to bring to fruition, not least because of the lack of relevant information on assets, etc., within the existing systems of departmental accounting. And as well as the major investment in new computer systems there will also be significant expenditure on staff recruitment and training. And if they are to work effectively the changes in accounting will need to be accompanied by changes in estimates and voting of funds towards a system of resource budgeting. The importance of budgeting has also been emphasized by the Treasury and Civil Service Select Committee.

It is early days to say how well these revised arrangements will work out and – most importantly – whether they will improve the operations of departments, strengthen accountability to Parliament and restore Parliament's ability to exercise effective financial control over supply. Historically, the last of these has always been weak, with little or no effective use of the financial and accounting information previously available; and it might be optimistic to see the new resource accounting information making a significant impact in this respect. It will also be crucial to ensure that, whatever the accounting system in use, the key safeguard of appropriation remains – i.e. that funds are used only on the designated services for which they are voted.

The NAO has been examining the introduction of resource accounting, the implications for Parliamentary control, and the extent to which views expressed by the PAC and the Treasury and Civil Service Select Committee have been taken into account. A report on the results of the NAO examination, with generally favourable provisional reviews, was published in 1996 and a continuing watch is being maintained as matters develop.

CONCLUSION

Any review of current audit issues and developments can only be a snapshot at a particular point in time, with further opportunities and threats around the corner. In such circumstances an audit body such as the NAO has to work hard to ensure that its examinations and reports make a worthwhile and positive contribution to current issues and concerns. Whilst remaining independent, and with an alignment that puts accountability to Parliament at the forefront of its priorities, the NAO's findings, conclusions and recommendations must command the respect of the departments and other bodies it audits as well as the confidence of the PAC. Audit cannot adopt a siege mentality when facing major changes; it must relish challenge; look forward not back; remain flexible whilst continuing to protect fundamental standards; recognize its own needs to learn and improve; and be accountable for its performance and results.

NOTES

1. Significant reservations and warnings have come from a number of sources:
   'New methods of enhancing efficiency, such as market testing, should not be carried to the point at which standards of service, of conduct and of accountability are put at serious risk... If the fastidiousness of civil service standards is perceived to decline, all citizens are diminished' (Lord Bancroft, former Head of the Civil Service, and Sir John Herbecq, former Permanent Secretary: letter to *The Times*, 25 February 1994).

'We must be wary of extending the contractual model over more and more areas of society and so displace ideas such as trust, professional ethic and vocation. When contract comes to dominate, it may drive out other values on which efficiency also depends' (Professor Raymond Plant: article in *The Times*, 1994).

And more than 200 years ago: 'The service of the public is a thing which cannot be put to auction and struck down to those who will agree to execute it the cheapest' (Edmund Burke: speech on economical reform, 1780).

2. Committee set up by the Prime Minister under Lord Nolan in October 1994. The Committee's *First Report on Standards in Public Life* was published in 1995 (Cm 2850, HMSO, 1995).

3. Lord Nolan identified the golden principles as: selflessness, integrity, objectivity, accountability, openness, honesty and leadership.

4. The cash basis of accounting was, for example, a serious concern of the Select Committee on National Expenditure 1918–19.

REFERENCES

HMSO (1988) *Improving Management in Government: The Next Steps*, HMSO, London.

HMSO (1991) *Competing for Quality: Buying Better Public Services*, Cm 1730, HMSO, London.

Committee of Public Accounts (1993–4) *The Proper Conduct of Public Business*, Eighth Report, HC 154, 17 January, 1994.

DISCUSSION QUESTIONS

1. What are the key features of the NAO's role in making departments, agencies and other bodies accountable to Parliament?

2. How can effective accountability be maintained as delivery of public services is increasingly dispersed?

3. What are the main opportunities and threats likely to arise from the contracting-out of public services, and how might these be dealt with?

4. How far and in what directions will value-for-money auditing need to develop to meet current and prospective changes in public sector organization and management?

5. Does 'traditional' financial audit have an increasing or diminishing role to play in the public service of the future?

6. What is the role and purpose of propriety and the proper conduct of public business in the NAO's examination, and how are these under threat as a result of changes in the organization and objectives of public administration?

Subject Index